Rugby World Cup Argentina 2023

Paul Tait

First published in 2012
© Copyright 2012
Paul Tait

The right of Paul Tait to be identified as the author of this work has been asserted by them in accordance with the Copyright, Designs and Patents Act 1998. All rights reserved. No reproduction, copy or transmission of this publication may be made without written permission.

No paragraph of this publication may be reproduced, copied or transmitted save with the written permission in accordance with the Copyright Act 1956 (as amended). Any person who does any unauthorised act in relation to this publication may be liable to criminal prosecution and civil claims for damage.

Paperback ISBN - 9781780923123
ePub ISBN - 9781780923130
PDF ISBN - 9781780923147

Published by MX Publishing Ltd, 335 Princes Park Manor, Royal Drive, London N11 3GX
www.mxpublishing.co.uk

Cover design by www.staunch.com

To my loving wife Denise. Thank you.

Contents

Prologue 4
Introduction 6

Part I: Building Recognition
Chapter 1: The Beginning (Pre Rugby World Cup) 10
Chapter 2: Rugby World Cup Amateur 16
Chapter 3: A Giant Leap – Wales 23
Chapter 4: Consolidation – Australia 30
Chapter 5: Global Shakeup – France 39
Chapter 6: Acceptance Confirmed – New Zealand 54
Chapter 7: Beyond – The Rugby Championship 71

Part II: Why Argentina
Chapter 8: Track Record in Rugby 87
Chapter 9: A Host Nation Prepared 95
Chapter 10: Approaching Professionalism 107
Chapter 11: Spirit of Rugby 120
Chapter 12: Contribution to Global Rugby 127

Part III: Global Impact
Chapter 13: Legacy for the Americas 153
Chapter 14: Tier One Model 183
Chapter 15: The Evolving State of Global Rugby 198

Part IV: Venues
Chapter 16: Level 1 Stadiums (Core venues) 217
Chapter 17: Level 2 Stadiums (Likely venues) 230
Chapter 18: Level 3 Stadiums (Possible venues) 238

Acknowledgements 249
Endnotes 250

Prologue

After searching on the internet and failing to find news on potential host nations for Rugby World Cup 2023 I started a rugby blog titled Rugby World Cup: Argentina 2023 in June 2010. I was inspired by the progress of Argentine rugby both on and off the field and also concerned about the hosting history of Rugby World Cup tournaments. Argentina had been unfairly treated by the structure of First Tier rugby and even after defeating powerful teams from the Six Nations tournament there were few moves being made to see Argentina enter the Tri Nations tournament. Finally after almost conquering the world in 2007 Argentina was added to the renamed The Rugby Championship in 2012 and, to my delight fit in easily and greatly contributed to the tournament in its first year. I am sure that in future years it will be hard to imagine a Southern Hemisphere competition without Argentina.

With Argentina offered a place in what became The Rugby Championship in the months following Rugby World Cup 2007 it came time to see just how much Argentina had to offer rugby as a global sport. Argentina delivered on the global stage and would finally have a First Tier annual competition to compete in. Could it host a Rugby World Cup? I first visited Argentina in 2003 when the country was still suffering greatly from an economic crisis. Latter that year, around a month before the World Cup, I was talking to my father, a New Zealander, about future World Cup´s and found myself arguing a case for Argentina to host a tournament. He was still bitter about the decision that saw Australia winning exclusive hosting rights after 2003 was supposed to see New Zealand act as a co-host. That decision proved to be both good and bad as New Zealand would go on to host Rugby World Cup 2011 on its own after Australia had, according to some, ended any chances of the World Cup returning to New Zealand.

The blog started as a means of exploring the idea on social media. It continues to be updated regularly and is entirely non-profit. Its aim is simple – create a platform for the possibility of Argentina 2023 to be seriously considered. It is not a blog based on wishful thinking. It is, in my view, a realistic goal and one which would tremendously benefit rugby globally. Shortly after beginning blogging it became evident that it was more than just about Argentina, it was about global rugby and in order for Argentina to host it needed to be offering not only something to the global game but also to its own region. The blog has covered rugby throughout the Americas from World Cup regulars Canada and the USA to places where the sport is new such as Cuba and Ecuador. The more time that I put into the blog the more convinced I became that not only could Argentina be a World Cup host but it needs to be.

This book would not have been possible without the remarkable work of the Argentine rugby players at France 2007. The tournament was ground-breaking for both the country of Argentina and the sport of rugby. The Argentine national rugby team, commonly known as, Los Pumas made history in defeating historically powerful teams including France, Ireland and Scotland en route to finishing third in the tournament and third in the IRB World Rankings. This result was no small achievement. It was massive as it meant that Argentina finished the World Cup ahead of highly fancied teams including Australia, New Zealand and hosts France. All three have previously hosted the Rugby World Cup. In fact, in finishing third in 2007, Argentina became the only Rugby World Cup semi finalist who has not yet hosted a Rugby World Cup.

Following the success of 2007 the sport has undergone significant changes in Argentina as adjustments have been made to change from the amateur to professional era. Los Pumas are now able to play in any city in Argentina and attract strong crowds. Home tests since 2007 have demonstrated this as the profile of the national team has resulted in rugby growing to previously impossible heights. It is this success combined with the history of rugby in the country which perfectly demonstrates the merits of Argentina hosting a Rugby World Cup. What had long been lacking was regular competition and 2012 marked an end to this with Argentina not only participating in The Rugby Championship but proving to a quality team.

Argentina's admission means it has now been officially accepted as an elite team backed by a responsible union. The opportunity to host Australia, New Zealand and South Africa in venues across the country further underlines the merits of Argentina hosting a Rugby World Cup. 2023 looms as the ideal time for Argentina to host because, aside from being the first time that it would have been hosted in the Americas, it will mark more than a decade of Argentina's involvement in The Rugby Championship. With England hosting in 2015 and Japan in 2019, it would logically be time for a Southern hemisphere country to host in 2023. Given that at this time Oceania would have hosted three World Cup's, Africa one, Asia one and Europe four, the Americas as a region will merit hosting the 2023 Rugby World Cup due to this fact alone. The question is not should Argentina host a Rugby World Cup. Rather the question is why shouldn't it?

Introduction

The Rugby World Cup and the sport of rugby union have, in one generation, gone from being a humble sport to being a truly global one. Significant changes have been realized off the field with the profile of rugby having been irreversibly altered to the extent that the global governing body of rugby, the International Rugby Board (IRB) says that the Rugby World Cup has now become established as one of the most important sporting events behind the Olympic Games and the FIFA World Cup.[1] Being able to be mentioned together with these events can suggest a number of things, one of which is that the sport is entirely different to when the sport's first World Cup match was played at Eden Park, Auckland in 1987.

However the rise of rugby to a global sport almost never happened. There had been attempts at creating such a competition before the 1980's but leading European rugby unions were not interested. The British and Irish unions were historically opposed to the creation of a Rugby World Cup and this was enough to prevent one from occurring. The British unions (or the home unions) comprised of England, Ireland (including Northern Ireland), Scotland and Wales were opposed to creating a Rugby World Cup as they did not want rugby to become a professional sport and preferred continuing the structure in place in which friendly and Five Nations matches were the order. Eventually, however, the push from Australia and New Zealand to have a Rugby World Cup was approved with a vote in Paris in March 1985 in which the Rugby World Cup was approved by 10 votes to 6. The home unions initially all opposed the idea with Australia and New Zealand being joined by France and South Africa which meant there were eight votes in favor and eight opposed. With no decision being able to be made, John Kendall-Carpenter of England took the bold action of changing his vote and from there the Rugby World Cup was born.[2]

During the twenty-four year history of the Rugby World Cup the sport has dramatically changed to attract an ever rising number of viewers. Rugby World Cup 2011 saw an increase of 60% in the number of hours viewed. People watching matches were also increasingly from all walks of life, rather than the categories of teenage boys and middle-aged men. In April 2012, the IRB reported that Rugby World Cup 2011 was watched by more young people and more females than any other tournament to date. The 5-45 age group increased by 6%

from that of 2007 while the number of female viewers boomed to the extent that 45% of viewers were women, compared to 25% for Rugby World Cup 1995.[3] The sport however has not changed entirely. The same unions who in 1985 each had two votes still carry two votes today. Together they account for sixteen of the twenty-eight votes on the IRB Council, giving them veto power due to the fact that together they hold a clear majority.

Despite the power being held by a select group, the IRB, nevertheless, consists of ninety-seven member unions and has an additional twenty associate members. Progress has been made, however, as in 1991 Argentina, Canada, Italy and Japan were added to the IRB Council but they were given one vote each not two. No other union has since been added. Instead regions, divided in continental terms have been added, all having one vote each. The governing bodies of Africa (CAR), Asia (ARFU) Europe (FIRA), North America and the Caribbean (NACRA), Oceania (FORU) and South America (CONSUR) all have one vote each as the six recognized regional associations. The remaining two votes are held by the IRB Chairman and Vice Chairman.[4] The concentration of power in the hands of a select few has seen rugby commonly being refered to as a sport run by an old boys club.

The system, perhaps not surprisingly, voted in New Zealand as hosts of Rugby World Cup 2011 ahead of Japan who had appeared the stronger contender. Upon losing the vote the President of the Japanese Rugby Football Union and former Japanese Prime Minister, Yoshiro Mori, appeared puzzled over not winning the hosting rights for Rugby World Cup 2011. He commented that "Many people supported our goal of making rugby global. We did not receive the exact vote but we think that a lot of sympathy was with New Zealand because they weren't able to host the World Cup in 2003. All the boys in the meeting were saying that we have to make rugby global, so why do we have to wait for another five or ten years to make this happen?"[5] Mori believed that Japan and rugby had been shortchanged in saying that "Our tender was much better than those of the other two (New Zealand and South Africa), everybody thought it would be of great value to the game to stage the Rugby World Cup in Asia. We had public support and there is a feeling that the game needs to be globalised. "It looks as if this was a sympathy vote for New Zealand because they couldn't stage the World Cup in 2003. Maybe it was the old boy's network of the IRB at work."[6]

The secret ballot utilized by the IRB meant that the voting results have never been made public. Some unions made it known who they had voted for but it was an exception to the rule. What was known from the outset, however, was that New Zealand had far more in common with the voters than Japan did due to the regular international competition between New Zealand and the members of the IRB Council. Indeed, historically, the sport has very much been Anglo dominated with France only added to the IRB Council in 1978, a year after winning its second Grand Slam Five Nations title. It took France sixty-eight years to be added to the Council after France had initially been admitted to the Five Nations in 1910. The slow pace at which rugby operated until the 1980's has become a thing of the past as the sport has a higher number of competitive teams than previously and, crucially, the sport is taken much more seriously outside of the traditional strongholds than it used to be. The voting, however, does not represent the sport as best as it could.

Looking at it from a regional perspective there are two associations whose members will not have hosted a Rugby World Cup following Japan 2019. They are CONSUR and NACRA who are, at times, combined for various purposes by the IRB. The World Cup Qualification system, for instance, sees the winner of NACRA advance directly to the Rugby World Cup as Americas 1 while the runner-up faces the winner of CONSUR to determine the Americas 2 qualifier. For France 2007 and New Zealand 2011 this saw the United States of America qualify as Americas 2 after having defeated Uruguay. While neither CONSUR nor NACRA have hosted a Rugby World Cup both regions have had two countries compete at Rugby World Cup's. All four have won matches and overall the Americas have done well on the global stage.

Combined, the Americas account for nineteen of the ninety-six member unions[7] of the IRB World Rankings. NACRA has eleven full IRB members and two IRB associate members while CONSUR has eight full IRB members[8]. With just under 20% of the IRB's member unions and a combined total of more member unions than the likes of all regional associations except for Europe (FIRA), the Americas would appear to deserve hosting a Rugby World Cup in the near future. Europe is confirmed to host its fourth Rugby World Cup in 2015 and Asia will host its first four years later. This will set two new records. Firstly, Europe will have hosted more Rugby World Cup's than any other region, and it will have, in fact, hosted 50% of all Rugby World Cup's. Secondly the Rugby World Cup will then have a final frontier – the Americas. This book aims to change this by exploring the potential of Argentina as a Rugby World Cup host nation.

Part I
Building Recognition

1

The Beginning

From humble beginnings rugby in Argentina has developed into a popular sport. The development of the national team has been a long process, with a history dating back to 1873. The sport was brought to Argentina that year by British immigrants who contested the first known rugby match in the country at the Buenos Aires Cricket Club in the neighbourhood of Palermo. Due to a lack of players the match was disputed between one team of thirteen players and another of eleven and was contested between a team known as *Bancos* (Bankers in Spanish) who had thirteen players and *Ciudad* (City) who had eleven.[9] At the end of the nineteenth century Argentina had its first rugby governing body and league with the creation of the River Plate Rugby Football Union and the River Plate Rugby Football Championship in 1899. The creation of the union was made following talks between four clubs – the Buenos Aires Football Club, Belgrano Athletic, Lomas Athletic and Rosario Athletic Club.[10] Three of the four clubs are from Buenos Aires with Rosario Athletic Club being from the Argentina's third largest city, Rosario, to the north east of Buenos Aires. The club, nevertheless, continues to this day in Buenos Aires's club elite competition run by the Unión de Rugby de Buenos Aires (URBA).

Over time the British origins of rugby in Argentina have faded into the past being replaced by Spanish names such as URBA and the Unión Argentina de Rugby (UAR). The UAR replaced the River Plate Rugby Football Union as the name of the governing body of rugby in the country in 1951 some forty-one years after the first rugby international in Argentina. The first international rugby match was played in 1910 with Argentina facing the British Isles in a non-international in Buenos Aires. The visitors won the match 28-3. Before the changing of the name to the UAR in 1951 Argentina had only played fourteen other test matches, winning for the first time in 1936 against neighbours Chile in Valpariso in two tests. In the post war years, Argentina played far more international rugby than previously with sixteen tests being played in the decade of 1948-1958 in comparison to the ten matches played from the first ever one in 1910. The post war matches quickly confirmed that Argentina was the dominant force in South American rugby as the team was able to complete comfortable victories in the first ever South American Rugby Championship in 1951. Argentina won the tournament after defeating Uruguay 62-0, Brazil 72-0 and Chile 13-3 in Buenos Aires. The following year Argentina achieved success against a European opponent for the first time as the South Americans drew 3-3 against Ireland in one of two home tests.

When Argentina next won against a European visitor, it came after a sixteen year wait. Argentina's 9-5 win over Wales in 1968 marked Argentrina's first ever win against a non-South American nation. It was also the first time that Argentina had played against Wales. The teams played each other two weeks later in a match which was drawn 9-9 in Buenos Aires. Before receiving Wales, Argentina had played in four more editions of the South American Championship playing the likes of Brazil, Chile, Peru and Uruguay. Argentina won every match with the lowest margin being an eight point win over Chile in 1961. However, the true test of the ability of Argentine rugby could only be measured against intercontinental opposition. Argentina's first ever test v Scotland was played the year after Wales had been conquered and Scotland's fate was the same with Argentina winning the first test 20-3 but the Scot's turned it around to win the second 6-3. The results were central to establishing a name for Argentine rugby as the UAR was becoming capable of securing both more matches at home and tours abroad.

Ireland's tour to Argentina in 1970 was the start of a groundbreaking decade of rugby as Argentina became a far bigger name in international rugby by defeating traditional heavyweights and, in doing so, putting South American rugby on the world map. Before the 1970's, Argentina's tours had been to Southern Africa rather than to Europe but this changed entirely following a first ever series win, with Los Pumas[11] defeating Ireland 8-3 and 6-3 in Buenos Aires in 1970. Despite not facing elite opposition in 1971, the year has gone down in Argentine rugby history as extraordinary. It was the year in which IRB Hall of Famer Hugo Porta made his international debut. He faced Brazil, Chile, Paraguay and Uruguay in the South American Championship. In 1973 Argentina's long awaited first ever tour took place with Argentina facing Ireland and Scotland abroad. It completed a record year in which Los Pumas played eight test matches. The year began with two home wins against Romania and was followed by four record breaking wins in the South American Championship which saw Argentina defeat Paraguay by 95 points, Uruguay by 55, Brazil by 98 and Chile by 57. The winning run did not continue in Europe as Ireland won 21-8 and Scotland won 12-11. Argentina returned to Europe for further tours in 1975 and 1976 with Argentina playing in France and Wales. The South Americans were winless but pushed Wales to the limit in losing 20-19 in Cardiff with Hugo Porta standing out.

In contrast to the 1973 and 1975 European tours in which Argentina played two tests, the 1976 tour featured only one test. The UAR had secured a home series against New Zealand which saw Argentina take on the All Blacks for the first time in history. Despite having played against South African sides in non-internationals,[12] Argentina had never faced the Springboks which made the 1976 matches v New Zealand the first ever between Argentina and a team from what is now The Rugby Championship. New Zealand returned home victorious having won the tests 18-9 and 26-6. The following year Argentina received France for two tests in Buenos Aires. The Europeans dominated the first test in winning 26-3 but Los Pumas made history seven days later with an 18-18 draw on July 02 to mark the first time Argentina had not lost against the French. Also in 1977 the UAR took a historical move by hosting the South American Championship in Tucumán, a city with a strong rugby presence. Los Pumas won the four tests in impressive style defeating Brazil 78-6, Uruguay 70-0, Paraguay 77-3 and Chile 25-10.

Argentina continued to face new teams in the late 1970's. In 1978 Los Pumas faced England and Italy for the first time and had a mixed tour. Argentina, like it had done in matches against the other Five Nations teams, drew v England. The 13-13 result was also Argentina's first ever appearance at Twickenham. Argentina's other tour match was not so memorable, however, as Argentina lost 19-6 vs Italy in Rovigo. Argentina toured New Zealand for the first time ever in 1979, playing tests in Dunedin and Wellington losing both tests by nine points in September. The following month, Argentina defeated Uruguay, Chile, Paraguay and Brazil in the South American Championship with the 19-16 win over Uruguay being the narrowest match ever played between the two sides. In the same tournament Argentina scored more than 100 points for the first time, defeating Brazil 109-3. The year, and decade, ended with Australia playing two tests in Buenos Aires. It was the first time the two countries had ever faced each other and the South Americans collected a further scalp with a 24-13 victory in the first test. Australia recovered to square the series with a 17-12 win but Porta's first test performance which included two conversions, three drop goals and a penalty had established Argentina as serious rugby nation.

Argentina was not able to secure as many test matches in the 1980's as it had in the 1970's. The decade started off well for Argentina with Los Pumas playing three tests in 1980. The first was a match in Buenos Aires against a World XV while the other two matches had Argentina facing Fiji for the first time. The South Americans were notably better than Fiji, winning the matches by scores of 36-22 and 34-22. The following year again had Argentina playing three international matches with Argentina hosting England on a two test tour in late May – early June and then hosting Canada in October. Like in 1978, Argentina played very well against the English, drawing the match 19-19 in Buenos Aires. One week later, however, England completed a six point win in the second test but the 12-6 win would be the last time England would play Argentina in the 1980's. Argentina's spring test v Canada was the first time the two countries had played each other and it would be the South Americans who were the stronger with Los Pumas winning the match 35-0.

The impressive results achieved from 1970-1981 would be overshadowed by the Falklands / Malvinas War in 1982 between Argentina and Great Britain. The then Argentine military dictatorship lead by Leopoldo Galtieri invaded and occupied the Islands leading to British retaliation and a war which was won by Great Britain.[13] While the war saw democracy return to Argentina it had negative impacts on rugby as not only England but also Ireland, Scotland and Wales cut ties with the UAR due to their outrage over the war which had killed 255 British servicemen[14]. None of the home unions would play Argentina at all before the inaugural Rugby World Cup in 1987. Tensions thawed at the end of the decade with global changes due to the end of the Cold War changing the global political landscape. This saw the rugby relations between Argentina and the home unions repaired and Argentina faced England, Ireland and Scotland in 1990 and Wales in 1991, as part of the World Cup.

The British and Irish boycott of facing Los Pumas seriously held back the progress of Argentine rugby by taking away 50% of what was the elite opposition. It meant Argentina hosted no visiting team at all in 1982 and would have to wait until November to play a test match. Argentina toured France and Spain losing twice against the French and defeating Spain 28-19 in the first international between the two nations. At this time test rugby against South Africa was off limits but it was common for teams to bend the rules and face South Africa in matches that were international games featuring teams playing under alternative names or simply not as official test sides. The British and Irish Lions, for instance played in South Africa in 1974 and 1980 and the New Zealand Cavaliers toured in 1986. Argentina was not an exception with Hugo Porta making history as he scored a try and kicked a South American team to victory over the Springboks in the apartheid country in 1982. The team was officially the South American Jaguars, in a move comparable to the Lions. This enabled matches in 1980, 1982 and 1984 to be played as no country was actually being represented. The make up of the team, however, was not a composite team despite the name suggesting otherwise, the teams 21-12 win over South Africa in Bloemfontein on April 03 1982 was a South Africa v Argentina match with all the players for the South American Jaguars being Argentineans.[15] For this reason the win should arguably be considered as Argentina's first win against South Africa.

1983 was a better year for scheduling and also a year which saw history being made. Argentina played six matches, starting with a 28-20 win over a World XV in June and followed by victories over Chile, Paraguay and Uruguay in the South American Championship in July. The matches against CONSUR opposition had been preparation for Argentina's first ever tour of Australia. The two test tour was another fine point in the career of Hugo Porta with Argentina winning the first test in Brisbane convincingly. The 18-3 victory saw the world class Wallaby team shut down with Porta reigning supreme against highly fancied players such as David Campese and Mark Ella.[16] Australia, like in 1979, recovered well to win the second test but would be unable to win the test series.

When Argentina next played test rugby the lines had already been drawn up and the rugby world had been forever changed. Argentina hosted France for two tests in June, three months after the decision had been made to create a Rugby World Cup tournament and for it to happen in 1987. The pattern that had emerged over the previous decade and a half continued in 1985 for Los Pumas as the team continued to collect new scalps in two test series. Argentina's 24-16 win over France marked the first time Argentina had defeated Les Bleus. France, however, hit back to win the second test 23-15. After defeating Uruguay, Chile and Paraguay in the South American Championship, Argentina did what many thought could not be done – perform against New Zealand. Argentina hosted the All Blacks for two tests in the spring with the visitors winning the first 33-20. The next weekend, however, saw Hugo Porta deliver a top class performance as he scored all twenty-one of Argentina's points in the 21-21 draw. New Zealand would go on win the inaugural Rugby World Cup unchallenged less than eighteen months later.

France returned to Argentina in 1986 for another two test tour looking to rectify the first test loss the previous year. Argentina, however, delivered a solid performance winning a tight contest 15-13. France reversed the result the following weekend with a 22-9 victory. Argentina was unable to compete well in Australia that year as the Wallabies humbled Los Pumas 39-19 and 26-0. It seemed the inaugural Rugby World Cup had come two years too late for Argentina. Los Pumas, however, had one final test to play. Three weeks before the tournament, Argentina faced Uruguay in Montevideo winning 38-3.[17]

2

Rugby World Cup Amateur Era (1987-1995)

1987
Despite not being a serious contender for the World Cup title in 1987, Argentina had firmly established itself as a genuine power in global rugby and entered the inaugural Rugby World Cup looking to finish second in the Pool to advance to the Quarter Finals. The South Americans, on paper looked to be destined for a place in the play-offs given its Pool opponents were Fiji, Italy and New Zealand. Argentina's wins over Australia in 1983 and France in 1985 and 1986 seemed to suggest that Argentina could match it with the best teams. Moreover, the 1980 matches between Argentina and Fiji saw Los Pumas win comfortably. However it had been a long time between matches and with Argentina unable to play as many test matches as it would have desired the team entered Rugby World Cup 1987 in an unprepared manner. When Argentina played its first ever Rugby World Cup match, in Hamilton vs Fiji in May 1987 the team failed to deliver and Fiji won the match 28-9 scoring four tries to one. There was more to it, however, than the South Americans simply having a bad day. The teams star, Hugo Porta, was at this time 36 years of age and Fiji's flair was something that Argentina was not so familiar with.

The opening loss all but ended Argentina's chances of advancing to the Quarter Finals but not entirely. Four days latter Argentina took on Italy in Christchurch and came out on top in a good contest in which both sides scored two tries each. Argentina's 25-16 win saw Porta kicking five penalties in comparison to Oscar Collodo of Italy who scored two. A short turn around saw Italy backing up its loss to Argentina by facing Fiji three days latter. The Europeans won a tight contest 18-15 which meant Argentina could make the Quarter Finals with a win or a draw against the All Blacks. Any chance of Argentina making the final eight of the inaugural Rugby World Cup were dashed by an impressive New Zealand performance with the hosts winning 46-15 to eliminate Argentina.

While it was still the amateur era the inaugural Rugby World Cup had changed the shape of rugby forever. The international calendar was already being organized unlike previously with World Cup's being the focus and teams needing to start preparation sooner rather than latter. With time it has been accelerated to the extent that the clearing out of aged players in favor of younger ones often happens immediately after World Cup's. One team who failed to make the necessary changes for Rugby World Cup 1991 was the World champions, New Zealand who failed to defend its title in large part due to having a number of aged players, especially in the forwards.[18] Argentina was another that did not adapt quickly enough. While new players were selected it was not always the case as Hugo Porta earned more international caps in the lead up to Rugby World Cup 1991. His final test came in 1990 with Porta coming out of retirement to face England, Scotland and Ireland in Europe.

1991
The period between the first and second Rugby World Cup's had high and low points for Argentina. Los Pumas recorded some impressive wins but also some big loses. After the inaugural Rugby World Cup Argentina completed 1987 with six additional test matches all in South America. Los Pumas warmed up for the South American Championship with a 40-12 win over Spain in Mar del Plata and then ran riot in Santiago with a 62-4[19] win over Paraguay and a 47-9 win over Chile. Argentina then closed out the year with two home tests against World Cup Semi Finalists Australia in Buenos Aires. The first test on October 31 was a 19-19 draw while the second made Argentina's loss vs Fiji seem bizarre as Argentina impressed with a 27-19 victory.

Australia had been defeated 30-24 by France at one of the greatest ever Rugby World Cup matches earlier that year. Australia looked to have secured victory late in the match only for France to level the scores and then went ahead with a try to Serge Blanco to win the match. France's win meant the team considered as the World Cup favorites[20] had been eliminated. While Los Pumas faced Australia twice in 1987, the team went on to play France four times in 1988 with two matches being played in Buenos Aires in June and France hosting Argentina in Nantes and Lille in November. The first test was an even contest which France won 18-15 but the Buenos Aires series was tied with Argentina winning the second test 18-6. France impressed at home winning by margins of 10 and 20 points.

While Argentina and all competing teams had been invited to play in Rugby World Cup 1987 the same was not true for the 1991 tournament. It was the first

Rugby World Cup and it had been organized in less than two years with no teams qualifying due to the short period of time between the decision to have a Rugby World Cup and the tournament itself. The eight Quarter Finalists from 1987 went on to automatically qualify for Rugby World Cup 1991 with the IRB determining the remaining eight places from a series of qualifying tournaments which were broken down into regions. This saw Argentina play in the Americas zone and take on Canada and the United States of America in a home and a way series played from September 1989-June 1990. Firstly, however, Argentina had three tests in June with a home test against Italy and a two test tour of New Zealand and then four matches in the South American Championship. The first test was a victory as Argentina defeated Italy 21-16 in Buenos Aires. Los Pumas, however, were overwhelmed by the All Blacks in losing by 51 points in the first test match and 37 in the second. Argentina completed its preparation for the Rugby World Cup Qualifying matches with a tough schedule of four matches in sevens days in defeating Brazil 103-9, Chile 36-9, Paraguay 75-7 and Uruguay 34-14.

Argentina started its 1991 qualifying campaign with a home match against the USA in November 1989. Like Argentina, the USA had won one of its three matches at Rugby World Cup 1987. That aside there was little to compare between the two sides and their match in Buenos Aires was the first time Argentina and the USA had ever played an official test match. Argentina was the better side, winning the encounter 23-6. The USA had lost its opening qualifying match by a similar score, 21-3 against Canada. The Canadians then defeated Argentina 15-6 at Burnaby Lake, British Colombia to give itself a strong chance of winning the Americas qualification series. The USA hosted Argentina in Santa Barbara, California and showed improvement but was defeated 13-6 by Los Pumas. This meant that the return match in Buenos Aires between Canada and Argentina would determine the final order of Americas 1, 2 and 3. Canada completed back-to-back wins in defeating Argentina 19-15 to qualify as Americas 1 and be drawn into Pool 3 which also included Fiji, Franca and Romania. Americas 2 and 3 had noticeably tougher asks as the Pools that the qualifiers would play in featured a team each from the Five Nations and either Australia or New Zealand. Argentina would join Australia, Wales and debutants Western Samoa[21] while the USA would take on England, Italy and New Zealand.

With the teams knowing who they would be going up against in the 1991 tournament which started in October 1991, the remaining matches served simply as preparation. Argentina had two home tests against England and split the series with England winning the first match 25-12 and Argentina winning the second 15-13. Argentina´s tour of Europe to complete the year saw Los Pumas play well against Ireland in losing 20-18 before England and Scotland completed massive wins by scores of 51-0 and 49-3. The same two sides would go on to reach the World Cup Semi Finals the following year. Argentina's match at Twickenham was overshadowed by the sending off of frontrower Federico Mendez who punched English secondrower Paul Ackford in a well documented incident.

Argentina had a sufficient number of tests in 1991 before the Rugby World Cup with four home tests and two away ones in neighboring South American countries. New Zealand toured Argentina playing two tests in Buenos Aires in July with the World Champions completing 28-14 and 36-6 victories. The following month Argentina played Chile in Santiago, winning 41-6. Argentina then completed the 1991 South American Championship in September and October by taking on Uruguay, Paraguay and Brazil just before the start of the global tournament. The South American Championship was played so late that Argentina's 84-6 win over Brazil took place just two days before the opening match of Rugby World Cup 1991.

Argentina's three Pool matches took place in Wales with the principality being one of five nations hosting World Cup matches. The tournament was officially hosted by England with Twickenham hosting the opening match and the final but the four other members of the Five Nations each hosted Rugby World Cup matches. Argentina started by taking on the favorite to win the Pool, Australia. The South Americans played well, pushing the Wallabies hard in a 32-19 loss. The next opponent was Wales who had been shocked in losing 16-13 to Western Samoa in its first match. The result meant Wales needed to defeat Argentina and also either needed Argentina to defeat Western Samoa or had to, itself, defeat Australia. Argentina again played well against Wales but was unable to win the match as the Welsh completed a 16-7 victory to eliminate Los Pumas from the tournament. Argentina then faced Western Samoa and lost 35-12 to exit the tournament winless.

1995

Like Rugby World Cup 1987, the disappointing campaign in 1991 did not seem to show the qualities of Los Pumas. On both occasions Argentina had gone through cycles of positive and negative performances which included some significant victories and some humbling defeats. The pattern of inconsistent results continued in the years between Rugby World Cup 1991 and 1995. In 1992, for instance, Argentina played six test matches with three of the tests being against France. Argentina were downed 27-12 and 33-9 by the French in Buenos Aires in July but ended the year with a 24-20 win in Nantes. It was a significant result as it marked the first time that Argentina had won a test match in France. The match was the third of Argentina's end of year European tour in which Los Pumas faced Spain, Romania and France. Earlier, however, Argentina had hosted Spain in Buenos Aires, winning 38-10 in September. One month latter Madrid was the setting for a return match which saw Argentina winning 43-34. Argentina then traveled to Bucharest to take on Romania and won the match 21-18 which meant that for the first time in history Argentina had gone undefeated in a European tour.

1992 was also significant for global rugby as it marked the return of South Africa to the global stage. South Africa had missed the first two Rugby World Cups and a lot of international competition due to the country's apartheid government. The system was withering away due to changing global perceptions of racism and in South Africa the apartheid legal set up was officially abolished from 1990-1991 which enabled South Africa to return to the international stage to face New Zealand and Australia in August and France and England in November 1992. The following year South Africa would play seven tests with two against Argentina in Buenos Aires. The Springboks won both tests but were given a tough outing in the first test which South Africa won 29-26. The year saw Argentina playing eight tests having earlier hosted Japan for two tests in May and having played in the South American Championship. Argentina won all six matches, starting with a 30-27 win against Japan in Tucumán and the winning 45-20 in the second test in Buenos Aires. Argentina again had few problems against its neighbors in defeating Brazil 114-3, Chile 70-7, Paraguay 51-3 and Uruguay 19-10. The latter of the matches doubled as qualifying matches for Rugby World Cup 1995.

By this stage teams were well into preparations for the 1995 tournament. South Africa's selection as the host nation had resulted in changes to the qualifying system. The tournament continued the format of sixteen teams divided into four pools of four but with South Africa hosting there were nine automatic qualifiers rather than eight. South Africa joined the eight Quarter Finalists from Rugby World 1991 – Australia, Canada, England, France, Ireland, New Zealand, Scotland and Western Samoa as automatic qualifiers. The remaining seven places were determined through qualifying which involved forty-three nations, eighteen more than the twenty-five who had played in qualifying matches for the 1991 tournament. Despite South Africa's participation Africa retained a qualifying slot which saw the Americas have only one qualifying slot. Canada's automatic qualification meant only one of Argentina or the USA would qualify for Rugby World Cup 1995 and similarly there would only be one qualifying place for Fiji and Tonga to contest.

Having won the South American zone in 1993, Argentina advanced to face the winner of the North American zone in 1994. The USA had won the zone after defeating Bermuda 60-3 in March 1994 which set up a home and away knock-out series with Argentina winning both matches - 28-22 and 16-11 to qualify for Rugby World Cup 1995. The matches were played in May and June with Argentina hosting Scotland for two tests in between. Argentina won both tests by narrow margins - 16-15 and 19-17 but, importantly, completed a home series win against a side that had won the previous international between the sides 49-3 in 1990. Argentina visited South Africa for two tests in October but was outplayed in losing by 20 points with the Springboks winning the first 42-22 and the second 46-26.

The year of the third Rugby World Cup saw Argentina play a record thirteen tests with three being World Cup matches. The World Cup started in late May which changed the international calendar that year. Argentina had four warm-up matches starting with home tests against Uruguay and Canada in March in what doubled as a first ever Pan American Rugby Championship. There was reason to believe that Argentina had a stronger team to that of Rugby World Cup 1991 as Los Pumas defeated Uruguay 44-3 and Canada 29-26 to win the American title. The subsequent tour of Australia, however, saw Argentina humbled with the World Champion Wallabies winning 53-7 in Brisbane and 30-13 in Sydney. It saw Argentina enter the World Cup as a team that had potential but would need to lift its game if it were to succeed in reaching the Quarter Finals. The Australian tour, however, did go down as a key moment in Argentine rugby history as IRB Hall of Famer Agustín Pichot made his debut in the Brisbane test at the age of 19.

The draw for Rugby World Cup 1995 was a tough ask for Argentina with Los Pumas grouped with 1991 runners-up England, Quarter Finalists Western Samoa and Italy in Pool B. The South Americans started the tournament by facing England in Durban and proved to be extremely competitive. Argentina not only scored the games two tries but the South Americans were also leading the match before the boot of Rob Andrew turned it around giving England a 24-18 victory. Three days latter Argentina was playing its second match of the tournament. Los Pumas travelled to East London to face Western Samoa who had defeated Italy 42-18 in its opening match of the tournament. Similar to the match against Fiji in 1987 it was a team that played a style of rugby that was not like the opponents Argentina had been facing in the years leading up to the 1995 tournament. The match was in many ways a continuation of the encounter against England with Los Pumas playing good rugby and being unlucky in not winning the match.

Western Samoa came from behind to win 32-26 which meant Argentina was eliminated from the tournament with one match still left to play.

The South Americans had a chance to leave the tournament with a win against Italy but instead exited the tournament winless and did so with a former Puma kicking Italy to victory. Diego Dominguez was born and raised in Córdoba and made his international debut for Argentina in 1989 after having initially been selected as a 20 year old in 1986 for Argentina's tour of France. The presence of Hugo Porta, however kept him out of the team and Dominguez opted to play for his mothers home country, Italy with whom he made his debut in 1991 and went on to play in three Rugby World Cups. Dominguez broke the Italian points scoring record and is one of only five players to have scored 1000 or more points in international rugby.[22] Since he stopped playing Italy has struggled to replace him and has lost a number of key matches due to goal kicking. The match between Argentina and Italy at Rugby World Cup 1995, however, was a good day for Italian rugby with the Europeans winning 31-25 with Dominguez scoring 25 points.

Despite being eliminated winless the year was far from over for Los Pumas who still had six tests to play. The first was in Asunción with Paraguay hosting Argentina in the South American Championship Argentina won 103-9. Six days latter Los Pumas faced Chile in Santiago winning 78-3 and then Argentina hosted Uruguay in Posadas winning 52-37. The year came to an end in October with Romania, Italy and France all visiting Argentina. The team's failure to convert good performances into wins at the World Cup was highlighted by Argentina's strong showing v Romania with a 51-16 win in Buenos Aires a 26-6 win over Italy in Tucumán. But the year did not end on a high as France completed a 47-12 win in Buenos Aires Indeed, the final Rugby World Cup before professionalism was, from an Argentine perspective, a case of what could have been. Argentina could very well have won all three matches. Instead, the team finished bottom of the pool.

3

A Giant Leap - Rugby World Cup 1999

Rugby World Cup 1995 was a turning point in the history of rugby. It was the last World Cup tournament before the start of professionalism. The sport was opened to professionalism on August 26 that year following a meeting in Paris in which the IRB officially removed restrictions on payments and related benefits to people associated with the sport. Rugby as a sport was deemed to be under threat in a number of important places, in particular Australia. The rival sporting code of rugby league had been attracting rugby players from Australia and New Zealand to play as professionals and thus change codes. However, a new movement at the time called Super League threatened the sport like never before with large salaries on offer to big name rugby players which was countered by rugby turning professional. In the case of Australia and New Zealand it saw the creation of SANZAR together with South Africa and a move to establish the Tri Nations and the Super 12 in 1996.[23] In Europe it saw the creation of the Heineken Cup in 1995 and an opening of doors which led to Italy turning professional and being admitted into the Five Nations, creating the Six Nations in 2000.

While progress was being made in Europe it was a different situation in Argentina. The UAR opted against transforming rugby in the country and decided to keep the game strictly amateur. The union was afraid of damaging the club scene in the country which in the case of Buenos Aires was and still is arguably the best in the world with over seventy clubs affiliated to URBA and fifteen others being invited members.[24] This saw a number of players take up professional contracts abroad and the UAR initially responded by making players based abroad non-eligible for Los Pumas. This saw Argentina lose players to other countries in a similar fashion to that of Diego Dominguez playing for Italy. Patricio Noriega for instance had earned twenty-five caps for Argentina, including playing in two Rugby World Cup's but was playing for Australia in 1998 after he had been signed to play Super Rugby for the ACT Brumbies in 1996. He subsequently played in France before joining another Australian side, the Waratahs in 2006.[25] He went on to play twenty-four times for the Wallabies.

With some players unavailable and the national team generally being reformed following disappointment in 1995, Argentina had a demanding task of winning tests against teams made up of players who had recently become professional. Los Pumas warmed up for its home June test series against France with an away 37-18 victory against Uruguay in Montevideo. Five players were making their test debuts including one of the finest props in world rugby over the past decade or so, Mauricio Reggiardo. He combined with Roberto Grau over the following two weekends to take on France in Buenos Aires. It was the start of a long term combination that would persist until Rugby World Cup 2003 with the pair both starting their final tests together against Ireland in Adelaide. Their debut together against France was not so memorable with France winning the first test 34-27 and the second 34-15.

Los Pumas were busy in the second half of the international season with the Pan American Cup which was played in the Canadian province of Ontario and featured Canada, Argentina, Uruguay and the USA. Argentina used the tournament with an eye to the future with nine players making their test debuts in the team´s first match of the tournament. Argentina took on the USA in Nepean with three big names of the future debuting - secondrower Carlos Ignacio Fernández Lobbe, tighthead prop Martín Scelzo and flyhalf Gonzalo Quesada. Argentina won the match 29-26 and four days latter took on Uruguay in Hamilton. The 54-20 victory featured Quesada scoring nineteen points and it also marked the debut of hooker Mario Ledesma. The third and final match of the tournament saw Argentina defeating Canada 41-21 in Markham to be crowned the Pan American Champions.

Argentina welcomed back a number of players for the end of year tests against South Africa and England. Argentina lost by scores of 46-15 and 44-21 in Buenos Aires against South Africa who was fresh from a first ever Tri Nations campaign and had a squad now consisting entirely of professional players. The second test against the Springboks was noticeable due to flyhalf José Cillay subsequently being dropped and replaced by Quesada. Cillay had been Argentina´s flyhalf at Rugby World Cup 1995 and, in being outplayed by Diego Dominguez he was unable to fill the boots of his predecessor, Hugo Porta. Quesada was selected at flyhalf for Argentina´s final test of the year, against England at Twickenham and he scored all of his sides points in the 20-18 defeat.

With the British and Irish Lions touring South Africa England took up the opportunity to play a two test series in Argentina in mid 1997. England contributed seventeen players to the thirty-five man Lions squad that year. This resulted in England fielding seven uncapped players but amongst them were some stars of the future including Richard Cockerill and members of the 2003 World Champion side - Danny Grewcock and Martin Corry. Despite not being the first choice English players they were all professionals unlike the vast majority of those representing Argentina. It was apparent in the first test which England won 46-20. The following week, however, Argentina turned things around to win 33-13. But there was no room for celebration as two weeks after the win Argentina played a two test series in New Zealand and was taken apart by an impressive All Blacks side that won the first test 93-8[26] and the second 62-10.

The heavy defeats gave Argentina a wake up call and it was taken seriously by the coaching staff who experimented heavily for the teams spring matches in the South American Championship. Fourteen players made their Pumas debuts in the 78-0 win over Paraguay, a further five debuted two weeks latter in the 58-17 win over Uruguay and six others debuted versus Chile in the team's 50-10 victory. A stronger Argentine squad was selected for the October tour of Europe in which Los Pumas defeated Romania 45-18, drew 18-18 with Italy and lost 32-27 against France. The three matches were all played in France as a part of a special Latin Cup won by the host nation. Los Pumas returned to host a two test tour with Australia visiting in November. Australia won the first test 23-15 while Argentina won the second 18-16. It was the last time that Argentina hosted a test series against a SANZAR nation. Of the fifteen starting players who lost the second test against Los Pumas eleven went on to become world champions two years latter as Australia won the 1999 Rugby World Cup.

A detailed calendar awaited Los Pumas in 1998 with the team playing thirteen test matches including World Cup qualifying matches and a first ever visit to Asia. The international season began in June with France touring Argentina and impressing with good wins in Buenos Aires by scores of 35-18 and 37-12. Argentina also hosted Romania for a one off test in Rosario in August, winning 68-22 in what was preparation for three other tests latter that month. The key matches of the year, however, were the Pan American Cup matches. The 1998 edition featured Argentina, Canada, Uruguay and the USA and the matches doubled as qualifying matches for Rugby World Cup 1999. The IRB had expanded the Rugby World Cup from sixteen to twenty participants following the 1995 tournament and this gave extra importance to the Pan American Cup matches as the results would play a part in the seeding for places in Rugby World Cup 1999.

Argentina hosted the tournament and came out on top after winning all its matches by impressive margins. The results in comparison to how Argentina and Canada performed in qualifying for Rugby World Cup 1991 suggested conclusively that Argentina had progressed as a rugby nation while Canada had almost certainly taken a few steps backward. Argentina opened with a 52-24 win over the USA with Quesada scoring 22 points. Three days latter Argentina defeated Uruguay 55-0 with a much changed side which set up an Argentina vs Canada match with the winner to qualify for Rugby World Cup 1999 as Americas 1 and the loser Americas 2. Los Pumas delivered a five tries to one performance in defeating the Canadians 54-28. On the same day the USA defeated Uruguay 21-16 to qualify as Americas 3. Uruguay were not eliminated, however, as Los Teros entered repercharge and went on to qualify as Repercharge 2 after having defeated Portugal and Morocco in 1999.

The qualification series confirmed that Argentina would be in Pool D together with Japan, Samoa and host nation Wales. It was a winnable group for Los Pumas and it was probably the fairest of the five pools in that there was no team that was, at the time, significantly better than the others. Wales had not made the Quarter Finals of Rugby World Cup 1991 due to a loss against the Samoans while the side missed out in 1995 due to a loss against Ireland. While Wales was joined by Argentina and Japan to form a competitive pool there was concern raised at the time that it was not a fair reflection of the global order of international rugby in that Pool B featured England and New Zealand, two Semi Finalists from the previous Rugby World Cup. It was, however, not the only pool lacking two teams from the Five Nations and Tri Nations tournaments as Pool C only had one with France being joined by Canada, Fiji and Namibia.

Argentina´s coaching staff had been unsettled in the post Rugby World Cup 1995 years. José Luis Imhoff had been the headcoach from 1996-1999 with José Fernández and Héctor Méndez also having responsibilities and former All Blacks coach, Alex Wyllie being an advisor. In 1997, however, it changed with Fernández no longer involved and in 1998 Méndez left the frame. 1999 started with Imhoff and Wyllie being the coaches but soon Méndez returned to replace Imhoff and then with the Rugby World Cup approaching Wyllie was officially the team´s only coach. The situation was nothing less than volatile with infighting within the UAR ultimately leading to Argentina not having a coach. Wyllie was, in the end, appointed as the coach[27] and had the task of guiding Los Pumas to the

Quarter Finals for the first time in Rugby World Cup history. It was therefore not a simple task of the coaching staff identifying probable players for the tournament and actively building a team.

The constant changes combined with the new structure of professionalism made the management of the team highly complicated. Nevertheless, many new players continued to be tried in 1998 with ten players, including Ignacio Corleto and Rodrigo Roncero, making their Pumas debuts in Tokyo in September. Japan ran out 44-29 winners but there was little to be taken from the match ahead of the World Cup encounter between the two the following year. In October Argentina took on Paraguay, Chile and Uruguay in the South American Championship winning the matches 59-0, 25-17 and 30-14 again with a number of new players being blooded. In total fifteen players represented Argentina for the first time with the two notable players being Rimas Alvarez Kairles who made his debut v Paraguay and Felipe Contepomi v Chile. In November Argentina completed a three test European tour. The tour started with a 23-19 loss against Italy with Dominguez kicking thirteen points. France had a big 34-14 win over Argentina in Nantes and Wales won 43-30 in Llanelli in a match which had Pichot and Contepomi forming a scrumhalf – flyhalf combination for the first time.

While Rugby World Cup 1995 was a turning point for global rugby, Rugby World Cup 1999 was a turning point for Argentine rugby. Despite the players still being predominantly amateur the team was breaking away from the second tier and leaving the likes of Canada and Romania behind. Los Pumas had four warm-up matches before the 1999 event with two home tests against Wales and away tests against Scotland and Ireland. The matches versus Wales were a sign of things to come as the same fixture had been chosen to open Rugby World Cup 1999 at the new Millenium Stadium in Cardiff. The South Americans played some good rugby in the June tests but it was the Europeans who came out on top with Wales winning the tests by scores of 36-26 and 23-16. In theory Argentina's match at Murrayfield should have been a loss because Scotland was the Five Nations champions and the players were all professionals. Not withstanding, Argentina delivered a strong performance to leave a mark ahead of the World Cup with a 31-22 victory over Scotland in which Quesada slotted sixteen points. Argentina's final warm-up match was against Ireland four and a half weeks before the kick-off of Rugby World Cup 1999. Given how the tournament transpired, it would prove to be the most important pre-World Cup match of the year. Ireland won 32-24 in Dublin.

Despite never having previously gone beyond the pool stage of a Rugby World Cup and not having a professional domestic structure Argentina was chosen ahead of Samoa and Japan to face Wales in the opening fixture of the 1999 tournament. Historically Argentina had had a bigger impact on global rugby than Samoa who was a newcomer after not having featured in the inaugural Rugby World Cup in 1987. Japan had, like Argentina, only won one match in the first three editions of the World Cup and similarly did not have a historical record of wins against the likes of Australia, England, France or Scotland. Argentina proved during the tournament opener to be up to the task as Los Pumas played well in going down 23-18 to Wales. Wales scored two tries to zero with all of Argentina's points coming from the boot of Quesada. The result meant Argentina had to win its two remaining pool fixtures. The team's second match took place at the historical Stradey Park[28] in Llanelli with Argentina looking for revenge after having been defeated by Samoa at Rugby World Cup 1991 and Rugby World Cup 1995. Quesada delivered a decisive performance in arguably the best game of his career as he scored 27 points in Argentina's 32-16 triumph. The team's remaining pool match was against Japan in Cardiff. The South Americans were in firm control against Japan with Quesada kicking 21 points to see Argentina qualify for the knock-out phase.

The unique format for Rugby World Cup 1999 was different to that of previous tournaments. With twenty teams instead of sixteen the tournament was structured on a five pool system with each of the Five Nations hosting one pool each. The winner of each pool qualified for the Quarter Finals while runners up and the best third placed team would play in a knock-out round to determine the three remaining Quarter Finalists. Wales had won the group despite having been defeated by Samoa. In defeating Wales, Samoa would join Argentina in the knock-out phase with Samoa facing Scotland at Murrayfield and Argentina facing Ireland in Lens. The two other teams were England and Fiji who played at Twickenham. The results saw Scotland advancing to the Quarter Finals to play New Zealand and England advancing to play South Africa while the winner of Argentina v Ireland would travel to Dublin to face France.

The elimination match was played on October 20 and saw Argentine rugby rise to glory as a South American country made up mainly of local amateur players defeated a strong European team to advance to the Quarter Finals. The 28-24 victory was a win based on merit with Argentina having come from behind with a stunning try on the left touchline to winger Diego Albanese. Quesada landed the difficult conversion and then slotted a late penalty to put Argentina four points clear. Ireland fought back hard and had a late opportunity to score a try. Ireland raided attacks on the Pumas goal line but was held off by a determined defensive unit. Four days latter Argentina was playing at the home of Irish rugby, Lansdowne Road against France in a Quarter Final. The choice of the venue was due to the match having been planned to be between Ireland and France. While Argentina had been playing Ireland France had been resting. Fatigue certainly appeared to factor in how the match unfolded with Argentina giving France a solid match and pushing the Europeans to the limit. France had stormed clear with early tries before a Pumas fight-back saw Argentina narrow the lead to seven points with eight minutes remaining. France though, scored two late tries to secure a 47-26 victory and eliminate Argentina from the tournament.

At the heart of Argentina's performance was Agustín Pichot who was heroic in his play and went on to be named by Sports Illustrated as Argentina's best player since Hugo Porta and having had one of the great individual performances of the tournament.[29] Pichot scored his second try of the tournament after having previously scored against Japan. His performances made him the obvious person to take over the Pumas captaincy and lead Argentine rugby into the new millennium. His colleague in the halves, Gonzalo Quesada was honored with the Golden Boot award for being the tournament's highest point scorer, scoring 102 points. Argentina's progress had been extraordinary and it would continue in the new millennium.

4

Consolidation – Rugby World Cup 2003

While Argentina was not making any moves to establish a professional rugby structure in the country the top players were increasingly in demand to join European clubs. Many more opportunities than previously became available to Argentine players after Rugby World Cup 1999. The increased number of contracts on offer had a huge impact on Argentine rugby that has forever changed the shape of Argentine rugby. The team that had defeated Ireland in Lens featured six players who were or had previously been professional players.[30] But nine other players who played in the knock-out match versus Ireland went on to become professionals. Some such as Quesada were signed and began playing professional rugby shortly after the tournament. Others were signed shortly thereafter which helped Argentine rugby kick-on and continue to evolve.[31] The market opened up especially in England and France and it helped solidify Argentina as a Tier One rugby nation by having the country's top players exposed to a professional regime in which they were training and playing full time just like players from the Tri Nations and Five Nations teams.

Former Argentine test centre, Marcelo Loffreda was named as the new Pumas coach in April 2000. His appointment saw a return to stability in the coaching circles after Argentina had gone through numerous changes between 1995 and 1999. Alex Wyllie worked well to restore order. He was well respected as a quality coach and being a foreigner he was not a part of domestic problems of the time. Loffreda was accomplished as both a player and a coach. On the international stage he had played fifty test matches from 1978-1994, with most of his international career seeing him play outside Hugo Porta. He was a product of the SIC rugby club and was the club captain from 1983-1992. After retiring in 1994 he became the SIC headcoach and guided the club to the URBA championship in 1994, 1997 and 1999. He took over the team at a good time with the buzz from 1999 far from over. His first test in charge was a World Cup rematch with Argentina taking on Ireland. A settled team was named with no players making their test debuts. Ireland was confident having had defeated France in an away match for the first time since 1972. Los Pumas, however, saw that Loffreda would have a successful debut as Argentina won the match 34-23 at the Ferrocaril Oeste Stadium in Buenos Aires. Argentina then travelled to Australia for a two test tour to take on the World Champions. Loffreda made some changes to the team with the interesting selection of Felipe Contepomi at fullback. The Wallabies won the Brisbane test 53-6 but Argentina played much better in the second test in Canberra in losing 32-25.

Los Pumas only had two further tests to play in 2000 – a home test against South Africa and an away test against England in November. The UAR took the bold move of relocating the Springboks test to the country's largest venue - River Plate Stadium. It hosted the Final of the 1978 FIFA World Cup with a capacity of 74,621 but today it hosts fewer due to new regulations seeing the venue now have a capacity of 64,000. The UAR's decision proved to be a good one as a record crowd of 60,000[32] attended the match. The spectators were given a quality showing with South Africa winning 37-33. More important than the result, however, was the match itself with Los Pumas showing a markedly improved performance to the previous outings against the Springboks. The occasion also underlined the sports growth in the country and Los Pumas would return to the River Plate Stadium the following year. 2000 did not end on a high note however as Argentina's away match against England was a disaster with the home side winning 19-0.

Argentina had a full program of international rugby in 2001. The international season started with a visit to Ontario as Argentina, Canada, Uruguay and the USA contested the fourth edition of the Pan American Championship. Loffreda selected ten uncapped players for Los Pumas's opening fixture against Uruguay in Kingston. It saw a team that was far from full strength face Los Teros but the side was selected for the specific purpose of the next Rugby World Cup. One of the players on debut was winger José Maria Nuñez Piossek who would go on to become the highest try scorer in the history of Argentine rugby. Argentina was given a good contest by Los Teros but held on to win 32-27. The second match of the tournament saw a number of changes and two other players were awarded their first test caps as an impressive Pumas team defeated the USA 44-16 in Hamilton. This set up the tournament's defining match with the undefeated sides of Argentina and Canada playing at Fletcher's Field in Toronto. Argentina scored the games only try in winning the match 20-6.

In June Los Pumas travelled to New Zealand for a one off test in Christchurch. Argentina was noticeably more competitive than in 1997 but was not able to match the standards of the home side which won 67-19. The side returned to Argentina to play a home test against Italy the following month. It was played at what had been the traditional home of Los Pumas, Ferrocaril Oeste Stadium and was the start of a solid run of performances in the second half of 2001. Loffreda got Argentina playing differently and the South Americans impressed in scoring four tries to one in winning 38-17. In November Argentina had a three match schedule which started with Los Pumas playing in Cardiff and Edinburgh and hosting the All Blacks in Buenos Aires. A masterful performance by Felipe Contepomi began the tour as he scored 25 points in the 30-16 victory over Wales at the Millenium Stadium. The following weekend he scored 20 points as Argentina defeated Scotland 25-16 at Murrayfield. Los Pumas then flew home to prepare for a home test at River Plate Stadium. The match has gone down in history as one that should not have got away as the South Americans led the All Blacks in the second half and looked to have sealed the victory with the game entering injury time. Contepomi, however, failed to find touch from a kick he made from behind his own tryline and it resulted in an All Black counterattack that saw Scott Robertson turn the match with a try at the death which gave New Zealand a 24-20 victory. The crowd was larger than that recorded for the test against the Springboks one year earlier as 70,000 fans attended the Pumas v All Blacks at the same venue.[33]

By virtue of reaching the Quarter Finals of Rugby World Cup 1999 Argentina did not need to participate in the qualification matches for Rugby World Cup 2003. This saw the 2002 international season divided into three sections. The first took place in late April and early May with Argentina facing Uruguay, Paraguay and Chile in the South American Championship. Argentina's first match of the tournament took place on the same day as the final match of the third round of South American qualification for Rugby World Cup 2003. Chile faced Paraguay and won 57-5 to advance to round four in which Los Condores would compete against Canada, Uruguay and the USA in home and away matches from June-October. The 2002 South American Championship served as preparation for Chile and Uruguay while Argentina used the event to experiment with the best Argentine based players and also blood young players with five debuting. Argentina hosted the tournament in Mendoza and won its three matches by scores of 35-21 against Uruguay, 57-13 against Chile and 152-0 against Paraguay. The victory against Paraguay is Argentina's largest ever win.

An important result occurred in Argentina's next test match against France at Velez Sarsfeld Stadium in Buenos Aires. It was the start of a notable run by Argentina against France which saw Los Pumas defeated France four times in a row from 2002-2004. It was also a continuation of what had started with the 2001 win over Italy with Loffreda succeeding in transforming the team into a consistently improving test side. The South Americans were not always able to be consistent though as after defeating France 28-27 Los Pumas lost 26-18 against England at the same venue. England was putting together an impressive record of its own which would see the team lift the World Cup in Australia the following year. Argentina's third and final June test match was against South Africa in the city of Springs in Gauteng province. The home side won the match 49-29.

Argentina returned to River Plate Stadium for the first of three November internationals as Los Pumas took on the Wallabies. It was an opportunity to see a preview of the opening fixture of Rugby World Cup 2003 as Argentina had been selected for a second time in as many tournaments to kick off a World Cup and this would be the final match played between the teams before the global event. The 2002 match was not as good as the previous two outings at River Plate Stadium as there was only one try scored. Australia won the game 17-6 with both teams then travelling to Europe to take on teams from the Six Nations. Argentina's first test in Europe was against Italy and the South Americans played strong to rattle Rome with a five tries to nil 36-6 victory. The final test of the year offered Argentina a chance to make history by defeating Ireland on its home turf but a strong Irish side controlled the match to defeat Argentina 16-7 in Dublin. This ended the year with Argentina having lost against both Australia and Ireland who were in the same Pool as Los Pumas for the following years Rugby World Cup.

An impressive calendar was planned for Los Pumas for the 2003 season. In all the year would see Argentina play tests against thirteen different opponents. It began in April with Uruguay hosting the South American Championship. Loffreda continued with the tradition of experimenting with local based players against South American opponents. The first assignment against Paraguay featured nine players winning their first Pumas caps. Amongst the debutants were Patricio Albacete and Juan Martín Hernández who were selected for the World Cup before becoming stars in France. The match, however, was highlighted by José Maria Nuñez Piossck who scored a Pumas record nine tries in the match which Argentina won 144-0. Three other players made their international debuts against Chile three days latter with Argentina defeating Los Teros 49-3 and then ending the tournament with a 32-0 win over Los Condores.

Loffreda mixed up his players for Argentina's two home tests against France in June as he looked to finalize his squad of thirty players for Australia 2003. The two tests were vastly different from each other with the first being a low scoring contest and the second being a highly entertaining one. The first test featured only one try scored by Nuñez Piossek. It was converted by Felipe Contepomi who also kicked a penalty in the 10-6 victory. The second test saw the Europeans cut down a 21-12 half time deficit and almost win but Los Pumas held on to win the match 33-32. Hernández, playing fullback, scored an impressive try which would see him retained in the position for the teams match in Port Elizabeth the following weekend. Eight days after winning by a single point, it was Argentina's turn as South African flyhalf Louis Koen landed a late penalty to snatch a 26-25 victory for the Springboks. Argentina had been playing positive rugby with Felipe Contepomi scoring a brilliant team try that started from within the Pumas 22.

Seven weeks after returning from South Africa Los Pumas started its third and final stage of preparation for Rugby World Cup 2003. Buenos Aires was the host venue for the fifth edition of the Pan American Cup. It was an important tournament for the Americas as it featured four teams who would all participate in the World Cup – Argentina, Canada, Uruguay and the USA. Los Pumas prepared for the event by hosting Fiji. The test was played in Córdoba and was an entertaining match with eleven tries being scored in a 49-30 Pumas victory. Argentina then demonstrated its dominance of the Americas as Los Pumas won its three matches to retain its Pan American Cup title. The 2003 event was the most recent edition of the tournament but it did not give the same results as earlier tournaments due to the USA defeating Canada 35-20 in a second round match. Argentina started the tournament well with a 42-8 victory over the USA and four days latter Los Pumas defeated Uruguay 57-0. Canada was not fielding a weak side but the team lost to the USA and then suffered a forty point loss against Los Pumas. Argentina's 62-22 victory is the largest win by Los Pumas against Canada.

Rugby World Cup 2003 saw a changed format to that of 1999. There were twenty teams like in 1999 but the teams were divided into four pools of five rather than five pools of four. This meant there would be no Quarter Final play-off matches as the top two teams from each pool would automatically advance to the Quarter Finals while the third, fourth and fifth placed sides from each pool would be eliminated. Another change to the tournament was that it was hosted by one nation with all forty-eight matches being played in Australia, compared to nine of the forty-one matches in 1999 being played in Wales. The tournament was originally planned to be hosted by both Australia and New Zealand but a contractual dispute between the New Zealand Rugby Union (NZRU) and the Rugby World Cup Ltd over signage rights at stadiums saw the John O'Neill led Australian Rugby Union (ARU) host the tournament on its own.

There was also controversy concerning the match schedules handed out to different competing teams. The same eight nations which have two votes each on the IRB Council were the same sides given the most time to play their four pool matches. All eight of Australia, England, France, Ireland, New Zealand, Scotland, South Africa and Wales had twenty-one or more days to play their four pool matches. It turned out to give them an advantage over their opponents as they were the same eight teams who made the Quarter Finals. It was a significant failure on behalf of tournament organizers to give the twenty teams an equal opportunity of achieving success in the tournament. For instance while Argentina opened the World Cup against Australia the Wallabies would play Ireland six days after Argentina had played its fourth and final pool match. In addition, England was yet to play its third match when Argentina had completed all of its four matches. Argentina was given sixteen days for its four matches but others had it tougher such as Italy and Tonga.

In April 2003 Italy had threatened to withdraw from the tournament. ARU spokesman Strath Gordon responded to Italy's unequal schedule of playing four games in fourteen days by saying the schedule given to Italy was justifiable as "The teams that travel are given extra time between matches." Italy was in Pool D alongside Canada, New Zealand, Tonga and Wales and needed to win three matches to make a debut appearance in the Quarter Finals. Gordon said that Italy had an advantage over others because it was to play three matches in a row at the same venue. Whereas Italy faced Canada, Tonga and Wales in Canberra after opening against New Zealand in Melbourne the Welsh were given twenty-one days for its four matches against the same teams with the games being played in three venues rather than two. Canada was given seventeen days and the pools strongest side, New Zealand was given twenty-two and the weakest of the five, Tonga was, like Italy given fourteen days for its four matches.[34]

The uneven scheduling justified by the tournament organizers ignored the key factor of match turn-arounds. Italy indeed did play both Tonga and Canada in Canberra, ahead of facing the Welsh but Wales had also played its previous match in Canberra. Despite facing New Zealand eight days after playing Italy the Welsh were also given two extra days to prepare for the crunch match against Italy. The schedule ultimately forced Italy to prepare to take on Wales with some key players, including Andrea Masi and Alessandro Troncon, in doubt. Italian coach, John Kirwan commented that he was unable to prepare his players. There was no time for training because the four day turn-around meant Italy could only recover and not actually train to take on Wales. Had Italy been given more days then the chances of the players being available would have been greater. Ahead of the Italy v Wales match both coaches of Canada and Tonga, Dave Clark and Jim Love, supported the idea by both saying that Italy were a stronger side than Wales.[35] Earlier in 2003 Italy had defeated Wales 30-22 in the Six Nations but Wales won the World Cup match 27-15.

The comments of Strath Gordon were ultimately confirmed by the IRB as not being accurate as IRB Chairman Syd Millar admitted that organizers had unfairly stacked the draw against less marketable countries to maximize profits. In planning certain matches to be played at certain times[36] the tournament organizers let down the sport of rugby by deliberately putting money ahead of sport. It resulted in Rugby World Cup 2003 having no real upsets at all in the forty pool matches. Conversely Tonga defeated France in 2011 thanks to a fairer system. The Tongans pushed Wales hard in losing 27-20 in 2003 but the game was played four days after Tonga had faced Italy while Wales's previous match had been seven days earlier against Canada.

The tournament kicked off on October 10 with Australia facing Argentina in Sydney. The home side had been criticized for not playing well following loses to England, New Zealand and South Africa earlier in 2003. There were also concerns over the selection of former rugby league players for the Wallabies with Mat Rogers, Wendell Sailor and Lote Tuqiri all in the match day 22 to face Argentina. The concerns faded during the tournament as all three proved to be outstanding players. Sailor's name would go down in history as he scored the first try of the tournament as Australia completed a 24-8 victory. Argentina had a disappointing performance with Contepomi having an off night with his goalkicking. Loffreda had selected him ahead of Quesada in a bid to play running rugby. Australia was never really challenged on the night but the Wallabies were given a late scare when Ignacio Corleto scored a try in the 72nd minute.

Four days latter Argentina was playing its second match of the tournament. The South Americans travelled up the New South Wales coast to take on Namibia in Gosford. Los Pumas won the match convincingly by winning and collecting a bonus point in the 67-14 victory. Loffreda had made fourteen changes to the team with only Diego Albanese starting against both Australia and Namibia. Argentina impressed in the forwards scoring two penalty tries and also had a better day in the backs with outside centre Martín Gaitán scoring a hat trick. Argentina scored eleven tries in all but the score sheet was noticeable in that none of the starting lineup from the Australian match scored points against Namibia.

Argentina had an eight day turn around to prepare to take on Romania in Sydney but the match could not be properly used to prepare for the vital match against Ireland due to that game being played four days after the match against Romania. Loffreda opted to field a team made up of reserves against Romania to ensure his top players would all be available for the fourth pool match. Only José Maria Nuñez Piossek started against both sides but it did not impact on the nature of the match as Los Pumas played attractive rugby in scoring seven tries to zero. The 50-3 win gave Argentina a bonus point but all thoughts were already on Ireland and the must win match at Adelaide on October 26. The do-or-die match between Argentina and Ireland went against the justifications for the uneven schedules made by the ARU. Ireland had played its previous match seven days prior and done so in Sydney. Argentina had also played its previous match in Sydney but had three fewer days to prepare despite the distance between Sydney and Adelaide being over 1300KM. Nevertheless the players were not fatigued like the Italians or Tongans due to Loffreda shuffling them to keep them in top condition for the clash against Ireland. The less than ideal schedule, however, meant that the players lacked game time together and Argentina had in fact played three entirely different teams in its first three matches.

The hard work that had gone into preparing a team for the World Cup and the positive results along the way were in many ways put on hold for the match against Ireland as Loffreda selected a defensive orientated team which featured Gonzalo Quesada at flyhalf and the impressive but young trio of Patricio Albacete, Martín Gaitán and Juan Martín Hernández on the bench. The latter two had been the Country's strongest backs in the wins over Romania and Namibia but Loffreda decided to select more experienced players as Argentina tried to play a simple but effective game of low-risk rugby with goal kicking expected to determine the outcome. Ireland had been leading 10-9 at half time after having scored the games only try when Argentina fumbled a lineout which Ireland was able to take advantage of with Keith Wood and Alan Quinlan combining with the latter scoring the try. Argentina fought back to hold a 12-10 lead but ill-discipline let down the South Americans and O'Gara took his opportunities to seal a one point victory that eliminated Argentina from the tournament. A disappointed Pichot congratulated Ireland on winning the match but also criticized the IRB for the unfair schedules as he commented that "Now the IRB have the eight countries they wanted in the Quarter-Finals."[37]

Six days after Argentina's early exit Australia took on Ireland in a World Cup match, yet it was a pool match not a Quarter Final. The John O'Neill led administration had planned the match schedule with the intention of maximizing profits. Syd Millar's latter confirmation of this left a bitter taste for many rugby fans. The selection of the date and location of the match between Australia and Ireland was intentional. The game was played on November 01 at Docklands Stadium[38] in Melbourne one day after another sporting match between Australia and Ireland, also played in Melbourne. The city is the home of Australian Rules football, a sport which rugby has historically had problems competing against throughout the country and especially in the state of Victoria. The day before the Wallabies faced Ireland, there was an International Rules Series match involving a mixture of rules from Gaelic Football and Australian Rules Football played at the Melbourne Cricket Ground.[39] The intention of the ARU in scheduling Australia v Ireland for the same weekend was to attract spectators from the International Rules Match by making it a double event to ensure a packed stadium for Australia's home World Cup match in Melbourne.

5

Global Shakeup - Rugby World Cup 2007

The loss against Ireland was hard for the players to take with television images of Los Pumas post match showing a devastated group of players. There was no blame laid on the players or team management, however, as Pichot remained the team captain and Loffreda continued on as coach. The share disappointment was a feeling that the players never wanted to feel again[40] and it was used as motivation for Argentina to succeed at Rugby World Cup 2007. The disappointment went beyond simply losing the match it had a lot to do with the frustration of Argentina having demonstrated from 2000-2003 that it can compete with the best teams yet was excluded from international competitions. While Italy had been added to the Six Nations in 2000 Argentina had no such equivalent. This is what would go on to highlight the 2004-2007 period with Los Pumas fighting to secure inclusion in a major rugby competition outside of the Rugby World Cup, that is either the Tri Nations or Six Nations.

It was a hard battle but a winnable one that Los Pumas could achieve by being humble and approaching each test match one at a time. While the captain and coach continued unchanged there were a number of players who would not play again for Argentina. So much so that five members of the staring lineup would never play again – Diego Albanese, Roberto Grau, Rolando Martín, Gonzalo Quesada and Mauricio Reggiardo. A sixth player, Santiago Phelan was on the bench and would also never be a Puma again. This relatively high turnover of players was not such a concern due to Argentina having an increasing number of players plying their trade in Europe. The loss of Grau and Reggiardo, for instance, was not felt at all as the trio of Omar Hasan, Rodrigo Roncero and Martín Scelzo were all playing in France. There were also a number of talented young players who after the World Cup went on to also play in Europe such as Patricio Albacete, Juan Martín Hernández, Lucas Ostiglia and Hernán Senillosa. It enabled Argentina to quickly recover and move forward.

Argentina also had the South American Championship to experiment with new players and the side which played in the 2004 tournament featured eleven debutants. The tournament itself, played in Santiago, was modified with Venezuela participating for the first time in place of Paraguay. Argentina won the event to be crowned South American champion for the twenty-fifth time. Los Pumas defeated Chile 45-3, Uruguay 69-10 and Venezuela 147-7 and did so with contemporary captain, Juan Martín Fernández Lobbe making his international debut. He was, at the time, a 22 year old and would have to wait until 2005 to get the call up to face Tier One opposition. There was more to the tournament than just blooding players, however, as Loffreda fielded a number of players who played in the June internationals. Of the team that faced Chile ten were in the match day 22 for the first home test against Wales.[41]

The two match home series against Wales was the first time Argentina had hosted the Welsh since Rugby World Cup 1999. Wales had come to life after eliminating Italy from Rugby World Cup 2003 as the team discovered magic in its reserve players with many of them starting in the final Pool match, against New Zealand. The underdogs gave the All Blacks a major scare as the lead continuously changed hands before New Zealand pulled clear to complete a 53-37 victory. One week latter Wales faced England in the Quarter Finals and was leading the match at halftime but the boot of Jonny Wilkinson turned the tide and England won. Amongst the players to stand out in these two matches were Brent Cockbain, Colin Charvis, Adam Jones, Sonny Parker, Ceri Sweeny and Shane Williams. All of them were in the starting lineup for Wales for the first test against Argentina in Tucumán. The match was highly entertaining with a total of eleven tries being scored. Argentina scored one more than Wales and it proved vital as the South Americans won the contest 50-44. Wales squared the series with a 35-20 win in Buenos Aires one week latter with Shane Williams scoring a hat trick. The following week Argentina was in Hamilton taking on New Zealand. The South Americans were well beaten with the All Blacks winning 41-7 due partly to Argentina missing a number of backs including Contepomi, Hernández, Gaitán, Pichot and Nuñez Piossek.

Argentina had three matches to finish the year. It faced France and Ireland in Europe and hosted South Africa in Buenos Aires. The series started with a visit to Marseille, a place where France had never lost a test. A determined Pumas side took on a French team that had won eight tests in a row and had one week earlier defeated Australia 27-14 in Paris. Los Pumas went into the game with a three match winning streak against France and for the Argentina players the opportunity of winning four in a row was boosted by the best players all being available for the first time since the World Cup. Los Pumas defied a lack of time together and produced a strong performance with the forwards setting a solid platform and

Contepomi having a good day as he kicked fourteen points. The 24-14 win saw Argentina score two tries to one with Ledesma being awarded man of the match. He commented post match that "It is a huge success for us. However four victories in a row is not much considering we lost 18 in a row before that. Perhaps we were more focused than the French and they had their minds on the All Blacks match next Saturday."[42] Such was the Pumas desire to be considered as equals and to be treated with the same respect as other leading teams.

Hot off the win in Marseille, the South Americans travelled to Ireland in a much awaited rematch of Argentina's one point loss in Adelaide. The match was played at Lansdowne Road in Dublin which had become the new home of Felipe Contepomi as he moved from England to Ireland to play for Leinster. He mirrored his performance against France by kicking fourteen points. Argentina looked to have won the match as the team was leading late in the game. However Ronan O'Gara landed a long range drop goal in the 79th minute to give Ireland a 21-19 victory. The Munster flyhalf scored all of Ireland's points as he kicked five penalties and two drop goals.[43] The match was also a preview of Rugby World Cup 2007 with the draw for the tournament having been made in May 2004. Although Argentina was not confirmed to be in the same pool as Ireland it was virtually assured given that Americas 1 would play in the group.

After the Dublin defeat the Argentine squad separated into two groups with all except two of the European based players returning to their clubs and the Argentine based players returning home to face the Springboks. The UAR knew that getting players released would be virtually impossible due to the match being played outside of the IRB international test windows of June and November but decided to host South Africa nonetheless. Stade Français released Hernández and Pichot but no other clubs released players. It saw Loffreda selecting six uncapped players for the match. The lack of international competition for Argentina meant the union had to make sacrifices to secure tests and consequently the test went ahead despite ten of the players who started against Ireland being unavailable. There were three players on debut who would go on to play in Rugby World Cup 2007 – Marcos Ayerza, Gonzalo Tiesi and Alberto Vernet Basualdo. The understrength Pumas were no match for the Springboks with the visitors winning 39-7 in a match that resembled the clash against the All Blacks earlier in the year.

Struggling to recieve international opposition, Argentina accepted an offer to face the British and Irish Lions in Wales in 2005. The match was to be a warm-up fixture and sending off for the Lions before the teams three test tour of New Zealand. The match was scheduled on the same day as the Heineken Cup Final which featured Stade Français and Toulouse, two teams with Pumas players. With the game taking place in May instead of June Loffreda was unable to call upon twenty-six players due to clubs not having to release them.[44] A number of players were made available but the team was very much thrown together with Loffreda making the most out of a tough situation. One month prior Argentina had a preparation match as Los Pumas took on Japan in Buenos Aires. No European based players were involved but Loffreda used this to his advantage by recalling Federico *Ninja* Todeschini for his first test in seven years. He scored 19 points in Argentina's 68-36 win and would go on to play opposite Jonny Wilkinson in Cardiff.

Todeschini's selection proved to be screwed. He had been playing in France's second division for Béziers but delivered when his country needed him and it changed his rugby career. Joining Todeschini against Japan were three players on debut, including Juan Manuel Leguizamón who scored a try. The team that Loffreda assembled featured only three regular Pumas – Felipe Contepomi, Mario Ledesma and José Maria Nuñez Piossek. Contepomi was named as captain and was moved to inside centre to enable Todeschini to start at flyhalf. Joining Contepomi in the centres was the returning Lisandro Arbizu who was selected out of position. Ledesma was joined by Federico Mendez and Mauricio Reggiardo in the frontrow with the latter having come out of international retirement for the match. Of the remaining players in the starting lineup four were amateur players based in Argentina and three were playing second division rugby in England.[45] The deck was stacked heavily but Argentina played with determination. Los Pumas started well with Todeschini landing penalties and Nuñez Piossek linking with Contepomi to score a try. The Lions fought back with a try but trailed 19-16 at the interval. Todeschini and Wilkinson traded penalties in the second half and with Argentina leading by three points the game went into injury time and Wilkinson secured a 25-25 draw in landing a penalty in the last play of the game.

Argentina celebrated the result like a win as the players knew they had sent a clear message to the global rugby audience. Los Pumas had been a quality team since the first World Cup in the professional era but was unable to play in a major rugby competition and had a tough time putting together a team for international matches due to the rules of player release. While the Lions faced the All Blacks Argentina played host to Italy in Salta and Córdoba as the UAR started a regular policy of distributing key home matches around the country. The teams split the series with Argentina winning the first 35-21 and Italy winning the second 30-29. Todeschini was continued at flyhalf and scored a total of 47 points in the two tests with Contepomi being the teams inside centre for the majority of the period leading up to the World Cup.

Eleven months after facing South Africa outside of the IRB international window, Argentina hosted the Springboks again but this time the players were available. It was Argentina's first of three November tests with the South Americans subsequently playing against Scotland and Italy in Europe. The Springboks were coming off a Tri Nations campaign while it was Argentina's first game in over four months. Loffreda wanted to defeat South Africa and for this to happen he selected a changed team that had a less defensive appearance to the one that had faced the Italians. The maneuver saw a different attacking style and it produced three impressive tries as Argentina appeared on course for victory as it held a 20-16 lead at the interval. South Africa was a superior side in the second half, however and went on to win the match 34-23.

At this time Loffreda was becoming increasingly bold in his selections as he was using the time to experiment with a variety of players as he began to put together his squad for Rugby World Cup 2007. Joining the squad for the European tests was Juan Martín Fernández Lobbe with the then amateur player being selected ahead of professional players to start against Scotland. Loffreda was shuffling his players against Tier One teams to a greater extent than he had from 2000-2003. At the same time, Argentina continued to accumulate more wins against these teams and, increasingly, do so in away matches. Los Pumas won a narrow game 23-19 against Scotland at Murrayfield and then defeated Italy 39-22 at Genoa. The match against Italy was important for the future as it was the first time that Juan Martín Hernández had played a test match at flyhalf. His selection for this match was a preview of things to come as Loffreda had a 9-10-12 combination of Pichot, Hernández and Contepomi. The same combination would be used throughout Rugby World Cup 2007.

Like the previous year, Argentina still had one test remaining after the completion of the IRB November international window. It saw Argentina hosting Samoa in December but not being able to secure the release of any European based professional player. Loffreda selected seven uncapped players for the match. Samoa, in contrast, had a strong side which included players based in New Zealand. The visitors won the match 28-12 and the UAR paid attention as it would be the last international against a Tier One or Tier Two side outside of the IRB international windows. Samoa's win included three tries, one more than what the locals had managed. Argentina's tries were scored by two players of the future – Juan Martín Fernández Lobbe and a debuting Horacio Agulla.

2006 was a year of changes in Argentine rugby. Los Pumas played some quality rugby to continue to enhance its reputation but there was a stand-off between the players and the UAR before any rugby had been played. Argentina was due to face Wales and New Zealand in June but the series became in doubt when almost sixty Argentine players, including a combination of European based players and the leading Argentine based players, threatened to take strike action against the UAR. The union was in financial trouble at the time due to it having lost a court case against a player who was badly injured and left a quadriplegic. The situation led to the UAR almost having to declare bankruptcy[46] and the UAR told the Pumas players that it would not be paying for their expenses during the June tests.[47] The players agreed to play the tests but the situation was far from resolved.

The three match home series featured two tests against Wales and one against New Zealand. The UAR made the decision to have the small Patagonian town of Puerto Madryn host the first test against Wales. Located in the Chubut province the town is far from being one of Argentina´s largest cities and is located around 1,100KM south of Buenos Aires. The decision was made to play there as part of the UAR´s desire to play home matches in different cities. Puerto Madryn was selected specifically to host Wales because it has a large Welsh speaking population. The city was founded in 1865 when around 150 immigrants from Wales arrived in a sailing ship from Liverpool.[48] Immigration continued in the country with most Welsh immigrants settling in Chubut. The province has 50,000 people who claim to have Welsh ancestry and 5,000 who speak the Welsh language.[49] Puerto Madryn received the visiting Welsh team with open arms for the match in 2006, putting on a festival week with the players seemingly having the support of the local population. On match day, however, it was clear that the real home team was Los Pumas.

The crowd was treated to an entertaining match with both teams scoring three tries each. Argentina held a 20-12 half time lead but Wales fought back hard with Argentina winning 27-25. Loffreda had gone for a centres combination of debutant Rafael Carballo and 20 year old Gonzalo Tiesi. Felipe Contepomi returned for the second test at Velez Sarsfeld and Argentina played very well in winning 45-27 with Todeschini scoring 30 points. The Welsh tour took place during the FIFA World Cup in Germany with Argentina´s soccer team having World Cup matches the day before both home tests. It meant that Los Pumas were unable to receive the normal level of press and it impacted on the crowd size for the Buenos Aires test. The situation was increased for Argentina´s third home test as Los Pumas took on the All Blacks at Velez Sarsfeld on the same day as a FIFA

World Cup knock-out match between Argentina and Mexico. The South Americans played a good match, leading 16-15 at half time and had a chance to win the match with New Zealand six points in front in the last minute. Argentina was camped deep inside the All Blacks 22 and went close to scoring but the visitors held firm to win the match 25-19.

Despite having played the usual three June test matches Los Pumas still had two international matches to play. Elimination at the pool stage in Australia 2003 meant Argentina would have to qualify for Rugby World Cup 2007 and the final stage of the South American qualification series took place in July with Argentina, Chile and Uruguay playing each other to determine who would join France, Ireland and two yet to be confirmed other nations in Pool D. Each country would play one home match and one away which saw Argentina face Chile in Santiago and host Uruguay in Buenos Aires. Loffreda selected a strong squad of players for the series but not a full strength one. Agustín Pichot was the captain of a team that featured twelve players who made the squad for Rugby World Cup 2007. Argentina scored ten tries to one against Los Condores and returned home with a 60-13 victory. The match against Uruguay was played in atrocious conditions with strong wind and rain making it difficult to contest a match. Pichot and his colleagues were restricted but happily won the match 26-0. The result meant Argentina won the twenty-seventh South American Championship and qualified for France 2007.

Having qualified for the World Cup and having played well the players were united behind Pichot and Loffreda but were yet to end the dispute with the UAR. In August six senior Pumas signed an open letter requesting the UAR to solve the issues with Ledesma saying that they were running out of patience.[50] The situation was resolved in time for the November international window which saw Argentina playing three away tests against England, Italy and France. There were some who wanted the dispute not to be solved, however as Paul Rees from the Guardian pointed out if Argentina's test against England were to be cancelled then England could have all its players available to face New Zealand in the reopening of the South Stand at Twickenham. The agreement between the clubs and union in England restricts players to three tests in November but England had added the All Blacks test to a schedule that already featured a test against Argentina and two against South Africa.[51]

Argentina's preparation had not been ideal for the tour. Pichot had been sidelined with injury and was yet to play for Stade Français. Rodrigo Roncero had broken a jaw playing for the same club and would miss the tests. Worse, however, was the team's preparation with Argentina only having four days to prepare for the game.[52] It was a unique opportunity for a strong Pumas side. No Argentine team had ever won at Twickenham with England winning the previous encounter 19-0 and going on to win Rugby World Cup 2003. Loffreda looked to play attacking rugby with Felipe Contepomi selected at flyhalf but the move did not last long as Federico Todeschini came on as a replacement in the 24th minute for Gonzalo Tiesi who left injured. This saw Contepomi move to the centres and Todeschini take over the goalkicking responsibilities. At half time England held a 10-9 lead but Argentina had looked like the better side. Todeschini put Argentina in front with a penalty and with it the South Americans took control of the match. He continued his fine run for his country by scoring 22 points, including a try, in Argentina's 25-18 victory. It meant he had scored 184 points in his nine tests since his recall against Japan in 2005.

Argentina's win was deserved and it was timely as it underlined the credentials of the team with the World Cup only ten months away. Loffreda showed just how united he was with the players in his post match interview. "It was very important, this victory for Argentina, not only because this is the home of rugby, the cathedral of rugby and because England have the best rugby tradition - they invented the game - but also because we can show the world that we are on the same level as the great rugby countries."[53] Two days before the match Pichot had told The Guardian that "we don't have the exposure to international competition and the time to prepare for games like this. We are passing through and next week all the headlines will be about South Africa and we will be forgotten until next summer. I think Argentina can be part of the Six Nations".[54] Less than six months earlier the players had threatened to strike but now the issues had been resolved and the team had conquered London. It meant the call to be added into either the Six Nations or Tri Nations could be significantly amplified as ignoring it or talking down Argentina's isolated situation had become unsustainable.

Los Pumas travelled to Rome to face Italy seven days latter and Loffreda showed confidence and a will to experiment as he made eight changes to the starting lineup. Gonzalo Longo captained the side in place of Pichot and Ignacio Corleto played his first test since Rugby World Cup 2003. He played on the wing with Hernández occupying fullback and Todeschini playing flyhalf. The 23-16 victory saw the visitors scoring two tries to one with Todeschini having another memorable match, scoring 18 points. It meant that if Argentina could defeat France in its final test of the year that the tour would be the most successful in the history of Argentine rugby.

Having the match played at the Stade de France made it a preview of the opening match of Rugby World Cup 2007 as Argentina had been, for a record third time, chosen to open the global tournament. Pichot returned as captain to partner Todeschini in the halves, the Contepomi twins were paired up in the midfield and the back three was Nuñez Piossek, Corleto and Hernández. Ten months out from the World Cup this appeared to be the backline for the tournament, making the match literally a test. Argentina, however, lost Todeschini in the first half as he was replaced in the 24th minute which forced a reshuffle. France was playing a superb match and had the better of play when Todeschini was on the field and when he had been replaced. Les Bleus held a 17-9 lead which became 27-9 in the 50th minute. The remainder of the match, however, was all Argentina as the Pumas forwards took control. Argentina scored two second half tries with the second seeing Felipe Contepomi and Juan Martín Hernández combine brilliantly with the fullback collecting his teammates kick and step his way around a defender. The conversion made it 27-26 with France holding on for the win and ending its four match losing streak against Los Pumas. After losing in Paris Pichot made the call for the Seven Nations repeating the frustration of having no international competition to play in outside of the World Cup.[55]

The South Americans next test would be in May 2011 some six months later with two tests taking place in Argentina. The opponent was Ireland with the Europeans having come off an impressive Six Nations campaign which included a record 43-13 win over England. The squad sent to Argentina, however, was not at full strength with coach Eddie O'Sullivan resting players ahead of the World Cup. Loffreda also fielded a weakened side as the Top 14 season had not yet finished. The UAR choose Santa Fé to host the first test and Velez Sarsfeld hosted the second. Both matches were well attended and both were won by Argentina with the first test being well disputed by both sides and decided by a late drop goal from Felipe Contepomi which gave his team a 22-20 victory. A two – nil series win was completed with a 16-0 win seven days latter. The following Saturday Argentina hosted Italy for a one off test in Mendoza with the players again being rotated. The 24-6 victory ended the final stage of matches before Loffreda would finalize his thirty players for the World Cup.

The squad was confirmed on July 28 but two of the players selected did not make it to the World Cup after they were ruled out of the tournament in August. Martín Gaitán had been a genuine contender to be Argentina's starting outside centre in the tournament but was forced into retirement following a heart attack that he suffered playing against Wales. He had played the full 80 minutes in Argentina's

27-20 loss at the Millenium Stadium but after complaining of chest pains he was rushed to the hospital where it was revealed that he had partially torn the wall of a coronary artery.[56] The team to face Wales was close to full strength but Loffreda had not named the strongest possible squad. Noticeably Todeschini was at flyhalf and Federico Serra Miras was at fullback while Hernández was left out of the match altogether and Corleto played wing.

Argentina´s final match before the World Cup was a match in Brussels that was officially not an international due to the home side, Belgium, being reinforced by veteran French players. Los Pumas won the match 36-8 scoring six tries to one. Loffreda choose Juan Martín Hernández at flyhalf. It was the first time he had played there for his country in two years and only the second overall. He had made the move from fullback to flyhalf for Stade Français in the 2006-2007 Season and had contributed significantly to the teams Top 14 championship victory over Clermont. The match versus Belgium came at a cost, however, as two players certain to start at the Stade de France, Gonzalo Longo and José Maria Nuñez Piossek, were injured.[57] Longo´s injury ruled him out of the first two matches of the World Cup while Nuñez Piossek would miss the tournament entirely.

September 07 2007 was the date in which the unthinkable happened. France lost the opening match of the Rugby World Cup. Everything had been done well. Before the match there was a memorable opening ceremony, the stadium was full and even the weather was ideal for the evening. But Los Pumas ensured that this World Cup would not go to script. Argentina played like it was the World Cup Final. It was not just about trying to reach the Quarter Finals it was also about recognition. The players still firmly believed that their results since Rugby World Cup 1999 had not registered with the sports authorities. The four wins in a row against France followed up by a one point loss had not achieved what Argentine rugby needed. There was still no tournament for Argentina to play in. There was only one more place to change this - at the World Cup and as the Argentine players sang their country´s national anthem it was clear that they were ready to leave an everlasting impression.

Loffreda developed a simple but effective game plan of a kick-chase approach in which he had identified a weakness in the French defense and Hernández at flyhalf was able to exploit this with high kicks and putting the ball behind the French back-three. The team was well prepared for this approach with every kick having a wave of chasers. It took France by surprise and the hosts struggled to counter the South Americans approach. Argentina was leading 9-3 in the 26th minute when France looked to have a half chance of a promising attack. Damian Traille caught a Hernández kick and fed Remy Martin but his loose pass found Horacio Agulla who combined with Manuel Contepomi who passed to Ignacio Corleto to speed clear and score the first try of the tournament and the only try of the match. The try stunned the players and the spectators and at 14-3 down France needed something special to change the match. Felipe Contepomi and David Skrela kicked penalties as both sides had chances but the key moment was early in the second half when Argentina withstood a three minute assault on the try line and was awarded a penalty. France never came close to scoring again as Argentina completed a 17-12 victory.

The result made the world stand up and take notice. The Telegraph called it a major upset and said that "Argentina shocked France in World Cup opener".[58] The BBC reported that "Argentina rocked tournament hosts France".[59] Pichot, in his fourth World Cup said "Argentina should be proud. I think we do exist."[60] It was an acknowledgement of two things – his country and the profile of Argentine rugby on the global stage. Back in Argentina the victory was in the headlines everywhere. La Nacion reported that "with courage and humility, Los Pumas achieved an eternal victory. It was an electrifying feeling, the image of a match conquered from the heart."[61] Argentina did exist and the players had achieved their first goal but it was only the beginning.

Joining Argentina and France in the Pool were Georgia, Ireland and Namibia. Georgia had qualified as Europe 3 behind Italy and Romania while Namibia had qualified as Africa 1. The tournament organizers had not repeated the scheduling flaws of Rugby World Cup 2003. For 2007 teams had more time between matches and less backing up. Teams had at least seventeen days for their four pool matches. But with five teams per pool there were still going to be teams having a short turn around. Argentina was one such team as four days after the tournament opener Los Pumas faced Georgia in Lyon. Loffreda made seven changes to the team and the South Americans completed a second win, collecting a bonus point in the final minute to win 33-3. It was far from a simple victory, however as all four tries were scored in the second half and the Lelos made Argentina work very hard to secure the bonus point.

Argentina's first two games were played four days apart while the third match took place eleven days later. The South Americans traveled to Marseille already planning to face Ireland but were not getting ahead of themselves as they firstly needed to ensure they defeated Namibia. The Africans, like Georgia scored the first points of the match with a penalty and gave Argentina a fair contest before Los Pumas pulled away. Argentina was leading 23-3 at the interval but was yet to score four tries. The match changed after the break with Felipe Contepomi securing the bonus point and Argentina going on to complete a 63-3 victory that included nine tries. Making his comeback against Namibia was Gonzalo Longo who was a secondhalf replacement. Loffreda wanted him starting against Ireland which saw him replace Leguizamón who had scored two tries against Namibia and played well in the first three matches of the tournament. The starting lineup was otherwise unchanged from the team that had defeated France. There were six Pumas and six Irish players returning from the 2003 match with the same coaches. It was, very much a grudge match after the previous two World Cups. A win for Argentina would see Los Pumas top the group and advance to face Scotland in the Quarter Finals. Ireland needed a bonus point victory to advance and needed to win by seven or more points.

In a match where both teams scored two tries each it was the playmaking of Hernández that proved the difference. He delivered an exhibition performance of flyhalf play as he took on the defense, linked well with his teammates and kicked three drop goals. After some missed penalty attempts Argentina opened the scoring with winger Lucas Borges scoring from a five metre scrum in the 17th minute. O'Gara kicked a penalty three minutes latter but Hernández cancelled it out in the following minute with a drop goal. Ireland took the lead with a try to Brian O'Driscoll as the tide looked like it may be turning but Hernández made it 11-10 to the South Americans with his second drop goal four minutes after the try. Argentina then scored the best try of the match. Corleto collected a high ball around 25 metres from his try line and passed to Hernández who put up a high ball and re-gathered it on the Irish 10 metre line and offloaded to frontrower Martín Scelzo in the tackle. Argentina kept the ball alive with four quick phases before Horacio Agulla went over in the left corner. The conversion gave Argentina an 18-10 lead. Ireland scored the only try of the second half with Geordan Murphy going over in the 47th minute. Argentina, however was in firm control and had the scoreboard ticking over as Contepomi added three penalties and Hernández kicked one drop goal to complete a 30-15 victory.

The result changed the face of the World Cup as it was Argentina and not France playing in the Stade de France in a Quarter Final against Scotland. Despite France being the host nation of the tournament Les Bleus played its Quarter Final in Wales. Argentina had successfully shaken up global rugby and Los Pumas were the story of the tournament. At home the World Cup success was having a significant impact with Gonzalo Longo appearing on the front page of La Nacion. The performances even saw changes to soccer scheduling. The kick-off of the Quarter Final coincided with the kick-off of Argentina's *Superclasico* soccer match between Boca Juniors and River Plate. The Associación del Fútbol Argentino (AFA) stated that it moved the match "in order to allow fans to follow the campaign of our remarkable national rugby team which is dazzling at the World Cup in France."[62]

The Quarter Final was a tight contest with both teams utilizing their forwards predominantly. It took sixteen minutes for the first points to be scored when Dan Parks landed a penalty from halfway. Argentina was, however, in control of this match throughout and went ahead 13-3 following two penalties to Felipe Contepomi and a try to Longo. The backrower had charged down a clearance kick from Parks and shown speed to beat Scottish winger, Sean Lamont to the ball as he recollected it to complete the try. Chris Paterson cut the lead to seven with a penalty late in the half but it was cancelled out by a penalty from Felipe Contepomi to open the second half. When Hernández landed a drop goal in the 54th minute Argentina looked to have sealed the match but it went down to the wire following a converted try to Chris Cuister in the 63rd minute which made it 19-13. No further points were scored, however, as Argentina had made history by qualifying for the Semi Finals.

The same fifteen players that eliminated Ireland and Scotland were retained for the Semi Final. The first Semi Final had seen England defeat France while the second would be disputed between the only two undefeated teams in the tournament. Argentina firmly believed it had a chance of winning but the coaching staff believed that in order to do this the team would need to adopt a different strategy. As such Loffreda had his players utilizing a more attacking game plan and at times it was effective as the South Americans were able to advance up field. It was, however, untested and South Africa was able to use this to its advantage. Of South Africa's four tries three were a result of Argentine errors. The first came from a Felipe Contepomi pass which was intended for Corleto but was intercepted by Fourie Du Preez. Bryan Habana scored the second after a turnover inside his teams half. He brilliantly chipped a kick over Lucas Borges's head and got the bounce to sprint over for the try. Contepomi had kicked two first half penalties but with the half coming to a close a Pichot pass curved downwards upon arriving at Hernández and he knocked it onto his foot. South Africa re-gathered the fumble with Danie Rossouw putting South Africa 24-6 ahead at half time. Los Pumas reduced the deficit to eleven points with a try to Manuel Contepomi but Argentina would not score again. With the South Americans advancing and time running out Hernández looked to put Corleto into a gap which would have seen the fullback score but Habana intercepted it and completed a 37-13 win. The Pumas errors proved to be the team's downfall. In general the sides were very evenly matched with South Africa controlling the lineouts and Argentina having the better scrum.

It was a devastating result for the South Americans. The players emotionally recovered by taking a day off to go to Euro Disney and then returned fully motivated to finish the tournament on a high. Argentina would face France for the second time, this time at the Parc des Princes. Historically teams disputing the Bronze Final (or the Third place play-off) had complained of it being pointless and that they did not want to be playing in it at all. On the eve of the 1999 Bronze Final New Zealand captain Taine Randall commented that "I personally think the play off for third is a waste of time, it's stupid, no one really wants to play it."[63] He was backed up Sean Fitzpatrick who captained New Zealand in Rugby World Cup 1991 and 1995. Fitzpatrick said "It was a total waste of time. Why punish these guys still further? They will be bruised, if not broken, in body and heart."[64] New Zealand lost the 1999 Bronze Final to South Africa but the Springboks were not exactly thrilled about playing either. Prop Ollie le Roux described the game as "a bit like kissing your sister" while England's Rugby World Cup 1995 backrower Dean Richards revealed how he had been out drinking with French players until 6am on the day of their playoff in 1995.[65]

The coaches of the two sides disputing the 2011 Bronze Final did not share the view of these four players from the Bronze Finals of Rugby World Cup 1991, 1995 and 1999. Rather it was a test match that was no less significant than the Semi Finals.[66] This changed perception was due to the 2007 Bronze Final delivering a quality match. Any suggestion that it was pointless or meaningless had not registered with Los Pumas.[67] The South Americans played their best rugby of the tournament, scoring five tries to one to defeat France 34-10. They played as a team and it was evident that the players were enjoying themselves. They were there to win with the prize of a Bronze Medal being far more than just a consolation. The match was not only dedicated to the people of Argentina but went beyond that. For Manuel Contepomi, Ignacio Corleto, Omar Hasan, Gonzalo Longo, Agustín Pichot and replacements Nicolás Fernández Miranda and Hernán Senillosa it was the last time they would ever play for Los Pumas.

The players celebrated the win with honor and pride, underlining the importance of the fixture. They had achieved greatness by tearing apart the traditions of which international rugby had stood. There was more to it than the historical Five Nations and Tri Nations sides. International rugby would be forever changed with Argentina having officially earned the right to be placed as equals to the sports best nations. The players had given the sport a massive wake up call. The tide had turned with IRB Chairman, Syd Millar calling for Argentina to join an expanded Tri-Nations tournament, saying the Pumas cannot be "neglected" any longer.[68]

Pichot's team had also made a significant impact back in Argentina. While changing the time of the *superclasico* match had been a highly significant moment it was only the tip of the ice burg. After the World Cup Los Pumas returned to Argentina and were received like heroes. Upon arrival in Buenos Aires the team was greeted by fans at the airport, giving the players a warm reception.[69] In addition, Pichot and his teammates received a Presidential welcome. The late Néstor Kirchner and his wife and current President, Cristina Kirchner honored the team. President Néstor Kirchener told Pichot that "it is a joy, thank you, all Argentines are proud of the outstanding performance by Los Pumas in the World Cup in France".[70]

6

Acceptance Confirmed - Rugby World Cup 2011

The Bronze Final in Paris was not only the final match for seven Pumas it was also the final game of the Loffreda era. He left the position after having been in charge for eight years with Argentina having played seventy-one test matches. His tenure saw Argentina win forty-seven matches and lose twenty-four giving him a 66.19% winning record.[71] He left Argentine rugby in an extremely healthy state both on and off the field and the next four years would see the sport flourish in the country. Playing numbers increased to the extent that the IRB announced that Argentina had 103,000 registered players in 2011. In comparison Australia had 86,952.[72] Loffreda was replaced in 2008 by Santiago Phelan who, like Loffreda, had been coaching in Buenos Aires. At age 29 Phelan was forced into early retirement. He took up coaching and succeeded in guiding Club Atlético de San Isidro (CASI) to the Buenos Aires title in 2005.

Before Phelan had been appointment, however, Argentina had a one off test against Chile in December 2007. The UAR selected the Andean city of San Juan for the match and with no replacement yet for Loffreda Les Cusworth was in charge of the team for the match. None of the players from Rugby World Cup 2007 featured which saw a staggering number of eighteen players on debut. Of them backrower Alejandro Campos and fullback Lucas González Amorosino would go on to make the squad for Rugby World Cup 2011 as would scrumhalf Nicolás Vergallo who was earning his sixth cap. The youthful side played well, scoring thirteen tries to one in a 79-8 victory.

Argentina had been promised nine international test matches per year and significant funding at the IRB Forum in Woking[73], England in November 2007 but it did not quite work out this way. The extra funding did happen as the UAR and the IRB combined to create a National High Performance program called PladAR.

Work began quickly and in February 2009 the UAR named a list of thirty-one amateur players to be trained and paid. The union also confirmed a project to construct facilities in Buenos Aires, Córdoba, Mendoza, Rosario and Tucumán. The injection of $2 million per year[74] enabled the program to become a reality and for the first time ever Argentina had a system that could effectively bridge the gap from amateur rugby to international rugby.

The promise of nine tests per year however did not eventuate. Argentina only played twenty-eight tests between Rugby World Cup 2007 and Rugby World Cup 2011. During the same period Australia and New Zealand each played forty-eight tests, South Africa and Wales played forty-three, England and Ireland played forty, France and Italy played thirty-eight and Scotland played thirty-five. Moreover nine of Argentina's twenty-eight tests were against Chile and Uruguay which meant Argentina only played 19 tests against Tier One opposition in 46 months. Excluding the matches in the South American Championship and the Rugby World Cup, Argentina played seven tests in 2008, five in 2009, six in 2010 and one in 2011. To complicate matters further the late finish to the Top 14 season in 2008 meant French based players would miss at least two of the three home tests in June.

Phelan was officially named as coach in March 2008[75] which gave him time to effectively prepare for the June test series in which Argentina would host Scotland and Italy. He named Felipe Contepomi as captain for the home series. Pichot had not officially retired but had made it known that 2007 was his final World Cup. Before June, however Argentina faced Uruguay in Montevideo in May. Twelve players made their test debuts. Amongst them were Gonzalo Camacho and Leonardo Senatore who went on to feature in Rugby World Cup 2011. Both players were also a part of the PladAR program as were most players who faced Uruguay and Chile during this period. Argentina's 43-8 victory featured seven tries.

A number of the players from the Montevideo test went on to play in the June series, replacing French based players who were unavailable. The starting XV continued to be dominated by professional players but players who had been out of favor were now finding themselves starting for their country. For the first test Phelan selected Alvaro Tejeda at hooker who was making his test debut at the age of 31 while none of the back three played in France 2007. The test took place in Rosario and was well attended. The home side won but were given a very difficult match from Scotland. Chris Paterson was on target, landing five penalties but the Scot's were unable to score a try. Argentina scored two with Tejada scoring a first half try and centre Gonzalo Tiesi scoring one on full time to complete a 21-15 victory. The sides travelled to Buenos Aires for the second test. It was played at Velez Sarsfeld in front of a full house but Los Pumas were unable to deliver. Despite the teams scoring two tries each Scotland won the match 26-14 with Paterson contributing 16 points. The third test was against Italy and was played in Córdoba on June 28, the same day as the Top 14 Final. Some players had returned from France but Phelan opted to rest some leading players such as Felipe Contepomi, Todeschini and the Fernández Lobbe brothers who had played against Scotland. The elder brother, Carlos Ignacio played his 65th and final test for his country. Hernández returned for the match against Italy but had to be replaced in the first half with a broken hand. It proved costly as Argentina was disorientated and Italy was able to claim a famous 13-12 win with a late try.

The lack of test matches saw the UAR accept an offer from South Africa to play a one off test in August. It was to commemorate Nelson Mandela's 90th Birthday.[76] Despite the match taking place outside of the IRB International Window Phelan was able to select most of Argentina's top players, albeit not all of them. Argentina started well with Contepomi on target with penalties as Los Pumas held a 9-0 lead after 24 minutes. From there it fell apart as South Africa scored nine unanswered tries to run away with a 63-9 victory. Similar matches would not be repeated in the subsequent years and Argentina would not face any SANZAR team again until Rugby World Cup 2011.

Argentina's November schedule was unique. It included four matches with two matches listed as official tests taking place on the same day. In South America Argentina faced Chile in Santiago. Argentina had fielded an amateur side with nine players making their debuts. Three of them played in the 2012 Rugby Championship – Martín Bustos Moyano, Martín Landajo and Tomás Leonardí. Argentina scored eleven tries and won the match 71-6. Meanwhile in Europe Argentina played the first of its three matches in the old continent with a test against France in Marseille. Argentina was missing first choice players Leguizamón and Scelzo which saw Alvaro Galindo and Juan Orlandi start with the latter debuting at tighthead prop. The match was played in wet conditions with no tries being scored and neither team really threatened the opposition's try line. France won 12-6 after kicking three penalties and one drop goal while Argentina kicked two penalties.

Argentina's second test took place across the border with Italy in Torino. Phelan made three changes to the team by playing different wingers and moving secondrower Rimas Alvarez Kairelis into the backrow. Los Pumas produced a solid albeit not brilliant performance but, importantly, were able to control the match. The 22-14 victory featured one try per team with the Italian try being scored in the final minute. Argentina's try was a piece of master class from Hernández who gathered an Italian kick and attracted defenders before kicking over the defensive line, re-gathering and offloading to Rafael Carballo who side-stepped a defender and went over for the try. Two players from the Rugby Championship - Santiago Fernández and Agustín Figuerola made their debuts.

Argentina's final test match of 2008 was against Ireland in Dublin. Argentina was rocked with the 10-12-13 combination being entirely changed. Tiesi and Contepomi were ruled out in the days leading up to the match while Hernández was ruled out 20 minutes before kick-off. Miguel Avramovic and Federico Martín Aramburu played in the centres while Santiago Fernández was named at flyhalf. Juan Martín Fernández Lobbe captained the side which also saw a new fullback with Horacio Agulla making his first test appearance in the position. The match carried extra significance due to it being the final match before the cut off date for IRB World Rankings. The positions of the twelve automatic qualifiers from Rugby World Cup 2007[77] were used to determine pool placements for Rugby World Cup 2011. Argentina entered the match against Ireland ranked fourth in the world but could fall to fifth if Ireland won by more than fourteen points. A loss by fourteen or less would mean Argentina would be seeded in the first of three layers which would likely mean a better draw for New Zealand 2011. The injury ravaged Pumas side survived, but only just. Ireland won the game with Argentina competing well but losing 17-3 thanks in large part to having no specialist goal kicker. The match featured only one try with Tommy Bowe scoring four minutes from full time. The result meant Argentina were still ranked fourth in the world and would eventually be drawn with England, Scotland and two qualifying teams.

The 2009 international season started with the South American Championship. Uruguay hosted the tournament in Montevideo and Argentina used it to good effect by having seventeen players debut against Chile. Of the debutants the star performer was Juan Imhoff who scored four tries in Argentina's 89-6 victory. He scored a try against Uruguay three days latter as Los Pumas wrapped up another South American title with a 33-9 victory. Two weeks latter Argentina was playing its first of two home tests against England. The first test, however, was played in Manchester. The UAR had made the decision to move the match from Buenos Aires in a bid to make a larger profit from selling tickets at more expensive prices. Around 40,000 people attended the match which would have pleased the UAR but the rugby played by Argentina was poor. Los Pumas started well with an early drop goal from Hernández but England took control running away with an impressive 37-15 victory.

The teams travelled to South America for the second test with the UAR again opting for another city to host the match. The selected venue was the Northern Argentine city of Salta. With a much smaller capacity than other stadiums it is not the largest stadium in the country but it was a good home test played at a packed stadium. Argentina was a different team from Manchester with the South Americans controlling the tempo of the match virtually from start to finish. At the helm was Hernández who the Guardian said "produced a master class, mixing up attacking kicks with some clever off-loading and incisive running".[78] He scored fourteen points and fed a flat pass to Horacio Agulla as he put the fullback past Andy Goode en route to setting up Gonzalo Camacho for Argentina's second try. The match would, however, be Hernández's fifth and final test in the years between the 2007 and 2011 World Cup's. His next test match would not come until Argentina faced South Africa in Cape Town in 2012. There was one final match for him in a Pumas shirt as Argentina faced the French Barbarians with Argentina having a good afternoon at Velez Sarsfeld in winning 32-20.

Argentina had played the June internationals without Felipe Contepomi. The Pumas captain had been a part of the Leinster side that won the Heineken Cup for the first time. He played the campaign at flyhalf and was in good form but injured his knee in the Semi Final against Munster in May and with it his international season was over before it began. In his place Fernández Lobbe again captained the team and Santiago Fernández played inside centre in June. For the November tour, however, Contepomi was joined by both Hernández and Marcelo Bosch on the sidelines with both requiring surgery. Phelan made the most of a tough situation by calling on the uncapped Martín Rodríguez Gurruchaga to form an amateur 10-12 combination with Fernández. They came through the tour well with both players enhancing their reputations and being signed to play in France the following season.

The tour, however, was tough with Argentina also missing key players in the backrow and on the wings. The first test was at Twickenham where Argentina was playing for the first time since 2006. Despite fielding a depleted lineup the South Americans played well and pushed England until the final whistle with Los Pumas coming close to scoring a try in the final minute. England held firm to claim a 16-9 victory. The following weekend saw Argentina face Wales at the Millenium Stadium. Argentina played well but leaked three tries and only scored one in the 33-16 loss. Despite losing by seventeen points the man of the match award went to Fernández Lobbe who was playing at 8 rather than 7 and was becoming recognized as one of the world's greatest players. He led the team again seven days latter at Murrayfield in a match in which neither team could play very much rugby due to freezing conditions. Scotland had come off a win over Australia the previous week but the South Americans ended the tour on a high with Rodríguez Gurruchaga drop kicking Argentina to a 9-6 victory. He returned to Argentina having scored all of his country's points on the three test tour.

2009 was more of a notable year for what happened off the field than what happened on it. Argentina overall had a bad year as a rugby nation but on September 14 the long awaited invitation from SANZAR arrived.[79] It was a relief to finally be added but it was not a celebration as the battle had been won not the war. There were other issues to be resolved such as finding a tournament for the PladAR players to compete in. Many players had been a part of Los Jaguares teams playing in the IRB Nations Cup or the Churchill Cup in the June international windows. The tournaments, however, were never enough as they only lasted two weeks each. A solution was found in December 2009 as Argentina was added to South Africa's Vodacom Cup.[80] The PladAR team went on to enter the competition in February 2010 and was called Los Pampas XV as will be covered in Chapter 10.

A number of the players from the Vodacom Cup made the Argentine test squad and were even selected ahead of European based professionals. For instance, Argentina's match day 22 for the first June test of the year included six players from Los Pampas XV[81] Three weeks before Scotland arrived for the two test series in June 2009, Argentina played in the South American Championship. Los Pumas won both matches of the tournament which was staged in Santiago, defeating Uruguay 38-0 and Chile 48-9. The home tests that followed were played in Tucumán, Mar del Plata and Buenos Aires. The decision to move the matches around paid off as the crowds were overall positive despite the FIFA World Cup being played in South Africa at the same time.

Tucumán was close to full for the first test and coincided with an Argentina versus Nigeria soccer match on the same day. The soccer team won 1-0 and the rugby team looked like making it a double as Los Pumas scored both tries of the match. Ill discipline cost the team a win, however, as man of the match Dan Parks gave the visitors a famous 24-16 victory. It was the first time Argentina had lost in Tucumán but, with the teams confirmed as opponents in Rugby World Cup 2011 it was noticeable how the Europeans were able to get on top as Argentina gave away too many penalties. The second test was dominated by cold rain and wind as

Mar del Plata seemed more like a Scottish city.[82] The rugby was far from attractive but Scotland was not interested in impressing. It just wanted a win to complete a first ever test series win in Argentina. The South Americans were left stunned having lost 13-9 and with a World Cup quickly approaching there was a lot of work to be done.

Los Pumas started work straight away and played its third test of the month, against France in Buenos Aires. Phelan made three changes with the most noticeable one being Nicolás Vergallo returning to start at scrumhalf. He had been out of favor following a disappointing performance in Manchester in 2009 but was given a chance for redemption at Vélez Sarsfield. He took the opportunity with open arms as he organized the forwards smartly and combined brilliantly with Contepomi as together they tore apart the Grand Slam winning French combination of Morgan Parra and François Trinh-Duc. In a performance which showed just how poorly Los Pumas had played against the Scot's Argentina broke the record winning margin set in the 2007 Bronze Final by completing a 41-13 victory. The eighteen point win featured four tries with Contepomi scoring two of them as he scored 31 points, surpassing his previous best record of 25 points against Wales in Cardiff in 2001. It also saw Juan Figallo making his international debut after he had previously toured Europe with the squad in November 2008 as a 20 year old.

The game was reassurance that Argentina was still a very capable team. There were obvious questions over consistency and not many tests left to establish who would be going to New Zealand 2011. With Argentina still without a tournament to play in the November 2010 tour of Europe would be the last test matches featuring the professional players before a squad was confirmed for the World Cup. The first of three tests took place in Verona and Phelan named a handful of fringe players in the starting lineup to take on the Italians. Gonzalo Camacho was back after having missed the November 2009 tour and the June 2010 home series due to injury. He was partnered by Lucas González Amorosino, who had struggled to get game time for Leicester all season, on the other wing. The pair came through the match with flying colors with both having outplayed their opposition players. Camacho was one of the best players on the field while the 22-16 Pumas victory had a lot to do with González Amorosino's clever kick and chase which gifted Rodríguez Gurruchaga a try and from there the game was won.

Fourteen of the starting players kept their places for the next match as Argentina faced France in Montpellier. The one change saw Patricio Albacete returning from injury to start in the secondrow in place of Manuel Carizza who had broken his arm against Italy. The match featured a host of different players on each team from the 2008 equivalent in Marseille but otherwise it was virtually the game repeated. Like two years earlier the game featured no tries, the conditions were dreadful and France won by six points, this time, by 15-9. World Cup preparation was not much easier in Dublin one week latter at a frozen and snow covered field at the Aviva Stadium[83] meant training on the field had been impossible. Phelan experimented somewhat with Marcelo Bosch starting for the first time since June 2008 and Julio Farías Cabello starting for the first time at the age of 32. Argentina started the game strongly and looked to have earned a penalty try as the Pumas scrum bullied the Irish but, instead, Ireland was awarded the resulting feed. It seemed to impact on the South Americans spirits as Ireland took charge and completed a comfortable 29-9 victory.

The World Cup year started in horror for Argentina as Hernández's participation was cast in serious doubt after badly injuring his knee playing for Racing Métro in a Top 14 match in March. He had time to recover but it was doubtful and at best Argentina would have to prepare without him. He underwent surgery and was monitored but when it came time to confirm the thirty man squad for the World Cup he was not ready and had to be left out.[84] Phelan had no test matches to finalize who the players would be so he instead relied a lot on the form of players in Europe and in the Vodacom Cup. The UAR did manage to secure a set of three home matches for June with the French Barbarians playing twice and Los Pumas taking on a CONSUR XV to be made up of players from all parts of South America. The international calendar officially started in May with Argentina hosting the years South American Championship in Missiones province. The team was captained by scrumhalf Tomás Cubelli who like a number of players had played in the Vodacom Cup that year but none of the players played that featured against Chile and Uruguay would go on to be selected for the World Cup. In all sixteen players made their test debuts with the most notable player being 20 year old backrower Tomás De La Vega. Argentina won the championship after defeating Chile 61-6 and Uruguay 75-14.

The three June matches were well attended in the host cities of Avellaneda, Resistencia and San Juan. Phelan used the matches to experiment as much as possible in order to finalize his squad in confidence. The first match took place at the Estadio Libertadores de América in Avellaneda, Greater Buenos Aires and saw Argentina win a close match 23-19. The French Barbarians reserved the result one week latter winning 21-18 in Resistencia. Argentina's final home match against the CONSUR XV (South American Invitational XV) was more about giving Los Pumas a fairwell than anything else and the team did not disappoint as

Argentina won 78-15. It did, however, give some players a chance to underline their credentials. One such example was Juan Imhoff who had been the top try scorer in the Vodacom Cup but was not expected to make the squad due to his lack of test rugby and because Phelan had a number of European based players to call upon. But Imhoff gave Phelan every reason to select him as he scored a first half hat-trick.

Indeed Imhoff did make the cut as he was one of three specialist wingers selected following a return to Pensacola, Florida for a fitness conditioning program. The squad featured seventeen forwards and thirteen backs, identical to what Loffreda had taken to Australia and France in 2003 and 2007. The squad included two uncapped players with Maximilano Bustos and Tomás Vallejos Cinalli being selected ahead of Juan Orlandi and Esteban Lozada. The squad featured only ten players returning from Rugby World Cup 2011. The significant turnover of players indicated just how difficult Phelan's job had been given the low number of international matches he had at his disposal and the pressure to win games. Of the final squad five played their rugby in England, nineteen in France and six were from the PladAR program in Argentina. But one player, Alvaro Galindo was ruled out of the tournament and replaced by Genaro Fessia.

Three weeks before the World Cup Argentina played a warm-up match against Wales. Loffreda sprung a surprise by selecting Juan Figallo to start in place of Martín Scelzo at tighthead prop. Figallo had come off an impressive season with Montpellier but had been playing loosehead prop. A minor surprise was the selection of Marcelo Bosch at outside centre. He was playing in place of the then injured Gonzalo Tiesi. Despite being a natural flyhalf Bosch was moved to the outside center position by his club, Biarritz for the majority of the 2010-2011 Season and the experiment was successful. Los Pumas had a good match in Cardiff with the South Americans dominating the first thirty minutes of the match. The team was unable to convert the pressure into points, however with only a single Contepomi penalty on the board in what was not one of his better matches with the boot. Wales turned the match by scoring two tries in the final five minutes of the half to lead 14-3 at the interval despite having been outplayed by the South Americans. Wales added penalties in the second half as Argentina was taken out of the game. Both teams scored one second half try and the Europeans won 28-13.

Phelan gave the reserves a start three days latter as Argentina faced Aviva Premiership side the Worcester Warriors. Leguizamón was the only player to start against both Wales and Worcester while Gabriel Ascarate, Lucas Borges and

Agustín Figuerola all started against Worcester despite none having been named in the World Cup squad. Argentina was disappointing but, nevertheless won the match with both tries being scored by left winger Juan Imhoff. The 21-15 win also featured good goal kicking from Nicolás Sánchez who was replacing Hernández and was thought of as being potentially important for Los Pumas from the bench. The two match tour was a sign of progress with Argentina playing significantly better than the team had against Ireland in November 2010.

The match against Wales proved to be a preview of things to come at the World Cup as Phelan made only one change for his sides opening match of the tournament. Gonzalo Tiesi returned with Bosch dropping to the bench. The tournament's opening match for Los Pumas was against England on September 10 at the new, indoor stadium in Dunedin. Argentina produced a similar performance to that of the first half against Wales as the South Americans had the better of play. In front of a capacity crowd Argentina seemed to be returning to the form of four years earlier. Argentina came close to scoring a try on several occasions early in the match. Tighthead prop, Juan Figallo was an inch away from the try line while captain, Felipe Contepomi went very close before being tackled and being subsequently forced from the match due a rib injury. Gonzalo Tiesi was also forced out of the match early on with a knee injury. They were replaced by Marcelo Bosch and Juan Imhoff with both replacements putting in quality performances. Bosch played at both centre and flyhalf during the match as he exchanged duties with Santiago Fernández. He made one clean linebreak which very nearly resulted in a try.

England was able to defend well but gave away penalties. Contepomi and Martín Rodríguez Gurruchaga were both used to kick the goals but neither kicker was able to kick to their usual standards with both missing kicks they would usually be expected to get. England's ace kicker, Jonny Wilkinson also had an off-night and complained that the Gilbert balls used at the tournament were poor in quality, lacking consistency in how they swung.[85] With so many missed kicks the scores remained low throughout the match and it took a late try by English replacement scrumhalf, Ben Youngs, to shake up the match as England took the lead for the first time in the contest. Argentina responded by playing its most attacking rugby of the night with Imhoff going close to scoring. Right winger, Gonzalo Camacho also had a strong match as England's fancied wingers were kept quiet.

The 13-9 result gave England four points and put the side in pole position to win the pool. Argentina collected a bonus point for losing by less than seven points. It meant that every other match was a must win, starting seven days latter in

Invercargill as Los Pumas took on Romania. The Eastern European nation was also unsuccessful in its first match having gone down 34-24 to Scotland. Romania had, however, given Scotland a major scare and was winning 24-21 with thirteen minutes left to play. A late rally from Scotland saw the Tier One side home. Four days after facing Romania, Scotland took on Georgia, also in Invercargill. The match was dominated by the conditions with strong rain and wind cutting down the chances of attacking rugby for both sides. Scotland was happy to take Georgia on in the forwards and the two sides ground each other down. Neither side was able to score a try with Dan Parks seeing his side home to a 15-6 victory. For Los Pumas a victory against Romania was an absolute must but the South Americans were under no illusions that it would be easy. Romania's strong showing against Scotland had been largely based on the teams resources in the forwards. The Scots were leading the pool after having won its first two matches. The loser of Argentina versus Romania would therefore have no chance whatsoever of making the Quarter Finals.

Los Pumas coach, Santiago Phelan was forced into a number of changes, particularly in the backs. Captain Felipe Contepomi and inside centre Gonzalo Tiesi were both out of the match with the latter out of the entire tournament. Phelan took the opportunity to experiment by selecting an entirely different 10-12-13 combination. Santiago Fernández was selected at pivot with Martín Rodríguez Gurruchaga moving from fullback to inside centre and Marcelo Bosch starting at outside centre. It was a new trio with two players swapping positions but it was, nevertheless, a reliable trio with all three players having completed solid seasons in France for their respective clubs - Montpellier, Stade Français and Biarritz. Bosch was starting at international level for the second time ever in the 13 shirt while Fernández and Rodríguez Gurruchaga were re-forming the Pumas combination from November 2009.

With Rodríguez Gurruchaga playing inside centre, Phelan opted to play Lucas González Amorosino at fullback. It was another selection which showed a will to test out combinations as despite having come through the Argentine system as a fullback / flyhalf, González Amorosino had only ever played for Los Pumas as a winger. The selection did appear partly controversial, however, as Montpellier's Martín Bustos Moyano had contributed immensely to the French clubs first ever appearance in a Top 14 Final. Phelan had left out the ace goal kicker in preference of González Amorosino who is a running fullback and a young and largely unknown winger, Juan Imhoff. Phelan named Imhoff, again, on the bench with Horacio Agulla and Gonzalo Camacho being retained in the starting XV as was scrumhalf, Nicolás Vergallo. No changes were made in the forwards from the pack that faced England but with the loss of Contepomi, Juan Martín Fernández Lobbe was named as captain.

Argentina´s superiority was never in question due to the status of the contest - Tier One v Tier Two. The two sides had not met since their Pool match in Sydney in Rugby World Cup 2003. Such was the seriousness of the match and the need of getting combinations right with Argentina set to face Scotland seven days latter in Wellington. The South Americans mission of creating opportunities proved successful and a number of players took their opportunity with both hands as the team won satisfactorily, 43-8. González Amorosino proved highly effective attacking from the deep as he made multiple line breaks and scored a try. With an eye to the match against Scotland the team´s two best tries were scored by forwards with Leguizamón casting memories back to Jonah Lomu as he ran over Florin Surugiu and Juan Figallo scored from a pick-and-go. Imhoff also proved his selection to be on the money as he went over for a second half try after replacing Camacho. It also caught the attention of Racing Métro who signed Imhoff after the World Cup.

Argentina´s defining match of the tournament took place eight days latter. Not only was it a must win match but it was against a team that that defeated Los Pumas twice in June 2010. The fortunes of both Argentina and Scotland depended on the outcome of the match. It was winner takes all and New Zealand´s capital city, Wellington, increased the stakes by turning on a rainy night with the teams playing in miserable conditions. Attacking rugby was off the agenda as the field was wet throughout the match, with rain continuously falling and often coming down heavily. The match was scheduled to be played in Christchurch. However, due to the tragic events of February 22 in which a 6.3 earthquake struck the city killing 185 people, destroying downtown and badly damaging the stadium,[86] all seven matches due to be hosted at AMI Stadium were relocated.[87]

Argentina and Scotland were two very evenly matched teams and the June 2010 matches appeared to give the Europeans the upper hand. One interesting point, however was that Scotland had won these matches without scoring tries. Argentina scored two tries to none in the Tucumán test while Jim Hamilton scored the only try of the Mar del Plata test. Furthermore Scotland was unable to score tries in either the 2009 win over Australia or the 2010 win over South Africa. The Scot´s also entered the do-or-die clash in Wellington having scored a relatively low number of four tries in its first two matches of the World Cup. The pair of Dan Parks and Chris Paterson had been crucial in Scotland´s wins during this period and both would play key roles against Los Pumas in Rugby World Cup 2011 but neither would be able to deliver the killer blow.

Scotland had selected the promising Ruardih Jackson at flyhalf with Dan Parks named on the bench. The move was an attempt to get Scotland playing more attacking rugby with Jackson being a more gifted athlete than the kicking expert which is Dan Parks. The weather complicated matters but the lack of tries was not through a lack of trying, as both sides did spin the ball. Both teams countered one another with a feature being well organized defensive lines and a highly competitive battle of the loose forwards at the breakdown. Argentina had gone into the game with the same eight forwards that faced both England and Romania. The 10-12-13 combination was modified again with Fernández continuing at flyhalf and Bosch at outside centre. This saw Rodríguez Gurruchaga back at fullback and Contepomi returned from his rib injury to play at 12 rather than 10. Horacio Agulla and Gonzalo Camacho were again the starting wingers for Los Pumas. Scotland's best attacking players were up against these two with Max Evans and Sean Lamont both receiving plenty of ball throughout the contest.

Argentina's major concern leading into the game was goal kicking. Both Felipe Contepomi and Martín Rodríguez Gurruchaga had contributed to Argentina's downfall v England. Both kickers also missed a number of opportunities against Scotland. Conditions made kicking highly complicated which saw the reliable Chris Paterson also not kicking to his usual standards. At halftime Scotland were leading the match 6-3 and Argentina were in trouble having lost two star players to injury. Loosehead prop, Rodrigo Roncero was injured as a scrum collapsed and Fernández Lobbe had a freakish knee injury as he landed awkwardly after contesting a high kick. Scotland looked the better side after the break and after Contepomi had made the scores 6-6 in the 64th minute the Europeans broke clear thanks to two drop goals with man of the match Ruardih Jackson slotting one in the 65th minute and his replacement, Dan Parks slotting a second seven minutes latter.

Argentina were at this point losing by six points and facing elimination from Rugby World Cup 2011. Los Pumas needed a converted try and only had eight minutes to score. From the restart, Argentina kicked high and short with backrower, Julio Farias Cabello re-gathering on Scotland's 10 metre line. From there scrumhalf, Nicolás Vergallo and the Pumas forwards gained some valuable metres upfield. Right winger, Gonzalo Camacho went himself from the base of a ruck and fed the ball to Patricio Albacete who was tackled 32 metres out from the try line in midfield. With Camacho having come off his wing replacement fullback González Amorosino moved outside Bosch. Los Pumas split the backs with Fernández on the left and Contepomi on the right - each having two backs to feed. Vergallo passed from the ruck to Contepomi who attracted two defenders before passing to Bosch who attracted Sean Lamont. Bosch held on just long enough to put González Amorosino into a half gap and from there he showed good pace to get passed Chris Paterson and he subsequently danced his way around Jim Hamilton, Mike Blair, Graeme Morrison and Max Evans to score a remarkable try. The scores were 12-11 with Felipe Contepomi needing the conversion to put his side in the lead. Having missed several kickable penalties earlier he was able to this time deliver as Argentina held a one point lead with seven minutes left.

Scotland had an opportunity to win the match in the final minute as Dan Parks lined up a drop goal ten metres from the try line. Argentina's rush defense put him off-guard, however as he was forced onto his left boot and was unable to land his attempt. It was not game over yet, however, as the match continued well over time. Contepomi had kicked the 22 metre dropout long with Scotland recovering it on its own 10 metre line. The Europeans, upon recovering the ball, attempted to break the line to score a miracle try from inside their own half. The ball was spun left and right but Argentina's defense proved to be rock solid. After several minutes of tackling, Los Pumas finally managed to turn over the ball with Bosch kicking for touch and the players were extremely elated. Veteran Pumas prop, Martín Scelzo, playing his fourth World Cup was in tears as he celebrated with his captain. Scotland, in contrast, were simply devastated as the loss meant they needed to defeat England the following week by over seven points or be eliminated from the World Cup before the Quarter Finals for the first time in history. Argentina's win proved to be the downfall of Scotland while it meant the South Americans would face Pool A winners, New Zealand in the Quarter Finals so long as they could defeat Georgia in Palmerston North seven days latter.

Argentina made five changes to face the Georgian Lelos with Marcos Ayerza, Mariano Galarza, Juan Imhoff and Leonardo Senatore all starting for the first time in the tournament. The other change saw Lucas González Amorosino, starting for the second time. Ayerza and Senatore replaced the injured Roncero and Fernández Lobbe while the other players were selected to enable the Phelan to have a recovered squad ahead of the Quarter Final. The injury list was a complicated matter for Phelan but with England having defeated Scotland 16-12 the night before Argentina's task was simplified. This meant Scotland was on 11 competition points and Argentina 10. A win or a draw would see Argentina advance. The Scot's failure to collect a bonus point against Georgia made life easier for Los Pumas to the extent that Argentina could still advance if they were to lose to Georgia. A bonus point loss would have been sufficient for the South Americans to finish second in the pool.

Georgia went into the match having beaten Romania 25-9 four days earlier. The win was remarkable in a number of ways. Romania, according to history, is Europe's seventh best side and had defeated France and Italy regularly during the communist era. Romania also did well against Scotland and Wales during the same period but it was not invited into the Five Nations due to the west's attitude towards the communist east. Romania, since 1989, has been a shadow of its former self but the Eastern Europeans had, nonetheless, defeated Zimbabwe, Fiji, the USA, Namibia and Portugal in previous World Cup's and the only campaign in which the Oaks had lost every match was in 1995 due to having to face Australia, South Africa and, what was then a very competitive, Canadian team. Since 2007, Georgia had gotten the better of Romania but the match was the first in which neither side could say it was not at full strength. Georgia's ability to boss Romania around the park was highly noteworthy and explained why both Scotland and England had been unable to score big wins unlike what was being written in many rugby websites and social networks.[88] England won 41-10 but the match was actually much closer with England only seven points clear at half time and Georgia having goal kicking issues that could have otherwise seen the a different score entirely.

Like in 2007, Georgia proved to be highly competitive in the first half of the contest. Imhoff went over in the 32nd minute for the first try. Argentina used the width of the field before the young winger was able to break tackles and accelerate to open the scoring. It counted for little, however, as Lasha Khmaladze scored for the Lelos seven minutes latter and with Malkhaz Urjukashvili's conversion Georgia held a 7-5 half time lead. Memories were reborn from 2007 when Georgia took it to the Irish in a match Ireland won 14-10 in Bordeaux. On that occasion the Eastern Europeans almost scored a try in the final minute. In Palmerston North, however the Lelos were unable to score a point after the interval which meant Argentina's two tries in the final fifteen minutes were hard for Georgia to swallow. The Lelos were able to return home knowing that not only had they defeated Romania but they had also prevented both Scotland and Argentina from scoring a bonus point. Indeed the Lelo's worst defeat had been talked of as flattering for England.[89] Argentina's 25-7 victory meant Los Pumas finished second in Pool B behind England and would face New Zealand in the fourth Quarter Final one week latter at Eden Park.

The winner of the Semi Final would go through to face Australia at the Semi Final stage. Australia had defeated South Africa earlier in the day in the third Quarter Final. With Wales beating Ireland and France beating England only New Zealand remained undefeated in the tournament. It underlined New Zealand's position as tournament favorites and the All Blacks were expected to be far too strong for Argentina. So much so that New Zealand's gambling agency the TAB had New Zealand paying NZ$1.02 for a win while Argentina was written off at NZ$15.[90] Rugby websites and social media were unanimous in saying this would be a big New Zealand win. Bet365 said Argentina could lose by as many as 35 points.[91] Planet Rugby decreased the margin to 20 but agreed that there was only one team that could win.[92]

Much of this was based on how good New Zealand was rather than anything else. There certainly was good reason to talk up the host nation. In the pool phase New Zealand had scored 240 points and 26 tries and was the only team to score a bonus point in all of its four pool matches. The team also had the second best tackling record after Scotland, it had the best lineout in only having lost three of its own throws, was one of only two teams together with South Africa to have won all its scrums and had won more opposition scrums than any other team.[93] Statistically there was only one possible result but in the sport of rugby there is a lot that figures cannot tell. Some examples are camaraderie, pride and passion.

New Zealand had been rocked by the loss of star flyhalf, Dan Carter in the days leading up to the final pool match against Canada. But Argentina was hardly entering the game in the best possible manner. Argentina was without Juan Martín Hernández, Juan Martín Fernández Lobbe, Alvaro Galindo and Gonzalo Tiesi. With both Fernández Lobbe and Galindo missing Argentina's starting backrow saw two Argentine based players starting – Julio Farías Cabello and Leonardo Senatore. A loss of players, however, is no excuse in a World Cup, less so in a Quarter Final and Argentina crafted a game plan to try to topple the All Blacks. The plan proved to be highly effective on defense as New Zealand struggled to break the line and despite match previews and statistics saying the side was dominant, it took over three quarters of the match for the All Blacks to score a try.

Argentina gave away five first half penalties and the penalties proved to be crucial as All Blacks scrumhalf, Piri Weepu kept New Zealand in control of the scoreboard. Leading 6-0 after 29 minutes the crowd was silenced as Argentina scored an impressive try with Farías Cabello diving over from a ruck close to the line. Senatore had broken past Kieran Read and Richie McCaw from a scrum two metres inside Argentina´s half. After getting past both All Black backrowers, Senatore ran clear and passed to Contepomi who gave a hot potato pass to Bosch who similarly fed Fernández who in turn spun it to Rodríguez Gurruchaga who ran 25 metres before being tackled two metres short of the try line. Camacho cleaned Piri Weepu out of the ruck and Farías Cabello dived over to the right of the ruck. Contepomi landed a sideline conversion which gave Argentina a 7-6 lead. The All Blacks regained the lead as Weepu saw the home team leading at the interval.

Argentina cut the deficit to two points in the 46th minute with Bosch landing a penalty kick from over 55 metres on the angle. His kicking style was not that of a long range kicker as he only took two steps before making contact with the ball. He had kicked one goal from two attempts against Georgia and could have possibly altered the outcome of the match against England had he been used. Leading 12-10 the All Blacks then looked to close out the match with Weepu adding two more penalties to give his side an 18-10 lead in the 60th minute. Argentina was unable to get the try that it needed and with New Zealand finally coming within range of scoring its first try, Rodríguez Gurruchaga went for an intercept rather than remaining in the defensive line. He came very close to catching the ball but his effort was not quite enough and Kieran Read went over in the 67th minute for New Zealand´s first try. The result was secured as Argentina was by now too far behind. New Zealand were able to score one more, however, as with three minutes remaining Cory Jane passed a miracle ball to Brad Thorn who scored a run in try. The final score of 33-10 did not feel like a true reflection of the match. Argentina had defended brilliantly despite losing scrumhalf, Nicolás Vergallo for ten minutes to a yellow card. Argentina exited the World Cup having had a mixed tournament but one that was, nevertheless, successful. Los Pumas had eliminated Scotland at the pool stage - something never done before and had scored some special tries. In general the team was young and the vast majority of players are expected to be playing at the Rugby World Cup 2015 in England.

7

Beyond – The Rugby Championship

Argentina made global headlines during Rugby World Cup 2007 but this was not repeated in 2011. A key difference between the two campaigns was that Los Pumas had increasingly been accepted as a top international side and now there was more expected of the team internationally than there previously ever was. This is what the Pichot lead team had been striving to achieve. While the team from Rugby World Cup 2011 was not as successful as the side from four years earlier the team had competed respectfully and exited the tournament with viewers all being aware of the quality of a side from South America. There would be no return to the old order of the Five Nations and Tri Nations sides.

The next step forward for the sports continued global expansion will not depend less on Argentina but, instead, it will depend on the country even more. Adding Los Pumas to the Tri Nations is no small matter. It means that Argentina is going to continue to improve and be a better side in the future. Historically teams have always developed on their own and have regularly played test matches against a small group of sides rather than a diverse set. Matches were predominantly regional in orientation with matches against the top sides less frequent due to distances of Australia, New Zealand and South Africa to Europe and also between each other. It has always meant that developing has long been a complicated task with representative teams having limited opportunities. This had long restricted the growth of rugby as a sport until recently. It took the creation of professionalism for rugby to become a global game and Argentina is the first country to really take the bull by the horns and transform from a team with potential to being a team which is now capable of winning the World Cup.

Argentina did not grow on its own. There was no professional competition set up by the UAR with the union centrally contracting players and having them trained as professionals. Nor was there a revolution with clubs becoming profit making entities that contracted players and paid for them to enjoy a quality lifestyle. Within Argentina the resistance towards professionalism was strong in 1995 and in parts of the country it continues this day. In Buenos Aires there remains a particular unwillingness to change with a real fear that it would destroy the vibrant club system in place in the capital. But in 2012 Buenos Aires is not all of Argentina and it is increasingly becoming less important in comparison to the remainder of the country. The state of amateurism in Argentina is changeable and the union has begun the process of transformation. This will be covered in greater detail in chapter 10.

Argentina became a global power without being able to develop players at home. This is vital to the future of the sport as it is not possible for every country to have its own professional structure. Nor does the possibility exist for all unions to join forces with neighbors or similar regional powers to form a professional competition. The Celtic-Italian League (Rabo Direct Pro 12) for instance, works for Ireland, Italy, Scotland and Wales but a similar system would not necessarily be viable elsewhere. A case in point being Super Rugby which works for Oceania´s leading teams - Australia and New Zealand but having Fiji added like Italy was to the Celtic League is a different situation altogether. Italy has a much larger population and is a more developed economy. There are also solid rugby relations in place due to the Six Nations Championship. Argentina became a top side due to the country´s leading players being exposed to professionalism. Fourteen players from the starting lineup that defeated France to open Rugby World Cup 2007 had played, at least, the 2006-2007 Season for European clubs. As such France by contracting Argentine players had greatly aided the developed of Argentine rugby to the extent that the French national team was defeated at home on a vitally important occassion – the start of the World Cup in France.

Not all rugby playing nations have sufficient infrastructure for professionalism. There are, however a growing number of professional teams requiring an increased number of players that they cannot find within their own borders. France has foreign players at all levels of club rugby from the Top 14 to the Fédérale 3. The top two levels of French rugby alone account for thirty teams and the clubs are all professional. Below them the clubs are not professional but it is, nonetheless, common to see imported players in the lower divisions. They are not strictly amateur as there are paid players but it is a significant drop off from the Pro d2. The club system is a success with a competitive league which is able to attract strong crowds as the product continues to expand. Attendances in the 2008-2009 Season for instance, grew 12% from the previous season.[94]

The crowds are larger because rugby is growing. The World Cup is a major product and as international competition has improved so have professional leagues. It is a mutual exchange in which clubs are able to raise their level and their profile by having a higher selection pool to choose from. This helps the sport by people becoming increasingly exposed to it and with both the level of players and teams improving. The clubs in turn pay the players and they then play for their country at a higher level than they otherwise would. It helps produce superior players, superior teams and superior rugby within the professional league and ultimately better World Cups. Juan Martín Hernández was fundamental to Stade Français's championship win in June 2007 and also to Argentina's World Cup campaign latter that year. Argentina developed through this system and so can others. In general it is not overly significant where people play but it does matter that they play professionally and do so at a high level. The better the quality of the league the better development a player will receive.

The French club season is long and challenging. Traditional powerhouses have fallen to the Pro d2 and even beyond. The bottom two at the end of the season are automatically relegated and clubs need reinforcements due to playing twenty-six league matches in the regular season and teams also disputing either the Heineken Cup or the Amlin Challenge Cup. There is also the matter of international matches during the season which clubs need to prepare for by having back up players. This requires large squads of over thirty-five players each and with fourteen teams it is not possible to find all these players from within France. Playing resources are stretched even further with Pro d2 clubs needing more players of quality to win promotion to the Top 14. In England's Aviva Premiership there is also not enough top level players from within England to cater for the demands of the twelve teams who dispute the competition. There are, however, enough players in the world to fill the void. Better players equate to better rugby and finding the right players is not an easy task but it is an impossible one without looking abroad. Crowds are also on the increase in England, albeit only slightly. The 2011-2012 Season saw an increase of 1.1%.[95] Combined France and England were responsible for twenty-six of the thirty-four man Pumas squad for the inaugural Rugby Championship. One other is contracted to a Welsh team.[96]

While this club system has seen Argentina become equal to the English and French test teams it has not actually made the French team deteriorate at all. France actually is the only team in the professional era to have played in the Semi Finals of every World Cup. Similarly, the English national side remains a strong team and has been to two World Cup finals in the professional era. Australia and France have too but nobody has been to three. The suggestion that signing foreign players damages ones national team lacks solid evidence. Wales in 2011 made the Semi Finals of the World Cup and in 2012 were undefeated in the Six Nations. Despite this Wales has only four professional teams and three of them have players who played for teams other than Wales at Rugby World Cup 2011.

While Wales was impressive in 2011 the same cannot be said of the team in France 2007. Even with Wales playing two of its four pool matches at the Millenium Stadium the campaign was forgettable and Wales was eliminated at the pool stage after losing 38-34 against Fiji. The Pacific Island nation had qualified for the Quarter Finals after playing some impressive attacking rugby in its four pool games. Fiji started with a 35-31 win over Japan in a match that could have gone either way. Four days latter Fiji defeated Canada 29-16 but opted to field a second string team against Australia in its third match and lost 55-12. The Fijian team that defeated Wales was not an amateur side featuring local based players. Twelve of the starting XV were professionals that played the previous season in Europe or Japan. Without professional teams for its players the Fijian side would have been significantly inferior as occurred when the teams met again at Rugby World Cup 2011 with Wales winning 66-0. On that occasion Fiji had less professional players but, more importantly, had few professional players playing in an elite professional competition[97] and even fewer playing in an elite competition and receiving regular game time. Fiji also faced South Africa in both tournaments. The 2007 Fiji was highly competitive in the Quarter Final match before South Africa ran away with a 37-20 victory. In 2011 however an inferior attacking Springboks team[98] defeated Fiji 49-3.

Georgia took a squad with plenty of professional players to New Zealand 2011. Of the thirty players selected twenty-three were based in France.[99] It was beyond debate that the Georgian team had improved remarkably since making its debut World Cup appearance in 2003 and the underlying reason for this was France. The team had an interesting World Cup in 2007 in defeating Namibia 30-0 and losing 14-10 against Ireland. In 2011 Georgia gave no team an easy match. Neither Romania nor Scotland scored a try against the Lelos. While Georgia narrowly lost World Cup matches against Ireland and Scotland what is stopping Georgia from kicking-on to defeat the Tier One sides in these contests is the level of rugby that the majority of players play in. Having players exposed to professional rugby is a major boost but in order to become equals players must be playing in elite leagues. Having players exposed to French club rugby saw Georgia significantly reduce its losing margin against England from 78 points in 2003 to 31 in 2011. But Argentina having its leading players almost exclusively playing in one of the Aviva Premiership, Pro 12 or Top 14 has enabled Los Pumas to go further than

Georgia. Despite having over two-thirds of its squad members in France the majority were playing in the lower division's not the Top 14 or Pro d2 in the 2010-2011 Season. Of the twenty-three French based players nine were in the Top 14 and not all were receiving regular game time.

The Georgian players were, nonetheless better prepared than Romania whose squad featured twenty players based in Romania, nine in France and one in England. Three of these players, Paulică Ion, Marius Tincu and Ovidiu Tonița, were playing in elite level competitions, notably less than that of Georgia. Romanian rugby is not strictly amateur, unlike Georgia. Since 2003 Romania has had a semi-professional rugby competition. The players are paid a similar salary to the average wage in the country. In 2003 there were twenty teams participating[100] compared to eight in the 2011-2012 season of the Super Liga (Romanian Championship). Romania also participates in Europe's second most important club competition, the Amlin Challenge Cup. But rather than have its club champion participate it has a team called the București Wolves which is made up of the best club players.

This is not to say that unions should not develop themselves. Relying exclusively on the professional market is a risk and individual unions need to actively develop to have systems of producing, targeting and preparing players. Argentina has long had a system that has done the first two of these but not the third. Potential Pumas have since 1951 played in the South American Championship. Preparing players for the top level has been eroding as a problem due to the high number of Argentine players in Europe but also because of the PladAR system and the UAR's desire to have a professional set up that works for Argentina. The 2008 rejection of making a professional competition in Argentina was not the end of the road. It was, rather an indication that the systems that are in place in other places are not necessarily going to work in the Argentine context. But Argentina remaining amateur is changing with a team being added to the SANZAR competition, Super Rugby very much being a work in progress.

With Argentina added to The Rugby Championship the international calendar has been otherwise unchanged. It is divided into four categories. The first of which is the South American Championship which took place in May. Chile hosted the tournament in Santiago and it was a four team event following the return of Brazil. Argentina fielded a side made up of Argentine based players with a mix of players from PladAR and completely amateur players. The first match was against Uruguay with Argentina fielding fourteen debutants. Leonardo Senatore captained the team which featured the international debut of Manuel Montero and Bruno

Postiglioni. Argentina won 40-5 six. Two more players made their debuts three days latter as Argentina played Brazil for the first time since 1993. On that day Argentina had won 114-3 and the winning margin repeated itself as Argentina won 111-0. Argentina scored seventeen tries with wingers Facundo Barrera scoring six tries and Manuel Montero three. Argentina won the title with a nine tries to zero 59-6 win over Chile. Both Barrera and Montero were again amongst the try scorers.

The second category of the international rugby season took place in June. With the UAR firmly pushing the growth of rugby in the country none of the three home tests were played in Buenos Aires. Instead Italy would play in San Juan and France would play in Córdoba and Tucumán. Phelan named a weakened squad for the three tests. Twenty-four players were rested[101] due to a long season which had started before the World Cup. All twenty-four players were involved in the European club season either playing in England or France. Argentina's admission into The Rugby Championship required a guarantee that the top players would all be available. Clubs would all be forced to release players under IRB regulation 9. The UAR collaborated with English and French clubs to ensure the players would be available and agreed to not field any players in June who would play in the August-October tournament.

Facing Tier One sides without twenty-four leading players is a tough ask and in many positions Argentina had its resources stretched. But it was, nevertheless, the best decision given the alternatives. Had Phelan used his leading players they would never have had a break. They would be playing rugby year-round which would not be in the best interests of player welfare. In any event the first home test took place on the same day as the Top 14 Final and only seven days after the Aviva Premiership Final and Top 14 Semi Finals. In other words, assembling and preparing a squad for the matches would have been very limited if all players had actually been considered. Phelan named a 30 man squad that featured 4 players from English clubs, 1 player from a Scottish club, 8 from France and 17 players from Los Pampas XV.[102] Felipe Contepomi was the captain having taken the decision to play in June but not playing in The Rugby Championship. Five players from the World Cup squad joined him for the June tests. It would be a true test of the PladAR program to have so many athletes playing for the national team. If Argentina could come out on top after facing the two Six Nations teams then it would be a sign that the program is working. Phelan had an advisor with the UAR having contracted Graham Henry. The All Blacks World Cup winning coach had no role in selection. His role was in his words to get "Argentina to score more tries."[103]

The first test was played on June 09 with a disappointing turnout in San Juan. It was scheduled at the same time as Argentina v Brazil in soccer. Italy scored the games first try with the referee awarding a penalty try from a scrum in which Argentina were missing Farías Cabello who had been yellow carded. Argentina's first try came in the 29th minute with Tomás Leonardí scoring. He had debuted in 2009 v England as an amateur and had developed through the PladAR system. He had a good match against Italy, making 20 tackles. Argentina came out strong following the restart with Contepomi landing one out of two early penalties to put Los Pumas six points clear. Italy hit back with a great solo try from scrumhalf Edoardo Gori following an Italian tighthead scrum. Playing in his 49th test, Rodrigo Roncero scored a spectacular try for a prop forward, let alone a 35 year old as he collected a blind-inside pass from Contepomi and got passed three tacklers. Senatore scored eight minutes later to secure the victory. Contepomi converted both tries and then scored a converted try of his own in the 77th minute. Italian veteran Mauro Bergamasco went over in the corner for the games final try which Riccardo Bocchino converted. The 37-22 final score was highly positive and the way Argentina had played gave room for optimism. For Contepomi it was more than just that, however as he completed a massive milestone as he overtook Hugo Porta to become the highest point scorer in the history of Argentine rugby, with 610 points. His personal tally of 22 points also made him the first Puma to reach 600 test points.

Going into the first test against France Argentina had a strong list of results against the French over the past decade. So strong, in fact, that Los Pumas had won seven of the past ten tests against France. Statistics, however, were not important at all in the build up to this match as the real story was not about previous results or about who was playing for the two countries. Rather, the bigger story was who was absent. Argentina fielded a side packed with players with shaven heads. The reason is a part of Pumas tradition. Upon making ones first appearance against a Tier One opponent it is customary to shave ones hair. The shaving occurs in the days that follow and for Belisario Agulla, Tomás Cubelli, Tomás de la Vega, Martín Landajo, Ignacio Mieres, Manuel Montero and Joaquin Tuculet who all featured in the win v Italy seven days earlier this meant they were all bald and ready to take on France in Córdoba.

Argentina fielded such an unknown side v France that only Contepomi and backrower Farías Cabello had played at Rugby World Cup 2011. The thirteen others were selected by Phelan for the purpose of developing depth with the team playing without twenty-four players. France, in contrast fielded six players from the 2011 World Cup Final. Argentina had eight Argentine based players, six French and one English in the starting lineup. Moreover, Phelan had not selected players from any French clubs involved in the Top 14 play-off's. France, on the other hand went for big name players from the likes of Clermont, Montpellier, Stade Français and Toulouse but could nevertheless not be called a full strength French team.

In front of a large and vocal crowd the match started with Morgan Parra kicking a penalty in the second minute. The South Americans responded swiftly with Belisario Agulla, the relatively unknown younger brother of Horacio Agulla scoring the games first try. In just the fourth minute Agulla intercepted a pass from François Trinh-Duc. The pass turned into a gift for Agulla as backrower Tomás de la Vega put in a solid tackle on Trinh-Duc which had the effect of taking the air out of the pass. Contepomi landed the conversion to make it 7-3 after four minutes. Parra kicked two penalties and Contepomi one before France broke clear down midfield and attacked the Pumas tryline. After several phases Trinh-Duc kicked wide to Jean Marcellin Buttin who caught the ball, attracted the tackle of Manuel Montero and off-loaded to Louis Picamoles who scored for France. Contpomi kicked his second penalty at the end of the half to make it a one point game with France leading 14-13 at the interval.

France looked to be heading for a victory after the interval as the Europeans were taking over certain areas of play with the South American scrum being dominated. Parra had kicked an early penalty to put France four points ahead before Argentine Tomás Leonardí was yellow carded for entering a ruck from the side when France was hot on attack. Parra put France seven points ahead with a resulting penalty in the 52nd minute. Contepomi made it 20-16 in the 56th minute at a time when France was looking dangerous but was not able to finish off chances. With three minutes left to play Fulgence Ouedraogo threw a loose pass near the Argentine 22 which was re-gathered by the home team with outside centre Joaquín Tuculet seizing the opportunity to attract defenders and kick ahead for Manuel Montero to collect and score a try. Contepomi converted the try making it 23-20 with two minutes remaining and succeeded in closing out the match for a victory.

Seven days latter the two teams met again, this time in Tucumán. The city again responded well by filling the stadium. The contest, however, was utterly different to the first test. France completed its biggest ever win over Argentina with a 49-10 victory. France produced a complete performance, playing well in all areas of the game to completely outplay the home side at the Estadio José Fierro. At the heart of the French victory was debutant scrumhalf Maxime Machenaud who replaced Morgan Parra and put on an outstanding display of attacking scrumhalf rugby. Outside him was the returning Frederic Michalak who alongside Maxime Mermoz had a very good performance but so did the backs in general as Florian Fritz, Yoann Huget and Benjamin Fall all played well. France's try scorers were Benjamin Fall, Yoann Huget (2), Maxime Machenaud, Maxime Mermoz and Alexandre Lapandry.

This heavy loss featured few positives but it did help clear up the picture as to who would be joining the players already named for The Rugby Championship. None of the players contracted to European players would make the squad based on the agreement that the UAR had reached with clubs. Following the completion of the home series Phelan named a thirty-three man squad to travel to Pensacola, Florida to undergo an intensive fitness performance program. The squad included the twenty-four players rested in June as well as nine players from Los Pampas XV[104] and Roncero who had previously announced he would retire following the June internationals. Shortly after returning to Argentina the squad was expanded to thirty-four with Manuel Montero being added.

The squad continued its preparation by training at the SIC club in Buenos Aires. The UAR had arranged for two friendly matches against Stade Français to be played in August. Phelan used a total of thirty players in the match. The first of which was played art Vélez Sarsfeld. The South Americans looked to have the game sealed but after having made thirteen changes the team lost its rhythm and was defeated 25-21. Argentina had played some great rugby in the backs with Horacio Agulla and Juan Martín Hernández performing particularly well. The teams two tries were created by these players with Agulla scoring the first after Hernández had off loaded in a tackle to put him into a gap. He then barged over former French test fullback, Jerome Porical to score. Argentina's other try came from an Agulla linebreak. Like the first he had come off the left wing to run a channel through the central part of the field. After attracting defenders he passed to Juan Imhoff who scored in the right hand corner. Argentina had issues in the forwards and in particular in the lineout with the South Americans not able to win enough clean ball. The one try that the French club scored came from a lineout on the Pumas try line. After Stade Français had secured the throw two Pumas forwards fell over which opened a huge hole for the try to be scored. It gave the Parisians the lead and ultimately the victory.

Six days later the two teams met in Santa Fé. The UAR wanted to ensure as many people as possible would have a chance of seeing Los Pumas play. The Buenos

Aires match had seen over 20,000 tickets sold while in Santa Fé a good crowd was also present. Argentina played better rugby but was not overly impressive in the 31-17 victory at the Estadio Brigadier General Estanislao López in Santa Fé. The three tries to two win was clean with Argentina able to put into practice what it had been training for. It came at a price with first choice hooker, Agustín Creevy leaving the field in just the second minute of play after fracturing a rib in a two man crunch tackle. Los Pumas scored good tries with Horacio Agulla and Juan Imhoff both impressing. Felipe Contepomi made it an appropriate farewell for Los Pumas. He played at inside centre for Stade Français and played a role in creating the first of Stade Français's two tries as he ran from inside his 22 and attracted defenders before offloading to a teammate. Contepomi said goodbye and goodluck to his close friends as they flew to Cape Town two days latter.

The Pumas players were buzzing about playing in The Rugby Championship. It was a massive triumph that the senior players had long dreamed about. Patricio Albacete compared the challenge to the World Cup. He said "It will be like a World Cup with the worst fixture of your life."[105] Albacete and been through it all. He had been to three World Cup's experiencing the highs and lows and had conquered Europe as a test player and also a club player. His brief summary was an account of what lay ahead. Going into unchattered waters is never easy and only time will tell as to how strong Argentina will be in the Southern Hemipshere tournament. It will not be fair to judge the team on its performances in its first years in the tournament. Italy, for instance took quite some time to adapt to the Six Nations with some big loses in its early years of the competition. The team is much more competitive now but remains in the bottom two annually. Nevertheless in 2012 it would be practically impossible to imagine the competition without Italy. Argentina, however, is a different example altogether with a history of results and a group of players that has far more strengths than weaknesses.

The historical debut of Los Pumas in The Rugby Championship saw a team playing from the heart but a team that failed to play as good as it can. The Springboks completed a 27-6 win in Cape Town scoring three tries to nil and deserving the win. The scoreline was not an accurate indication of the match as the teams were quite evenly matched in most areas. Argentina's lineouts issues of recent years vanished as Eusebio Guiñazú had an accurate match finding the jumpers. This was notable because Argentina used both secondrowers and all three starting backrowers as lineout jumpers. Both teams were penalized at scrum time but both won their own ball cleanly with Santiago Phelan getting a good scrum throughout the match even when he changed both props for the final quarter. The distribution to the backs was clean too. All in all the set piece was a success.

The result, from a historical standpoint was good in terms of defense but bad in terms of attack. Leading into this match the average score had been South Africa 42-21 Argentina. On the one hand Argentina won a battle as the home team scored three tries which was not enough to collect a bonus point. On the other hand it is worrying that the efforts of changing the style of play that involved employing Graham Henry did not see Argentina genuinely come close to scoring. All three of the South African tries were soft scores. None were the result of substantial period of attacking play. They were not constructed by phases at all. When South Africa did actually have sustained periods of attack on or close to the Pumas tryline they were unable to score. Argentina held off the waves by always winning a penalty or forcing Springbok handling errors.

In professional sport seven days can be a long time and Argentina demonstrated this in the return match in Mendoza, seven days after losing in Cape Town. Los Pumas stuck to its guns and produced a controlled display of rugby that South Africa struggled to combat. Argentina played an organized style of rugby that worked well even without Juan Martín Hernández who had been ruled out injured. He was replaced by Nicolás Sánchez who played well at flyhalf. The match was nothing less than history making. A case of bad luck in the largest degree cost Argentina victory. With the South Americans leading 16-9 a kick from Marcelo Bosch was charged down by Frans Steyn with the same player collecting the rebound to score the Springboks only try. It secured a 16 all draw in a match in which the home side was vastly better than the visitors for the majority of play. After the try Bosch was upset and at the end of the match he was extremely emotional. But such is test rugby that no players dared blame him. As a player Bosch has been through more hard luck than virtually anybody. He has had two career damaging injuries requiring shoulder and knee reconstruction.

South Africa had the first chance with a long range penalty attempt from Frans Steyn but it was slightly off target. It was a long attempt from inside the South African half and he would have a second opportunity in the match which would similarly not find the mark. Martín Rodríguez Gurruchaga playing fullback opened the scoring. His 11th minute penalty made it 3-0 to Argentina. Six minutes latter it was 10-0 as Argentina attacked well up midfield with Eusebio Guiñazú making good yards and keeping the ball in play. Several phrases latter Juan Figallo took a two man tackle and handed the ball to Santiago Fernández who went under the posts for a try which Rodríguez Gurruchaga converted. Morné

Steyn made it 10-3 in the 33rd minute with a penalty before Rodríguez Gurruchaga ended the scoring in the first half with his second penalty. At the interval Argentina led 13-3.

In the secondhalf Morné Steyn scored first with a penalty in the 49th minute. Three minutes later Rodríguez Gurruchaga cancelled it out with a penalty of his own but it would be the only Argentine points in the secondhalf. The South Americans controlled play for the first twenty-five minutes of the secondhalf before the opportunistic chargedown. Only one minute earlier Argentina had almost put the result beyond doubt as Santiago Fernández attempted a dropgoal but it missed the mark. Had it gone over Argentina would have won regardless of Frans Steyn's try. The match ended South Africa's perfect record against Argentina. The loss against the South American Jaguares has been defended as not being against Los Pumas but the draw in Mendoza meant there is no team that has Argentina has not either defeated or drawn against.

Argentina's third round match was against New Zealand in Wellington. Like the World Cup match against Scotland the game was dominated by atrocious conditions with strong rain and wind greeting the players. The All Blacks had a strong wind advantage in the first half but it died away altogether in the second. The match was similar to the Quarter Final in Auckland. New Zealand led 6-5 at halftime and was being seriously challenged. The only try of the first half came from a New Zealand mistake. Centre Ma'a Nonu knocked on and Argentina spun the ball with Gonzalo Camacho being tackled two metres short. From a ruck Rodrigo Roncero went over to make it 5-3. With fifteen minutes of the match remaining it was still anyones to win as the All Blacks led 9-5. A key moment in the secondhalf came in the 58th minute when Julio Farías Cabello was yellow carded, giving the All Blacks a one man advantage. With him off the field New Zealand was able to take control and scored its first try of the match through left winger Julian Savea. The youngster was handed a simple try after three Pumas went in to stop centre Conrad Smith which left New Zealand with two unmarked men. It made the scores 14-5 and effectively ended the South Americans chances as time was running out. New Zealand scored a second try in the 71st minute with Corey Jane scoring from a scrum on the Pumas 5 metre line. With the conversion it was 21-5 with eight minutes remaining. Argentina had an opportunity to score a second try of its own and came close. Camped in the New Zealand 22, Argentina drove hard but the All Blacks were able to hold up the Pumas maul. With slow ball Vergallo passed to Hernández in midfield who darted back before feeding Camacho. The Exeter Chiefs winger came to within several metres of the line before being tackled. It was not the final play of the game but it was as close as Argentina would get to scoring in the secondhalf.

There were many positives to come out of the match for Argentina. In the week leading up to the match there had been countless comments by New Zealanders on allblacks.com, facebook and other social media saying this would be a New Zealand win by at least forty points. The New Zealand commentary team was full of praise for a number of Los Pumas players. Former All Blacks scrumhalf Justin Marshall was impressed with Rodrigo Roncero, Juan Martín Fernández Lobbe, Juan Martín Hernández, Marcelo Bosch and Martín Rodríguez Gurruchaga. Argentina had already shown that it deserved to be in The Rugby Championship. In the previous round Australia had failed to score a point against the All Blacks at Eden Park. Yet Argentina gave New Zealand a scare and again proved to have superb defense that New Zealand, like in 2011, could only penetrate in the final quarter.

Argentina's fourth match of the competition was its first against Australia since 2003. It was the first international match ever played on the Gold Coast and was also at the smallest venue of the competition, Skilled Park with a capacity of 26,000. The match was not a sell-out and nor were Australia's home matches against New Zealand in Sydney and South Africa in Perth. The Wallabies had produced a superb secondhalf comeback in Perth and Argentina was not expected to be able to win due, arguably, to historical stereotypes. Nevertheless Argentina had the game in the bag holding a 19-6 lead after 56 minutes as Juan Martín Hernández landed his third penalty goal of the match. But from there Argentina would not score again while Australia would go over for two converted tries and a penalty to win after Argentina had held the lead for the games first 68 minutes. Scores were 6-3 in Argentina's favor at the interval after Hernández had landed one penalty more than Berrick Barnes. Argentina took control after Barnes's second penalty early in the secondhalf as replacement backrower Tomás Leonardí charged down a kick and went over for the first try in the 48th minute. Two minutes latter Argentina were leading by ten points as Hernández broke the line before feeding Juan Imhoff who sped around Nick Phipps and passed to Julio Farías Cabello who scored while being tackled. But Australia recovered to scrape home with two late tries and a penalty to win 22-19.

Australia's comeback showed one clear difference between the teams - the superiority of the replacements. A theme throughout the first four matches was that although Argentina has the depth every time Santigao Phelan went to the bench to replace a tired player the team seemed to drop a level. A second factor was goalkicking. While Berrick Barnes was on target to convert both of his country's tries the same cannot be said of Juan Martín Hernández who otherwise had a stunning game. He tackled more than any of his teammates and did so from flyhalf. He helped create the try of the match as he ran the ball from the deep and overall the match was another to show his credendials as a playmaker. He has an overall game which lacks one component - goalkicking. He missed both conversion attempts which could well have ended the match before the Australian fightback had begun. Hernández has kicked for Argentina previously, but it has not been common. He had a key role in Argentina's 2009 win over England but otherwise has tended to not kick the goals. Professionally it is similar. Hernández has kicked for all of Stade Français, Natal Sharks and Racing Métro but it has been the exception rather than the rule.

The performances of Los Pumas have not gone unnoticed internationally. Those less familiar with Argentine rugby have been shown that there is a world class team from South America that was able to hold South Africa to a draw and then lead Australia 19-6 several weeks later. It is the start of something that will inevitably see Argentina continue to receive more plaudits. Two time World Cup winner, John Eales would not suggest that the Australian team is weak or a shadow of past teams. Rather he wrote "I think it more accurately reflects Argentina's rise."[106] At the same time those more familiar with Argentine rugby have been echoing the quality of Los Pumas. French international coach, Philippe Saint-Andre believes that Argentina's performances in The Rugby Championship have shown that the South Americans have surpassed France and that the preparation that the players have gives them an enormous advantage. He said "Argentina is more than just a good team. They drew with South Africa when they deserved to win. In New Zealand, until the yellow card, they were keeping up very well. I believe Argentina will improve."[107] Saint-Andre is familiar with Los Pumas as a player and a coach. He notably coached Fernández Lobbe at both Sale and Toulon.

Another separate point to consider about Argentina is the youth system in place. Argentina has been a permanent member in the IRB Junior World Championship and before that the IRB under 19 and under 21 World Championships. In the most recent edition Argentina was a Semi Finalist in the tournament held in South Africa in June. Los Pumitas were in Pool C alongside Australia, France and Scotland. The South Americans won the group after defeating France 18-15, Australia 15-3 and Scotland 17-12. The side was eliminated by the host nation 35-3 in the Semi Finals and subsequently lost the Bronze Final 25-17 to Wales. The team had a number of impressive young players including fullback Santiago

Cordero who set up a jaw-dropping try against France and secondrower Juan Cruz Guillemaín who signed for Stade Français shortly after the tournament. Italy, in contrast finished bottom of the standings in 12th position after losing all its matches. Its final match was a 19-17 loss against Fiji which means Italy will play in the 2013 IRB Junior World Trophy rather than the IRB Junior World Championship.

Part II
Why Argentina

8

Track record in rugby

Part I elaborated on the performances of Argentine rugby in the international arena to illustrate that Los Pumas are amongst the best test teams in the world. Part II will look into off the field aspects to better understand whether or not Argentina is capable of being a host nation. The aspects have been subdivided into five separate sections, each of which is one separate chapter. Firstly, chapter eight will look into whether or not Argentina has a track record in hosting rugby events. Secondly, chapter nine will examine whether or not the country is ready to host a World Cup. Thirdly, chapter ten will look into the state of Argentine rugby and professionalism. Fourthly, chapter eleven will consider the possibility of Argentina as a host nation given the meaning or, the spirit of rugby. Lastly, chapter twelve will examine Argentina's contribution to global rugby by focusing on Argentine players playing abroad.

Not only have all previous Rugby World Cup hosts been nations who have strong teams that have all made the Knock-out stages or won the World Cup but they have also all been nations who have a rich history or, perhaps it could be better put, have a track record in rugby. Japan, of course, is going to change this in 2019 when it becomes the first Asian nation and first non-Tier One nation to host a Rugby World Cup. There is, however, little difference between Argentina and previous hosts when considering the staging of tournaments outside of the Rugby World Cup. Argentina has hosted tournaments at the development level such as youth rugby events, regional events and rugby sevens events. But did it host them effectively or, in other words, has the UAR been a good host?

Youth Rugby
In June 2009 The IRB announced Argentina as the host nation for the 2010 IRB Junior World Championship. The tournament is held once a year with the objective of giving young players the opportunity of competing for their country

against future stars from other countries. Since 2010 it has been a twelve team tournament with Under 20 level players being given the opportunity of having a feeder competition to international level. It replaced the former IRB under 19 and IRB under 21 World Championships. The tournament features the best 12 teams from the world who compete in three groups of four and it is followed by a play-off's series in which a champion is crowned and all competing teams finish with an official placing. It is organized by the IRB in conjunction with the host union.

The first IRB Junior World Championship was played in Wales in 2008 and Japan was the 2009 host nation. The third edition was played in Argentina. The IRB had selected Argentina as the host nation by highlighting that Argentina has the necessary infrastructure, that playing numbers were on the rise and that the UAR had successfully implemented the High Performance strategy (PladAR).[108] The move, knowingly or not, underlined Argentina's credentials as a future Rugby World Cup host. In announcing Argentina as the host nation IRB Chairman Bernard Lapasset said "The Championship is hugely important to the IRB in terms of providing a platform for the next generation of international Rugby stars to showcase their skills on the international stage and develop into elite athletes. It also plays a significant role in increasing global playing standards. Argentina has the facilities and infrastructure to ensure that the Tournament will be organized to a very high standard which is vital for its success."[109]

The tournament was hosted in the litoral region in the Entre Rios and Santa Fé provinces located northwest of Buenos Aires. The region was selected not only for its facilities but also because of the the objective of the UAR and IRB - reaching out to new Rugby fans in an area where there has been significant growth in participation in recent years.[110] The thirty match tournament was played in three different venues - the Estadio Brigadier General Estanislao López stadium in the city of Santa Fé, Club Atlético Estudiantes in Paraná and the Estadio Newell's Old Boys in Rosario. Games were distributed equally with each venue hosting ten matches.

The attendances on the opening day were double the size of those recorded in Wales 2008 and Japan 2009. The record breaking attendances involved more than 30,000 spectators with 16,000 attending the two matches in Rosario, 10,000 in Santa Fe and 4,000 in Parana. IRB Tournament Director Philippe Bourdarias was impressed by the amount of interest from the Argentine public. He said "We were expecting lots of people but not so many. The truth is that the numbers have exceeded our expectations. There were 30,000 people among the three stadiums and we really loved it. It is the best start of an IRB Junior World Championship as regards influx. Generally the attendance is high on the last day, but it was never like this first day."[111]

Five years earlier Argentina was hosted the IRB under 21 World Championship. It was the fourth time the event had been played after South Africa, England and Scotland had hosted the previous editions. Like the 2010 IRB Junior World Championship the 2005 IRB under 21 Rugby World Championship was played away from Buenos Aires. It was played entirely in Mendoza province with the matches being played at five venues. Four of the venues were rugby clubs – Chacras RC, Liceo RC, Maristas RC and Mendoza RC. The final was played at the Estadio Malvinas Argentinas, the same venue that hosted Argentina´s debut home match in The Rugby Championship.

Americas Rugby Championship
Mendoza is Argentina´s fourth largest city behind Buenos Aires, Córdoba and Rosario. Similar to Rosario hosting the 2010 IRB Junior World Championship, Mendoza was chosen to host the IRB under 21 Rugby World Championship because of the UAR and IRB´s interest in expanding rugby in the country. Córdoba also hosted an international event in 2010, the second edition of the Americas Rugby Championship. The inaugural tournament was played in Canada and it was a two stage event divided into a Canadian section and an intercontinental section in which development teams from Argentina and the USA would compete.

It started with four Canadian sides competing in a round-robin competition which doubled as the Canadian Rugby Championship. The tournament replaced the North American 4 to become the leading international competition in North America below test level. The North American 4 had existed from 2006-2008 and featured two teams from Canada and two from the USA – Canada East, Canada West, the USA Falcons and the USA Hawks. It had been so successful as a bridge from domestic rugby to the test arena that over 80% of the players representing Canada and the USA at Rugby World Cup 2007 had participated in the tournament.[112] The Americas Rugby Championship however had four regionally defined Canadian teams. The two strongest Canadian provinces – British Colombia and Ontario had a team each while much of the remainder of the country was divided into one of two teams. The western provinces of Alberta, Manitoba and Saskatchewan, also known as the prairies, combined to form the team known as the Prairie Wolfpack. The fourth team drew on the five eastern provinces of New Brunswick, Newfoundland & Labrador, Nova Scotia, Prince Edward Island and Quebec. It was named The Rock.

After completing the round-robin section the two top sides, from the Canadian Rugby Championship would go on to qualify for the Semi Finals of the Americas Rugby Championship. It was divided into a Canadian Semi Final and an Argentine v USA Semi Final. The BC Bears and The Ontario Blues qualified for the Canadian Semi-Final, which the Bears won 12-8. The Argentina Jaguars would be the opposition after defeating the USA Select XV 57-10 at Inifinty Park. The BC Bears v Argentina Jaguares final was played at Fletcher's Fields on October 17 and was won 35-11 by the South Americans. The Ontario Blues claimed third place after defeating the USA Select XV 27-24 earlier in the day.

The tournament structure changed for the 2010 tournament. Argentina, Canada and the USA all competed again with Argentina and the USA playing under the same names as in 2009. In 2010, however, there was only one Canadian team, which was called the Canada Select XV. The fourth competing team was Tonga A which despite not being from the Americas was included. Córdoba hosted the competition in October the month after the completion of the Canadian Rugby Championship. The four Canadian sides played each other in the same format as 2009 but it produced different results with The Rock winning the final 19-8 against the Prairie Wolfpack. Players from the four teams were considered for the Americas Rugby Championship with the Canada Selects XV being an amateur test side similar to the USA Select XV and the Argentina Jaguars.

The tournament format was also altered with all four teams facing each other in a round-robin format spread over 11 days. However, like the 2009 event it was local with no foreign based players involved. Tournament Director, Tom Jones said "These four teams represent the best of domestic players in each of their countries and many of them will travel to New Zealand in one year for Rugby World Cup 2011."[113] Indeed players went to play in New Zealand 2011 with seven players from Argentina's squad playing in the World Cup.[114] The event was also a way of analyzing the PladAR system and Los Jaguars impressed in successfully defending its title. The Argentine team defeated the Canada Select XV 49-14, the USA Select XV 45-12 and Tonga A 28-20. The Canada Selects XV finished second and the USA Selects XV was third.

Rugby Sevens
The 2012 Americas Rugby Championship had been rumoured to be returning to Argentina with Córdoba, Mar del Plata or Rosario suggested as potential venues.[115] But it was instead played in Canada. While Córdoba hosted the 2010 Americas Rugby Championship and Rosario the 2010 IRB Junior World

Championship Final Mar del Plata is also no stranger to an international rugby event. The city hosted the 2001 Rugby World Cup Sevens from January 26–28. It was the first time a major rugby tournament had been held in South America and was the third edition of the competition. The inaugural tournament took place at Murrayfield in 1993 after the Scottish Rugby Union (SRU) had proposed for the IRB to create a World Cup of the abbreviated form of the sport. It was accepted and Scotland would be the host nation for historical reasons. Scotland is the birth place of Rugby Sevens after an assistant butcher, Ned Haig, from Melrose suggested a tournament of abbreviated rugby be played. On April 28 1883 the tournament began and 12 days before its 110th anniversary Edinburgh hosted the first Rugby World Cup Sevens tournament. The SRU had also had the innovative idea of commemorating the union's centenary by staging an invitational Rugby Sevens tournament at Murrayfield in 1973. The tournament led to the creation of the Hong Kong Sevens in 1976.[116]

As Nigel Starmer-Smith pointed out in 1986, the Hong Kong Sevens was ahead of its time. The first edition of the event was played eleven years before the first Rugby World Cup and it had quite a role to play in the transformation of rugby from a select sport into something entirely different as rugby started to become a cosmopolitan international competition. It enabled teams perceived as non-traditional or even non-rugby nations to have a chance to show their worth. Starmer-Smith noted that South Korea and Western Samoa were every bit as good as Japan and Tonga.[117] The inaugural Rugby World Cup one year latter would not feature Western Samoa because it was not considered good enough unlike neighbors Fiji and Tonga. Incredibly, despite not having qualified for Rugby World Cup 1995, Fiji was crowned Rugby Sevens World Champions in 1997 after defeating South Africa 24-21 in the final. The tournament involved fourteen of the sixteen nations from South Africa 1995 with the Côte-d'Ivoire and Italy not participating.

The Hong Kong Sevens also helped modernize rugby as the event was one of the first rugby events to attract major sponsorship as airline Cathay Pacific sponsored the 1976 tournament.[118] Economic success saw the tournament become a permanent fixture on the rugby calendar as not only the first regular competition of its kind but also the world's premier Rugby Sevens event. The late Bill McLaren, known as the voice of rugby, wrote in his 1991 book *Talking of Rugby* that "I remember a big South Sea Islander saying that, in his view, the Hong Kong sevens were really the Olympic games of Rugby Union. Certainly, the Hong Kong event encapsulates all the really good things that the game has to offer – splendid organization, wonderful sporting spirit, universal camaraderie, admirable field behavior, the most enjoyable crowd participation, the chance for emergent rugby nations to lock horns with the mighty men of New Zealand, Australia, Fiji, Wales, Scotland and the Barbarians. There is, too, scintillating running and handling which is what the game is supposed to be all about."[119]

With the exception of the inaugural Rugby World Cup Sevens tournament in Scotland no other tournament has been hosted by a nation which has also hosted a Rugby World Cup. Scotland hosted five matches in Rugby World Cup 1991 including a Quarter Final and a Semi Final. In 1999 in hosted eight World Cup matches including one Quarter Final and in 2007 it hosted two pool matches. The 2005 Rugby World Cup Sevens returned to Hong Kong with Fiji winning its second title after defeating Australia 29-19. While in 2009 it was played in Dubai with Wales becoming world champions after defeating Argentina 19-12. The 2013 event will be played in Moscow. Not only is Scotland the only nation of these to have hosted Rugby World Cup matches and a Rugby World Cup Sevens tournament but it is also the only one to have won matches at a Rugby World Cup. Neither Hong Kong nor China have ever qualified for a Rugby World Cup nor has the United Arab Emirates while Russia played at a Rugby World Cup for the first time in 2011, losing against Australia, Ireland, Italy and the USA. Moreover in Rugby Sevens Scotland is on its own in having competed at every Rugby World Cup Sevens tournament to date.

Argentina, in contrast, has competed at every Rugby Sevens World Cup tournament with its best result coming in Dubai in 2009 when Argentina finished second. In 1993 Argentina won the Plate Final but four years latter it lost a Plate Quarter Final. The South American side was outside of the title contenders in both tournaments. Argentina, was, nevertheless selected as the host nation for the 2001 Rugby World Cup Sevens tournament. Argentina hosted the event in Mar del Plata, 400KM south of Buenos Aires despite the city only having previously hosted one international rugby match – Argentina v Spain in 1986. The Estadio José María Minella had previously hosted the 1995 Pan American Games and matches in the 1978 FIFA World Cup but in rugby terms it was yet to host anything of this kind. The final day of the event was a success with a crowd of 30,000 present.[120]

Argentina had done significantly better than in previous editions of the Rugby World Cup Sevens. The hosts had made the Cup Quarter Finals for the first time with Argentina taking on South Africa. The tournament was won by New Zealand who fielded a star-studded team including players such as Mils Muliaina, Rodney So'oialo and Jonah Lomu who scored three tries in the final. Argentina had its own share of star players with Agustín Pichot and Felipe Contepomi both playing in the 14-12 Quarter Final victory against South Africa which saw Argentina advance to face New Zealand in the Semi Finals. New Zealand won the match 31-7 and then won the World Cup after defeating Australia 31-12.

Mar del Plata was a host venue for the inaugural season of the IRB World Sevens Series in 1999-2000. It was, however, dropped from the series as were a number of others as the tournament changed significantly over the following decade. The inaugural season featured a ten leg circuit with Brisbane, Dubai, Fiji, Hong Kong, Mar del Plata, Paris, Punta del Este, Stellenbosch, Tokyo and Wellington all hosting one stage each. The 2012-2013 season features nine legs too but only four of the cities from the inaugural season continue as hosts - Dubai, Hong Kong, Tokyo and Wellington. Tokyo, however only returned for the 2011-2012 season. Australia and South Africa continue to host a leg each but in different cities. New additions over time have included England, Scotland and the USA. The Australian leg is played on the Gold Coast and South Africa's is in Port Elizabeth while the 2013-2014 Season will mark the return of Argentina.

The return of Argentina as a host union will not see the event take place in Mar del Plata. Rather, the capital city of Buenos Aires province, La Plata will host the tournament. The city is located 60KM from the national capital of Buenos Aires and has a well equipped modern stadium that makes it the country's leading venue. It hosted the opening match of the 2010 Copa America and also hosted the Pumas v All Blacks match in the 2012 Rugby Championship. From an Argentine perspective hosting the event in La Plata makes perfect sense due to the city's location, population and the timing of the event. The spring conditions of late October make for encouraging rugby and also for strong crowds. From the IRB's perspective the La Plata Sevens is a part of the sports preparation for inclusion in the Olympic Games in 2016 in Rio de Janeiro and an acknowledgement of the progress of South American rugby. IRB Chairman Bernard Lapasset said: "These are exciting times for South America, where participation has grown by 25 per cent in the last four years owing to the prestige and profile of Rugby World Cup, the IRB and CONSUR's investment and development strategies and Olympic Games inclusion. Argentina continues to be the beating heart of the South American success story and we very much look forward to working in partnership with the Argentine Rugby Union and the Argentina government to deliver an event that will capture hearts and minds, benefit Rugby throughout the Region and mark another significant milestone as we countdown to Sevens' Olympic Games debut in Rio in 2016."[121]

Argentina as a Rugby Sevens host is also a decision backed by sponsors. From a commercial standpoint the inclusion of La Plata was a reflection of the success of the event since its inception, its commercial prowess its and also an interest in the South American market. Giles Morgan, Group Head of Sponsorship and Events, HSBC Holdings said: "Since HBSC's involvement in the Sevens World Series, attendance has grown by almost 100,000 fans to 547,500 for the 2011/12 season, and broadcast coverage has reached record levels around the world. For HSBC the sponsorship enables the bank to engage with its customers and staff in key markets around the world, and with ten host cities across six continents."[122]

9

A host Nation Prepared

Having considered Argentina's history in hosting international rugby events the country would appear to be of merit as a World Cup host nation but what about Argentina as a host in general? Would Argentina be a suitable candidate to host Rugby World Cup 2023? Or would it be a risk to big to take? To answer this there are some general points to consider. Firstly, does the country have a history in staging large events? Secondly, is the country stable? Thirdly, is it of a sufficient size to successfully host a Rugby World Cup? Fourthly, is it an affordable place to attract a high number of visitors? Finally, does the country have the necessary infrastructure to cope with the demands of hosting a Rugby World Cup? In addition to hosting key rugby events other than the Rugby World Cup Argentina has hosted a number of major events such as the Formula one from 1953-1998 in Buenos Aires and also global sporting tournaments including athletics, basketball and soccer dating back to 1950 with Buenos Aires long being one of the predominant sporting centers of Latin America.

Hosting Sporting Events
The Argentine capital played host to the first ever Basketball World Championship in 1950. The sports governing body, FIBA or the International Basketball Federation had decided in 1948 to create a world championship to take place every four years. It was to be played in the years between the Olympic Games which saw the first event played in 1950. The FIBA Congress had met during the 1948 Olympic Games in London and awarded hosting rights of the inaugural tournament to Argentina. FIBA also decided that there would be ten teams with the three Olympic medalists qualifying automatically and being joined by regional qualifiers – the two best teams from Asia, Europe and South America, plus the host nation. Financial restraints, however, prevented Asian sides from competing and their places were taken by Spain and the former Yugoslavia.[123] Argentina won the tournament with the USA finishing second and Chile third.[124]

The tournament was a success with Luna Park attracting 25,000 fans as Argentina defeated the USA 60-50.[125]

Forty years latter Argentina hosted the tournament again. It was the eleventh edition and was played in 1990. Like the 1950 edition the final was played at Luna Park in Buenos Aires but unlike the inaugural competition the 1990 edition featured multiple venues. There were a total of six cities hosting matches with Buenos Aires being joined by and Córdoba, Rosario, Salta, Santa Fé and Villa Ballesta just to the north of Greater Buenos Aires. The competition was won by the former Yugoslavia who defeated the former Soviet Union 92-75 in the final. The USA claimed third spot after defeating Puerto Rico 107-105.[126] In hosting for the second time Argentine joined Brazil as a two time host of the tournament. Spain will join the select club in 2014 when it hosts the event for the second time. Another curiosity is that when Argentina hosted in 1990 it meant Latin America had hosted eight of the eleven tournaments. In naming Spain as hosts of the 2014 FIBA World Championship a first time bidder, China missed out. Like Argentina 1990, Spain 2014 will be an event with six venues. It will be a new tournament however as it was renamed the FIBA Basketball World Cup.[127]

The selection of Argentina as the 1990 host was an acknowledgement of the country as a reliable host nation. It was also a reflection of the level of the national team which has long been a quality side and continues to be up to this day. Argentina finished international competition in 2011 ranked third in the world.[128] In addition to utilizing six venues at the 1990 tournament rather than only one in 1950, the tournament had expanded to included sixteen teams. While having a shorter history the Rugby World Cup provides a useful comparison as it has expanded from sixteen to twenty teams and like basketball the hosts have operated on a rotational format. In basketball, since 1970 the subsequent host nation has always been from a different continent. Similarly, in rugby the World Cup has always changed continent from one tournament to the next. The difference, however has been that Europe has hosted every second World Cup since 1991 and this trend will continue to at least 2015 when England hosts the eighth Rugby World Cup and Europe's fourth overall.

The Pan American Games are the Americas regions version of the Olympic Games. It features nations from the continents of North America and South America. The first edition of the Pan American Games took place in 1951 in Buenos Aires. The thirteen day event involved 2,513 competing athletes from twenty-one countries. The event featured eighteen different disciplines with

Argentina scoring the highest number of medals, 150.[129] The 1951 event was not the actual origin of the Pan American Games. In 1932 Latin American delegates had proposed a regional event be established for the Americas. This led to the first ever Pan American Sports Congress in 1940 where the sixteen countries present selected Buenos Aires to host the inaugural Pan American Games in 1942. The Games had to be postponed due to World War II. When the first post-war Olympic Games were held in London in 1948 a second Pan American Sports Congress confirmed Buenos Aires to host the Games in 1951.[130]

Argentina hosted the Pan American Games for the second time in 1995. It was the twelfth edition of the Games and took place in Mar del Plata. Argentina became the third country in the Americas to host two editions of the Pan American Games, after Mexico and the USA. The 1995 Games were significantly larger than the 1951 Games. The number of participating countries had increased to thirty-four and there were 5,114 athletes competing in forty-two disciplines. The Games did not come without problems as the organizers left a number of competing athletes frustrated during the build up to the event. The games were, nonetheless, well attended with a capacity crowd of 30,000 spectators attending the opening ceremony at the Estadio José María Minella.[131] Argentina finished in fourth place with 159 medals. The USA dominated the event by collecting 425 medals.[132]

Regularly referred to as the most popular sport in the world, soccer is often used as a benchmark for other sports. In the case of the World Cup it is a benchmark. The FIFA World Cup is the biggest single-event sporting competition in the world.[133] As such the ability to host a FIFA World Cup is a useful indicator for the Rugby World Cup. Of the nations to have hosted a Rugby World Cup three have hosted a FIFA World Cup - England in 1966, France in 1998 and South Africa in 2010. While Rugby World Cup 2019 host, Japan co-hosted the 2002 FIFA World Cup with South Korea. In total there have been nineteen FIFA World Cups with Germany and Mexico each hosting two tournaments. The remaining fifteen FIFA World Cups have been hosted in different countries with one of them being Argentina.

The eleventh edition of the FIFA World Cup was played in Argentina in 1978. It can provide useful insight into Argentina as a potential Rugby World Cup host. While Rugby World Cups involve forty-eight matches the 1978 FIFA World Cup featured thirty-eight. It was a sixteen team tournament with matches played in seven venues in six Argentine cities. Buenos Aires was the principal city, contributing two venues including the Estadio Monumental Antonio Vespucio

Liberti which hosted the Final. The five host cities were Buenos Aires, Córdoba, Mar del Plata, Mendoza and Rosario. With the exception of Mar del Plata they are the country's four largest cities. In order to prepare for hosting the tournament new stadiums were constructed in Córdoba, Mar del Plata, Mendoza and Rosario while the Estadio Monumental Antonio Vespucio Liberti and the Estadio José Amalfitani were both upgraded. The country was prepared to host a successful tournament and did so with 1,610,215 people attending matches at an average attendance of 42,374 people per match.[134] The Argentine team also delivered as Argentina won the World Cup for the first time by defeating the Netherlands 3-1 in the final.

The nature of the victorious campaign however has long been surrounded by controversy which started before the tournament and continued during the tournament itself. Before the World Cup there had been calls from several competing nations to boycott the tournament. Led by the Netherlands, the protest was against General Jorge Rafael Videla who had staged a military coup d'état that deposed of Argentina's elected president, Isabel Martinez de Peron. The dictator's totalitarian regime was actively violating human rights in what was known as the Dirty War. From 1976-1983 Argentina's military Junta killed more than 30,000 Argentine citizens,[135] including Omar Actis, president of the World Cup Organizing Committee, who was assassinated by guerrillas. The situation calmed down eventually as General Videla exercised some diplomacy and guaranteed there would be no bloodshed during the competition, and the boycott was cancelled.[136] His reign as a brutal dictator continued after the tournament until democracy was restored in 1983. After a long road to justice Videla was convicted of the systematic kidnapping of babies and children during his tenure and sentenced to 50 years in prison in July 2012.[137]

The scale of Argentina's 6-0 victory over Peru was so unexpected that it has long been considered that Peru accepted a bribe to throw the match. Argentina required a four goal victory to advance to the final. A failure to do so would see Brazil advance instead. It was reported in the Times of London in 1986 that in exchange for enabling the elimination of Brazil Argentina shipped 35,000 tons of free grain to the Peruvian port of Callao, and its central bank agreed to unfreeze a $50-million line of credit for Peru.[138] In 2012 Peruvian Senator Genaro Ledesma told a court that the result had been agreed upon before the match by the dictatorships of the two countries. Mr Ledesma asserts that Videla accepted Peruvian political prisoners on condition that Peru deliberately lost the World Cup match by enough goals to ensure Argentina progressed to the final. Ledesma said in court: "Videla needed to win the World Cup to cleanse Argentina's bad image around the world.

So he only accepted the group if Peru allowed the Argentine national team to triumph."[139]

While athletics has the Olympic Games on a global scale and the Pan American Games on an American regional scale soccer has the FIFA World Cup and the Copa America. Argentina like Brazil and Chile has hosted both tournaments. All ten members of the South American Football Confederation (CONMEBOL) have hosted the Copa America and Argentina has hosted it more times than any other country. Argentina has hosted nine Copa America tournaments - 1916, 1921, 1925, 1929, 1937, 1946, 1959, 1987 and 2011. The most recent of the tournaments provides the best insight into the possibilities of Argentina hosting Rugby World Cup 2023.

It was a twenty-three day event played across Argentina with eight cities hosting matches. The same eight cities have all played host to Argentine rugby matches in the professional era. The Estadio Monumental Antonio Vespucio Liberti in Buenos Aires, the Estadio Mario Alberto Kempes in Córdoba and the Estádio Malvinas Argentinas in Mendoza were all returning venues from the 1978 FIFA World Cup. They were all renovated ahead of the tournament as was the Estadio 23 de Agosto in Jujuy, the Estadio Padre Ernesto Martearena in Salta and the Estadio Brigadier General Estanislao López in Santa Fé. The construction of the Estadio Unico Ciudad de La Plata in La Plata and the Estadio del Bicentenario in San Juan were both completed in 2011. The opening fixture was played in La Plata and the final in Buenos Aires. Argentina had a disappointing campaign, losing to eventual champions Uruguay at the Quarter Finals stage. But the tournament was another example of the country's ability to successfully host a large sporting event as over 1.5 million people attended the tournament.

Is it a Stable Country?

At the time of hosting the 1978 FIFA World Cup there were concerns surrounding the tournament due to Argentina's military junta. When Argentina was awarded the hosting rights to the tournament it was not a democracy. The FIFA Congress named Argentina as the host nation on July 06 1966 in London. The hosts for 1970 and 1982 were also confirmed with Germany and Spain given hosting rights. All three nations were the sole bidder for each of these tournaments.[140] Argentina was awarded the hosting rights only nine days after a military coup d'etat in Buenos Aires. On June 28 1966 Argentina's democratically elected president

Aruro Allia had been overthrown by a military coup d'etat lead by General Juan Carlos Onganía. It was the fifth of six coups imposed by the Argentine military in the twentieth century[141] and only four years after the previous one. Nevertheless, Argentina was awarded the right to host the 1978 FIFA World Cup.

It is fair to therefore conclude that Argentina was awarded the hosting rights of soccer's premier tournament when it was not a stable country. After having been awarded the tournament democracy did return in 1973 but it would not endure as the military took control again in 1976 with the sixth and final coup d'etat of the twentieth century. The World Cup went ahead as Videla's dirty war was able to be talked down during the tournament. The problems preventing democratic stability in Argentina were around long before Videla's military coup d'etat. Political Scientist Paul H. Lewis traces the origin of the Dirty War to the coup d'etat of 1930 and to the rise of former General and President Juan Peron whose regime led to the polarization of Argentine society.[142]

Democracy returned permanently in 1983 following the costly war with Great Britain over the Falkland Islands. Sustaining democracy in the country has succeeded and after a period of disturbance in the latter half of the 1980's it has been consolidated and there have been no signs of a return to a non-democratic Argentina. The new Argentina was free from military terror and the population was free to choose its government. The transition was not clean and swift however as the democratically elected government did not inherit the greatest economic conditions. As such there were four unsuccessful military uprisings during the late 1980's.[143] The economy was so unstable that the inflation rate was 5103% in 1989.[144] When Carlos Menem took the presidency in 1989 he transformed the economy by privatizing state-owned businesses and pegging the value of the Argentine peso to the US dollar. His radical free market reforms stabilized the economy as inflation[145] fell from 84% in 1991 to 17.5% in 1992 and 7.4 % in 1993.[146]

The economic restructuring proved successful in repairing the problems of 1989 but global economic issues of the following decade severely influenced the Argentine economy. Financial crises across Asia, Russia and Turkey from 1997-2001 meant Investors were less willing to invest in developing countries.[147] In December 1999 Menem was succeeded by Fernando de la Rua who had won that year's presidential election. De la Rua fought to save the economy but ultimately was unable to do so as the crisis worsened in 2000 and 2001. He resigned as president on December 21 2001 after rioting had broken out killing at least 22 people on the streets of Buenos Aires.[148] de la Rua's replacement, Adolfo

Rodriguez Saá attempted to find a solution but resigned as president six days latter. Eduardo Duhalde replaced him and with Argentina broke and facing economic Armageddon the country defaulted on a debt repayment of US$132billion. The peso had lost two-thirds of its value overnight.[149]

Duhalde resigned in May 2003 and called for an early election. The economic policies had been a disaster to the extent that 50% of the population was living below the poverty line during the crisis.[150] Duhalde was replaced by the late Néstor Kirchner who led the country from 2003-2007 and was succeeded by his wife, Cristina Kirchner who is into her second term as president after winning reelection in 2011. The Kirchner's turned around the crisis to in 2010 give Argentina the fasted growing Latin American economy with a growth rate of 9.2%. Furthermore the poverty rate had been cut by more than half since 2007.[151] In 2010 the unemployment rate was 7.9%,[152] and one year latter it was 7.2%.[153] In comparison South Africa which hosted Rugby World Cup 1995 and the 2010 FIFA World Cup is estimated as having an unemployment rate of 24.9%.[154] In short, the Kirchner's have given Argentina economic and political stability with the country having recovered dramatically to be considered as a reliable and suitable candidate to host Rugby World Cup 2023.

Population

Is Argentina large enough to successfully host a Rugby World Cup? In a word, yes. Argentina is the second largest country in South America and the eighth largest in the world[155] making it much larger than most countries to have hosted a Rugby World Cup. Australia which co-hosted in 1987 and hosted alone in 2003 is of the nine nations which will have hosted World Cup matches by 2019, the one with a larger territory than Argentina. Australia has a large population compared to Rugby World Cup 2011 hosts, New Zealand. Argentina, however, has a population of almost twice that of Australia and ten times that of New Zealand. With 42 million inhabitants Argentina is the thirty-second most populated country in the world and the third in South America after Brazil and Colombia.[156]

Argentina has a large population that would give the Rugby World Cup a good domestic audience in addition to catering to the needs of the tournament as a financial entity. While Buenos Aires is easily the country's largest city it is not dominant as a sports hub to the same extent as most of the Six Nation's capital cities. England, for instance, is dominated by London to the extent that the English rugby team plays all of its home matches at Twickenham. Argentina has sizeable cities in the north and west of the country which give it plenty of options for hosting matches. The south of the country is sparsely populated but there are certain places that could be considered. Since the World Cup was expanded to twenty teams in 1999 there have been eleven or more venues used to host matches. Part IV will look into the possible venues that could be used for Argentina to host Rugby World Cup 2023.

Affordable Destination

Argentina had been an expensive tourist destination during the Menem regime but after the economic collapse it became much cheaper. It has increased since 2002 due to the stabilizing effect of the economy and due to the natural effects of inflation. It, nevertheless, remains a very affordable destination for people with valuable hard currency such as the British Pound, Euro or the US Dollar. Whilst the exchange rates are subject to change the rates are significantly favorable to travelers on these currencies. In September 2012 USD$1 was ARS$4,69 while €1 was worth ARS$6,07 and £1 was worth ARS$7.59.[157] The travel guide company, Lonely Planet ranked Argentina as the seventh best value destination in the world in its 2011 top ten list. It sited that in addition to the attractions the benefits of visiting Argentina are its low hotel prices and quality and affordable food. The guide says that "best of all, you get great quality food, wine, lodging and transport throughout Argentina for your money."[158] In other words, Argentina is an affordable destination and there is no reason why a Rugby World Cup in the country would not be appealing to rugby fans and casual visitors from around the globe.

While not making the Lonely Planet's 2011 Top Ten list New Zealand is, nonetheless, a relatively cheap destination. Its performance as a Rugby World Cup host nation can provide important insight into what can be expected economically. In February 2012 New Zealand's Ministry of Economic Development reported that 133,000 tourists had ticked on their arrival cards that they went to New Zealand for Rugby World Cup 2011. The Ministry of Economic Development's Tourism Research and Evaluation Manager, Peter Ellis said "we're confident between 60 and 75 percent of the rugby visitors' expenditure can be regarded as a net increase in tourism spending – that is, an increase over what would have been spent by visitors if there had been no world cup in New Zealand. Taking into account sampling uncertainty, our best estimate is that tourism expenditure in 2011 was between $220 and $340 million higher as a result of the Rugby World Cup."[159]

The tournament was therefore a huge economic success for the country but it ultimately operated on a loss. Preparation for the event cost NZ$300million (US$249million)[160] with the redevelopment of the prime stadium, Eden Park, alone costing the government NZ$150 million.[161] New Zealand needed to invest in its stadiums for the tournament and it was costly but necessary. Argentina, in contrast, has relatively little work to be done on redeveloping stadiums because for the most part they have already been recently upgraded. The eight stadiums which hosted the 2011 Copa America were all either new or upgraded making it a much simpler task of Argentina hosting a Rugby World Cup than that of New Zealand 2011.

In May 2012 Rugby New Zealand 2011 (RNZ 2011) announced an official loss of NZ$31.3 million from staging the tournament. The figure came as good news as it was NZ $8 million lower than what had been forecast.[162] The event was a huge success for the sport and the country as it enhanced the profile of both. It did however cost a lot to organize and the country's low population meant it was a different situation to a larger country preparing like France for 2007 or England for 2015. In 2007 no stadiums were significantly redeveloped. France used the same ten venues from Rugby World Cup 2007 plus one stadium from each of Scotland and Wales. For 2015 there are not to be any major redevelopments comparable to that of Eden Park. As will be covered in Part IV Argentina like France and England does need to invest in such a significant project as that of Auckland's Eden Park.

Making a profit from hosting a Rugby World Cup is not a given as New Zealand illustrates. Any country intending on hosting a major sporting event needs to have sufficient infrastructure or the loss suffered could be significantly larger to that of New Zealand 2011. This can, in some cases, mean building from scratch. But the lessons of major sporting events have been clear for all to see. The costs involved are extremely high and there needs to be long term planning so that venues are used in the long term future and not just for the major event itself. Montreal hosted the 1976 Olympic Games and built a new stadium, Olympic village and other facilities to put on a successful event. It went down in history as a lesson as it cost Canada US$1.48 billion and took 30 years to pay off.[163] It outlined the need for sensible investments and a need for a host to have a large budget. But history would repeat itself and on a much larger scale in Athens, the host city of the 2004 Olympic Games.

Like New Zealand with rugby, Greece is considered a sacred place for the Olympic Games. The country has a population of over double that of New

Zealand but at 10.7 million it is significantly smaller than Canada which has a population of 34.3 million[164]. Like Canada, little thought was put into making it a sustainable investment. It was, like New Zealand 2011 more about national pride. Greece was determined to host the 2004 Olympic Games. Many Greeks had been outraged following the country's failure to secure the 1996 Olympic Games with politicians and journalists reacting angrily when Atlanta beat out Athens for in 1990 the right to host the Games.[165] Determined the host the Olympics, Greece bid for the 2004 event and won but was so costly that Montreal dwarfs in comparison.

It is a relevant and important lesson considering Greece's 2012 default and Argentina's default a decade earlier. Greece overtook Argentina for defaulting on the highest debt in history. Five years after hosting the Olympic Games Greece had a debt of US$447[166] making the 2004 Olympic Games the worst investment in the country's history. Argentina cannot go down a similar road but in order to host Rugby World Cup 2023 it need not do so. The cost of hosting the event was too high for Athens or Greece to handle but it did not stop the government spending money that it did not have. In 2011 seven years after hosting with the country close to bankruptcy the head of the International Olympic Committee, Jacques Rogge, admitted that hosting the Olympic Games aggravated the country's debt problem. The government estimated the cost at $11 billion.[167] The lesson is that without a clear plan of what to do with the facilities after the event has finished there is no way that the money put into hosting the event will ever be received back. The investments made for the 2011 Copa America mean Argentina 2003 would not be similar to any of Montreal 1976, Athens 2004 or New Zealand 2011.

Transport
Argentina is a large country but one well served by transport services. It is possible to travel by car, bus or airplane easily and safely making it a simple task for visitors. The infrastructure is sufficient to cope with the demands of hosting a Rugby World Cup. There are nationwide companies which operate in all the cities likely to be considered for the tournament. Not only do they cover all the cities but they do so frequently with an abundance of options. Visitors will be able to take long but comfortable trips from Buenos Aires to other major cities such as Córdoba or Mendoza by bus. There are many different companies to choose from with buses regularly departing giving visitors the choice of travelling by day or through the night. The inter-city buses offer a variety of options ranging from *común* (economy) to genuine first class experiences. The cheapest options are far from being uncomfortable but it is common to spend a little more and receive quality services including air-conditioning, toilets, TVs, complimentary snacks

and a seat which folds down into a bed or a semi-bed on overnight trips. It costs around AR$20 to AR$50 extra to get a sleeper class or semi-sleeper seat and it gives passengers wider and almost flat seating which is far more comfortable.[168]

In New Zealand 2011 it was common for visitors to get around in rental cars. The option is also available in Argentina. The popular rental car website, rentalcars.com has rates for car rentals in Argentina starting at US$40 per day[169] allowing those who want more control over their travels the opportunity to affordably get around the country. It is a potentially ideal way of travelling between cities to attend pool matches for small groups of two-five people. It would enable visitors to follow their team around while also having sufficient time to see the attractions. In New Zealand 2011 Ireland played its four pool matches in New Plymouth, Auckland, Rotorua and Dunedin. The team was well supported with a sea of green present at every match. Many of the fans traveled by rental cars or campervans to get from Rotorua to Dunedin for the crunch match against Italy which meant a road trip of over 1200KM and a three hour ferry ride linking New Zealand North and South Islands.

In Australia 2003 it was impossible for fans of some teams to rent cars or travel by bus. The distance from Perth to Melbourne is over 3000KM and Sydney is even further. Of the venues used for the 2011 Copa America the largest distance was that of Buenos Aires to San Salvador de Jujuy. The cities are very far apart at a distance of 1654KM but unlike Perth both have other cities located nearby which also hosted matches in the 2011 South American soccer tournament. This is not to say that Argentina does not have an airplane service to cater to the demands of hosting a Rugby World Cup. The country has multiple airline carriers with the largest being Aerolineas Argentinas which services twenty-seven Argentine cities.[170]

There is also a government project to construct a high speed train linking the country's three largest cities of Buenos Aires, Rosario and Córdoba and possibly also Mar del Plata. It would be the first system of its kind in South America. The TGV trains would travel at speeds of up to 320 km/h and have up to nine trains per day[171] making a Rugby World Cup in the country increasingly tenable. The proposal will see cities become increasingly interlinked as the travel time will be significantly decreased. It would be much faster than bus trips. Buenos Aires to Rosario would decrease from around four hours to a journey time of 85 minutes and a trip from Rosario to Córdoba would take 90 minutes.[172] President Néstor Kirchner announced the plans in 2006 and in April 2008 the government finalized a deal with a consortium led by the French company Alstom. It was estimated to cost US$4 billion and due to start but had to be put on hold due to the global financial crisis. Alstom announced it was on hold indefinitely, because the French bank Natixis had run into major troubles and could no longer put up the necessary financing leaving Argentina with nothing. The project remains on hold but the government has purchased high performance trains, with maximum speeds of half that of the planned bullet trains. When complete they will operate in a larger area of the country.[173] The high speed train project nevertheless remains a possibility and could well be completed over the coming decade.

10

Approaching Professionalism

The player strike threats were very much real in 2006 and they proved to play a significant role in the players respect for one another and also in revolutionizing the union. The UAR and the players came to an agreement with rugby developing significantly off the field. The UAR has established itself as a stable union and has actively resolved a dispute between itself and URBA. The Buenos Aires Rugby Union had reacted to the creation of the PladAR system negatively out of a fear that it would damage their clubs and even see many disappear. This attitude was predominant in 1995-1996 when other rugby nations were turning to professional rugby. In Argentina it saw the game remain strictly amateur and no change was shown by URBA between then and the creation of PladAR in 2009.

Following the establishment of PladAR URBA voted to block PladAR players from playing for their clubs in URBA competition as they contended that it gave then an unfair advantage over the players who were purely amateurs. The players concerned were highly disappointed and the UAR attempted to change URBA's position. While URBA was opposed to allowing PladAR players in its competition none of the countries other provincial unions prevented PladAR players from playing for their amateur clubs. It was simply a Buenos Aires problem and this was significant because Buenos Aires had long been the country's dominant union. The power of URBA was visible at Rugby World Cup 2007 when twenty-six of the players were from Buenos Aires.[174] Its power had been fading, however, as other unions were becoming more successful. The squad for Rugby World Cup 2011 was still dominated by Buenos Aires but this time twelve of the thirty players were not from Buenos Aires.[175]

So much change was made in Argentina following Rugby World Cup 2007 that URBA no longer had such a powerful position. In 2009 the UAR´s new president did not come from Buenos Aires. Instead the elected president was Luis Castillo from Tucumán. His appointment enabled changes to be made with the country´s unions able to overpower URBA. The capital's union still remained firmly against PladAR but not all clubs were happy. La Plata, for instance sent a letter to URBA requesting that all PladAR players be free to play for their URBA clubs.[176] With pressure from many parties including the UAR the decision to not allow PladAR players to play in URBA was overruled and players were able to play. The issue was far from being resolved permanently, however, and a special vote took place in April 2011 which saw a law passed to once and for all enable Buenos Aires´s PladAR players to play for their clubs. The decision was a major victory for the professional future of rugby in Argentina. The vote was won 75 to 78.[177]

In July 2011 the chairman of the UAR´s subcommittee on high-performance, Manuel Galindo, said "Our idea in the future is our union will have most of the players on contract in Argentina and only a few stars playing in Europe – about ten would be the best."[178] It is nothing short of a revolution on the part of the UAR which had been utterly opposed to professionalism. The plan is a part of consolidating Argentine rugby to ensure the national team continues to be strong while the domestic game is strengthened. It was the official start of Argentina as a professional rugby country and while there is yet to be a professional league or team based in the country the beginnings have certainly been firmly established.

It marks a dramatic move away from developing players through the European club system but not an abandonment of it entirely. Rather it is a desire to have the top players in Argentina at the full disposal of the training staff. With The Rugby Championship taking place during the early months of the European season some clubs have not reacted well to the changes. The Leicester Tigers insisted on releasing Horacio Agulla due to his certain participation in the tournament and Racing Métro President Jacky Lorenzetti said he would not be signing more Pumas. The hard talk threatened to change the future of Pumas in Europe but has not amounted to much as more players have joined European clubs. Agulla transferred to Bath while his Pumas teammate, Marcos Ayerza extended his contract at Leicester. Racing Métro extended the contracts of both Juan Imhoff and Juan Martín Hernández.

The European club game demands a large number of highly skilled players and this will ensure that Pumas players continue to be in demand into the future. But with the UAR now interested in creating a professional team there is a strong chance that the best players will be playing their rugby in Argentina. It would be in their interests to do so as it would mean a shorter season and more time to prepare for international duty. Galindo knew that the June 2012 home tests would not be real test matches because those under contracts to European clubs would be rested. Here in lies the UAR's solution to the problem as the union not only wanted the top players centrally contracted but is offering them something they have never had before and not only that but it is on track to have Argentina fully integrated into SANZAR by having Los Pampas XV become a Super Rugby team. Overtime there is also the real possibility of having an Argentine conference integrated into Super Rugby. Should Los Pampas XV successfully become a Super Rugby team and perform then teams based in the likes of Buenos Aires, Córdoba, Cuyo, Rosario and Tucumán could potentially be bases for Super Rugby teams eventually.

The uniqueness of Argentine rugby makes such a move longterm. Argentina cannot be rushed into playing Super Rugby as the local market needs to firstly be able to sustain a team. The UAR is actively looking at it from this perspective. The goal is Super Rugby but it will occur after firstly playing in the Vodacom Cup and Currie Cup. Argentina's intention of playing Currie Cup rugby is both well known and well advanced. Negotiations are well underway for Los Pampas XV to play in the 2014 Currie Cup.[179] It would further encourage the growth of PladAR players and consequently ensure an increased number of players for international selection. It will greatly benefit international rugby. Phillipe Saint-Andre believes that Argentina has firmly adapted to international rugby in the professional era and that it has overtaken France in organization.[180]

Los Pampas XV was created from the PladAR program for the simple reason of having something sustainable. But it is the means to an end rather than the end in itself. As mentioned in Chapter 7 Argentina became powerful without any professional structure whatsoever and it is a model that other nations can follow and some actively are doing so. The success of Los Pumas was achieved with significantly limited resources from the UAR compared to what other Tier One teams receive from their unions. The creation of PladAR was intended to close the gap and in many ways it has certainly succeeded as players now have funding and exposure to a semi professional competition, the Vodacom Cup. Moreover, the unions change in direction of hosting matches throughout the country is a major part of actively capitalizing on the success of Los Pumas in a bid to expand the market.

This also achieves the objective of seeing rugby thrive into the future by increasing exposure and encouraging opportunities to more players from more parts of the country. Argentina is moving on and the success of the 2011 Vodacom Cup is not the heights that the union is chasing. The Vodacom Cup is highly useful for Argentine rugby and in winning the 2011 tournament it underlined that significant results can be achieved with serious work. Galindo stresses the need for the UAR to make money from additional sources other than just Los Pumas. While the Los Pampas XV venture in the Vodacom Cup is a rugby investment it is not a cheap exercise. It is paramount that Argentina has or finds a way of having a tournament that is self-financing. It is not the simplist of tasks but the UAR is certainly on the right track and The Rugby Championship means that the budget available to the UAR will become larger than ever before. Galindo pointed out in 2011 that 35% of the UAR´s total budget was invested at the grass roots level and in the country there were 250 elite players from a total of around 100,000. This is from an annual budget of around AR$10 million. At the same time England, in contrast had a budget of £170 million.[181]

In saying "10 players would be best" Galindo is talking about making a system that works for Argentina. It does not mean copying what other Tier One unions have because no Tier One unions actually have the same system as another. New Zealand has a system that ensures there will always be a factory like production of players. Many teams in its national competition, the ITM Cup operate on a loss[182] but, like Los Pampas XV in the Vodacom Cup, it is necessary to ensure there is a constant supply of players who could be All Blacks. To play for the All Blacks one needs to be playing his rugby in New Zealand. Playing abroad instantly makes a player non-eligible. Australia applies the same system but without a national competition. In England and France the countries both have fully professional and highly profitable domestic leagues with France having two more teams than England in the elite division. Italy and Scotland have two teams each in the Rabo Direct Pro 12 while Italy also has a ten team semi professional competition called the Campionato Nazionale Eccellenza. Scotland´s only professional teams are those in the Celtic-Italian League - Edinburgh and the Glasgow Warriors. Ireland and Wales both have four teams. The Irish ones are provincial – Connacht, Leinster, Munster and Ulster. The model in Wales is regional with the Dragons based in Newport, Blues in Cardiff, Ospreys in Swansea and the Scarlets in Llanelli. Both have helped their respective national teams improve tremendously but in Wales the regions have not been successful in capturing the imagination of the public.

None of these models are really applicable to the state of Argentine rugby and the professional direction that is being undertaken. Rather, the most similar of all Tier One set-ups would be that of South Africa. The top players are almost all playing in the country but not exclusively. Playing abroad is discouraged in some circles but it does not make a player ineligible. François Steyn left South Africa to play for Racing Métro from 2009-2012 but remained firmly in the Springboks. Similarly Ruan Pienaar has long been in the Springbok frame as a scrumhalf or flyhalf and continues to be despite playing for Ulster. Both Steyn and Pienaar played at Rugby World Cup 2011 while under contracts abroad. South Africa's selection policy is to only pick players based abroad under special circumstances and this is, in essence, what Galindo wants for Argentina.

Argentina is not looking to replicate South Africa's domestic structure so closely though. South Africa has five Super Rugby teams as well as two domestic competitions – the Currie Cup and the Vodacom Cup. The Currie Cup is the premier competition and, like the ITM Cup it is played parallel to the international season which means neither All Blacks nor Springboks are able to play in both the domestic and international competitions. The Currie Cup in 2012 was reduced to a six team competition while eight teams dispute the second division. It was downsized due in large part to the impact of Super Rugby which has had significant impacts on the domestic competitions in both South Africa and New Zealand. Those opposed to professional rugby ever being established feared such consequences could significantly damage URBA clubs.

But Argentina's professional future does not need to have any impact at all on URBA. The URBA competition can continue to be played in the second half of the year unaffected while the country's national provincial championship, the Campeonato Argentino can also continue unaffected in March. The UAR has no intention of altering either competition. Professionalizing the Campeonato Argentino is not the answer. It could be in the future but at this point in time it would not be sustainable economically as it would not generate enough money to pay the players wages. The Los Pumas brand is highly marketable but like in Australia having a domestic professional competition is not likely to succeed. The UAR collaborated with South African Rugby with this in mind and had Los Pampas XV created for the 2010 Vodacom Cup. It was the beginning of something bigger with an eye to the team, over time, becoming integrated into Super Rugby.

Super Rugby is Argentina's road to sustainable development and it will become increasingly obvious over time now that Argentina plays in The Rugby Championship. Italy's involvement in the Celtic League came about after more than a decade of Italian participation in the Six Nations. Relations between the UAR and the three founding SANZAR unions will change dramatically and for the better. Rugby supporters from all three countries will also become far more acquainted with Argentine rugby which will also see significant changes. Exposure to more Argentine players will open more doors and it will make it a far simpler task for Argentina to enter a Super Rugby team. Before that, however, existing Super Rugby teams will be far more aware of the Argentine players and be far more likely to sign them. To sight just one example second rower Manuel Carizza was off contract with Biarritz after the 2011-2012 season. His involvement in the 2012 Rugby Championship will have increased his profile from a Southern Hemisphere perspective and Super Rugby teams will now have a much greater awareness of him and he stands a much greater chance of playing Super Rugby as a result.

Los Pampas XV is certainly a team on the right path to entering Super Rugby. In its first two seasons it functioned more as an academy than a team itself given the high turnover of players. In some ways it worked to the advantage of European club rugby by giving them a better look at Argentina's emerging players. The teams first season of Vodacom Cup rugby took place in 2010. It was the thirteenth edition of the competition but was the first to feature foreign teams. Joining Los Pampas XV as debutants was the Welwitschias from Namibia. The two sides were in separate groups with the Argentine side playing in the Southern section against seven South African teams. The season was disappointing for the South Americans as the team managed three wins and four losses from its seven matches. It saw the team finish in fifth place of the Southern Section and meant it was eliminated without reaching the play-offs. The tournament was nonetheless, a genuine success for the players and union. The experience of playing in a South African competition and playing entirely outside of Argentina was a priceless opportunity.

The team was in no way a weak side it just failed to gel. Of the squads thirty-two players nine were signed to play in the 2010-2011 European season. Six were signed by French clubs. Agustín Figuerola signed with Brive, Agustín Creevy signed with Clermont, Martín Rodríguez Gurruchaga signed for Stade Français, Martín Bustos Moyano and Santiago Fernández joined Montpellier and centre Miguel Avramovic returned to France to join Agen. Benjamín Urdapilleta signed for English club the Harlequins, Mariano Galarza joined Leinster and Horacio San Martín joined Aironi. The team had not had a long time to prepare but the high turnover of players and the team's failure to reach the Quarter Finals would see noticeable changes for 2011.

Los Pampas XV were certainly a different team altogether in 2011. On paper the team appeared to not be as good as that of 2010 but coach Daniel Hourcade assembled a group of quality players who had solid preparation and were given the motivation of not only making the Argentine test side but possibly also making the squad for Rugby World Cup 2011. The season proved to unearth a host of players who had previously been outside of the Pumas radar. Some teams had changed from the Northern to the Southern Section and vice versa. Los Pampas XV remained in the Southern Section but moved to be based in Potchfestroom. The South Americans had a solid season which started before the tournament itself when Agustín Creevy and Mariano Galarza both made the decision to return from Europe in attempts to get more game time. Creevy captained the side through an undefeated campaign which saw the team finish top of the Southern Section and then defeat the Free State Cheetahs and the Sharks XV to qualify for the final. In qualifying for the final the Argentine team had won its Quarter Final and Semi Final matches by defeating two feeder Super Rugby teams with the same mascots.

Los Pampas XV qualified for the final after playing what South African site Super Sport called "wonderful attacking rugby".[183] The style of play was a significant change from the traditional way of Argentine rugby and underlined the professional attitude that had taken over in the management of the PladAR program. Argentina was not simply playing in the Vodacom Cup to decrease the gap from domestic club rugby to the international stage. It was much more than that. The players were being systematically drilled for the future with Argentina looking to change its style of rugby to be able to compete at a higher level than previous teams. A large part of this meant rotating players regularly as actually winning the competition was not the overall motivation of the team managers. The real reason for playing in South Africa was what it could mean for Pumas players and teams in the immediate and long term future.

The final was an important day in the history of Argentine rugby. The final was played on May 13 at Olën Park in Potchfestroom and was against the Blue Bulls. Los Pampas XV were crowned champions with a 14-9 victory which completed an uncompleted campaign. Running rugby was absent from the final as wet conditions dictated play and the importance of the occasion dominated. The match featured only one try, scored by inside centre Agustín Gosio in the first half. The South Africans had the better of the early stages of the half but the Argentine side defended well with the forwards able to shut down their Blue Bulls opposites. Leading 8-0 at the interval Los Pampas XV went further ahead with a 43rd minute penalty to Nicolás Sánchez. His replacement, Santiago González Iglesias kicked a 57th minute penalty to give the South Americans an edge. But Marnitz Boshoff kept the Blue Bulls in touch throughout by kicking penalty goals in the 49th, 62nd and 77th minutes. It ensured the game would not be decided until the final whistle. The championship win was proof of the merits of professionalism in Argentine rugby. It had not only underlined the team as the basis of a future participant in Super Rugby but had also unearthed a sizeable contingent of potential Pumas. A total of thirteen players from the campaign were selected for Argentina´s June matches against the French Barbarians with some of them picked ahead of European based professionals.

Nine players from the championship winning squad went on to make Argentina´s thirty-man squad for Rugby World Cup 2011[184] while eleven players were signed by European clubs for the 2011-2012 Season. Two players signed to play in the Aviva Premiership with hooker Matías Cortese joining Gloucester, fullback Joaquín Tuculet joining the Sale Sharks and Agustín Gosio joined London Scottish to play in the English second division. Prop Mauricio Guidone also signed for a second division club, but for Mont de Marsan in France´s Pro d2. Seven further players were signed by Top 14 clubs. Nahuel Tetaz Chaparro signed for Stade Français, Belisario Agulla joined Agen, Juan Imhoff joined Racing Métro, Nicolás Sánchez joined Bordeaux-Begles, Leonardo Senatore joined Toulon and Agustín Creevy and Maximilano Bustos joined Montpellier.

Julio Farías Cabello took over from Agustín Creevy as captain for the 2012 Vodacom Cup campaign. His appointment was one of many changes for the new season as Los Pampas XV defended its title with a vastly different squad. Of the sixteen forwards from the 2011 squad seven did not return in 2012 while only six of the fourteen backs were returning. It was a combination of players having left for Europe and also fresh faces in the PladAR system being preferred. Manuel Montero, for instance, debuted in the 2012 Vodacom Cup and went on to make the Pumas squad for The Rugby Championship. A year earlier Juan Imhoff was the leading try scorer in the competition but he was not in the 2010 squad. What the PladAR system has been able to do for Argentine rugby is greatly influence the historical structure which has seen players from certain parts of the country advantaged over others. Those in the URBA Top 14 for instance have been more visible and have had greater chances of making Pumas's squads. Imhoff never played in URBA competitions. Rather he played for Duendes in Rosario.

The 2012 Vodacom Cup was not as successful as the 2011 campaign as the South Americans were unable to defend their title. Los Pampas XV was eliminated after losing a Quarter Final 26-18 to the Griquas. The team qualified for the knock-out stage after having won four and lost three matches in the Southern Section. It was an up and down campaign with Daniel Hourcade happy to rotate the starting lineup every week. It gave more players the opportunity of receiving game time and enabled the Pumas selectors a better look at all the players. It was more necessary in 2012 than in 2011 or 2010 due to Argentina's admission into The Rugby Championship. Santiago Phelan knew he would not be able to field European club players in both The Rugby Championship and in June internationals. He surprised many by naming seventeen Pampas players in his thirty man squad to face Italy and France in June.[185] Of the seventeen players three had been in the World Cup squad and some others had been fringe players in 2011 but the vast majority was selected to face Tier One opposition for the first time. Phelan's selections were enforced but were nonetheless nothing short of audacious. It was a reflection of just how far the UAR had come since the creation of PladAR. The investment in young players was truly succeeding as the next generation of potential Pumas was being given the opportunity that their predecessors could have only dreamed of. It was a system in which the players could put their faith in and they were given preparation for the international arena. While Manuel Montero debuted after playing in the Vodacom Cup Horacio Agulla had debuted after playing for Hindú in Buenos Aires. This remarkable change is just the start of professional rugby infrastructure in Argentina.

The next step is already underway with Argentina looking to have a team in Super Rugby. South Africa has long had geographical issues with Super Rugby. With Australia and New Zealand located close to each other it gives their teams an advantage. This perception played a role in South Africa's interest in having Argentina added to SANZAR competitions. It would level the playing field from a geographical standpoint and also achieve the long term objective of having more international teams to compete against. Shortly after Argentina's official confirmation in The Rugby Championship after Rugby World Cup 2011 South African Rugby's vice president Mark Alexander made it clear that the ambition needs to be adding Argentina to Super Rugby. He said "It's about having players available. I think this is a start, to get commercial partners back home because it's quite a costly exercise to run a franchise considering the cost of players, with time there could be a franchise coming out of this region and if we want to grow the game we are serious about our partnership with Argentina and this is a new market for us and a growth area."[186]

Increased economic opportunities also fit in well with what Galindo had been searching for. Argentina need professional rugby but it needs to be in a sustainable way that will endure and strengthen. It cannot operate on a loss. Alexander agrees that Los Pampas XV have the basis to be a Super Rugby team and that there were South African Super Rugby teams interested in some Pampas players. He said that "There are a lot of talented players in the Pampas team, a lot of franchises were looking at contracting players, but due to the gentleman's agreement we have with Argentina we asked our franchises to refrain from contracting the players so they could play as a unit, develop as a unit. But there's a lot of talent here, a lot of players who are eligible to play in South African franchises. There were twelve players who could be signed by franchises, they're good players, they are talented, they are ball players, we'll work with them."[187]

The hands off approach from the South African franchises continued in 2012 with all the PladAR players again available for the Vodacom Cup. But the most noticeable point to come out of the Vodacom Cup season was that only three players signed to play for European clubs - centres Lisandro Gómez Lopez and Gabriel Ascarate signed for Stade Français and Carcassonne while while prop Nahuel Lobo joined Montpellier as a medical joker. There has been no exodus to Europe like in the 2010 and 2011 campaigns. The major reason for this is not a changed attitude from the clubs who would not have use of the players for the entire season due to the October finish of The Rugby Championship. Rather it is due to the UAR's growth in professionalism. Like Galindo had stated in July 2011 the intention was to centrally contract players to have them playing in Argentina and be at the full disposal of Argentine rugby. Confirmation of this came on February 17 2012 when the UAR announced that ten players had been centrally contracted by the union.[188]

The players who signed are all centrally contracted to the UAR and six of them made the squad for The Rugby Championship. It could have been eight but two players were unavailable due to injury. In announcing the ten player list UAR President Luis Castillo said: "The contracts with this group of players is the UAR's first step to allow for better player development and, in turn, to ensure we have over a period of time, the same group of players that will expand the pool of potential international players for tournaments to come."[189] The UAR had guaranteed the services of all players for the year but the details of each individual contract were not revealed. Upon making the announcement Castillo hinted that some could be extended for two additional years. Galindo joined Castillo in expressing his optimism about this new relationship between the players and the UAR. He said "The professionalization of the High Performance is a key aspect in the preparation for The Rugby Championship. We met with the players to make our proposal official and explain what it is. They were enthusiastic and they know the effort that is making the UAR take this forward."[190]

The list included three players who represented Argentina at Rugby World Cup 2011 - Julio Farias Cabello, Mariano Galarza and Genaro Fessia. Galarza did not play for Argentina in 2012 however as he was injured during the Vodacom Cup. This saw Julio Farías Cabello receive increased game time in the secondrow. Fessia was signed but did not make the squad for The Rugby Championship and he is not expected to be signed again. His place is likely to go to Leonardo Senatore who returned from France to play in the latter stages of the Vodacom Cup and featured from the bench in The Rugby Championship. Farías Cabello has been rumored to be retiring after the 2012 November internationals and, if so, could be replaced by a number of Los Pampas players or potentially Manuel Carizza should he return from France. Another second rower Santiago Guzmán signed too and should be resigned in 2013 despite missing out on selection for The Rugby Championship. Centre Gabriel Ascárate was another contracted to the UAR. He had been expected to make the squad for The Rugby Championship but missed out after injuring himself against France in June. He should be resigned for 2013 and should be joined by 27 year old Gonzalo Tiesi who returned from seven years of professional rugby in England and France to play for SIC in the URBA Top 14 in 2012.

The five other players signed by the UAR all played in The Rugby Championship. They were all selected after coming out of the June tests with improved reputations. They are all seen as long term players for Los Pumas with all likely to be strong contenders to make the Rugby World Cup 2015 squad. Backrower Tomás Leonardí was a key player against Italy and Tomás De La Vega was similarly impressive against France in June which saw both named ahead of Genaro Fessia who had been used regularly by Santiago Phelan since 2009. Bruno

Postiglioni was moved around the frontrow in the Vodacom Cup, playing in all three positions. His future lies at hooker and he is another that has a good chance of being a long term player for Argentina. The scrumhalf pairing of Martín Landajo and Tomás Cubelli both signed despite neither having been amongst the top three players in the position during Phelan's first four years as headcoach. The UAR saw great potential in both players and they both played well in the Vodacom Cup and also in June to earn places in the squad for The Rugby Championship. The inclusion of both is a reflection of the union's desire to play a more attacking brand of rugby. They do not follow the pattern of distributing scrumhalves that Argentina has tended to produce and use at international level.

Of the ten players signed it was clear that the UAR was focusing on areas in which Argentina has less depth. It was an attempt of providing the coaching staff with a guaranteed supply of players in the event that the leading players are unavailable due to injury or due to the rules that the union agreed to with European clubs to not play players in both the June Internationals and The Rugby Championship. No props were signed due to Argentina having sufficient players of quality playing in England and France in these positions. While the ten players were selected with test rugby in mind their selection went far beyond simply having players available. The players that were selected also underline the changes in thinking within the UAR of trying to adapt and play a different style of rugby than that which Pumas teams have tended to play since the game became professional in 1996. Having both Cubelli and Landajo signed despite both Nicolás Vergallo and Agustín Figuerola being professional players in France had more to do with Argentina adjusting to professionalism than ensuring Phelan could play tests without its French based players in June.

The list is set to expand to be increasingly larger and the UAR will have much greater control over players. The new found revenue from The Rugby Championship will ensure there is a constant flow of money to invest in enlarging the number of players under contract. There are examples of players actively being encouraged to return from Europe. One interesting such case is 24 year old Juan Pablo Socino. The flyhalf / centre had been in the sights of the FIR with the Italians looking at him as a potential Italian international flyhalf. It would continue the tradition of Argentine players of Italian descent playing for Italy. French based Argentine second rower Leandro Cedaro had been in the sights of Santiago Phelan to play in the 2012 June tests but in May he announced he had instead chosen to play for Italy. He went on to play for Italy A in the June 2012 IRB Nations Cup in Romania.

In the case of Socino, the opposite occurred as he turned down an offer to play for Italy and was named in the Los Jaguares squad for the June tournament. Socino was selected after having impressed in England's second division, the RFU Championship for Rotherham and Nottingham. He was named at inside centre in the Dream Team for the 2010-2011 Season and again in 2011-2012. Scouts had been paying attention to his progress with one of Italy's two Rabo Direct Pro 12 sides, Benetton Treviso looking to secure his signature. Socino, however, turned down the offer as well as offers of staying in the RFU Championship and, in fact, cut short his contract with Nottingham by one season so that he could return to Argentina and focus on making his way into the senior squad. His return to Argentina saw him join PladAR, giving the coaches full access to him and ensuring he has a stable future in Argentine rugby. He is highly likely to play for Los Pampas XV in 2013 possibly at inside centre given the options available to Phelan at flyhalf. But before then he is in France playing for Pro d2 side Dax as a Medical Joker on a short term contract.

The changes will stretch beyond seeing Argentina playing a game that is likely to see Los Pumas score more tries. It will also mean that when Argentine players are exposed to Super Rugby, either for existing teams or for an Argentine team, that they will be far better prepared. The coming years will see the landscape become utterly different and changes are, indeed already in motion. For instance Nicolás Vergallo is an example of a Puma linked to a possible move Super Rugby. The policy of desiring players to be based in Argentina has already proven successful and with lesser players likely to be signed by European clubs the player base will likely be higher than it presently is. With the increased profile of the sport in the country and additional funding seeing rugby's popularity grow it is just a matter of time before Argentina has a team in Super Rugby. The new revenue streams will give the UAR the option of maintaining a team in the Vodacom Cup or Currie Cup which in turn will see that the gap from club rugby to Super Rugby will be eased.

11

Spirit of Rugby

Rugby is a sport involving immense physical contact but one driven by principles of pride, humility, teamwork, and fair play. Los Pumas at Rugby World Cup 2007 had such a profound impact on global rugby not only because of the results but because of the spirit in which the victories were achieved. As covered in Chapter 5 Agustín Pichot and his players made a massive statement and brought a new meaning to the Bronze Final. But before the start of the opening match Argentina had made a definitive impact as a fired up Argentine team was overrun by emotion during the singing of the national anthem. The team had been led out not by Pichot but by Rodrigo Roncero. Such was the custom of the scrumhalf captain that he liked to be the last man out of the changing rooms not the first.

Pride
Roncero led the players onto the field and the television images said it all. Argentina was highly focused and highly emotional. France, in contrast, looked relaxed. It was the tale of two teams as the Pumas focused all their frustration over failing to play much international rugby, having had a disadvantaged schedule four years earlier and having even threatened to strike against the UAR fifteen months before the World Cup. The emotion was clear as the players gathered and waited for the national anthem. The structure of the Argentine anthem used in Rugby World Cups is different to most other nations as it opens with a long instrumental section before it is time for the singing. As the players were lined up together with the music playing waiting for their cue to start singing the cameras caught players drowned in the moment. The majority of the team was close to being in tears with the honor of representing Argentina there and then telling a powerful story of the journey of Los Pumas and the meaning of the Rugby World Cup. When it came time to sing the players all sang loudly with emotionally packed expressions beaming off their faces. It was a powerful image that will stand forever in the echoes of time.

The South Americans had left their mark on global rugby without even playing. Anthems had traditionally been taken for granted as something necessary but were thought of as more of a formality than anything else. Welsh international Ryan Jones missed the World Cup through injury and was a blogger for the BBC throughout the tournament. He was one of many to take notice of the South American players. He wrote: "Their national anthem typified this determination and the sight of hardened competitors publicly displaying the depth of their emotion for this occasion was awe-inspiring. It just shows what this tournament means to individuals, teams and entire nations - and the television footage of the Argentine fan struggling to fight back his tears during the anthem will be one of France 2007's enduring images."[191]

Argentina is a proud nation. It is a country that has suffered significant setbacks such as losing a war in 1982 and financial meltdown twenty years latter. All the players were all too familiar with both and were playing for the pride of a nation even for those who are not accustomed with the sport. Pumas pride is something that most teams can only dream of having. For Los Pumas it is the mental preparation of defending the nation and is something that Argentina can offer to the global game on the greatest stage of them all. Argentina could put on an amazing show in hosting Rugby World Cup 2023 by taking the pride to the people and host a tournament that is different to its predecessors. That is not to say that other teams do not have pride. All teams do, just in different ways. The New Zealand version is tied to the Haka with players and fans both seemingly more emotionally involved during the performance of the pre-match ritual than during the performance of the national anthem.

Others are simply not so evidently emotionally involved. South Africans, for instance place great importance on their anthem. It was specifically written for a new country, one to replace the horror of a racist past. The anthem is split into three sections with the lyrics being divided into Zulu, Afrikaans and English. The players sing with honor and pride of the new country that was born in 1994. The Springbok players are every bit as committed to playing for their country as Los Pumas are for theirs. The difference, however, is the visible emotion shown by the Argentine players. It is something that is sometimes attributed to Latin culture as the emotion of the occasion can be overwhelming. It is something that is not a part of Anglo culture and is therefore rarely seen in the performance of the national anthems by rugby's traditional powers. Indeed of rugby's traditional powers France is the only one that was not a part of the British Commonwealth. The English translation of the shortened version of the Argentina national anthem that is performed for rugby matches is as follows:

May the laurels be eternal, (Sean eternos los laureles)
the ones who knew how to win, (que supimos conseguir)
the ones who knew how to win. (que supimos conseguir)
Live crowned in glory... (Coronados de gloria vivamos)
Or let us swear to die gloriously! (o juremos con gloria morir!)
Or let us swear to die gloriously! (o juremos con gloria morir!)
Or let us swear to die gloriously! (o juremos con gloria morir!)

When the Buenos Aires born politician, Vicente López y Planes wrote the lyrics in 1813 he could have had no idea that Argentina´s national rugby team would follow through with the anthem in Paris in the Semi Final of Rugby World Cup 2007. The players lived crowned in glory as they played like they were indeed defending their country in war throughout the tournament. In losing to South Africa the players were badly defeated and they knew it but they stayed true to the words of their country´s anthem as they *died gloriously*. Post match the players were a wreck with the likes of Ignacio Corleto, Juan Martín Fernández Lobbe, Juan Leguizamón, Agustín Pichot and Juan Martín Hernández all shown crying at the Stade de France in utter disappointment. Argentina, died gloriously that evening and bounced back extremely well to defeat France five days latter to claim Bronze Medal and to *live crowned in glory*. The inspiring performance of Los Pumas in France in 2007 has left a permanent mark on global rugby. The players efforts in triumph and failure won over a nation and that same nation should host Rugby World Cup 2023. In a post match interview in Spanish an emotional Pichot said "Thank you, thank you for all the effort you have put in, for the dream you have believed in, because it believed we had come here to get something. It is in sorrow that we could not follow, because we played to win ... we played to try to impress and we did not play well."

Upon defeating France neither Pichot nor Marcelo Loffreda were sending warnings to other teams. They were both very humble in their post match interviews and took the teams next two matches incredibly seriously. Argentina would face Georgia four days after the opener and then Namibia eleven days latter. The matches against these sides were the focus. There was no looking ahead to the match against Ireland. As Loffreda said "We are overcome with happiness, but we shouldn't get above ourselves because it is only the first match. We have given ourselves a good start and we need to take advantage of it. We are going to take it game by game."[192] These comments came from a man who was throwing his arms in the air when referee Tony Spreadbury had blown fulltime. Pichot similarly displayed humility and thanked France for assisting the development of his players in saying "For myself, coach Marcelo Loffreda and the rest of the team this result is very important. We are not the best technicians, we are not even the most physical, but we play with heart. This won't sink in for a while. We won't know what we have done, because you never know the context, but this team has a hunger to write history. As a team, we just want to make history for Argentina rugby." Many of the Pumas play in France, and Pichot added: "France has helped us to develop, taking us in as their sons. We thank them."[193] There is no denying that French clubs were at the forefront of Argentina's victory that evening in Paris. But such words from a man who had played the match of his life to lead his country to perhaps it's most important victory ever were words of humility. In a sporting context being humble in victory and gracious in defeat are vital but too often do not happen.

As pointed out in the previous chapter the state of Argentine rugby off the field had improved considerably by Rugby World Cup 2011. The players in the 2007 campaign were significantly disadvantaged but managed to finish third in the world. Four years latter the players were closer to having the same luxuries of the Tier One sides. The gap had closed but financially it had not closed by much at all. The Pumas players were given an allowance of US$700 per week during Rugby World Cup 2011[194] which was more than enough for the players to spend leisurely when they were not preparing for matches. Argentina's first opponent in the tournament had it very differently and the squad had made it known to the RFU before the World Cup that they needed to be well paid. The Daily Mail confirmed that the England squad had threatened to hold a sit-in on the team coach at the eve-of-departure dinner over a pay dispute. After the tournament RFU director of elite rugby Rob Andrew said that "It is very disappointing that a senior group, led by Lewis Moody, disputed the level of payment for the World Cup squad, which led to meetings with RFU executives."[195]

The English players were paid £8,545 per man per match during the pre-World Cup warm up matches against Wales and Ireland and were then paid £41,666 each for their World Cup campaign. It could have been significantly more however as each player would have been awarded with a bonus of £8,334 had England won its Quarter Final match against France. This would have seen each player paid a total of £50,000 in appearance fees and a bonus of £25,000 for reaching the Semi Finals.[196] The motivation of not only playing for World Cup glory but also being handsomely paid for winning was not restricted to the RFU. Rather England was just the tip of the iceberg. Welsh players were offered similarly lucrative incentives to win the World Cup following a payment deal signed by the Welsh Rugby Union and the players association. The deal meant that any player who appeared in every round of a successful 2011 World Cup campaign would take home £100,000.[197]

The Australian Rugby Union and the players association agreed to change the payout that Wallaby players would get from the tournament. But unlike England and Wales the overall income per player per match was decreased from AU$10,000 (£6,600) for the pool games, reduced from AU$13,000 (£8,600) in 2007. It was a strategy to reward the players by offering a much larger pay check for winning the tournament. The adjustments meant that the players would be paid an AU$110,000 (£72,800) bonus each if Australia won the World Cup. ARU CEO John O'Neill said that "We believe this agreement gives the players an opportunity to be well and deservedly rewarded if they achieve the ultimate and return from New Zealand as Rugby World Cup champions. Winning the Rugby World Cup would have enormous flow on benefits for the game in this country, so it is only fair the players have an opportunity to receive a tangible benefit if they reach the highest achievement level our game offers. ARU also acknowledges that this exciting group of players is prepared to back itself and reduce match payments to maximize their incentives should they win the tournament."[198] Australia's pay cut proved unsuccessful as the Wallabies were eliminated from the World Cup at the Semi Finals stage.

The two teams who contested the final also paid their players very well for winning the World Cup. The systems used by New Zealand and France were nonetheless vastly different from each other. The French players had an agreement with the FFR that they would be paid €180,000 each if France won the World Cup Final. A Semi Final win was also extremely well paid with the players earning €140,000 each for reaching the World Cup Final. In New Zealand dollars this worked out to be NZ$241,364 per player for reaching the final and NZ$310,383 for winning the tournament. The All Blacks had a deal with the NZRU to also be paid for winning but in becoming World Champions the All Blacks players actually were paid less than the amount that the French players made for losing the final. The All Black bonus was worth NZ$100,000 per player for winning the final.[199] Before the tournament had begun every All Black was paid $7500 for every seven days they were in camp, worth an extra $160,000 per year in earnings. The Pumas, in contrast received close to ten times less than what the All Blacks were paid.[200]

Money was not a factor motivating the Argentine players in the tournament. It was simply about playing for ones country and doing ones best. Some call it playing for peanuts others call it the spirit of rugby. In 2009 Pichot looked back at the 2007 World Cup campaign by denying that his players were professionals with the hearts of amateurs. He said "We were professionals, doing a professional job. However, it didn't mean we were interested only in money. Money was the by-product for us, not the purpose.[201]

Support

A second important part of the spirit of rugby is what goes on off the field. This is not in terms of the player's personal lives or even rugby clubs but it is instead a third force – the supporters. Having a sizeable fan base to call upon is something vital for hosting a World Cup. The team needs to be well supported to be a reliable option from a financial perspective. Russia's successful qualification for Rugby World Cup 2011 made headlines and deservedly so. The team had completed an amazing feat. It had qualified after drawing 21-21 with Romania in the Southern Russian city of Sochi. But the occasion was not one of Russia's finest moments as the IRB's announcement on rugbyworldcup.com showed a Russian player celebrating in an empty stadium.[202] The celebrations were certainly made in the spirit of rugby but unfortunately the attendance took something away from the occasion as all the positive press could not disguise the fact that the team had not been well supported at its actual matches.

Similarly simply attracting fans to matches is not enough. In other sports, such as soccer host nations can be from anywhere. A bid just needs to show that the nation can host the World Cup. This saw Qatar awarded the hosting rights for the 2022 FIFA World Cup. In rugby terms this means the United Arab Emirates should consider making a bid to host a World Cup. The 7evens stadium in Dubai has a proven track record in hosting Rugby Sevens events and the crowds are strong. By using this and other UAE and possibly neighboring Gulf state's facilities rugby could have its World Cup in the region too. But there is more to it than this. A crucial part of the spirit of rugby is having knowledge of the sport and what its significance is. This does not mean that a nation needs to be capable of winning to host. Japan meets this criteria fine. On the other hand it does mean that it is vital to have a reliable supporter base. The UAE plays international rugby in the Asian Five Nations but fails to attract sizeable crowds.

The African nation of Madagascar is very well supported, so well in fact that 40,000 people attended the team's historical 57-54 win over Namibia at the Mahamasina Stadium in Antananarivo in July 2012.[203] The sport is becoming increasingly popular in the country and Madagascar could well be a participant at a World Cup sooner rather than latter. It is an extremely positive sign for the future of rugby in Africa and globally as the sport continues to break out of the historical shackles of being a sport hugely and almost solely associated with the British Commonwealth. Madagascar embodies the spirit of rugby and highlights the need for Rugby World Cup´s to be taken to new places. This does not mean Madagascar should host a World Cup any time soon but it does mean that if there are nations that do tick the boxes then they would be better for the future of the sport than by returning to familiar places. For this reason despite Madagascar being located far closer to South Africa than to either Japan or Argentina this does not mean a World Cup in South Africa would bring greater long term benefits to rugby in Madagascar.

In the age of television a World Cup in Argentina is better for the future of rugby in much of Africa than one in South Africa could ever be. Moreover Argentina hosting Rugby World Cup 2023 would be better for Italian rugby than Scotland hosting. Italy has good crowds for international rugby and has great relations with its Six Nations colleagues but the manner in which European World Cup´s have been hosted is not really helpful for Italy. Teamwork does not mean dividing World Cup´s amongst multiple hosts or enabling a smaller union the opportunity of hosting some World Cup matches. It means standing tall. Like the UAR the FIR likes to spread matches around the country and is attempting to become a team with a larger supporter base and a more educated one. The home nations, in contrast, play at their national rugby stadiums almost exclusively. It is arguably a contradiction of the spirit of rugby as the notion of teamwork involves sharing not centralizing in the largest places. While Rugby World Cups have been concentrated in the most powerful rugby nations, the home matches of the four nations have also been concentrated in small parts of their own nations.

12

Contribution to Global Rugby

The emergence of Argentina in the new age of professional rugby was due chiefly to a continual exodus of players to professional rugby. Through the exposure to top flight rugby Argentine players have developed to be at the same level as the best athletes from Tier One unions. Over time the number of players being exported from Argentina increased sufficiently so that virtually all of Argentina's best rugby players were playing abroad. The players were playing abroad for two reasons. Firstly, clubs now had money to sign quality players from abroad and Argentina happened to have some. Secondly, the move to professionalism meant teams needed to have much larger squads than previously and survival in the professional age was different to what it had been in the amateur age. In many cases teams who fell from the top division in either England or France struggled to return and even dropped further. The success of a number of Argentine players increased the profile of Argentine rugby and ultimately saw a constant flow of players abroad. In turn it saw Los Pumas become increasingly more competitive and the team consolidated itself as the world's best and most consistent team from outside of the old eight. It has also been the biggest contributor of players to the professional game of all nations never to have hosted a Rugby World Cup.

Super Rugby
When the game became professional there were some paid players and with time the number of Argentine players in Europe steadily increased particularly in England and in France. The first wave of emigration was small with only a scattering of Argentine players playing professional rugby. It was reflected in the squad for the first Rugby World Cup in the professional era as in 1999 nine of the thirty-one Argentine players were professionals.[204] The transition to professionalism was marked by a noticeable difference between the Super 12 in

the Southern Hemisphere and the club game in Europe. In the early years the Southern Hemisphere had a significantly better product and the unions were better organized.

The centralization of resources into fewer teams enabled the quality of rugby to be higher as Australia had three teams, South Africa four and New Zealand five. Teams from all three countries imported players and this saw some notable Argentine props playing professionally in the Southern Hemisphere in either the Super 12 or in domestic competitions. Patricio Noriega joined the ACT Brumbies in 1996 and played five seasons of Super Rugby for the Australian side. Federico Mendez played for the Natal Sharks in 1996 and from 2002-2005 and then joined Western Province for the 2005 Currie Cup. Roberto Grau played for Transvaal (Golden Lions) in 1996-1997 and Omar Hasan played for the Hurricanes in 1997 and then the Brumbies in 1998. All four players played in multiple World Cups with Noriega being a duel international after playing for both Argentina and Australia at World Cups.

After the initial seasons of Super 12 rugby teams were no longer signing Argentine players and were in general virtually self-sufficient. The difference in competitiveness of the Hemispheres was well talked about before and during Rugby World Cup 1999. The then Welsh international coach, Graham Henry called for Europe to copy the Super 12 in a bid to close the perceived gap. He said "We need badly a Super 12 type competition in the Northern Hemisphere. There has to be a stronger bridge for players between club level and the international arena. The unions have to work together as they do in the south."[205] New Zealand coach John Hart backed up Graham Henry´s call for a European version of the Super 12 but his team was eliminated by France in a World Cup classic.

Regardless of the result of the 1999 Semi Final it was firmly established at the time that Europe had only made partial adjustments towards professionalism and more were needed. The result was not the creation of something similar to the Super 12 but it did close the gap by a significant margin. The Heineken Cup became a bigger event while adjustments to the English and French Leagues saw the quality of rugby rise in both nations. In France the first division changed from the Top 16 to the Top 14 which has gradually succeeded in becoming more and more competitive as historically powerful teams such as Biarritz and Perpignan have been threatened with relegation in recent times.

Celtic Rugby
Ireland joined Scotland and Wales to form the Celtic League in 2001 and by Rugby World Cup 2003 it had replaced the previous competitions entirely. The biggest changes were in Wales where the nation's professional competition, the Welsh Premier Division was scrapped and the number of professional teams decreased from nine to five and they were remodeled to be regionally based following the structure that had succeeded in the Southern Hemisphere. It achieved its objective of seeing the Welsh team become more competitive but had some bad effects on Welsh domestic rugby due to the historical division of teams complicating the creation of new teams. The five teams were reduced to four after the first season as the Celtic Warriors were put into liquidation.[206] The success of Wales at Rugby World Cup 2003 followed by a Six Nations Grand Slam in 2005 appeared sufficient evidence that the transformation was succeeding.

A reduction of teams in Wales did not put an end to importing players. Rather, the period between Rugby World Cup 1999 and 2003 saw a huge increase across Europe in imported players. Argentina's squad for Rugby World Cup 2003 had been gone from partially-professional in 1999 to being predominantly-professional with a noticeable increase in professional players across both the forwards and backs.[207] It saw Argentina perform at a noticeably higher level than in 1999 despite failing to make the Quarter Finals. The difference was not seen in how Argentina did against the Tier One teams but how it did against the Tier Two sides. The margin of its wins over Namibia and Romania was noteworthy and happened despite the majority of the starting players from the matches against Australia and Ireland not being used. Argentina simply had far more professional players than either Namibia or Romania did in their World Cup matches.

In losing 16-15 to Ireland in Adelaide Argentina had a team with many more professional players than in their 1999 encounter. Ireland was fully professional in both tournaments but in entering the Celtic League the national side benefitted and proved to be much more successful than during the earlier years of professional rugby. Ireland lost all three matches against Australia between 1996 and 1999 but has won four and drawn one out of the ten tests between the countries since 2002. Results have also been better against South Africa since the advent of professionalism. In the ten tests from 1906-1995 Ireland won one and drew one. Conversely since 1996 Ireland has won three out of the ten tests and all the wins have been since Ireland entered the Celtic League.

Ireland
With its four provinces as professional teams, Ireland has taken on professionalism successfully with Leinster, Munster and Ulster all having won the Heineken Cup. The six titles between them is equal to that of English clubs and more than French clubs who have won the Cup five times.[208] No side from Italy, Scotland or Wales has won the European championship and Irish superiority is also apparent in the Celtic League. In the ten year history of the competition Irish sides have won it six times and Welsh sides three times. The most successful team is the Ospreys with four championship titles, one more than Munster.[209] The impressive results of Irish provinces have unquestionably seen the Irish test side perform better than previously but the strength of teams has been effected in no small way by the contribution of imported players. Arguably the most important player from outside of the Republic of Ireland and Northern Ireland to have played professionally for an Irish team is Felipe Contepomi.

The former Pumas captain played professional rugby in England, Ireland and France with his seven years at Leinster being the highlight of his career. It was his second of four professional teams in Europe after he started his professional career for English club Bristol after Rugby World Cup 1999. Leinster was both career defining and changing for Contepomi as the team´s style of play and abundance of quality Irish internationals enabled him to develop into a genuine attacking player. He had come off a disappointing World Cup campaign in Australia both from a team and individual standpoint. Leinster enabled him to become one of the best flyhalves in European rugby. During his time with the Irish province Contepomi was a Celtic League and a European Champion. He was a key player in the 2008 Rabo Direct Pro 12 (then called the Magners League) champion winning campaign and also the 2009 Heineken Cup. He had to miss the final, however, after undergoing knee surgery following a serious injury in the Semi Final win over Munster. The impact he was having on Leinster rugby was rewarded with him being named as the competitions best flyhalf in the 2006-2007[210] and 2007-2008[211] season´s Dream Teams.

He left Ireland to play for Toulon in 2009 and did so having written his name into the Leinster record books. Contepomi had become the all time leading point´s scorer for the province in both the Rabo Direct Pro 12 by scoring 877 points including fifteen tries.[212] Moreover Contepomi is also the highest point´s scorer in the history of Leinster having scored 1225 points. His impact was so strong that before him no player had ever scored more than 600 points for the province.[213] His time in Ireland had also seen him become a global super star which saw him nominated as one of four players for the 2007 IRB player of the year. His time was also highly productive off the field as Contepomi became a qualified doctor, having completed his studies in Dublin, during his time playing for Leinster. The Royal College of Surgeons in Ireland conferred him with the medical degrees of MB BCh BAO (National University of Ireland) LRCP&SI in 2008. This saw him not only playing rugby in Dublin but also practicing medicine at Beaumont Hospital.[214]

Leinster signed Mariano Galarza for the 2010-2011 Season. Like Contepomi Galarza was a medical student. He was signed to bolster the clubs resources in the second row as both Leo Cullen and Kevin McLaughlin were out of action during the initial part of the season.[215] He decided to leave the province to return to Argentina to rejoin the PladAR set up ahead of the 2011 Vodacom Cup. His short time in Ireland saw him play nine matches, including four in the Magners League.[216] He had a good Vodacom Cup season which earned him a spot in the squad for Rugby World Cup 2011. The province was also the home of former Pumas prop, Juan Goméz from 2007-2009. After receiving limited game time he took up an offer to play for Leeds Carniegie. He initially joined the English club on a lone but latter extended his stay. Ireland was also the home of another Argentine prop, Federico Pucciariello. He never played for Los Pumas because he instead represented Italy despite being from Argentina and returning there after retiring from rugby. Pucciariello played for Munster for four years, averaging 21 games per season. He was a part of the teams resurgence as it won a first ever Heineken Cup in 2006 and he also featured in the teams near win against the All Blacks in 2008.[217]

The future of Argentine players in Ireland is not so bright due to the Irish Rugby Football Unions (IRFU) decision in 2012 to restrict the number of foreigners. The changes, which take effect in 2013, will mean that Leinster, Munster and Ulster are only allowed to sign one non-Irish qualified player per position between themselves. With only one foreign player per position it means that a great deal more players will have to be found from within Ireland. No scrumhalves, for instance, can be signed from abroad due to the presence of Ruan Pienaar at Ulster. In other words Leinster and Munster are now unable to sign foreign scrumhalves and will only be able to do so if Pienaar were to leave the isle. Ireland believes the strategy to be an important part of the future of the Irish test team. It is designed to give the Irish test team two experienced players in every position. The IRFU statement said that "The overall objective of the new policies is that there will be a minimum of two Irish qualified players per position playing in the Heineken Cup and RaboDirect Pro 12 as first choice selections."[218]

Scotland

Professional rugby in Scotland has not achieved the same success as Ireland. Both on the field and off it Scottish rugby has suffered tremendously in the professional era. The transition from amateurism has not succeeded as the professional teams have neither been able to attract sizeable crowds nor win championship titles. Unable to find the right set up for Scotland, the Scottish Rugby Union (SRU) has changed the professional teams and renamed them since 1996. In the beginning there were four teams with the traditional regions each having one team each – Glasgow and Edinburgh had teams while the Border Reviers were based in Netherdale and the Caledonia Reds based in Aberdeen and Perth. Financial debt saw the reduction of the teams from four to two with the Edinburgh Reivers and Glasgow Caledonian both being removed. The Border Reivers returned for the second edition of the Celtic League which angered Caledonia[219] but it was not long term as Borders was scrapped again in 2007. Since then there has only been two professional Scottish teams – Edinburgh and the Glasgow Warriors. Neither Edinburgh nor the Glasgow Warriors retain any attachment in name or representation to the former teams of Borders and Caledonia.

It has been a long term problem for the SRU and no real solutions have been discovered. The problem has always been economic – the SRU has been heavily in debt during the professional era due in part to the redevelopment of Murrayfield. When Gordon McKie took over as CEO in 2005 the SRU owed £20million. Upon resigning in 2011 the debt had been reduced significantly but still stood at £15million.[220] McKie had seen Scotland improve on the pitch too with the test team having defeated Australia in 2009 and South Africa in 2010. There were improvements domestically with the Glasgow Warriors making the Semi Finals of the Rabo Direct Pro 12 in 2011-2012 and Edinburgh reaching the Heineken Cup Semi Finals. There is yet to be any sign of a return of either Caledonia or Borders and the likelihood of either having professional rugby continues to remains remote. Without the SRU's debt being cleared or substantial investment Scotland will never have more than two professional teams.

Edinburgh's appearance in the Semi Finals of the Heineken Cup was extremely significant but it occurred despite the team finishing second to last in the Rabo Direct Pro 12. The team concentrated its efforts on the Heineken Cup to such an extent that it won six and lost fifteen matches in the Pro 12. The chances of Edinburgh making the play-offs again are unknown but the odds are against it from happening. A massive problem exists of retaining athletes as they are simply not paid what they are worth. Irish rugby journalist George Hook said: "No player worth their salt wants to stay in a structure where they cannot earn enough money to justify playing professionally. Without top names to attract fans through the gate and maintain sponsorship, the problems will only increase. Performances have to suffer."[221]

The situation has seen a number of Scottish internationals take up contracts abroad but still an overwhelming minority. Of the thirty man squad that toured Australia, Fiji and Samoa in June 2012 twenty-two players had played the 2011-2012 Season in Scotland.[222] Professionalism has, therefore not seen an exodus of players abroad but it has not ensured the best players are all playing in Scotland. Richie Grey for instance left the Glasgow Warriors for the Sale Sharks. Nevertheless the SRU is trying to replicate Ireland's success of having a solid structure, good attendances, competitive teams in the Rabo Direct Pro 12 and Heineken Cup competitions and, ultimately, a quality test team.[223] Despite a lack of teams and most Scottish players playing in Scotland today and throughout the professional era both Edinburgh and the Glasgow Warriors have employed the services of foreign players, amongst them have been players from Argentina.

The players that have tended to play for the Scottish teams have not been the most famous players. In general they have been fringe Pumas players. The major reason for this is the contracts offered by the SRU have never been as good as those on offer elsewhere. This has not meant that the Argentine players in Scotland have received limited game time. To the contrary some have been regular starters and have gone on to even be captain. Bernardo Stortoni played fullback for the Glasgow Warriors from 2007-2011. He had joined the club after previously playing in France and England. His best years as a professional were his four years in Scotland. He played 69 matches for the Glasgow Warriors in the Rabo Direct Pro 12[224] and his first match as captain saw his countryman, Federico Martín Aramburu debuting for the club. Aramburu had also joined the team to see out his professional career. He had previously played for Biarritz, Perpignan and Dax in France and was the captain of Dax in his final season of French rugby in

2008-2009. His move to Scotland was successful as he played more than 40 matches[225] and he was a part of the team that reached the Rabo Direct Pro12 Semi Final in 2012. Like Stortoni, Aramburu captained the team on several occasions. In his final home match he captained the team and was man of the match in a 24-3 win over Connacht.[226] Another Pumas winger to have played for the club was José Maria Nuñez Piossek who also ended his professional career at Glasgow. He signed for the 2008-2009 season but received limited game time due to injury. He had earlier played for Bristol, and subsequently played in France for Clermont, Castres and Bayonne.[227]

When Argentina drew 25-25 with the British and Irish Lions in Cardiff in 2005 Nuñez Piossek and Stortoni were in the starting lineup as two members of the back-three. The third was Francisco Leonelli who also went on to play rugby in Scotland. He played seven Celtic League matches in the 2006-2007 season for Glasgow[228] and fifteen matches the previous season for Edinburgh.[229] Leonelli was unique in playing for both Scottish teams and after playing one season for each team he moved to England to play for Saracens from 2007-2009. Edinburgh was also home to a replacement back from the Lions v Pumas match as winger Lucio Lopez-Fleming played twelve matches for the side in the 2006-2007 Season.[230] Three Argentine forwards have also played for Edinburgh in the professional era. The most well known is Esteban Lozada who featured at Rugby World Cup 2007 and subsequently played for Toulon from 2007-2010. He signed for Edinburgh in a bid to receive more game time and played a total of twenty-five matches in the Rabo Direct Pro 12 and Heineken Cup.[231] After two years at Edinburgh, Lozada returned to France to play for Agen in the Top 14. Lozada was joined by prop Ulises Gamboa for the latter part of his second season while fellow prop Augusto Allori played eighteen matches in the 2007-2008 Season[232] for Edinburgh.

None of the players are still in Scotland because all have either left for to play elsewhere or have retired from rugby. But this does not mean that Argentine players will stop playing in Scotland. To the contrary, it will remain an attractive place for players and both Edinburgh and the Glasgow Warriors know very well that they have got good value for their money from the South Americans they have previously signed. The policy of attempting to replicate Ireland is not likely to influence the signing of imported players and there are no official limits placed on who can be signed unlike in the case of three of the four Irish provinces.

Wales

Wales has not been a common place for Argentine players. In fact since the creation of the regional system only one player has been signed – Tomás Vallejos Cinalli. The Pumas secondrower signed for the region after having played the past two seasons for the Harlequins who won the 2012 Aviva Premiership. He also played in Italy from 2007-2010 for Parma. The same team is now the basis of the new Italian Rabo Direct Pro 12 franchise, Zebre. Manuel Carizza had been rumored to be joining the Scarlets after not having signed a new contract with Biarritz but the rumor seemed to have been nothing more than confusion over which Pumas second rower would in fact be playing for the Llanelli based side. Vallejos Cinalli´s move to Wales was somewhat of a surprise due to the fact that Welsh regions do not have a record of signing Argentine players.

The signing is rare and not likely to be followed by others. Wales simply does not have the same kind of budget as what is available to Aviva Premiership and Top 14 clubs. This has had a double effect of Wales not having the same kind of imported players as that seen in England, France and Ireland. Wales is in a position between that of Scotland and Ireland. While Scotland has struggled to sustain professional teams and grow in the professional era Wales has succeeded but not to the same extent as Ireland. Like Ireland Wales has had one weak team since the reorganization into a regional structure of five and then four teams. The Dragons have consistently been the weakest of the four regions and there has been a trend of its top players leaving to play for a different region.

The curious lack of Argentine players comes down to two factors. The first is that Welsh regions simply have less of a need for them than the case of Edinburgh and the Glasgow Warriors. This is principally due to Wales having a superior production line of rugby players than that of Scotland. While Wales has succeeded in winning Six Nations Grand Slams in the professional era and making the Semi Finals of Rugby World Cup 2011 it has also been World Champions in Rugby Sevens and Semi Finalists in the IRB Junior World Championship. Neither Scotland nor Ireland have come close to matching Wales in this area. The Welsh system may not be attractive to the local population with the marriage of Swansea and Neath to form the Ospreys being an example of something that is not supported by history and fans have not got behind the team. Leinster and Munster have left the Welsh for dead in this manner.

The second reason for Welsh sides not contracting as many Argentine players as Scotland is financial. The players that the Scottish teams have been signing have not been top of the line players. They have tended to be players either at the end of their careers or players outside of first choice Pumas squads. Scotland has shown an inability to have a player factory which has seen the likes of Bernardo Stortoni and Federico Martín Aramburu have successful careers in place of potential would be Scottish backs. They have been cheap buys for the Scottish teams and the Welsh sides have not really needed them because they have a much larger stock of players of quality as evidenced in Rugby Sevens and the IRB Junior World Championship. The money that the Welsh regions do have at their disposal is not enough to attract the same kinds of players that Argentina has had playing in England and France since Rugby World Cup 1999.

English and French clubs continue to widen the financial gap between themselves and the Celtic unions. It means that the chance of Vallejos Cinalli playing with or against Pumas in Wales is extremely low. In late 2011 the WRU announced significant spending cuts for the nation's four professional regions. The cuts which were in effect a salary cap for the regions, took effect for the 2012-2013 season. The salary cap limited the budget per region to £3.5million which has been suggested will significantly increase the likelihood of players leaving Wales to play outside abroad due to offers elsewhere, particularly in the Top 14. The likes of Lee Byrne, James Hook and Mike Phillips being joined in France by a host of others is increasing.[233] All three left the Ospreys for the 2011-2012 Season with Byrne joining Clermont, Hook joining Perpignan and Phillips joining Bayonne. While the Ospreys now have a salary cap of £3.5million Clermont spent €24.1million, Perpignan spent €15.3million and Bayonne spent €17.2million in the 2011-2012 season.[234]

Italy
Not content with an inability to win regularly against First Tier nations, the Federazione Italiana Rugby (FIR) actively sought a solution that would mean the country's international players were better prepared for international duty. Since entering the Five Nations to make it the Six Nations Championship in 2000 Italy had improved as a test team but it had not been able to deliver where it mattered most - at the Rugby World Cup. As covered in Chapter Four Italy's 2003 campaign was highly complicated due to a restricted number of days for its four pool matches. It depleted the team's chances of making the Quarter Finals and four years latter adjustments had been made. Italy had a similar tournament which saw a big loss against New Zealand followed by wins over Romania and Portugal and then the crunch match against Scotland. Italy scored the games only try and had a penalty kick with two minutes latter to seal a victory but it was unsuccessful. The one point loss saw Scotland advance to face Argentina at the Stade de France while Italy was eliminated. After the tournament Italy took the

bold move of investing in a new and proven coach, Nick Mallet. The English born South African raised coach led the Springboks to Bronze at Rugby World Cup 1999 and looked to change how Italy played to try to find a way of winning more matches. In his first two years the results were not what the FIR had desired but Italy was playing a different style of rugby. But the biggest change came in professional rugby. After the team lost all three of its home internationals against Australia, Argentina and the Pacific Islands (Fiji, Samoa and Tonga combined) in November 2008 the FIR looked to the Celtic unions to possibly have Italy added to the Magners League.[235]

A proposal was officially made and it was accepted by all of Ireland, Scotland and Wales and it saw two Italian Super Teams put together for the 2010-2011 season. To make the teams as competitive as possible they would see players from existing Italian teams join while the Italian Super 10 would be reconstructed. It was a model different to the three Celtic unions. While Ireland was provincial, Wales regional and Scotland based on the two largest cities the Italian set up saw no team based in Rome, Milan, Naples or Venice. Rather the FIR used the base of the two most successful Italian sides - Benetton Treviso and Viadana. Benetton Treviso continued on as a Super team while the other was called Aironi and was based in Viadana. Both cities are in Northern Italy, the traditional heartland of Italian rugby. Upon the confirmation of Italy's involvement in the Celtic League FIR President, Giancarlo Dondi said that "I am sure that the Magners League will bring benefits to all Italian rugby and will have a positive impact on the competitiveness of our national team"[236] Welsh Regional Rugby Wales chief executive Stuart Gallacher supported Italy's inclusion. He said: "We have been supporting this move for some months. We are always looking to extra revenue and the Italians give us all two extra home games each and, given time, the Italians will be a force to be reckoned with in our league and it will make the league much more competitive. They have great plans to bring all their international players back from Europe to Italy and that would raise the profile of the tournament."[237]

The growth from a ten to a twelve team tournament has increased the exposure of the league to a new market and made it more attractive due to it having more teams but not having lost much, if any, competitiveness value. Since being added the Italian teams have not been able to win or make the Semi Finals but have attracted the return of most Italian players from France and England. More importantly it has resulted in the Italian test team looking better prepared than previously with Italy upsetting the apple cart like never before with a Six Nations win over France in Rome in 2011. The problem of finding adequately prepared players in all positions could finally be becoming a thing of the past thanks to the competition provided in the now Celtic-Italian League. The gap between the Rabo Direct Pro 12 and international level is significantly less than that of the former Super 10 and international level.

Things have not been altogether smooth for the Italian sides off the field as Aironi's stay in the Rabo Direct Pro 12 lasted just two seasons. The North-Western Italian side was less successful on the field than Benetton Treviso and its failures were compounded in early 2012 when the FIR revoked the team's license after it was reportedly €4million in debt.[238] Aironi was quickly replaced by a new team called Zebre which is based in the larger city of Parma. Aironi's two seasons of professional rugby saw the team finish bottom of the Rabo Direct Pro 12. In the 2010-2011 Season Aironi won only one match in the Rabo Direct Pro 12. It did, however, defeat Biarritz in a Heineken Cup match. The 2011-2012 season was better for Aironi with four wins but this was little compensation and the FIR wanted to rectify the problems by having fewer non-Italians at Zebre.[239] While Aironi were gone Benetton Treviso was in no danger of being replaced with the North-Eastern Italian side having had satisfactory results in its first two years as a Super club. It finished in 10th place on both occasions but managed sixteen wins in the Rabo Direct Pro 12. The team could have finished much higher on both occasions particularly in 2011-2012 but its early season form vanished in the second half of the season.

The efforts at utilizing the teams as much as possible for the benefits of the Italian test team have not meant the players have been exclusively Italian in nationality or eligibility. Argentina has been one of the major contributors of players to the Italian teams. Benetton Treviso have three Argentine players in its squad today - props Ignacio Fernandez Rouyet and Pedro Di Santo and hooker Franco Sbaraglini. All are from Argentina but none have played for Los Pumas. Nevertheless Rouyet and Sbaraglini have played for Italy and Di Santo has represented Italy A. The trio was joined by four other players from Argentina - Augusto Allori, Diego Vidal, Gonzalo Garcia and Gonzalo Padro in the 2011-2012 season. But none of the four remain at Benetton Treviso. Garcia has transferred to Zebre as one of four Argentine players in its squad for its inaugural season. The team also secured two Argentine players from Aironi - Matias Aguero and Luciano Orquera. A fourth Argentina player is also playing for the side - Luciano Leibson but former Aironi players Gabriel Pizarro and Pablo Canavosio are not.

Despite being bottom of the table both seasons Aironi was notably better in its second season and one player who had a lot to do with the teams victories was flyhalf Luciano Orquera. He had joined the team from French club Brive and upon debuting after Rugby World Cup 2011 the team did achieve better results. He scored all his teams points in the 27-13 win over Benetton Treviso in December 2011. The following month he scored fifteen points in the 20-6 win over Connacht and in March he scored eleven points in the 21-17 win over Munster. Orquera missed out on playing in the teams other victory as it was during the World Cup. He was playing for Italy alongside five other players from Argentina. He started in the crunch match of the tournament, against Ireland in a 10-12-13 all-Argentine combination with Gonzalo Garcia and Gonzalo Canale playing in the centres. The Italian tighthead prop was the long serving Leicester Tigers Argentine prop, Martín Castrogiovanni while Stade Français's Argentine backrower Sergio Parisse was the captain.

Sergio Parisse is the biggest name in Italian rugby right now and has proven himself to be one of the best backrowers in world rugby. He is arguably the biggest name in Italian rugby since Diego Dominguez, who is another Argentine. The quantity of Argentine players in Italy remains high but the number of Argentine players becoming Italian internationals has decreased. Previously it was very common for players to quickly become a part of the Italian set up upon beginning their careers in Italy as was the case of Castrogiovanni, Garcia and Orquera. But Canale and Parisse were two exceptions who had moved to Italy as teenagers. This was, indeed, the exception though as most Argentine players representing Italy had moved to play professional rugby. The sixty-four time capped Santiago Dellapé retired in 2011 from test duty. He could have been a PladAR player had the structure existed eight years earlier. He, like Castrogiovanni went on to have a successful career in an elite professional league. Another example is Pumas prop Juan Pablo Orlandi who was playing for Rovigo when Santiago Phelan selected him for his debut. He had become eligible for Italy and had an offer to play for both countries.

Before Italy's entrance into the Celtic League there was an even bigger presence of Argentine players in Italy. It has leveled out a bit with the Super Teams due to their concentration of the best Italian players and the establishment of PladAR. Many of the PladAR players are precisely the type of players who had been lost to Argentina in years gone by and it suggests that fewer Argentine players will be playing in Italy in the future. The teams also featured more capped Argentine players with some quite notable players having played in the Italian domestic competition. While Orlandi played for Argentina in 2008 two World Cup Bronze

Medal winners also spent time there. Lucas Borges started five of Argentina's seven matches in France 2007, scoring three tries. After the tournament he played for Benetton Treviso. While Argentina's starting outside centre Manuel Contepomi went into the tournament after having played the previous season for Rovigo.

England
The birth nation of rugby has been a common destination for Argentine players, being second only to France. Since the beginning of professionalism in 1996 England has long been a destination for Argentine players. It saw the beginning of the professional careers of the previous two Pumas captains, Agustín Pichot and Felipe Contepomi and also the current captain, Juan Martín Fernández Lobbe. All three were a part of Argentina's historical 25-18 victory over England at Twickenham in 2006. However neither Pichot nor Contepomi were still playing in England at the time. The match was a defining moment not only in Argentine rugby history but also in English rugby history. It showed just how good the country's rugby players were and although the result was received as a shock in England it was more an indication of the changes in global rugby with historical stereotypes becoming a thing of the past.

The match defined the career of Pichot and all his teammates. For the older players it was an extreme high in an international career that was plagued by a lack of test matches and extensive problems with the UAR. It was also a beaming light that the younger players may have a chance of participating in a quality rugby event outside of the World Cup. The team was dominated by professional players with only one starting player being based in Argentina - winger Pablo Goméz Cora. The result proved to be a turning point in Argentine rugby. It was this game that caught the attention of many people ahead of Rugby World Cup 2007 to the extent that it started the changes that would see the UAR finally take steps towards professionalism. The players were playing for their country and many of them were crying following the win. It was share joy as they gathered in the middle of the field with Pichot telling his players the importance of what they had done. But behind the scenes was a union that the players were anything but happy with.

In the lead up to the 2009 encounter at Twickenham the then retired Pichot recalled the 2006 victory and pointed out that certain members of the UAR would have preferred England to win. He said "You know, they really hated us," recalling the day he led Argentina to a first, life-changing victory over England at Twickenham, only to discover that certain members of his own national union would have preferred another defeat. "They called us mercenaries because we were playing professional club rugby and turned their backs on us. After the game, they did not even come to the dressing room to congratulate us. It was a very low point, maybe the lowest."[240] Ten months latter the defense of amateurism in Argentine rugby had been severely eroded as Argentina took the World Cup by storm. The players that had threatened to strike against the UAR in mid 2006 had seen their dreams come true as the union's position had changed 180 degrees. In Pichot's words: "After the World Cup in 2007, many of those who had previously thought we were wrong to pursue the professional option by playing our club rugby in Europe conceded that we had been right after all.[241]

In his post match television interview as the winning captain of the 2006 match, Pichot said "this is the best day of his life." He mentioned the importance of playing and winning at the home of rugby and also thanked the friends he had made while playing in England for Richmond and Bristol. The clubs have been victims of professionalism in England as many small town clubs have been dropping out of the premiership due to financial demands. Pichot's first professional contract was from 1997-1999 with Richmond and he then joined Bristol for four years before departing for France after Rugby World Cup 2003. He played a total of 90 matches for Richmond and Bristol[242] and formed an impressive combination with Felipe Contepomi which started in the 2000-2001 season. Contepomi played a total of 45 Premiership matches in his three seasons with Bristol, scoring 573 points including 19 tries.[243] The team reached the final of what was then called the Zurich Premiership in the 2001-2002 Season. His twin brother, Manuel played for Bristol in the 2005-2006 Season.

Pichot and Contepomi were the starting scrumhalf – flyhalf combination in the 2006 match at Twickenham but neither was playing professionally in England. Many others were though as a total of six of the country's starting lineup were contracted to clubs playing in the English elite domestic competition, which had changed its name to be called the Guinness Premiership. The centre combination consisted of Miguel Avramovic and Gonzalo Tiesi. Avramovic was playing professional rugby for the first time for the Worcester Warriors. He would go on to play in France for Montauban and Agen with whom he joined in 2010. Tiesi was into his second of three seasons with London Irish. He transferred to the Harlequins in the 2007-2008 Season after France 2007. He played a total of 40 matches for the English clubs[244] with his best run of form coming in the 2007-2008 Heineken Cup campaign with his defense being the strong point of his game, particularly in the Harlequins two Heineken Cup wins over Stade Français. He also scored some good tries and was arguably in the best form of his career. His contribution to the Harlequins that season was so good that he was named in Guinness Premiership Dream Team of the season by Sky Sports.[245]

In addition to the centre pairing there were four forwards from Twickenham triumph who played in the 2006-2007 Guinness Premiership. Argentina's starting loosehead prop was Marcos Ayerza who had joined the Leicester Tigers that season in what was his first professional contract. He has had a very successful career with Leicester which has seen him become one of Argentina's most notable exports to England. Ayerza is now into his seventh year playing for the club. Since arriving he has been a Heineken Cup finalist and a three time English Premiership Champion. He started for the Tigers in the team that won the 2007 Guinness Premiership Final and the 2009 and 2010 Aviva Premiership Finals. He also started for the club in the 2008, 2011 and 2012 finals which Leicester lost. In other words, Ayerza has started in the English Premiership Final every year since he arrived in England. The significance of this is that the Leicester Tigers happens to be the most successful club in the history of English rugby. It has been the champion of England nine times with the next best being Bath and the London Wasps who have both won six titles each.

Ayerza has been a top player for the club since his arrival. He has held down the loosehead prop position throughout his time and passed the mark of 150 matches for the club in May 2012 against Bath at Welford Road.[246] His contribution to Leicester has seen him recognized as a standout player in England as he joined Tiesi in the 2009 Sky Sports Dream Team.[247] His stay in England is set to be a decade long as he is signed to with Leicester until Rugby World Cup 2015 and has a strong chance of being Argentina's starting loosehead prop for the tournament. He has long been a replacement for Rodrigo Roncero who also played in England. Roncero played for Gloucester from 2002-2004, playing 22 matches.[248] He then moved to France to play for Stade Français in 2004. It saw him face, amongst others, Martín Scelzo who had played for the Heineken Cup winning Northampton Saints from 1999-2001. Scelzo played a total of 18 matches for the club[249] before moving to France.

While the Contepomi brothers both played for Bristol they were overshadowed by the Fernández Lobbe brothers at the Sale Sharks. Carlos Ignacio Fernández Lobbe or *Nacho Fernández Lobbe* started his professional career in France in 2000. He played one season for Bordeaux and three for Castres before joining the Sale Sharks in 2005. His three year stay saw him become an English champion after winning the 2006 Guinness Premiership Final against the Leicester Tigers. He started in the secondrow[250] just like he did in the 2006 Pumas win at Twickenham and played the 2006-2007 Season for the club with his younger brother, Juan Martín or *Corcho*. Carlos Ignacio departed Sale to join the Northampton Saints on a two year deal from 2008-2010 which continued his success story. His qualities saw him captain the team in his first season while his brother was captaining his former club, the Sale Sharks. Carlos Ignacio retired in 2010 only to come out of retirement to end his playing career with Bath. He played 84 matches for English Premiership teams[251] while Corcho played 46 matches.[252]

Corcho Fernández Lobbe captained Sale in his final season but unlike Nacho he was not an English Champion. He played for the club for three years before leaving for Toulon. Despite not winning the premiership his final season for Sale saw him leave with a bang as not only did he captain the club but he was named in the Sky Sports Dream team as the best number eight in England and was also chosen as captain.[253] One year before he joined Toulon his Argentine backrow colleague, Juan Manuel Leguizamón had also left England for France. Leguizamón started in the 2006 win at Twickenham while he was into his second of three seasons with London Irish. His three year stay saw him play 39 matches for the club[254] before moving across the English Channel. He joined Stade Français after Rugby World Cup 2007 and then moved to Lyon in 2011.

When Argentina and England met in Dunedin in the Pool B World Cup match in 2011 the number of English based players in the starting lineup was two compared to twelve contracted to French clubs. The two players were Horacio Agulla, who played the previous season for the Leicester Tigers and Gonzalo Camacho who played for the Harlequins. Both players entered the World Cup in good form with Agulla being Leicester's starting right winger in the Aviva Premiership Final as Leicester were defeated by Saracens. Agulla had joined Leicester after having previously played three seasons in France for Dax and Brive. His move to Leicester saw his reputation significantly enhanced, particularly in his second season. In total he played 48 matches for the club, scoring eight tries with seven coming in the 2011-2012 season.[255] His form saw him rewarded with two prestigious awards at the 2012 Leicester Tigers Supporters End of Season Awards. He won 2012 Player of the Year and Try of the Year[256] and had earlier won Leicester Tigers player of the month on two occasions.[257] The club did not resign him due to his involvement in The Rugby Championship which saw him move east to play for Bath. This did not stop him being named in the ESPN Dream Team for the 2011 2012 Season as the best right winger in England.[258]

In the 2010-2011 Season Camacho's club did not do so well in the Aviva Premiership but did impress in the Amlin Challenge Cup. The team won the final

19-18 after defeating Stade Français with a late try. The try was the only one of the match and it was scored by Camacho. Somewhat surprisingly he left the club to join the Exeter Chiefs for the 2011-2012 Season which saw his appearances in his first three seasons as a professional total 30 matches.[259] In May 2012 he was officially recognized as having made a massive contribution in England when he won the prestigious Gatorade Game Changer of the Season. To find a winner, Gatorade used a formula devised by Opta Sportsdata, the official Statistics provider of the Aviva Premiership, to award points for metres gained, number of carries, turnovers won and tackles made.[260] He had been a key player for his club, the Exeter Chiefs who he helped qualify for the Heineken Cup for the first time as the club finished 5th in the 2011-2012 Aviva Premiership. He was joined by fellow Argentine international, Ignacio Mieres in the starting lineup for most of the season. Mieres, known in Argentina as *Cangu,* had joined the club after stints in France with Stade Français and Perpignan but had never been able to get regular game time. This changed in the 2011-2012 season as he was a standout for Exeter. Cangu played 22 matches in the season, scoring 211 points and being one of the finds of the season.[261]

The case of Horacio Agulla sent warnings to players currently playing in England and potential future players as Leicester were happy to see their star winger leave the club so that they could have the full time service of an alternative player. But the effect it is likely to have on Pumas players in the nation does not appear to be so strong. Of the thirty-three players who were named for the Pumas squad in the lead-up to The Rugby Championship only three are based in England – Agulla, Ayerza and Camacho. In comparison twenty-three were signed to French clubs. The significant difference between Pumas in England and France has come about due in large part to the Aviva Premiership's Salary Cap. While French clubs had budgets of up to €33.1million[262] for the 2011-2012 Season the Salary Cap in England limited the spending to £4million.[263]

France
France is home to the leading domestic rugby competition in the world, the Top 14. It is the largest money making domestic competition with both television viewers and match attendances regularly growing. In 2011 French pay-tv broadcaster Canal Plus signed a five-year contract with the Top 14 organizers, the Ligue Nationale de Rugby (LNR) believed to be worth up to US$228 million.[264] The tremendous success of professional rugby in France can be broken down into four factors. Firstly, the LNR has succeeded in producing a calendar that serves French Rugby. Secondly, teams playing in the Top 14 are increasingly from larger cities than previously. Thirdly, the sizes of the stadiums continue to increase.

Finally the use of imported players has bolstered squads and has increased the quality of the league.

The changes have seen the Top 14 become the leading competition anywhere. While it has grown and improved the big leagues of the Southern Hemisphere – the ITM Cup and the Currie Cup have suffered. They have decreased greatly in quality because of the Super Rugby calendar and The Rugby Championship. Without the All Blacks and Springboks playing, the product is not the same. In France there are no such problems due to club matches stopping for the November Internationals and the Six Nations Championship. Quite simply when the Top 14 is being played the players are available and when France is playing test rugby there are usually no club matches. The preference for the Heineken Cup still exists, but it is not a significant difference - not like in Super Rugby. As such the French league has never lost its quality or level of respect and clubs continue to get richer.

In France and England teams are looking for alternatives to their traditionally small stadiums. There are also games transferred to the largest stadiums in both countries. A club match in London between Saracens and Harlequins attracted a world record of 83,761 fans to Wembley Stadium in March 2012 for a regular season club match.[265] It broke the record set up Stade Français. The Parisian club has been using the Stade de France regularly since 2006, for up to four home games a season. Other clubs have followed suit in moving matches to larger venues. Racing-Métro has occasionally used the Stade de France, Toulon has used the Stade Velodrome in Marseille, Toulouse regularly uses the Stadium Municipal, and Bordeaux-Begles uses Chaban-Delmas. The use of big venues has been highly successful and it has seen teams even playing home matches in Spain. Biarritz and Bayonne have both used the Anoeta Stadium in San Sebastian while Perpignan transferred a Heineken Cup Quarter Final to the Olympic Staidum in Barcelona and attracted a sellout crowd.[266] In addition Montpellier and Clermont have recently upgraded their stadiums.

To ensure sustainability means ensuring survival because the bottom two teams are automatically relegated to the Pro d2. Having a quality squad of players has proven to be essential. Clubs cannot just use players from the local region or even just from France. Argentina's win to open Rugby World Cup 2007 featured nine players in the starting lineup who were contracted to French clubs in the season leading up to the tournament. The players were exceptionally well prepared thanks to European clubs, with France having the highest number of World Cup Pumas.

But, despite this, there is no reason to say that the French team is suffering as France is the only country that has qualified for the semifinals in every World Cup since the beginning of professionalism. The movement of players has made the league increasingly competitive with surprising results occurring with more regularity.

The injection of money into French rugby has significantly changed the shape of French rugby with the traditional hot-bed of France´s Southwest having fewer teams in the Top 14 with the number of clubs from the region almost decreasing year by year. In place of many small town teams are clubs based in larger cities around the country. Examples of teams from the Southwest that are no longer in the Top 14 are Albi Auch, Beziers, Brive, Colomiers, Dax and Pau. They all dropped out of the Top 14 because they simply did not have good enough players which predominantly was a result of most other teams have a higher budget. The four clubs from the 2011-2012 Top 14 season with budgets of over €20million were Clermont, Racing Métro, Stade Français and Toulouse.[267] Unsurprisingly they happen to be from larger cities than the majority of other teams. While the five teams with the lowest budgets were Agen, Bordeaux-Begles, Brive, Castres and Lyon.[268] Two of them were relegated to the Pro d2 and of the five four are located in southwestern France.

The Southwest continues to have the majority of teams in the Top 14 but there are fewer than previously. More importantly the likes of Montpellier, Racing Métro and Toulon have all established themselves as amongst the leading French clubs in recent years. This marks a fundamental change from before Rugby World Cup 2007. The 2006-2007 Top 14 Season featured eleven teams from what can be considered France´s southwest, according to the European Parliament Constituency.[269] They were Agen, Albi, Bayonne, Biarritz, Brive, Castres, Montauban, Montpellier, Narbonne, Perpignan and Toulouse. That season Agen and Narbonne were relegated with the final being contested between two of the three teams from outside of the southwest – Stade Français and Clermont. The 2011-2012 season, in contrast featured six teams from outside of the South-West – Clermont, Grenoble, Racing Métro, Stade Français and Toulon.

Since 2007 there has also been a clear change with big city teams succeeding at the expense of many small town teams. For instance Montpellier has gone from being threatened with relegation in 2007 to being a finalist in 2011. Teams winning promotion from the second division in the professional era have increasingly been firstly from different parts of France and secondly from larger cities. Together with Toulouse and Bordeaux Montpellier was used to host World

Cup matches in 2007. Its transformation has come about due to a solid junior rugby set up that has produced François Trinh-Duc, Fulgence Ouedraogo, Louis Picamoles and Julien Tomas, amongst others and the clubs contracting of foreign players. The significance of this is that rugby matches have become more popular in a number of large French cities that have both rugby and soccer clubs playing at the elite level. Toulouse has had larger crowds for rugby than soccer since 2005 while in 2010 Stade Français averaged 34,722 per match compared to Paris's soccer equivalent Saint-Germain which averaged 33,522 the same season.[270]

Teams from the Southwest are being relegated to the Pro d2 reguarly. In the 2011-2012 season Brive was relegated and in 2009-2010 Albi and Montauban were. In 2008-2009 Dax and Mont de Marsan were relegated, in 2007-2008 Albi and Auch were relegated, in 2006-2007 Agen and Narbonne were relegated, while in 2005-2006 Toulon and Pau were relegated. It is clear what is happening – Southwestern teams are being relegated more than others and they happen to be small town teams. It is not only teams from this region, but in the vast majority of cases it is. Every year since the Top 16 became the Top 14 one or both relegated clubs have been from the Southwest. Moreover, although Lyon was relegated in May 2012 one of the two teams winning promotion was the nearby Grenoble which is a big city with a sizeable stadium to host important games.

It is not all doom and gloom for Southwestern France's small town teams but it is a highly complicated situation for some of them. With Bordeaux-Begles now in the Top 14 the likelihood of Agen moving home matches to the Chaban-Delmas Stadium is low. It is the largest sizeable stadium near Agen and by quite some distance. The same is true of Brive which was relegated. Another club who could be in danger is Castres who faces a similar problem to Agen in that its closest big city is Toulouse. Biarritz is smaller than Castres but is located very close to the Spanish border near San Sebastián. Castres does not have any such luxuries with Toulouse, Montpellier or even Bordeaux being potential locations for moving matches but all have Top 14 teams. Castres's home ground, the Stade Pierre-Antoine, is the smallest in the Top 14. Even after improvements in 2008, the stadium is still small. When Castres hosted Munster a Heineken Cup match in November 2011 it moved the match to the 18,754 capacity Stade Ernest Wallon in Toulouse.[271] In 2007 the city of Castres was estimated at having a population of 43,347 compared to 44,812 in 1990[272] making it significantly smaller than the Southwest's largest cities of Bordeaux, Montpellier and Toulouse. It has still managed to be competitive in the Top 14. However, the trend of Southwestern

French clubs being relegated must be alarming to the club as derby matches are decreasing.

The Top 14 is notorious for having imported players and this is something that has assisted in the evolution of the country's domestic rugby and also the Rugby World Cup. The 2007 and 2011 tournaments featured more competitive performances from Tier Two and Tier Three nations due in large part to the exposure of players to professional rugby, mainly in Europe and especially in France. It has coincided with an increasing number of world class players from more places playing in the Top 14. A significant exporter of players to France is Argentina. Such is the quantity of Argentine players in the country that it is more a case of finding teams that do not have Pumas players rather than ones that do. In the 2011-2012 season twelve of the fourteen clubs had players from Argentina. The number of Argentine players per club ranged from Clermont and Perpignan with one player each to Montpellier and Stade Français with six each. Argentina had more than enough players across all positions to field a thirty-man World Cup squad made up only of French based players.[273] Of the Argentine players in the 2011-2012 Top 14 nineteen players were in the Pumas squad for Rugby World Cup 2011 and there were a further four players who did not play in New Zealand 2011 that played in France 2007.[274]

The high number of Pumas in France has coincided with a lower number of Pumas playing their rugby in England. This is due mainly to the clubs superior budgets in the Top 14 with players being paid larger salaries than in the Aviva Premiership. The Salary Cap placed on the Aviva Premiership clubs of £4 million is significantly lower than the €8.7 million that the Top 14 clubs can use to pay their players.[275] As such the average salary per player in the Top 14 is higher than in England and squads in the Top 14 also tend to be larger than in the Aviva Premiership for the same reason. In 2010 the average Top 14 player was earning US$153,700 compared to US$123,000 earned by the average player in the Aviva Premiership.[276]

Professional clubs have contributed to Argentina's healthy state. But development is a two-way street. While it has seen Los Pumas emerge to be a global power it has also seen the Argentine players assist the development of local players. Argentine players play with and against French players. It lifts the level of competition in the Top 14 by having a larger supply of quality players. In preparing to face Los Pumas in Montpellier in 2010 French international prop Thomas Domingo told French site rugbyrama that "I could not have had better teachers. Above all they are intelligent players who think a great deal about how to improve their scrummaging. And they're shrewd as well." He was referring to his Clermont teammates Mario Ledesma and Martín Scelzo[277] who had appeared in four Top 14 Finals in a row for the club. After losing in 2007, 2008 and 2009 they finally won the French Championship in 2010. Both players had highly successful careers in France with Ledesma playing more than 100 Top 14 matches.[278]

Many other Pumas have had a significant impact on their clubs performances in France. So many have been regulars for Top 14 clubs to the extent that the last time a Top 14 Final did not feature Pumas was in the 2000-2001 season. Ignacio Corleto was a try scorer in the 2003 Top 16 Final. His club Stade Français won 32-18 against Toulouse and then defeated Perpignan 38-20 the following year to win back-to-back titles. Corleto was again on the score sheet. He was joined in the starting lineup by Juan Martín Hernández and Agustín Pichot. Hernández became a French champion in his first season as a professional. On the opposing team was Rimas Alvarez Kairelis who started for Perpignan. Stade Français were beaten finalists the following season as Biarritz won the 2005 Top 16 Final 37-34. They did so with Federico Martín Aramburu on the bench while Hernández, Pichot and Rodrigo Roncero all started for Stade Français. Biarritz defended its title the following season in what was now the Top 14. The team won the 2006 Final 40-13 against Toulouse with Aramburu again on the bench while Omar Hasan started for Toulouse.

2007 was not only the year that Argentina caught the attention of rugby followers globally. It was also the year that it contributed a record number of players to a French final. Stade Français's 23-18 victory was historical because it saw a foreign captain win the championship for the first time. Pichot led the team in a halves combination that saw him playing with Hernández who had made the move from fullback in January that year. Also in the team were Roncero and Mario Ledesma's brother, Pedro Ledesma who conbined to start as the two Parisian props. The match was also testament to the complements Thomas Domingo went on to make in November 2010 as three of the four starting props in the match were Argentineans. Martín Scelzo scrummed against Roncero and Mario Ledesma starting at hooker. Gonzalo Longo was a secondhalf replacement for Clermont while the Argentine-Italian pair of Sergio Parisse and Gonzalo Canale also played.

The star of the 2007 Final was Hernández who put in an outstanding performance and was subsequently recognized as the best player in France, winning the 2007 joueur de l'année or Player of the Year award, the *Oscar du Midi Olympique*[279] and also the same award at the *Nuit du Rugby*, or the Night of Rugby.[280] He was, notably, the first ever non-Frenchman to win the player of the year award. The accolades meant he was the undisputed top player in France in the season leading up to Rugby World Cup 2007 and he underlined his form with a superb performance to see the Parisians crowned French Champions. The 2007 Final had given viewers a good look at what he could do at flyhalf in a big match situation. Former All Blacks flyhalf, Simon Manix said during commentary of the Rugby World Cup 2007 opener that "Hernández almost won the Top 14 Final by himself."

His performance saw Stade Français come from behind to win match after being behind 12-0 and it was Hernández's second half display that turned the match. He kicked 5 goals from 5 attempts, scoring thirteen second half points but more importantly he was in the right place at the right time to do his magic. In the 51st minute, Hernández created an attack near his own 10 metre line. He chipped over the defense and retrieved his own kick before offloading to a teammate in the tackle. This play put the Parisians well inside the Clermont 22 and resulted in a penalty goal. In the 61st minute Hernández combined with Christophe Dominici to set the French winger on a 40 metre run before slotting his third penalty. Stade Français found itself 18-16 behind in the 74th minute and following a break from Julien Arias Hernández came close to scoring a try as he was tackled one metre short. Four phases later Hernández threw a long cut-out-pass, skipping four players, to put Australian international Radiki Samo over in the corner in the 78th minute. Hernández landed the conversion to seal the victory. Curiously the only points that he was not involved in was his teams other try, scored by Pichot.

Stade Français had a good campaign in the 2007-2008 Season but was eliminated by Toulouse at the Semi Finals stage. Toulouse won 31-13 with Patricio Albacete and Omar Hasan both starting. Hernández played at flyhalf and was joined by Corleto at fullback, Roncero at loosehead prop and Parisse at number eight. The match was Corleto's final match as a professional after he missed the subsequent season due to injury. Toulouse went on to win the Final with Albacete and Hasan both becoming French champions. Hasan finished on a high after retiring from rugby to take up a career as a baritone singer. On the opposing front row were Mario Ledesma and Martín Scelzo who lost a second straight French final. Ledesma had possibly his finest season of rugby and was named in the Top 14 Dream Team for the 2007-2008 season at the Nuit du Rugby. Joining him were three other Pumas – Roncero, Albacete and Hernández.[281]

The same four Semi Finalists from 2008 were back in 2009 with Toulouse facing Clermont and Stade Français facing Perpignan. It would turnout to be Hernández's final match for Stade Français as he would go on to sign for South African side the Natal Sharks. Perpignan won the final 22-13 with Rimas Alvarez Kairelis becoming a French Champion. Earlier in 2009 he had retired from international rugby. His long time Pumas teammates Ledesma and Scelzo were on the losing side while his secondrow partner, Albacete was again named in the Top 14 Dream Team as he had established himself as the leading secondrower in France.[282] He was joined in the Dream Team by Juan Martín Fernández Lobbe who had played a key role for Toulon in transforming it into one of France's premier clubs.

The following season was the final one before the World Cup making it crucial for all players of all nationalities in the Top 14 to receive lots of game time and play well. It proved to be a key season for Los Pumas as a number of players who had broken into the senior squad impressed. It was also a history making season with Montpellier making the Final for the first time. It had gotten there by defeating Racing Métro 26-25 with a one time capped Puma, Martín Bustos Moyano being the hero. He kicked Montpellier into the final with a penalty in the 79th minute. Montpellier had been leading 20-6 following a try to Santiago Fernández but Racing Métro fought back strongly and the Parisians took the lead with six minutes remaining only to be denied by the Córdoba winger. Juan Figallo was also playing for Montpellier. He had a solid season as the teams loosehead prop. Regular game time gave Santiago Phelan the confidence to select him at tighthead prop ahead of Scelzo at Rugby World Cup 2011.

The Final was a close match but not a great one in terms of quality as Toulouse was crowned champions without scoring a try. It was an occassion to showcase the global game with Argentina, Fiji, France, Georgia, Samoa and South Africa all being represented. A new generation of Argentine players was a feature of the Montpellier performance and the trio of Bustos Moyano, Fernández and Figallo would be joined the following season by three other Pumas after the World Cup. The contribution of Bustos Moyano is perhaps the most interesting considering his lack of opportunities with Los Pumas. He has not only been able to establish himself as a key player but has also already become the clubs all time top points scorer. In just two seasons he has scored 545 points and has been nothing short of a true revelation. His contribution highlights the contribution of Argentineans to French rugby which can be described as a trade system that has seen the development of Argentine players, amongst other nationalities, in exchange for the growth of French rugby.

Part III
Global Impact

13

Legacy for the Americas

A Rugby World Cup host nation has the responsibility of hosting the sports premier event and delivering a memorable occassion. It is hosting on behalf of all rugby communities big and small, established and in formation. New Zealand 2011 represented Oceania and a large part of New Zealand's World Cup was about creating a legacy for the Pacific Islands. Nobody is closer culturally to the regions Second and Third Tier nations than New Zealand is. It is a key region including World Cup regulars Fiji, Samoa and Tonga and also developing nations such as the Cook Islands and Papua New Guinea. Seven months after the completion of the World Cup Rugby World Cup Ltd announced that NZD $34million was going directly to Oceania to assist with competitions, development, training and education initiatives.[283]

In addition to leaving a financial legacy there was also a rugby legacy and New Zealand delivered an extremely rare scenario by having all of Fiji, Samoa and Tonga play in the tournament's largest stadium. New Zealand opened against Tonga at Eden Park while the Fiji v Samoa pool match was also played there. When the draw had been made for Rugby World Cup 2011 it appeared logical that New Zealand v France would be the tournament opener but instead the choice was Tonga. This was in part to see the All Blacks play two matches in Auckland to get a good return from ticket sales but it was also to give Tonga a chance that is likely to never repeat itself – opening a Rugby World Cup. This was a key legacy for Tonga just as it was for Fiji and Samoa. None of the three will likely ever be capable of hosting Rugby World Cup matches either alone, together or as subhosts with the official home nation being a different country. The extraordinary decision of opening with Tonga contrasts to the nation's two matches played in Montpellier during Rugby World Cup 2007. The crowds of 25,214 for Tonga v USA and

24,128 for Tonga v Samoa attracted the smallest crowds of the forty-two matches played in France.[284]

Hosting a successful World Cup means representing the region and this is something that Argentina can arguably do well. The region in question is not South America, nor is it Latin America. Rather it is the Americas as a whole. A significant legacy would likely be left behind for the region should Argentina host Rugby World Cup 2023. In addition to Argentina the region is home to three other countries that have played in a Rugby World Cup at least twice – Canada, Uruguay and the USA. All of them would gain a lot from Argentina hosting a World Cup and so would other CONSUR nations, particularly Brazil and Chile who are a part of CONSUR A alongside Argentina and Uruguay. So much growth has been occuring following the success of Los Pumas in France 2007 that there are 25% more rugby players in South America now than there were in 2008.[285] This chapter will take a look at each of these countries in an effort to better understand what the sport can gain from Argentina hosting Rugby World Cup 2023.

Canada
The world's second largest country is one with a deep tradition in rugby. The sport has been played in Canada longer than it has in Argentina. It was originally introduced in the 1860's with the first recorded game being played in Montreal in 1864. The sport spread across the country in the late nineteenth century and after stagnating during World War I it gained popularity to eventually be played nationwide. The governing body was first founded in 1929. It was originally known as the Rugby Union of Canada but changed its name to Rugby Canada in 1974.[286] Rugby Canada has succeeded in seeing the Canadian test team establish itself as one of rugby's true developing nations. Canada has competed at every Rugby World Cup and since the creation of the IRB World Rankings in 2003 it has mostly been ranked as the 13th or 14th best team in the world. Since rankings began Canada has been positioned between 11th and 16th.[287]

Like the First Tier rugby nations of Australia, England, Ireland, New Zealand, Scotland, South Africa and Wales Canada is a part of the British Commonwealth. Rugby is a major sport in all these nations but in Canada it is not as strong due in large part to geography. The share size of Canada has historically complicated matters because of the great distances involved.[288] A simple match between two teams from different provinces can be very expensive and can mean players need to take several days off work to get to the game and to return home. It is a similar story to Australia, a country that until recently was far from being a genuine rugby nation. In the amateur era rugby in Australia was severely concentrated in the eastern coast states of New South Wales and Queensland. The same two accounted for the teams that played in Super Rugby until 1995. Since professionalism the sport has been able to grow. Starting in the Australian Capital Territory (ACT), Australia has established new teams that have succeeded due to Super Rugby and funding has been awarded to them. After the Brumbies succeeded in the ACT the ARU added the Western Force in 2006 and the Melbourne Rebels in 2011. This is why Australia has been able to remain one of the best teams in the world in the professional era while Canada is firmly a Tier Two rugby nation.

In the inaugural Rugby World Cup Canada competed against Ireland, Tonga and Wales and exited at the pool stage after winning one match, 37-4 against Tonga. Four years latter the Canadians made rugby history by reaching the Quarter Finals. Canada's first match of the tournament was against 1987 Quarter Finalists Fiji in Bayonne. The North Americans won a low scoring match 13-3 with Scott Stewart scoring the games only try. Canada followed it up four days later with a 19-11 victory over Romania in Toulouse. Both teams scored two tries each but Canada were victorious thanks to a drop goal from Gareth Rees and three successful kicks at goal from Mark Wyatt. It was a phenomenally important win for Canada, its most significant win in Rugby World Cup history. It set up a match against France with the winner facing England at the Quarter Finals stage and the loser facing New Zealand. France entered the match as heavy favorites after having defeated Romania 30-3 and Fiji 33-9. France finished top of the group with a 19-13 win in Agen. Canada troubled the All Blacks at times before losing 29-13 in Lille.

The final years of amateurism were the best for Canadian rugby. The North Americans completed some impressive wins against Tier One sides, most notably in 1993. Canada hosted England while the Lions were touring New Zealand and as such, Canada's home matches against England were officially non-internationals. It was, in effect, a strategy utilized to make it a win-win situation for England. Should England lose it could blame it on the Lions and claim it was just a training match. A win, in contrast, would be a way of saying that England rugby had considerable depth that was strong and formidable. It meant that Canada's 15-12 win at Burnaby Lake went down in history as being a non-international. Latter that year, however, Canada was not denied a famous win on a technicality as the North Americans defeated Wales 26-24 in Cardiff. Al Charron's late try secured what, to this day, remains Canada's greatest rugby triumph. It was also notable due to where it was played. The venue was the one that has since been upgraded and renamed the Millenium Stadium. Not only did Canada win in Wales but the home side was unable to score a try with Neil Jenkins's boot being responsible for all of the Welsh points.[289]

The Cardiff victory was not a one off magical performance. The following year Canada defeated France 18-16 in Nepean. IRB Hall of Famer, Gareth Rees kicked the Canadians to victory but the most remarkable point to come out of this was not that Canada won but that this was the same month that France defeated New Zealand twice to claim a series win in New Zealand. Canada's strength at this time was evident in international matches against the USA. Canada regularly defeated its neighbor by comfortable margins. It was also too strong for Japan and completed a good 22-10 away win over Fiji in Nadi in 1995. There was reason to believe Canada could repeat its feet of 1991 but the draw was far from friendly. Being drawn with both Australia and South Africa at Rugby World Cup 1995 meant Canada's chances of advancing to the Quarter Finals were extremely difficult. Canada opened its campaign with a 34-3 win over Romania before losing 27-11 to Australia and 20-0 against the Springboks.

The advent of professional rugby lifted the level of all teams who exposed their players to professionalism but Canada missed the boat and it has proven to have had telling consequences. Fiji, with players involved in Super Rugby and elsewhere completed a 38-22 win over Canada during Rugby World Cup 1999. In the same tournament Canada had been leading against France before losing 33-20 and it completed its largest ever World Cup win as the North American country defeated Namibia 72-11. But having lost against Fiji and France meant Canada was eliminated. Four years latter Canada had a sporting chance of making the Quarter Finals as it was grouped with Italy, New Zealand, Tonga and Wales. Despite dropping-off from its level of competitiveness of the 1990's, the North Americans were still able to push teams hard during the 2000-2010 decade. At Rugby World Cup 2003 Canada gave Wales a good first half but was overwhelmed by New Zealand in the second match. The result meant Canada's chances of reaching the Quarter Finals were over. But Canada nevertheless played good rugby against both Italy and Tonga. The North Americans collected a bonus point in losing 19-14 to Italy and finished the World Cup with a 24-7 win over Tonga.

Canada left the 2003 tournament with a win but having achieved what was a shadow of its success from decade earlier. Canada started Rugby World Cup 2007 against the pools second seed, Wales. Canada gave Wales a scare and it took the secondhalf introduction of Stephen Jones and Gareth Thomas to change the match. Canada had turned around a 9-0 Welsh advantage to lead 17-9 before Wales mounted a secondhalf comeback.[290] Canada traveled to Cardiff to face Fiji in a must win pool match against Fiji who had come off a 35-31 win against Japan. Neither Fiji nor Canada could afford to lose as both were chasing the dream of a Quarter Finals appearance. Canada were highly disappointed and failed to deliver a good performance, losing 29-16. Having been elimated Canada was now playing for honor as was Japan. The match went down to the wire with Japan scoring a converted ty in overtime to level the scores at 12-12. With only Australia to play Canada were now set to exit a World Cup winless for the first time. Canada played well against the Wallabies but lost 37-6.

The most important thing to come out of Canada's participation in Rugby World Cup 2007 was not its draw with Japan, but, rather the importance of having twenty teams at Rugby World Cup's. The tournament had been overshadowed by the IRB's apparent decision to decrease the number of participants from twenty to sixteen teams for Rugby World Cup 2007. Just two days before Fiji eliminated Wales from the tournament BBC Wales revealed that Rugby World Cup 2011 would have four fewer competing countries.[291] The same team had very nearly lost against Japan in its opening match of the tournament. While Argentina had started the tournament by winning against the hosts, Canada v Japan served as a reminder that great games do not require Tier One teams and that both Canada and Japan are vital participants of World Cup's. IRB chairman Dr Syd Millar agreed in saying that: "The developing nations at Rugby World Cup 2007 have produced significantly enhanced performances since RWC 2003."[292] What he did not include, however, was that the match schedules for 2003 had been unfairly balanced against most teams that fit into the category of developing nations.

Canada was drawn in Pool A for Rugby World Cup 2011. It faced France, Japan, Tonga and the host nation, New Zealand. Canada started its campaign against Tonga and was considered to be the underdogs by rugby writers. The teams previous World Cup wins over Tonga in 1987 and 2003 were not being used to say the North Americans had an advantage. Rather Tonga were genuinely thought of as better and expected to win the match. The BBC called the Canadian 25-20 win "the first upset of the Rugby World Cup"[293] while Television New Zealand called the called the win a shock.[294] The result proved to be one of the biggest in the World Cup due to what would subsequently happen in this pool. France had failed to find form in its first three matches as it had a tough time against Japan and Canada before being defeated badly by New Zealand. It had recovered from a slow start against Japan to claim a 47-21 win and after a similarly slow start it recovered against Canada to win 46-19. France was then humbled 37-17 by the

All Blacks but had, nonetheless, confirmed itself in the Quarter Finals. Canada's win against Tonga meant the Pacific Island nation had lost its first two matches and needed bonus point wins against Japan and France to advance to the Quarter Finals. Tonga did impress against Japan but its 31-18 win did not feature four tries. Tonga went into its final pool match on five points while France was on ten. Tonga showed just how important Second Tier Rugby Nations are with a 19-14 victory over France but was not to advance due it its loss against Canada. The North Americans contribution saved France from early elimination and highlighted its capabilities.

Canada did play well against France in its second match but was overrun in the closing stages as France scored two of its four tries in the final three minutes. The match was played in Napier, the same city for Canada's third match of the tournament. It was a rematch of the 2007 draw in Bordeaux but there had been two matches since then with Japan winning a two match home series comfortably in November 2009. The 46-8 and 27-6 results certainly gave reason to believe that Japan was a better team than Canada on paper. With Canada still to face New Zealand this was its last winnable match and it was Japan's final game. The Japanese had targeted at least two wins[295] but had a disappointing tournament despite starting promisingly against France. The loss against Tonga meant the best Japan could achieve was one win and the Asians looked like making this happen with a strong performance against Canada. Japan was leading 23-15 in the 73rd minute but Canada fought back with an unconverted try by Ander Monro and a Monro penalty to level the scores at 23-23 in the final minute. It put Canada into third place in the Pool but Tonga's win over France saw Tonga finish third. The North Americans final match was played five days later and it saw the host nation defeat Canada 79-15 in Wellington.

Overall Canada has a satisfactory World Cup record. But a lack of resources, the size of the country and the sports amateur status have worked against Canadian rugby. But despite the difficulties Canada has still been able to prove its worth as a country that is indispensible to the Rugby World Cup. It is also a country that could potentially host a Rugby World Cup in the future either alone or together with the USA. Canada has previously hosted the IRB Womens World Cup. The 2006 tournament was played in Edmonton and Canada performed well, finishing in fourth place. The city has also played host to international mens matches as have many other cities across the country. Canada does not have a fixed home stadium. Rather, like Argentina it moves its home fixtures around. The two strongest rugby provinces of British Colombia and Ontario tend to host regularly.

For instance Canada played host to Georgia in British Colombia in 2012 and Italy and the USA in Ontario.

The June 2012 test against Italy was played at BMO Field in Toronto. Italy won the match, as expected, but there were two key points to come from it. Firstly, Canada had played well and given Italy a genuine hard fought contest. Canada was leading the match 13-9 at halftime but Italy showed superior fitness to complete a 25-16 victory. The home team's downfall had a lot to do with the battle of the frontrows with Martín Castrogiovanni, in particular, impressing against Canada. The match was also notable for having a sizeable crowd of 12,220.[296] Ten months prior the same venue had played host to a test match between Canada and the USA and attracted a crowd of 10,621.[297] These two crowds were strong for Canadian rugby and they have virtually assured Toronto of hosting the biggest test match each year. Ireland is to visit in June 2013 with BMO Field likely to be seriously considered as the host venue. The stadium could also be a part of something even bigger. Its success in tests against the USA and Italy could well see it used to host Rugby Sevens to give Canada a home leg in the annual IRB World Sevens Series.

While results have not been what they were twenty years ago for Canada the country continues to produce its share of talented players. The most noticeable feature of Kieran Crowley's thirty-man squad for Rugby World Cup 2011 was that only nine of the players were contracted to professional teams. Moreover, of the professionals only Jamie Cudmore and DTH van der Merwe had been playing at the top level in the 2010-2011 Season.[298] Both Cudmore and van der Merwe went into the World Cup in good form. Cudmore was a French Champion in 2010, a runner up in 2007, 2008 and 2009 and a Semi Finalist in 2011. Van der Merwe had played nineteen matches for the Glasgow Warriors in the 2010-2011 Magners League[299] The seven remaining professional players were either playing in the English second division or were to begin playing professionally after the World Cup.

Argentina and Canada have a link that previously saw them compete in the Pan American Championship from 1995-2003. More recently, however the relations between the nations have been different, but nevertheless continue. In European professional rugby players from both countries have been teammates. Cudmore became a Top 14 Champion together with Mario Ledesma and Martín Scelzo while van der Merwe formed a wing partnership with Federico Martín Aramburu in Scotland. When Pichot became the first foreigner to captain a French club to the title he did so with Canadian secondrower, Mike James in the starting lineup.

On that evening in Paris James and Cudmore actually faced off on opposing teams. One of Pichot´s understudies at Stade Français was Morgan Williams who played for the club in 2005-2006 and captained Canada at Rugby World Cup 2007. Other Canadian international players have also teamed up with Pumas. In the 2011-2012 Season, for instance, both Adam Kleeberger and Agustín Gosio played for London Scottish.

Relations between Canada and Argentina have continued to tighten in recent years. The mutual development program through the Americas Rugby Championship has seen players from both nations go on to make their senior test team after representing the Canada Selects XV or Los Jaguars. The tournament is fostering a relationship similar to that of Japan with the Pacific Islands through the Pacific Nations Cup. All unions benefit in both cases. In the case of Canada, the Americas Rugby Championship is aiding both established home-based players and emerging players. Into the future it will continue to offer mutual benefits to both country´s and will see both becoming more interconnected. The tournament is a clear example of why what is good for one country is good for both. It is also showing that Canada is a definitive Tier Two nation and one that does have the potential to become a Tier One side. The Americas Rugby Championship is crucial to helping Canada develop a better test team. While Argentina hosting Rugby World Cup 2023 would be a big boost to Canadian rugby. It would show Canada what is possible for the future. Canada is not in a position to launch a bid for a Rugby World Cup just yet but should Argentina host a nationwide tournament in 2023 it would send positive waves into North America. In Canada, like in Argentina rugby is an important sport but it is not the biggest. This does not mean hosting a World Cup is not going to happen but having Argentina host, like having Japan host in 2019 will be a significant boost for the region.

USA
While Canada has slipped behind Tier One teams that it had defeated in the latter stage of the amateur era the professional era has been nothing short of revolutionary for rugby in the USA. The common reference of the sleeping giant has long been thrown around in reference to the huge potencial that exists for rugby to take off in the country and for the USA Eagles to become a Tier One team. Indeed the USA has been doing better at Rugby World Cups and more recently has been having more of its players exposed to professional rugby. Playing numbers have been rising with the interest in the game continuing the reach new heights. The governing body of the sport in the country, USA Rugby has been an innovator in seeing the sports popularity rise and is actively undertaking policies to ensure that it will continue to do so.

In 2010 the Sporting Goods Manufacturers' Association's (SGMA) annual survery of sporting participation which involves over 120 sports showed that rugby is the fastest growing team sport in the USA. That year SGMA executive Mika May said the number of people playing the full-contact version of rugby increased from 750,000 to 1.13million, with women making up a third of the total.[300] The findings were supported by a second report. The Centre for the International Business of Sport (CIBS) in 2011 reported that rugby participation in the USA had increased by 350% since 2004.[301] With growth comes progress and this is what has happened over the period broadly starting from Rugby World Cup 2003. A greater player base has enabled the USA to have a superior national mens team and the USA Eagles have achieved better results during this period than before it.

The USA played in the inaugural Rugby World Cup, losing 47-12 to Australia, 34-6 to England and beating Japan 21-18. The win over Japan would be the only time the USA would win a World Cup match in the amateur era. In the 1991 World Cup the USA was winless after facing England, Italy and New Zealand but most worryingly was in 1995 when the USA failed to qualify. The major reason for not qualifying was the system and not the ability of the team though as the return of South Africa to test rugby in 1992 meant that the sixteen team World Cup format would feature the host nation and an African qualifier, rather than just one African nation like in 1987 and 1991. The Americas in effect, lost two qualifying spots. Canada was an automatic qualifier after making the Quarter Finals in 1991 while Argentina and the USA faced-off as the winners of the South and North American qualifying zones. Argentina qualified after winning the two matches 44-33 on aggregate.

The USA returned for Rugby World Cup 1999 with the Americas now having three slots. The USA Eagles faced Australia, Ireland and Romania in Pool E which took place in the Republic of Ireland and Northern Ireland. The USA lost its first match 53-8 against Ireland and then had a heartbreaking 27-25 loss against Romania. It left the tournament winless after losing 55-19 to Australia. The tournament was not a total failure for the USA though and, curiously the USA was the only team that scored a try against Australia in the tournament. The USA qualified for Rugby World Cup 2003 but not easily. It had lost against Canada, Uruguay and Chile and entered repercharge after Canada and Uruguay qualified as Americas 1 and 2. It then had no problems in defeating Spain in the repercliage qualification series to earn its place in Pool B of Rugby World Cup 2003 alongside France, Fiji, Japan and Scotland.

The change of having five teams per pool rather than four made it more interesting for Second Tier teams. The USA could now target two matches as winnable rather than one, or none as was the case in 1991. The USA indeed targeted its matches against Fiji and Japan as its key games and game very close to defeating the Fijians. It was the first game for the USA while Fiji was backing up after facing France four days earlier. Heading into the final minutes Fiji was leading by six points with the teams having scored one try each. But Kort Schubert scored a try near the left touchline in the final minute. Mike Hercus had the chance to secure victory for the USA but his conversion attempt sailed wide. It gave Fiji a 19-18 win. The team's second match was not as memorable as the USA lost 39-15 against Scotland but the third match was history making as the USA scored a record five tries in its 39-26 win against Japan. Its final match was a 41-14 loss against pool winners France.

Rugby World Cup 2007 saw the USA grouped with England, Samoa, South Africa and Tonga. The team was less experienced than in 2003 with key players including Hodges, Luke Gross and Dan Lyle no longer playing. The USA had a young team with Mike Hercus now the captain. The USA began the tournament against reigning champions England and did well to restrict England to three tries – not enough for a bonus point. The 28-10 loss was the test debut of Taku Ngwenya who would go on to score two impressive tries. After a four day turnaround the USA played its second match and it did not go well as the USA lost 25-15 against Tonga in a game that the Eagles should have won. The pool was extremely unpredictable with South Africa defeating England 36-0 but almost losing to Tonga before winning 30-25. After defeating the USA Tonga upset Samoa 19-15. Samoa then lost to England before facing the USA in its final match. The North Americans started poorly just like what had happened against Tonga, but the USA came back to lose 25-21. Its final match against the USA was a big 64-15 loss but the lasting memory of the match was Ngwenya who scored the try of the World Cup after famously out stepping and sprinting past Bryan Habana.

During this period the result of rugby's increased profile were becoming clear on the field as the USA Eagles had a greater supply of quality players. Ngwenya went on to join Biarritz after the World Cup. Todd Clever was signed to play Super Rugby for the Lions and then play in Japan while Chris Wyles went on to play for Saracens. All three have achieved significant success and were key players at Rugby World Cup 2011. The clubs saw the development of all three into genuine world class players. In 2010 Ngwenya was a Heineken Cup finalist and in 2011 Clever was a Japanese Champion with Suntory Sungoliath and Wyles won the Aviva Premiership. The growth of the sport in the USA has also seen positive spin offs such as increased television exposure. When the USA Eagles took on Ireland in the team's first match of Rugby World Cup 2011 it was available live in the USA on NBC. It was one of seven matches that were broadcast live on the network.[302]

The match against Ireland marked the tenth anniversary of the 9/11 terrorist attacks. It was important not only from a national standpoint but also from a sporting one as the USA rugby community had lost two of its own in the attacks. Rugby players Mark Bingham and Jeremy Glick had battled hijackers on board United Airlines Flight 93. The players began the day at a church service to mark the occassion[303] and when it came time to play they delivered a strong showing. Twelve years earlier the USA had by forty-five points against Ireland and had conceded eight tries. In 2011 however the USA conceded only three tries in losing 22-10 and prevented Ireland from scoring a bonus point. The match showcased how far the USA had come since 1999 and that overtime the USA could well make the step to becoming a Tier One rugby nation. The team then faced Russia who was making its debut appearance at a Rugby World Cup. The USA scored the games only try in the first half and then was happy to play out the secondhalf to complete a 13-6 win. Its remaining matches were against two Tier One sides and were played four days apart. The USA decided to field a second-string team against Australia and lost 67-5 before ending its campaign with a 27-10 loss against Italy.

The tournament was a testiment to how much progress can be made when enough players are exposed to professionalism. It was the first time in Rugby World Cup history that the USA had fielded a side made up predominantly of players who ply their trade as professional players.[304] The loss against Australia underlined this as the team was predominantly amateur. Moreover, secondrower Hayden Smith was the only player to start against both Russia and Australia. The trend of having more professional players at each Rugby World Cup does not look like slowing down and this will aid the development of the USA Eagles into the future. Exposing players to professionalism will continually be simplified due to the improvements that have occurred off the field in recent times. The USA has an ever improving domestic setup and joins Argentina and Canada in the Americas Rugby Championship which is ideal for fringe players.

Like anything in American sport rugby needs to be marketable to a large audience if it is to succeed. The annual USA Sevens has continued to be successful and the move originally from Los Angeles to San Diego and then on to Las Vegas has been highly successful. The 2012 USA Sevens featured over 64,000 spectators with a North American record of 30,112 attending the event on the Saturday, which was the second of three days.[305] Tournament director, Dan Lyle said "Growing the game in the States is a challenge as we know but it can be done, we are proving it can be done and we are on our way." Lyle sees a great future for the event, saying it could become as big as the biggest of them all, the Hong Kong Sevens. He said: "I think with the third day we could become as big as Hong Kong now, we are a similar size stadium, 40,000 give or take, so we could put 120,000 through the gates over the three days. We are similar to Hong Kong and Dubai in that we are not exactly indigenous to rugby. While they have a 30-year head start they are still at 40 or 50% from their own market and we are 75% out of ours."[306]

Las Vegas is certain to stay on as a host venue for the Sevens World Series but looms as having more to offer than just an annual leg. Las Vegas could very well host the Rugby Sevens World Cup event in 2017, should it continue. It would be the first mens World Cup to be played in North America. There is plenty to support the idea such as the successful hosting of the IRB Junior World Trophy which was played in June 2012 in Salt Lake City. The tournament was a massive success both on and off the field. The USA won the competition after defeating Japan 37-33 in front off a capacity crowd at Murray Rugby Park. The victory meant the USA qualified for the 2013 IRB Junior World Championship which will be played in France. Off the field the event helped the sports profile in the country. The CEO of USA Rugby Nigel Melville said: "It's an exciting time for Rugby in the USA. It continues to develop and grow stronger. Being able to attract international events like the JWRT to our shores certainly helps us in that process."[307]

The role of Sevens is paramount to the future development of a superior USA Eagles team. USA Rugby is investing heavily in Rugby Sevens ahead of the 2016 Rio de Janeiro Olympic Games. Preparation is well under way with a milestone in the history of rugby in the USA having occurred on November 30 2011. The union announced that it would be signing twenty-three athletes as professional rugby players. It is a joined venture between USA Rugby and the USA Olympic Committee (USOC) and includes both mens and womens rugby. The players have been given full training in the Olympic Training Center in Chula Vista, California. The group includes fifteen men and eight women. Their contracts provide monthly stipends, meals, world-class training facilities, and high-performance support services at the OTC.[308]

The development of rugby in the USA has been noted by groups outside the USA to the extent that USA Rugby was asked to make a bid to host Rugby World Cup 2023. The bid could include Canada as a co-host, according to Nigel Melville who confirmed that the union had been asked to bid, but did not say who had had made the request."We were asked during the World Cup, whether we would be prepared to bid for 2023. Also Canada is interested in some sort of joint bid ... could we do it together as North America? There would be opportunities in Toronto and Vancouver, and obviously bringing the tournament to North America would be a tremendous boost for us all."[309] The likelihood of the USA hosting soon is not strong for the simple reason that the USA does not have a track record, outside of the Rugby Sevens.

Argentina could be a useful guide to the possibility of a World Cup in North America. It has a record of moving matches around the country and attracting good crowds. It also has a record of receiving few home test matches. The USA's regular home venue of Infinity Park is too small for World Cup consideration but Houston is not. The city hosted the USA v Italy in June 2012 with a record crowd of over 17,000 in attendance.[310] A World Cup in Argentina would be much more significant to the chances of the USA hosting the tournament than would a World Cup in any other Tier One Nation. Argentina and Italy are the only Tier One Nations to never have hosted World Cup matches but they are vastly different to one another due to the geographical size of Argentina. Only Australia is bigger but Australia had already co-hosted a World Cup before 2003 and it had an extensive history of international rugby with many more incoming matches than Argentina. The USA needs to not only host teams like Italy in large venues but also other teams too. The USA v Canada should not be hosted at Infinity Park. The venue is still good for receiving the likes of Georgia and Uruguay but bigger venues are needed for other matches and it is essencial that they are spread around.

In regional rugby terms the USA and Argentina are neighbors. They both have similar organizational policies with both having recently moved to professionalism. Playing numbers have been increasing significantly in both countries as the profile of rugby has grown greatly, particularly in the twenty-first century. They are both future candidates to host a Rugby World Cup but the next step for both unions countries should not be the same. The greatest legacy of Argentina hosting Rugby World Cup 2023 from a U.S. standpoint is that it will provide genuine insight that could see North America host too. NACRA's close relations with CONSUR have long been strong and they would improve with a World Cup in South America. Above all else the Americas would be taken much more seriously by virtue of Argentina hosting a Rugby World Cup. The historical stereotypes surrounding international rugby would be further eroded with North America being a winner.

Uruguay
Uruguay has a record in the South American Championship which makes it the undisputed second best rugby nation in South America. It is a two time Rugby World Cup participant and has a better record than regular tournament participants including Japan, Namibia and Romania at World Cups. The country also has a long rugby history, longer in fact that all of Argentina, Australia, New Zealand and South Africa. In May 2011 the IRB's weekly rugby program, Total Rugby, featured a piece on the oldest rugby club outside of Europe. The club is not from a traditional power or former English colony such as Australia or New Zealand but rather it is from Uruguay. The Montevideo Cricket Club (MVCC) has rugby roots going back to 1861 with the first match on record being listed as taking place in 1880 between Uruguyans and British settlers. 2011 marked the 150th anniversary of the club and the Twickenham Museum of Rugby recognized it as the eighth oldest rugby club in the world. The seven older clubs are all either British or Irish.[311]

The club has played in the Uruguayan national championship, the Campeonato Uruguayo de Rugby since it was created in 1950 and had its first ever match in the championship against Carrasco Polo Club which has won a staggering twenty-four national titles since 1950. The MVCC was successful in the early days of Uruguayan championship rugby, winning the national title in 1951, 1953 and 1956 but since this time it has been unable to compete at the same level. Instead clubs such as Carrasco Polo Club, the Old Christians Club and Old Boy's have become the Uruguayan rugby powerhouses. Between them the three clubs have won fifty-four of the sixty-five titles in the history of the Campeonato Uruguayo de Rugby. The last time a team other than one of these three were champions was in 1975. Carrasco Polo won the 2011 Championship while the 2010 champions were Old Boy's who, coincidentally, were crowned champions for the first time after it had been joint champions with Club de Rugby La Cachila in 1975.[312]

The Old Christians Club is arguably the most famous Uruguayan rugby club abroad. It made a significant contribution to global rugby in 1972, but not by playing. The country's most well-known contribution to the global game did not occur at a Rugby World Cup but actually far earlier. It was in 1972 when a plane carrying members of the Old Christians Club crashed in the Andes Mountains while flying from Mendoza to Chile. Caught in freezing conditions without any communication the players and family members of the Old Christians Club rugby team faced the impossible. The story has been well documented, notably in a book titled *Alive: The Story of the Andes Survivors* written by British writer Piers Paul Read and published in 1974 and a 1993 movie directed by Frank Marshall simply titled *Alive*. It is one of the most amazing stories of survival in human history.

The flight departed with forty passengers and five crew members on October 12 from Montevideo. The plane was forced to make a stop on the Argentine side of the Andes due to bad weather conditions that day. On October 13 the plane took off from Mendoza flying a different route to Santiago due to bad weather conditions but the pilot miscalculated the turn through the Planchon Pass and the plane crashed. After losing its tail and wings it slid down hill before stopping at an elevation of 11,800 feet. The crash killed twelve of the passengers and crew members and severly injured others.[313] Rescue efforts were abandoned ten days after the crash leaving the survivors starving high in the freezing mountains. Having no food, the survivors resorted to eating the flesh of those who had not survived the crash.

After two months Nando Parrado, Roberto Canessa and Antonio Vizintín said goodbye to their colleagues and left the site to search for a way out of the mountains. They endured physical and emotional trauma which tested them to the limit. They had nowhere near enough water to attempt what amounted to a 40 mile trek. The trio set off westward, scaling a peak. Upon reaching the top it became evident that they were surrounded by mountains and that much lay ahead if they were to be rescued.[314] Parrado and Canessa continued on while it was agreed that Vizintín would return to the wreckage so that the food they had would give them a greater opportunity of surviving and reaching help. The exhaustion that they faced almost led to their deaths but after ten days they descended from the mountains finding a river and seeing what looked like cows in the distance.

On December 20 Canessa spotted a man on a horse on the opposite side of the river. The following day the pair woke up very early, still alone. There were two men wearing farmers clothing on the other side of the river but they could not talk due to the extreme noise produced from the river. Parrado wrote with a pencil *Vengo de un avión que cayó em las montañas...* The message read "I come from a plane that fell in the mountains. I am from Uruguay. We have been walking for ten days. My friend is wounded. There are more than fourteen people injured on the plane. We need to get out of here quickly and we don't know how. We don't have food. We are weak. When are you going to come get us? Please. We can't cope with walking. Where are we?"[315] Parrado threw it across the river wrapped around a stone and the farmer rushed to get help after having thrown them some bread.[316]

Ten hours after leaving the farmer returned with medical help and a military escort to rescue Canessa and Parrado. News of their remarkable survival had reached journalists who reported the news on December 21[317] while fourteen people remained in the plane. Parrado assisted the Chilean military in locating the plane and after being trapped in the mountains for seventy-two days all sixteen survivors were rescued by December 23. Upon returning to Uruguay the survivors were welcomed as national heroes. In his book *Miracle in the Andes*, Parrado recalls that their survival became a motive of national pride. In his words their ordeal was celebrated as a glorious adventure. So much so that the population compared it to Uruguay's heroic conquest of the 1950 FIFA World Cup[318] in which Uruguay defeated Brazil in the final in Rio de Janeiro.

Should Argentina host Rugby World Cup 2023 the tournament could be used to honor the memories of those involved in the tragedy – both the survivors and the deceased. The tournament would be an opportunity for all of South America and not just for Argentina. 2023 will mark the 51st anniversary of the plane crash and should the tournament continue to be played during September and October, like it will in 2015 and 2019, then the anniversary would take place likely around the time of the Semi Finals. A host of possibilities exist such as having the incident remembered at the opening ceremony with a tribute being made with the survivors present in unison with Argentineans. Rugby has an ability to bring people together and Parrado, Canessa and the others are every bit as much important to the history of South American rugby as are Los Pumas.

A powerful theme to emerge from Nando Parrado's book is how rugby in Uruguay is a sport based on collectivity. Rugby helped shape his life and tought him invaluable lessons which would help him during his time in the Andes. He learned that the sport teaches not just values of friendship but also gives players character that units them as brothers. He noted comparisons in rugby to his catholic upbringing – discipline, devotion, austerity and respect. He learned this at the Stella Maris High School in Montevideo and was also encouraged to ignore the natural passion of soccer. While he learned values from rugby soccer was teaching people how to be selfish. Soccer's foundations of glory to the point's scorer are not replicated in rugby where it did not matter who scored a try it belonged to all fifteen players on the field. Over time Parrado came to see that the Christian Brotherhood had been correct in promoting rugby to them and not soccer.[319]

Twenty-Seven years after the plane crash, Uruguay became the second South American country to play in a Rugby World Cup when it made its debut at Rugby World Cup 1999. Uruguay had qualified after defeating Chile and Paraguay in South American qualifying matches and subsequently defeating European and African teams – Portugal and Morocco in repercharge. Los Teros were grouped with Scotland, South Africa and Spain and played all three of its matches in Scotland. Spain was also debuting at the World Cup which made their clash a virtual World Cup final for both teams. Uruguay was captained by the oldest player in the tournament, Diego Ormachea whom at 40 years of age performed well, scoring one of Uruguay's five tries against Spain. The South Americans won the match 27-15 while all of the European's points came from the boot of Andrei Kovalenko.

After defeating Spain Los Teros faced Scotland at Murrayfield and played well considering it was a World Cup debutant. The tournament featured two other debutants but neither won a match. Scotland had come off a loss against South Africa but there was never any real doubt that it would win its two remaining pool matches. Scotland completed a 43-12 win over Uruguay in a match that was overshadowed by a poor attendance of 9,463. But it got worse for Uruguay's third match as a record low of 3,000 attended the match at Hampton Park in Glasgow.[320] The match was against the reigning World Champions, South Africa who were heavy favorites and expected to have won by a massive margin. The Springboks scored five tries to zero in a 39-3 victory that was more a testament to how well Uruguay had defended than anything else. The South Americans were unable to score a try but the side did very well in defence compared to a number of other sides in the same tournament.

The thirty-six point loss was comparably a major victory for Uruguay. Elsewhere match results between Tier One nations and teams from Tier Two and Three had been significantly different. In Pool B Italy had lost 101-03 against New Zealand and Tonga had lost 101-10 against England. Canada had defeated Namibia 72-11 in Pool C and Wales had beaten Japan 64-15 in Pool D. These results were similar to what was expected of South Africa against Los Teros. Uruguay´s points in the game were scored by Diego Aguirre of Carrasco Polo Club. He went on to play in France for Union Sportive Tours rugby in the Fédérale 1 in 2004-2005 and he captained Uruguay at Rugby World Cup 2003 and was also the teams leading points scorer with nineteen points in the tournament. He retired as the highest capped Uruguayan of all time in 2007 with 74 test caps.[321]

Uruguay succeeded in qualifying for back-to-back Rugby World Cup tournaments after Los Teros qualified ahead of the USA to be Americas 2. The South Americans were given a tough assignment - drawn in Pool C alongside England, Georgia, Samoa and South Africa. The team began its campaign against the Springboks in the Western Australian captial of Perth. Los Teros lost the match 72-6 but were not as dominated as the scoreline suggests. Uruguay actually put up a good fight before fatigue set in after the interval. It did not get any easier though as four days latter Uruguay played Samoa. Uruguay was given a split schedule for the tournament with four days separating its first two matches and again four more separating its final two matches after a thirteen day break. As such Uruguay had to rotate a number of players and despite scoring two tries, the South Americans were overpowered by Samoa who won 60-13.

The key match for Uruguay was its third one – against Georgia in Sydney. The two earlier matches were preparation for Georgia while the final match, v England was of secondary importance. The crucial game was the most winnable one and Uruguay was extremely motivated for the occasion. It was clear before the kick-off with players singing the Uruguayan national anthem with more determination than in its previous matches. Uruguay played its best rugby of the tournament scoring three tries to zero in a 24-12 victory. One of the telling images of the tournament occurred after the final whistle. Uruguayan players ran into the stands to celebrate the win with their supporters. It was a lasting memory of importance for Uruguayan rugby and the Rugby World Cup. There is more to play for than just winning the tournament itself and Uruguay showed this vividly.

It was mission accomplished and the final match against England was the team´s worst performance of the tournament. The eventual champions won the match 111-13 but Uruguay did have its moments. Former Stade Français prop Pablo Lemoine scored a good try while backrower Rodrigo Capó Ortega put in a huge tackle on his opposite, Lawrence Dallaglio which neither player will likely ever forget. Capó Ortega was just 22 years old but was already playing professional rugby in France. He joined Castres in 2002 and to this day remains at the Top 14 club having made more than 200 appearances.[322] He went on to captain his country and led the team into represcharge against Portugal with the winner advancing to Rugby World Cup 2007. Uruguay was favorite to qualify as Portugal had never played in a World Cup before but the Europeans won the first match 12-5 in Lisbon. Uruguay responded by winning the second 18-12 but ultimately did not qualify as Portugal had scored one more point on aggregate. It was heartbreaking for Los Teros but the team could not blame anybody else as they played 79 minutes with one less player after secondrower Juan Bado had been red carded in the first minute of play.[323]

Uruguay faced a similar situation to qualify for Rugby World Cup 2011. Los Teros had topped South America but lost against the USA. This put Uruguay into repercharge and Los Teros faced Kazakhstan who had qualified as Asia 2 behind Japan. Uruguay won the match 44-7 at the Estadio Charrúa in Montevideo to advance to face Romania in the Rugby World Cup Final Place Play-Off. Romania had reached the final after defeating Tunisia (Africa 2) in Buzau. The first of two matches took place at the Estadio Charrúa and Uruguay managed to turn around a deficit to draw the match 21-21 at fulltime. It was, in effect, a loss because it put the teams at 0-0 heading into the return match in Bucharest. Romania was a different team at home and was able to put in a five tries to two performance. The 39-21 win secured the final spot at Rugby World Cup 2011 and meant it retained its proud record of having played at every Rugby World Cup.

Uruguay is firmly established as the fourth best rugby nation in the Americas and it has good relations with all of Argentina, Canada and the USA. Uruguay continues to face Argentina in the South American Championship and also has faced both Canada and the USA in the defunct Churchill Cup and in friendly internationals. Like Argentina, Uruguay has had a comparably small number of international matches in comparison to similarly ranked teams in the IRB World Rankings. Between Rugby World Cup 2003 and its repercharge matches against Portugal in 2007 Uruguay played fifteen internationals. It had five games in 2004 with wins of 20-13 against Chile and 92-8 against Venezuela in the South American Championship. Los Teros finished second in the tournament behind Argentina. In October Uruguay hosted Georgia and Portugal defeating Georgia 17-10 and Portugal 30-3. In 2005 it played five tests for two wins and three loses. Its lonely home test was a 24-18 win over Japan, the only match ever played between the two nations. Uruguay played five tests in 2006 too with the final two being qualifying matches against the USA. It had earlier faced Portugal in Montevideo winning 20-14 but would have no test matches in 2007 before facing the team in its home and away repercharge matches.

Consolation for the lack of preparation for the World Cup qualifying matches came later. Having been eliminated Uruguay played Italy, Spain and Chile to end a forgettable year against Europerans. Los Teros lost to Italy and Spain in Montevideo but defeated Chile in Santiago. After Rugby World Cup 2007 Uruguay received a much improved calendar with the matches doubling in some years compared to the total that it had played between 2003 and 2007. In June 2008 Uruguay played three tests in the IRB Nations Cup. The South Americans lost against Georgia and Romania but defeated Russia 23-19. In November Uruguay played in Sandy, Utah in a preview of qualifying matches for Rugby World Cup 2011. The South Americans started well but were defeated 43-9 by the USA. 2008 ended with a 46-12 win in Montevideo against Chile while 2009 started with Uruguay hosting the South American Championship. In total Uruguay played eight tests that year but was disappointing. Uruguay defeated Brazil, Chile and Paraguay but lost to Argentina, Romania, Russia and the USA. 2010 was similar with wins over Brazil, Chile, Paraguay and Kazakhstan but loses against Argentina, Canada, Romania and Russia.

In failing to defeat Romania in 2010 Uruguay essentially began its preparation for Rugby World Cup 2015 in 2011. It did not have the best of years, though. An experimental team played in the South American Championship in Argentina with Los Teros defeating Brazil and humbling Paraguay 102-6 but ultimately having a bad tournament, losing against Chile for the first time since 2002. Los Teros toured Portugal and Spain in November for two tests after warming up against Los Jaguares. Los Teros turned around a loss against the Argentine side by defeating Portugal 16-9 in Lisbon. It was potentially a fresh start to leave behind the dark years that have followed Rugby World Cup 2003. Uruguay rose to 19th in the IRB World Rankings and could have gone higher but lost 16-13 against Spain after being 16-0 down at halftime.

Uruguay returned to the IRB Nations Cup for the 2012 tournament. Its inclusion was to give it a chance of playing against similarly placed sides from Upper Third Tier and Second Tier rugby nations.[324] Six teams participated in the tournament which was organized with a view to growing and developing Rugby around the world. Central to this strategic aim is providing Tier Two and Tier Three Unions with an expanded and competitive international competition calendar. Uruguay played three matches losing 29-9 against Romania and 19-13 against Russia. Los Teros saved its best for last by defeating Portugal 35-7. Overall the team's performance was sufficient to suggest it could qualify for Rugby World Cup 2015 with Russia potentially being its repercharge opponent if the higher ranked nations of Georgia and Romania qualify as Europe 1 and 2.

The IRB Nations Cup has been a welcomed tournament for Uruguayan rugby. The superior international calendar has not eliminated one problem – a lack of home tests. Uruguay has been playing more away matches than home matches and by a noticeable margin. Since Rugby World Cup 2003 Uruguay has played thirty-seven tests abroad and only nineteen at home.[325] Like Argentina its geographical position has seen it receive the short end of the stick in international rugby. The lack of international rugby in Uruguay has been so high that since Rugby World Cup 2007 the only home matches have been against South American opposition or have been World Cup Qualifyers. While Uruguay has faced Georgia, Portugal, Romania, Russia and Spain since 2007 all matches have been played in Europe. The 2011 tour of Iberia was competitive but needs to be played more regularly. The same teams should be playing in Uruguay and Chile similarly to Argentina hosting one or more Six Nations teams every June. Change may be happening at long last as Portugal toured Chile and Uruguay in November 2012.

Another of the major obstacles that has complicated matters for Los Teros has been the wide gap between Uruguayan club rugby and international level. Argentina worked together with Uruguay and Chile to try by having both nations compete in the Campeonato Argentino de Mayores – the Argentine National Championship. They were added to the Zona Campeonato, or the Championship Division to compete against the eight leading Argentine provinces. Divided into two pools of five Chile faced Córdoba, Salta, San Juan and Tucumán in pool 1. While Uruguay faced Buenos Aires, Cuyo, Mar del Plata and Rosario in pool 2.[326] Both Chile and Uruguay won one of their four matches in the competition. Chile defeated San Juan 28-27 and Uruguay defeated Rosario 22-15. The inclusion of foreign teams was exciting for the region and is a sign that CONSUR has its focus in the right direction. Such endeavours are likely to assist the development of both nations to enable them to be stronger on and off the field. The invaluable experience of providing the players with a higher level of rugby can only help make the test teams improve. The relationship is only going to become tighter over time and with it the benefits of Argentina hosting a Rugby World Cup will spill over its borders to a greater extent.

Chile
In rugby terms what is good for Argentina is good for Chile. Argentina's western neighbour is a Third Tier rugby nation that has shown promise but has been unable to kick-on. It has been a permanent feature of the world's top 30 nations

since the establishment of the IRB World Rankings spending the majority of the time ranked as the 24th best team in the world.[327] Like Uruguay, Chile has a small contingent of professional rugby players but it does not have any clear stars to compare to Rodrigo Capó Ortega. Perhaps the most notable Chilean is Sergio Valdés who has had a long career in France, mainly in the Pro d2 but also in the Top 14. He has played for Stade Aurillacois, Racing Métro, Auch and since 2011, Pau. Another player of note is Cristian Westenenk who has played for Manly in the Shute Shield competition in Australia.

Like Uruguay the majority of players at test level are not professionals and it has clearly impacted on the team's performances. Chile has remained a country with few players exposed to professional rugby while both Georgia and the USA had teams at Rugby World Cup 2011 whose starting players were principally professionals. Results against South American opposition have essentially been unchanged in the professional era with Chile predominantly, but not always, being third in the continent. In contrast, matches against teams from other continents show a drop off in performance from Chile. In 1999 Los Condores hosted Spain in a pre World Cup match for the Europeans. Chile won 20-18 but most remarkably was that it was a one off match and was Chile's first match against a European nation since hosting and defeating Spain in 1995. Since then Chile has faced Georgia and the USA twice each and has a record of one win and one loss against both countries. Similar to Uruguay Los Condores have not progressed in the years following Rugby World Cup 2003.

Like Argentina and Uruguay Chile is another that has had to endure a low number of international matches. The wins against the USA and Georgia did not see the country receive regular international competition outside of the South American Championship. The Pumas struggle, in many ways, has been a South American rugby struggle. The push to be added into a Tier One competition coincided with a drop-off of incoming tours to not only Uruguay but also Chile. The last time Chile hosted a European team was in 2007 with Spain defeating Chile 30-25 in Santiago before that years World Cup tournament had started. Test match rugby in general has been thin with Chile playing as few as two tests per year on more than one occasion. The biggest year was 2002 when Chile played ten tests. The number was so high due to Rugby World Cup Qualification. The IRB had altered the system for Rugby World Cup 2003 following Argentina's automatic qualification. It combined both North and South America to have Canada, Chile, Uruguay and the USA battle it out for two qualification places and the third best to enter repercharge.

All four of the participants won matches and three of the four were very evenly matched. Chile started with a win over Uruguay and also won its home match against the USA. It was not able to play so well on the road however as Chile lost against all three and also lost its home match against Canada. It had, nonetheless finished joined with the USA on ten points but was eliminated by virtue of the USA having a superior points for and against record. The qualifying system was a great innovation for the Americas and it gave Chile a schedule which has since not come close to having been replicated. The exciting qualifying format proved to be a one off as it would not be repeated for Rugby World Cup 2007, perhaps understandably due to Argentina needing to qualify unlike in 2003. But it could have been repeated for 2011 or 2015 but instead the IRB has decided to have North and South America separated until the final stage.

Having defeated two teams that had qualified for Rugby World Cup 2003 there was reason to believe that Chile could be turning the corner. Chile needed more test rugby and in a year with limited opportunities it received a home test in 2003 against Fiji, losing 41-16. The following year it hosted both Portugal and Georgia winning 30-24 against Georgia but losing 28-9 against Portugal who were the then European Nations Cup Champions. Chile toured Europe in 2005 to play against the same two sides but was unable to achieve the same kind of success. Portugal won 31-18 in Lisbon and Georgia won 29-6 in Tblissi. Since then Chile has not played a match outside of South America. Conversely, both Georgia and Portugal played at Rugby World Cup 2007 with Georgia having a good tournament even though it had lost against Chile three years earlier.

Without additional tours Chile has, instead simply played in the South American Championship. It has played two matches against non-South American opposition – the 2007 match against Spain and a test against Tonga in 2010. The clash with Tonga was played in September and as such professional players were not available for selection. Chile was missing players including Cristian Westenenk, Sergio Valdés, Francisco de la Fuente, Cristián González and Sebastián Gajardo while Tonga fielded a domestic based amateur side. It meant that the test match was between the best Chilean based players and the best Tongan based players and it turned out to be an evenly fought contest. According to IRB World Rankings it was the 24th best team hosting the 16th best but the teams were considered vastly different due to Tonga having a World Cup record of appearing in every tournament except for 1991 and Chile having never qualified.

The scoring started after ten minutes of play in the first half when Los Condores flyhalf, Javier Reyes, kicked a penalty. Tonga hit back in the 16th minute with a try to Taumei Hikila which Michael Toloke converted before Reyes slotted a second penalty goal in the 33rd minute. Tonga responded immediately with Damien Fakafanua scoring Tonga's second try and Toloke adding the extras. A blow out was not on the cards however, as winger Diego Schachner scored for Chile at the end of the first half. It took Tonga three minutes after the restart to score again through Petuliki Mateo, which Toloke failed to convert and at this stage Tonga was winning 22-11. Reyes kicked three penalties - in the 44th, 48th and 57th minute and replacement Francisco Cruz slotted another in the 76th minute. Tonga kicked one in the 46th minute and Toloke also scored a second half try but Chile kept fighting. Tonga was being penalized for constant violations and as the game drew to a close Tonga collapsed a Chilean maul close to the try line which gave the referee no choice but to award a penalty try to the hosts. With Cruz's conversion Los Condores had ended the match proudly to close proceedings at 32-30 to Tonga.[328]

Chile's premier domestic rugby competition is the Torneio Ado Super 12 by Hyundai, or simply the Super 12. It is a twelve team competition played from June to October. All teams face each other in eleven rounds before the top four meet in Semi Finals and the winners dispute the final. Rugby is practiced throughout Chile but, like the population it is concentrated in and around the capital. Of the teams disputing the 2012 Super 12 eight are from Santiago– Alumni S.C., Craighouse Old Boys and Girls (COBS), Old Boy's, Old Red's, Old Georgian's, Principe de Wales Country Club (PWCC), Stade Français and Universidad Católica. The remaining four are from the cities of Viña del Mar and Concepción which both have two teams each in the 2012 competition. Viña RC and Old Mackayans RFC are from Viña del Mar while Old John's and Los Troncos are from Concepción. The Super 12 is a healthy national competition which is seeking to resolve the problem of Chile not being able to transfer its success at junior level to seniors. Despite having a healthy number of 16,000 rugby players distributed throughout Chile's sixteen regions[329] Chile has been unable to consistently deliver against Uruguay. This alone has haulted the growth of Los Condores. Chile has both many more rugby players and a much larger population. Uruguay has a population of 3.3 million compared to Chile whose population is slightly more than 17 million.[330] While Uruguay had 7,460 players in 2011[331], Chile had over 9,000 more.

At junior level Chile has a solid record. It has competed at the IRB Junior World Trophy on three occasions – 2008, 2009 and 2012. It has finished in the top three on two occasions with its best performance coming in the inaugural edition of the competition which Chile hosted in 2008. All sixteen matches were played in

Santiago and it was a great tournament for South America as the final was disputed by Chile and Uruguay. The Chileans had won Pool A with three solid victories - 33-10 against the Cook Islands, 20-6 against Namibia and 14-3 against Romania. The run came to an end in the final after Uruguay was crowned champions with a 20-8 victory. It was a significant occasion and was well attended with close to 7,000 spectators attending the final. Uruguay had earlier defeated South Korea 67-8, Jamaica 82-0 and Georgia 20-16.[332] Upon confirming Chile to host the tournament the IRB's Head of Rugby Services, Mark Egan said "The IRB is delighted that Chile and the city of Santiago will host the IRB Junior World Trophy next year. Chile has a heritage of hosting major Rugby Tournaments including the FIRA run 32-team Under 19 Championship in 2001, an IRB Sevens World Series Tournament in 2002 and is also a regular host of CONSUR Regional Tournaments."[333]

Chile finished third in the 2009 competition. After winning two out of three pool matches it went on to defeat hosts, Kenya in the Third Place match 19-17. It had impressed against South Korea and Papua New Guinea winning 50-17 and 50-22 but lost 26-20 against Romania who went on to win the tournament. Chile returned for the fifth edition of the tournament in 2012 and started its campaign impressively, defeating Russia 53-19. It finished third in the Pool, however as it lost 54-25 against hosts the USA and 41-14 against Tonga. But Chile added to its list of victories against Rugby World Cup nations by defeating Canada 43-31 to finish in fifth place. This meant that although Chile has never qualified for a Rugby World Cup tournament it has defeated Canada, Namibia, Romania and Russia at the junior level. Its success at the junior level and its ability to successfully host tournaments were again recognized as Chile was chosen as the host nation for the 2013 IRB Junior World Trophy.[334] This will make Chile the first country to host the event twice.

Chile's confirmation as tournament hosts came two months after a history making result for Chilean rugby. On Saturday May 05 the Chilean Under 20 team defeated the Argentine Under 19 team (Los Pumitas) by 33-14. It marked the first time in the century long history of Chilean rugby that a national selection had defeated an Argentine rival.[335] Argentina did have an age disadvantage but this should not take away anything from Chile's triumph. Eight players from the Argentine team played in the 2012 IRB Junior World Championship the following month. The result puts Chile in a good position to prepare a quality team to participate in the qualifying matches for Rugby World Cup 2015. At the senior level Chile also had a victory against a respected opponent that same weekend. Los Condores defeated the Ontario Blues 19-17.[336]

The results highlight the need for more regular future home matches at both the junior and senior level. Chile should certainly be a stronger team in the coming years as its top domestic players can now, compete in the Campeonato Argentino. The participation of Argentina in The Rugby Championship has spilt over to Chile with advertizing packages to attend Argentina v South Africa in Mendoza appearing on Chilean rugby sites, including the home page of the Federación de Rugby de Chile (FERUCHI). Chile's involvement in the Campeonato Argentino is also likely to further enhance the strong relationship between the governing bodies of the two countries – the UAR and FERUCHI. Moreover, Chile has a strong relationship with Uruguay both on and off the field. It will likely always have a special bond with Uruguay due to the plane crash and subsequent events of 1972.

Brazil
The largest country in South America and the fifth most populated in the world[337], Brazil is a country experiencing significant progress in rugby. Like Chile it has more rugby players than Uruguay and rugby is also a sport played in most of the country. In 2011 it was confirmed that for the first time ever Brazil had 10,000 registrered players.[338] However, a greater number of players does not always mean stronger performances. Brazil has a growing number of players but the majority continues to play in low level competitions. This is what continues to separate Uruguay from both Chile and Brazil but the gap is decreasing in both cases. Both have been growing sufficiently to have realistic chances of over time rising to the required standard to qualify for a Rugby World Cup. The growth has occurred despite a lack of international rugby for the countries test teams.

The sport has traditionally been limited to the countries southern and south-eastern states, with São Paulo being particularly dominant. More recently it has been changing with the sport spreading so much that there are few states that do not have rugby clubs. The growth has been recent and has been so extensive that the number of rugby clubs has increased to give Brazil over seven times as many clubs today as it had in 2005. Today Brazil has close to two hundred and thirty clubs while in 2005 there were only forty.[339] In 2012 there were official tournaments with registered players in the states of Minas Gerais, Paraná, Rio de Janeiro, Rio Grande do Sul, Santa Catarina and São Paulo. In addition there were a number of other tournaments across Brazil, mainly interstate but not entirely. The state of Mato Grosso do Sul, for instance, had four teams playing a reduced version of rugby – twenty minute halves.

The expansion has seen the sport's historical base in São Paulo city eroded. The city continues to have a massive footprint in Brazilian rugby but it no longer has the strongest team in the country. The most successful team in the country's history is São Paulo Athletic Club (SPAC) which has won the Brazilian Championship twelve times since its first edition in 1964. It won the championship six times in a row from 1964-1969 and then five times in a row from 1974-1978. It has, however, not won since 1999. SPAC together with Bandeirantes, Pasteur and Rio Branco represent the four strongest clubs historically in São Paulo and together they have won twenty-two Brazilian titles and continue to be amongst the strongest teams in the country. Other teams from São Paulo have also previously been strong. So much that in the history of Brazilian rugby São Paulo clubs have accounted for forty-one of the fifty championship winning teams.

More recently it has not been a team from São Paulo city winning. Since 2002 São José Rugby has won eight national titles and is the largest contributor of players to the national team. The city is located 94KM from São Paulo and is one of only three non-São Paulo clubs to have won the Brazilian Championship. The two others are Niteroí from Rio de Janeiro state which has won the title six times, most recently in 1990 and Desterro from Florianopolis in Santa Catarina state which has won three times, most recently in 2005. The seven mentioned clubs are still amongst the strongest in Brazil with all competing in the 2012 Campeaonto Brasileiro de Rugby, or the Super 10. The three others are Belo Horizonte, Curitiba and Farrapos from the southern city of Bento Gonçalves. The competition expanded from eight to ten teams in 2011 with Belo Horizonte and Farrapos entering. This marked a change in Brazilian rugby as the fronteirs of the sports leading competition had expanded into the states Minas Gerais and Rio Grande do Sul.

Similar growth has occurred wherever established compeitions exist. The historical strength of clubs from São Paulo city meant teams from other parts of the state were not able to compete. New teams face a daunting task similar to a Third Tier nation facing a First Tier nation. This led to the creation of the Liga Paulista do Interior (LIPAR) in 2002. It was created by four clubs from the cities of Campinas, Jundiaí, Presidente Prudente and Ribeirão Preto in 2002 and has grown to become the largest league in Brazil. Its level of competition remains inferior to the level of the top sides in the state but has greatly assisted the development of new teams and a number have gone from LIPAR to play in the Paulista A or Paulista B competitions which are of a higher level and involve teams from the capital. For instance in 2010 the team from Ribeirão Preto, Raça

Ribeirão Rugby played in the Paulista A and won its opening match 21-14 against SPAC in São Paulo.[340] Raça Ribeirão's participation in the league saw a player, Marcelo Danesin selected for the national team. He would play for Brazil in 2010 and 2011 despite not playing at all in the Super 10. His selection was a sign of the future of Brazilian rugby and the potential that can be unlocked from further expansion away from the country's largest cities.

The emergence of new teams each year in official competitions has two points of origin – Argentina and Television. The rise of Los Pumas and the growth of Brazilian playing numbers and clubs are not coincidental at all. They are connected extensively so much so that the rivalry between the countries in soccer is not replicated in rugby. Brazilian rugby players are overwhelmingly followers of Los Pumas. Arguably the best player Brazil has ever produced, Fernando Portugal said: "For a long time we did not want to recognize the strength of Argentine rugby on the world stage. We didn't have many exchanges with the country, even though it is so close. Perhaps the rivalry between the two nations, as for example in soccer, has contributed to this fact. But today I have peace of mind in saying that we are proud of the achievements of Los Pumas and they represent South America so well on the world stage of this sport. We have begun to strengthen ties with this country to obtain more knowledge about the game."[341]

Fernando Portugal started playing rugby as a teenager. A native of São José dos Campos he was exposed to rugby at a younger age than most players. In his career he has been a Brazilian champion for São José and Bandeirantes and has played international rugby for Brazil, including captaining the Sevens team. He has also played professional rugby abroad. In 2005 he left Brazil in hope of playing professionally in Italy. He was signed to play in the second division, the Serie A for Segni and played for the club for two seasons before returning to Brazil. He has held down the inside centre position for Brazil throughout his career and one of his centre partners has been Moisés Duque. Aged 23, Duque was signed by French club Blagnac to play in the Fédérale 1 in 2012. He became the first Brazilian to play professionally in France[342] and could well go on to play in a higher division. Like Fernando Portugal, he is from São José dos Campos and has had a lot to do with the club becoming the best in Brazil.

São José dos Campos was the host city for Brazil's regional play-off against Trinidad & Tobago in 2008. Brazil won 24-12 which saw it advance to face Chile and Uruguay. It won 55-20 on aggregate following a 31-8 victory in Malabar. While it has been tough for Chile and Uruguay to host international rugby it has been even tougher for Brazil. The match against Trinidad & Tobago was the only time Brazil has played a home test since Rugby World Cup 2007. Since then all of its matches have taken place abroad. It has been a result of a lack of rugby in general but also Brazil's position as either the strongest from CONSUR B or the weakest from CONSUR A. Brazil entered CONSUR B in 2000 and hosted the inaugural edition in São Paulo and comfortably won the championship with a 53-0 win over Peru and a 30-12 win over Venezuela. Brazil defended its title over the next two years but finished second in 2003, 2004 and 2005. The 2003 tournament was won by Venezuela for the first time while Paraguay won in 2004 and 2005 after it had left CONSUR A to play in CONSUR B.

The rivalry between Brazil and Paraguay has always been important and from a Brazilian perpective it has been a key source for judging the contemporary national team. In total there have been nineteen matches between the countries. The first took place in 1970 with Brazil winning 12-3 in Asunción. Brazil had been the better team in the 1970's and 80's with six wins from the eight matches but it then lost seven in a row from 1991-2005. Since then, however Brazil has been firmly restablishing itself as the fourth best in South America. Brazil won all four matches from 2008-2011 and won the most recent match with a record 51-14 victory in Puerto Iguazú, Argentina. Brazil has also improved its performances against Chile and Uruguay in recent years. The last two home matches against either side were against Chile with Los Condores winning 46-6 in São Paulo in 2002 and 57-13 in 2005. Brazil entered CONSUR A in 2009 after being undefeated in CONSUR B from 2006-2008. It had nonetheless lost heavily against CONSUR A opposition in Rugby World Cup qualifying matches in 2009. Brazil was defeated 78-3 by Chile and 71-3 by Uruguay but has since done considerably better. It has not won against either side but has not come close to conceding as many points. Against Chile Brazil lost 31-08 in 2010, 25-6 in 2011 and 19-6 in 2012. Against Uruguay Brazil lost 26-10 in 2010, 39-18 in 2011 and 27-15 in 2012.

The improved results received attention internationally and Brazil was invited to face Hong Kong, Kenya and the United Arab Emirates in the 2011 Emirates Cup of Nations in Dubai. It was the first time Brazil had played test rugby outside of South America and Brazil entered the tournament with the intention of being champion. It was not to be, however as Brazil lost its opening match 27-25 against Kenya and its final match 37-3 against Hong Kong. Brazil did play well against the UAE, winning 66-3. As a result of the two losses Brazil dropped out of the World's Top 30 in the IRB World Rankings.[343] Brazil's participation was more of a discovery than anything else. For both players and officials it enabled them to better understand the demands of international rugby. No doubt the CBRu need to address the lack of matches in Brazil for the level of the national team to grow. While Brazil has not hosted test matches since 2008 it has hosted visiting teams such as Edinburgh University in 2011.

The lack of home tests is very different to Brazil's South American standing in Sevens rugby. Brazil has hosted the past two editions of the CONSUR Sevens and will also host the 2013 event. Both CONSUR and the CBRu have targeted the 2016 Olympic Games as key to Brazilian rugby and they are working together to see that Brazil can successfully stage the sporting event. The ambitions of the CBRu do not stop with the Olympic Games though. In 2011 the President of the CBRu, Sami Arap made it known that Brazil intends on being considered as a host nation for Rugby World Cup 2023.[344] Arap's intentions remain unknown, despite having said he intends on bidding. What he could have possibly been seeking was attention as Brazil is a country improving but one without an international program that meets its needs. One thing that Brazil needs is Argentina and it will continue to do so into the future. Fernando Portugal is a firm believer of this and he believes Argentina should host Rugby World Cup 2023. He said: "Rugby in Argentina is perceived as it is in some places in the world. It fills our eyes with envy to see what our "hermanos" (brothers) have done with this sport. Not only do I think that Argentina could host a Rugby World Cup, but it should. The world of rugby, in which the Argentines absurdly contribute to its growth, having players in almost every major world championship, must repay this work with a World Cup. And we will take a piece, since we're so close. Who knows some games could be held in Brazil?"[345]

14

Tier One Model

The division of rugby playing nations into tiers serves to establish a clear basis for present and future ability, setting a platform for sides to know where they lie and just how much work they need to do to advance to a superior tier and also not fall down to an inferior one. The IRB World Rankings has ninety-six nations but the top two tiers account for only the top eighteen sides.[346] Of the sides considered as being in the Top Two Tiers all except Georgia have competed at every Rugby World Cup since it became a twenty team tournament. The First Tier consists of ten sides - Australia, Argentina, England, France, Ireland, Italy, New Zealand, Scotland, South Africa and Wales. The same teams account for all places in the Six Nations Championship and The Rugby Championship. The Second Tier consists of eight sides - Canada, Fiji, Georgia, Japan, Romania, Samoa, Tonga and the United States of America. In New Zealand 2011 these eighteen sides were joined by Namibia and Russia. As expected, no Tier Two side made the Quarter Finals of the tournament and neither Namibia nor Russia won a match which goes to show the tier's are a good reflection of the global rugby order.

The Tier system was officially changed in 2008. Replacing it was a four category system which has identfied seventeen teams as belonging to the top category - High Performance. They are the same ten from the First Tier and seven of the eight from the Second Tier. The nation missing is Georgia which has been placed in the Performance category together with Namibia, Portugal, Russia, Spain and Uruguay. IRB Chairman, Bernard Lapasset said that: "Unions such as Georgia, Portugal, Spain, Namibia, Uruguay and Russia will benefit from increased development funding as Performance band Unions." The third category was termed Targeted and includes China, Germany, India and Mexico. The remaining teams were classified as Developmental. Lapasset commented on the four category setup in saying "This new banding structure better identifies Unions in terms of their development status and record on the international stage. It allows for a more specific development grant investment system based on a Union's potential to progress through the bands," said Lapasset.[347]

Despite neither the tiers nor the bands being geographically organized at all the IRB and Rugby World Cup Limited operate on a regional structure which in the case of Namibia, for instance, has seen the African nation qualify for the past four World Cup's, despite never having come close to winning a World Cup match. Namibia, a Tier Three nation, has been Africa's best for the past twelve years but has seemingly only participated at World Cup's due to Africa being given a direct qualifying spot. This controversy highlights a major failure of the global rugby authorities to create a fair system for all competitors. It gives African Tier Three sides a massive advantage over all Tier Three nations from all other regions - Asia, Europe, Oceania and the Americas. While Namibia qualified for New Zealand 2011 after defeating no teams from Rugby World Cup 1999, 2003 or 2007 Russia qualified after defeating teams from each of these World Cup's - Portugal, Romania and Spain.

The sides that Russia faced also happened to also have significantly higher placings in the IRB World Rankings than the sides Namibia played against. Russia officially qualified on February 27 2010[348] when it was ranked 16th in the IRB World Rankings. It qualified after drawing an official qualifying match against Romania which, at the time, was ranked 19th in the world. It had previously defeated Portugal which was ranked 21st in the world, Spain which was 23rd and Germany which was 26th. At the same time Namibia was ranked 22nd in the world. At this time Namibia had already qualified for the tournament having won the African section of Rugby World Cup qualification in November 2009.[349] At its time of qualifcation, Nambia was ranked 23rd in the world and qualified by virtue of defeating Tunisia in home and away matches. Tunisia was, at the time, ranked 28th in the world. Earlier Namibia had faced Cote d'Ivoire in home and away Semi Final qualification matches, drawing the first 13-13 and winning the second 54-14. While in the group stage Namibia had defeated Senegal 13-10 and Zimbabwe 35-21. Of these sides the highest ranked at the time of Namibia's official qualification was the Cote d'Ivoire which was 39th in the world. Senegal was 62nd and Zimbabwe was 46th. Morocco was ranked higher than these nations, in 32nd place but it had been eliminated by the Cote d'Ivoire.[350]

The automatic qualifying place handed to the top African side does not appear to be based on having the World's top twenty ranked nations compete at a Rugby World Cup. Instead it suggests that the IRB desires to ensure Africa is represented with South Africa and a Third Tier nation. The policy provides African nations with something to strive for and Namibia has faced a variety of different teams in the African final. In 1999 Namibia lost 20-17 against Tunisia but recovered to defeat Zimbabwe 32-26 to qualify for final round of African qualification. It was undefeated against the Cote d'Ivoire, Morocco and Zimbabwe and qualified as Africa 1. In 2003 Namibia qualified after having drawn a two match series with Tunisia on aggregate. Namibia won the first match 26-19 in Windhoek but lost the second 24-17 in Tunis. The tie was resolved by the number of tries scored and Namibia's superior total saw the Southern African nation qualify for Australia 2003. In 2007 Namibia defeated Morocco to qualify. Overall the competitiveness has been good in Africa but there have not been results at World Cup's to support the region being awarded an automatic spot. Zimbabwe lost all its matches in Rugby World Cup 1987 and 1991, the Cote d'Ivoire was winless in 1995 and Namibia has been winless in the four subsequent tournaments. Nevertheless Africa's guaranteed position has not come into question even though tournament performances and IRB World Rankings appear to suggest its more to do with geography than merit.

On a global scale the IRB World Rankings have come to have greater significance since Rugby World Cup 2007. The global rugby authorities decreased the number of qualifying teams from twelve to eight with not only the Quarter Finalists automatically qualifying but also the teams that finished third in each pool. This has meant Tier One teams are no longer involved in Qualifying matches and that some Tier Two teams are also able to directly qualify. For instance, Fiji's defeat of Wales in 2007 did not mean Wales needed to qualify as Wales finished third in its pool. It has cut down on the number of Tier Two teams involved in qualifying with Fiji and Tonga automatically qualifying for New Zealand 2011 alongside Italy and Ireland and Samoa and Tonga automatically qualifying for England 2015 alongside Italy and Scotland. The change from the model used previously sees the IRB divide the twelve automatic qualifiers into three groups of four teams. Known as bands they are drawn randomly slightly less than three years before a World Cup tournament to give the tournament organizers plenty of time to adequately plan the logistics of hosting the competition.

IRB Chairman Syd Millar commented that: "In an innovative move the IRB World Rankings will be used to seed the 12 automatic qualifiers from RWC 2007 in France into a draw for the four pools for RWC 2011. The Rankings are now very well established and provide us with a credible and succinct way of seeding teams for the Rugby World Cup pool draw. The pool draws for previous tournaments, including RWC 2007 in France, used results from each respective preceding tournament to seed teams for the allocation draw. However, the RWCL Board felt that the Rankings are a more accurate record of a team's position at any given time and will provide the best possible chance of evenly matched pools emerging from the draw."[351]

For Rugby World Cup 2011 the draw was conducted in December 2008 and by March 2009 match scheduling including venues was confirmed.[352] The tournament was all but ready well in advance and for 2015 it is going to be precisely the same with the draw taking place in December 2012 to replicate that of Rugby World Cup 2011. The tournament's twenty competing teams will be divided into five bands with the top three being the automatic qualifying teams from Rugby World Cup 2011. They are to be officially allocated into Band 1, Band 2 or Band 3 depending on where they are ranked on December 03 2012. The top four according to IRB World Rankings will make up Band 1, the countries ranked fifth-eighth will be Band 2 and the remaining automatic qualifyers will be Band 3. Joining them will be Oceania 1, Europe 1, Asia 1 and Americas 1 in Band 4 and Africa 1, Europe 2, Americas 2 and Repercharge winner in Band 5.[353]

The use of Rankings to determine seedings can only mean that the rankings system is considered accurate. Current IRB Chairman Bernard Lapasset echoed the views of Syd Millar in saying: "The format of seeding teams for the Rugby World Cup Pool Allocation Draw using the IRB World Rankings is a credible, succinct and a proven method that reflects form, stimulates interest and is backed by our Unions."[354] It is, no doubt a fairer system than the system used for Rugby World Cup 2007 which had Argentina significantly disadvantaged in comparison to Rugby World Cup 2003 Quarter Finalists Scotland and Wales. While Argentina was drawn to face both France and Ireland Scotland had an easier draw of facing New Zealand and Italy while Wales faced Australia and Fiji. Had that tournament featured a draw made in December 2004 based on rankings then it would have seen a different draw altogether. On December 06 2004 Argentina was ranked 7th in the world with 77.63 points. Wales was 8th on 76.91 and Scotland was 9th on 74.65.[355]

The changes have made it more difficult for a lower ranked team to receive a favored draw similar to how Scotland was drawn with Italy while Argentina was drawn with Ireland. But the changes have not impacted on the teams outside of the top twelve. The remaining eight qualifying teams are not based on rankings in any way. Instead they are based almost entirely on regions. Seven of them advance to the World Cup after winning regional qualification while the final place is determined by repercharge. The runners-up from the regional qualifying matches in Africa, the Americas, Asia and Europe will play-off in the same way to that of Rugby World Cup 2011. The winner of the Africa v Europe match will face the winner of the Americas v Asia.[356] There is no place for a team from Oceania as the winner of the 2013 Oceania Cup will face Fiji to determine who advances.[357]

No explanation has been made for Oceania not recieving a place in repercharge but the obvious reason is that beyond Fiji there are no teams who really could qualify. The competing teams will be American Samoa, Cook Islands, Niue, Papua New Guinea, Solomon Islands, Tahiti and Vanuatu[358] who are all Tier Three nations and in August 2012 all were ranked outside of the world's top 50 based on the IRB World Rankings.[359]

Needless to say the IRB World Rankings make it clear that Fiji will have no problems in qualifying and that none of the Oceanian sides are likely to challenge the runners up from Africa, the Americas, Asia or Europe. The expansion of eight to twelve direct qualifiers has changed Oceania's qualification greatly. The qualification for Rugby World Cup 2007 in Oceania saw the Cook Islands defeat Niue and Tahiti in Oceania east and then defeat Papua New Guinea who had won Oceania west with wins over the Solomon Islands and Vanuatu. The Cook Islands then faced Tonga who had finished third in Oceania behind Fiji and Samoa. The Oceania section of 2007 Qualification showed a disadvantage of the system. In knowing the distribution of teams into Pools for Rugby World Cup 2007 Fiji was able to plan its way through its matches to see that it finished second and not first. There was a greater prize for finishing second in Oceania than finishing first. Oceania 1 would face both England and South Africa in the Pool Phase while Oceania 2 would face Australia and Wales. Fiji, Samoa and Tonga played each other home and away in the qualification matches with Tonga being winless. Both Fiji and Samoa were confirmed participants with Fiji happy to let Samoa win big against Tonga to create a large difference in points scored. It meant that Fiji needed a 36 point win over Samoa in the final qualification match to qualify as Oceania 1.[360] Fiji won 21-15 which saw it receive an easier draw.

While Namibia has arguably been the biggest winner from the changes, the biggest loser has been South America. Unlike Africa, Asia, Europe, North America and Oceania there is not an allocated spot awating the winner of the continents Rugby World Cup qualification matches. While the top side from every other continent automatically qualifies, the top South American side enters a play-off against the runner-up from North America. The winner of the North America v South America play-off qualifies for the World Cup as Americas 2. Not only is it a system that contradicts the paths of other regions but it also ignores the Tier structure because North America has two sides from the second tier but South America has none. Having Uruguay win the South American qualification series and then face Tier Two sides while Namibia advances directly to the World Cup after only facing Tier Three sides, ranked considerably lower is a contradiction of the words used by Syd Millar and Bernard Lapasset. It is not ensuring the best

187

teams are at the World Cup. Instead it is simply ensuring Africa has two teams with one of them being South Africa. Gifting Africa an automatic spot is also questionable given the performances of nations from other regions. Uruguay, for instance, has won two World Cup matches from a total of seven played. The qualification system appears to largely discredit Uruguay's victories.

The tough demands of qualifying for a World Cup added to a lack of international matches both at home and abroad place South American nations in a disadvantaged position globally. Nevertheless Argentina remains a regional leader. As covered in Part I there is little to suggest that South American teams are closing the gap on Argentina. To the contrary, Los Pumas are a permanent Tier One side that continues to match it against the best. Without its professional players, Argentina is still far too strong as demonstrated in the 2012 South American Championship. Such matches do little for Argentine rugby but are crucial to the growth of the likes of Brazil, Chile and Uruguay. Argentina's annual participation provides potential Pumas of the future a chance but, more importantly, the tournament acts as a measuring stick for Argentina's opponents. Argentina has played Brazil twelve times, Chile thirty-five times, Paraguay eighteen times, Peru twice, Uruguay thirty-four times and Venezuela once since the creation of the South American Championship in 1951.[361] Conversely of the nine other Tier One sides no team plays in an annual regional competition comparable to the South American Championship.

Africa
The governing body of African rugby, the Confederation of Africa Rugby (CAR) has thirty-seven members with only South Africa being a First Tier rugby nation. All others are from the Third Tier. Including South Africa there are twenty-three countries which are either full or associate members of the IRB.[362] The CAR is responsible for organizing rugby in the continent. The continents major competition is the African Cup which in 2012 featured twenty-two countries divided into four divisions.[363] Teams involved in the top three divisions are involved in the African section of Rugby World Cup qualification with the winner of the 2014 African Cup set to qualify for England 2015 as Africa 1. The qualifier will be one of eight countries – those in the 2012 Division 1A and the Division 1B. The winner of the 2013 Division 1B will be promoted to the Division 1A to dispute the 2014 African Cup. It will swap places with the bottom placed team from Division 1A which will not play in the 2014 African Cup and will thus not be in contention for a place in the World Cup. For 2013 Division 1A will feature, Kenya, Madagascar, Uganda and Zimbabwe while Division 1B will be contested between Botsuana, Namibia, Senegal and Tunisia.[364] Madagascar entered Division

1A after winning promotion from Division 1B. It defeated Namibia 57-54 in the final in July 2012. It was a celebrated occasion for African and global rugby. A crowd of 40,000 watched the match at the Mahamasina Stadium in Antananarivo.[365]

The African Cup is a new competition. It was first played in 2000 featuring five teams – Morocco, Namibia, South Africa, Tunisia and Zimbabwe. In an attempt to level the playing field South Africa sent an amateur side similar but not equal to Argentina in the South American Championship. Argentina's matches see test caps awarded unlike South Africa's in the African Cup. The South African Amateurs competed in the tournament four times winning in 2000 and 2001 while also making the final in 2006. South Africa provided good competition and helped lift the standard of play but has not participated since 2006. The African Cup is vital to rugby in the continent. While there are many rugby playing nations that, aside from South Africa are all categorized as Tier Three the difference in ability is extremely varied. Of the four sides confirmed for the 2013 Division 1B there is a gap of over fifty places in the IRB World Rankings separating Namibia from Botsuana.[366]

Although Namibia has had up and down results in the African Cup it has been the most successful team with titles in 2002, 2004, 2006 and 2008-2009. Outside of the African Cup and the World Cup it has faced teams including Georgia, Portugal, Romania, Russia, Samoa and Spain. But it has had a lack of opportunities against South Africa. The World Cup match between the nations in 2011 was only the second time they had ever played each other. The first took place in 2007 in a warm-up match for that year's World Cup. South Africa won the match 105-13 in Cape Town. It was a clear sign of the huge gap that exists but nothing has been done in terms of international competition to try to bridge it. Jacques Burger is arguably the best player Namibia has ever produced. He captained Namibia at Rugby World Cup 2011 and has pleaded for more tests. He suggests that without more matches Namibia will never improve. He is not just speaking of Namibia but of Africa and the Third tier in general. He said "We need to play against better opposition in order to lift us up, to a level where we would like to be."[367] Quite simply Burger would like to have a neighbouring country like Argentina which plays in the South American Championship annually.

Oceania
Unlike African nations Oceanian teams have a track record of merit at Rugby World Cup's. The region is the home of the current World Champions, New Zealand and fellow two-time World Champions Australia. It is also home to Fiji,

Samoa and Tonga, three Tier Two rugby nations that have all had a dramatic impact at Rugby World Cup's. Fiji and Samoa are both two-time Quarter Finalists while Tonga has defeated six countries - the Cote d'Ivoire, France, Italy, Japan, Samoa and the USA. The five countries are all a key part of Rugby World Cup tournaments and are second to only Europe in terms of quantity. At Rugby World Cup 2011 Oceanian and European nations accounted for thirteen of the twenty competing teams and all four Semi Finalists. Oceania's governing body, FORU has twelve full IRB members and three associated members.[368] The home page of FORU states that the Federation of Oceania Rugby Unions is responsible for representing the interests of members and to promote the growth of Rugby throughout Oceania.[369] The region has six different competitions[370] which try to fulfill the objective of the organization.

The two most important FORU tournaments are the Oceania Cup and the Pacific Nations Cup. The Oceania Cup is a development orientated competition featuring Tier Three rugby nations. The most recent edition of the tournament was in December 2011. It was hosted and won by Papua New Guinea. The only time it has not won was in 2008 when Niue won and Papua New Guinea did not participate.[371] The teams involved are ranked outside of the world's top fifty nations[372] and are significantly behind the level of Fiji, Samoa and Tonga. By virtue of winning the Oceania Cup Papua New Guinea faced Samoa in 2009 with the winner qualifying for Rugby World Cup 2011. Samoa was too strong, winning the two matches 188-19 on aggregate.[373]

The Pacific Nations Cup is a Tier Two competition featuring Fiji, Samoa, Tonga and Japan. The inclusion of Japan is due to the similar level and needs it shares with the three Oceanian teams. The tournament used to feature six teams with both Australia and New Zealand participating. Both teams used developmental teams – Australia A played in 2007 and 2008, the Junior All Blacks played in 2006, 2007 and 2009 and the New Zealand Maori played in 2008. Unlike Argentina in the South American Championship and South Africa amateurs in the CAR the Australian and New Zealand players were professionals, contracted to Super Rugby teams. The tournament gave fringe players and returning players an opportunity to stake a claim for the test side and many from both Australia and New Zealand went on to make the team. For instance of the Junior All Blacks team that defeated Fiji 35-17 in 2006 there were three players who would feature for New Zealand at Rugby World Cup 2011.[374] The tournament was played during the Tri Nations which meant a greater number of players were active in international colors but neither of the Tier One teams would be permanent. The first to leave was Australia and in late 2008 the ARU confirmed that Australia withdrew from the tournament due to the cost of fielding a side.[375] New Zealand followed one year latter.

While Oceania is powerful on a global scale the regions rugby structure does not appear to be providing the Tier Two nations with a suffcient number of test matches. Fiji, Samoa and Tonga play more rugby than Chile, Namibia and Uruguay but none play enough against First Tier nations. From June 1995 to August 2012 Fiji played 114 test matches. Of these twenty-four were against Tonga, twenty-two against Samoa, eleven against Japan and ten against other Tier two nations. During the same period Fiji played nine tests against Tier Three nations and the remaining twenty-seven were against Tier One nations.[376] In other words, Fiji has averaged fewer than two tests per year against Tier One opposition in the professional era. Partly to blame is the perceived lack of resources in Fiji to host test rugby. This would explain why around two-thirds of Fiji's tests during this period were away matches. Of the twenty-seven Tier One tests Fiji played only five at home. Fiji nevertheless won three of these matches and lost two. In 1998 Fiji hosted France and Scotland and completed a 51-26 victory over Scotland. It defeated Italy 43-9 in 2000 and 29-18 in 2006 while it lost 37-25 against Scotland in June 2012.

Samoa has played 105 test matches during the same period. Of these thirty-nine matches were against Tier One nations and sixty matches were against Tier Two nations.[377] Samoa played roughly three-quarters of its matches abroad, hosting only twenty-seven matches during this twelve year period. Of its home tests just four were against Tier One nations. Samoa hosted France in 1999, Italy in 2000, Ireland in 2003 and Scotland in 2012. Of these four matches it won one, defeating Italy 43-24 but very nearly won a second as Scotland claimed a late 17-16 win. Scotland was also supposed to play in Samoa in 2004 but the match was transferred to Wellington. Samoa moved its home test there in hope of attracting a large crowd to in a bid to make more money for Samoan rugby. The experiment was a one-off with Samoa losing badly, 38-3 in wet conditions. Like Samoa, Fiji had moved a home match to New Zealand. The 2002 match between Fiji and New Zealand was played in Wellington, attracting 25,000 fans.[378] Clearly a better take than the profits generated from hosting the Junior All Blacks in 2006. In hindsight neither Fiji nor Samoa appear to be happy that they moved their matches against Tier One opposition. They both hosted Scotland in June 2012.

Tonga played less rugby than both Fiji and Samoa and hosted only twenty-six test matches in the same twelve year period. Tonga hosted two tests against Tier One opposition – a 20-16 win over France in 1999 and a 40-19 loss against Ireland in

2003.[379] In total Tonga played one hundred test matches, twenty of which were against Tier One nations but outside of Rugby World Cup's the number was much lower. So much so that Tonga only played eight tests against Tier One opposition in twelve years. Although Tonga came close to defeating South Africa in Rugby World Cup 2007 it would play no tests against Tier One opposition until Rugby World Cup 2011. It only played seventeen tests between the two World Cup tournaments.[380]

The fundamental problem facing Tonga is no different to the difficulties that Fiji and Samoa have. There is no Oceania Cup involving Australia, New Zealand and the three Tier Two nations. Opportunities have historically been limited. Australia has played four tests against Tonga, all in Australia.[381] In comparison there have been thirty-six matches between Argentina and Uruguay and ten have been played in Uruguay.[382] The successful opening of Rugby World Cup 2011 was notable in that it worked with a Second Tier nation. It was the third time New Zealand and Tonga had met in a World Cup match and only the fourth overall. Outside of Rugby World Cup's the teams have only met once, in 2000. It was New Zealand's first test of the year and was seen as a warm up match for the two test series against Scotland. The All Blacks 102-0 victory on Auckland's North Shore was not the result either team desired after Tonga had given New Zealand a good contest, especially in the forwards, the previous year at the World Cup. The nature of the match effectively meant Tonga would lose out on future tests.

In total there have been nineteen matches between Australia and Fiji. The first was a two match series played in 1952. Australia won the first test but Fiji won the second 17-15. Of all matches between the countries three have been played in Fiji, fifteen in Australia and one was played in Montpellier during the 2007 World Cup. The professional era has seen a decline in matches between the nations. Fiji's most recent home test was in 1984 and since then there have only been six tests. 1984 was also the last time New Zealand played a test in Fiji. It was the third time Fiji hosted the All Blacks out of a total of nine test matches between the nations. The most recent game was in 2011.[383] A crowd of 15,000 attended the match in 2011[384] while 20,000 had attended the Fiji v Junior All Blacks match in Suva in 2006.[385] Of the three Pacific Island nations Fiji is the only one to have hosted either the All Blacks or Wallabies.

In the professional era it has been tough to secure home matches partly because of ability but not entirely. An equally, if not larger, problem has been the allure of playing extra tests abroad to receive a profit. While tests in the Pacific Islands cannot offer the ARU or NZRU revenue tests against Tier One sides can. With cash flow being all important in the professional era the likes of England and Wales have both hosted Australia and New Zealand more than previously. Wales has hosted New Zealand for a test during every All Blacks end of year tour since Rugby World Cup 2003. The All Blacks played at the Millenium Stadium in 2004, 2005, 2006, 2008, 2009 and 2010. No November tours in World Cup years explain why there were no matches in 2007 and 2011. Australia, however, did play a post World Cup match after both the 2007 and 2011 tournaments. The Wallabies have, in fact, played a test at the Millenium Stadium every year since 2005. In addition both All Blacks and Wallabies played again in Wales in November 2012. Wales defeated Australia in 2005 and 2008 and drew in 2006 but lost all its matches against New Zealand. The closest match was a 26-25 loss in 2004 but it was followed by a 41-3 loss in 2005 and a 45-10 loss in 2006. In comparison Argentina lost by four points in 2001 and six points in 2006 against the All Blacks in Los Pumas' only home matches against New Zealand in the professional era before entering The Rugby Championship.

During the same period England has hosted Australia, New Zealand and South Africa five times each. Like many of Wales's home matches against Tri Nation's teams the All Blacks 2008 match at Twickenham was an additional match. It was added to the schedule which included matches against Australia, South Africa and the Pacific Islands. The RFU and the NZRU agreed on the match worth an estimated £7 million with New Zealand taking a significant portion as an appearance fee.[386] It was the All Black's fifth and final test match of the tour. In search of additional revenue Australia and New Zealand had started their European tours in Asia. In an historical day for rugby a Bledisloe Cup test was played in Hong Kong on November 01 2008. The teams would repeat the fuxture in 2010 and would also play in Tokyo in 2009. Following confirmation of the 2008 Asian Bledisloe Cup test John O'Neill commented that "the rewards that can be generated in this part of the world are extremely significant."[387] Such rewards cannot be generated from playing in Fiji, Samoa or Tonga.

Between 2007 and 2011 Samoa played an away test against both Australia and New Zealand. The tests were notable for the results and for the scheduling. New Zealand hosted Samoa in September 2008. As it was outside of the IRB international windows Samoa could not get access to many of its professional players. Only one player, George Stowers, started the match and would also play against Wales in the key World Cup match in 2011. Nevertheless the 2008 fixture was a test match and New Zealand won it 101-14. Less than three years latter Samoa played Australia in Sydney and won 32-23. The two matches are both the lowest moment and greatest moment of Samoan rugby history. They were a clear example of the needs of the Second Tier and how teams require not only international competition but matches at appropriate times.

Europe
European international rugby is arguably the best organized of all the IRB's recognized regions. It is also the largest with forty-seven member unions spread over seven divisions.[388] Its system of dividing countries by ability gives the regions team's appropriate competition. The promotion / relegation policy means the teams all have to regularly perform. Teams like Germany and Ukraine have come and gone from the ENC Division 1A while World Cup regulars Georgia and Romania have long been there. Five of the six teams in the 2012-2014 competition have Rugby World Cup experience.[389] It is, however, not a perfect system as there is no promotion from Division 1A to a higher competition. Unlike in the FIRA operated tournaments the six members of the Six Nations Championship face no danger of being relegated. In 2012 while Belgium switched places with Ukraine Georgia did not switch places with the then Six Nations wooden spooners and the competitions only winless team, Scotland.

The lack of a bridge between Europe's First and Second Tier teams is only part of the problem. A larger one is the share lack of matches between Six Nations teams and ENC Division 1A teams. In the professional era Australia, New Zealand and South Africa have played few internationals against neighbouring countries and so have Six Nations teams with Romania not having played against a Six Nations opponent outside of Rugby World Cup's since 2006. In the first decade of professionalism Romania played against all six teams but it last played against England in 2001, Italy and Wales in 2004, Ireland in 2005 and France and Scotland in 2006. Georgia has overtaken Romania as the seventh best European nation but has only played Six Nations teams eight times in history. The first two were World Cup qualification matches against Ireland in 1998 and 2002 while the third was a warm-up match for the 2003 tournament with Italy winning 31-22. Georgia's five other matches were World Cup games. Spain has played two matches. It faced Italy in 1999 in a World Cup warm-up match and hosted Australia in 2001 in Madrid. Portugal and Russia and have only faced Six Nations teams at World Cup's or in qualification matches.[390]

Within the Division 1A competition is not as tight as it is in the Six Nations. Georgia's record in the 2010-2012 competition saw it win eleven of its twelve matches with its one loss being 25-18 against Spain. Georgia won eight and drew one match in the 2008-2010 competition and won nine out of ten in the 2006-2008 competition. In addititon Georgia has done well against visiting teams from

Second Tier nations. It has notably recorded wins over Canada, Tonga and the USA in its only home matches against such rivals. Georgia is a country seemingly meriting matches against Tier One teams with lower ranked members of the Six Nations potentially being suitable but with the Six Nations tournament having a closed door and no warm-up matches there is no room in the calendar for Division 1A teams.

Romania no longer hosts visiting teams from the Six Nations. Instead it plays home matches in the Division 1A and hosts the IRB Nations Cup. The last time Romania hosted a test match against a Tier One nation was in 2006 against France in Bucharest. Les Bleus won the match 62-14. It hosted Scotland in 2005 losing 39-19 and Italy one year earlier losing by one point, 25-24. Prior to that Ireland played in Bucharest in 2001 winning 37-3 and France won in 1997 and 2000. Pre-professionalism France was also the last to play in Romania, winning 37-20 in 1995. In the era of amateur Rugby World Cup's Romania hosted England once, France four times, Italy three times, and Scotland once however Romania did not host Ireland during this period. Of these matches Romania defeated Scotland 18-12 in 1991, Italy 9-3 in 1987 and 26-12 in 1994 and also defeated Samoa 33-24 in 1989. None of the other Division 1A nations have hosted Six Nations teams. Professionalism has made it harder for the Division 1A teams due to the gulf between amateur and professional players and this has seen less opportunities for international rugby. The plight of Romania is a concrete example of what is at risk should regions fail to look after their members. There is a lot at stake and Romania almost did not qualify for Rugby World Cup 2011, only seventeen years after completing a convincing win over Italy.

At first sight it may appear likely that the simple reason for no regional competitions is the clear differing abilities between nations. While Italy has been able to fit into the Six Nations and establish itself as a permanent member on even terms with Scotland this does not mean Georgia is a good comparison. Nor does it mean that Fiji, Samoa or Tonga could perform with the same success against Australia and New Zealand in an Oceania Cup. Nevertheless such an explanation does not answer why the Tier One has the Six Nations and Tri Nations but excludes the Second Tier and has no process of admitting them. If the reason for their exclusion was simply based on ability then Rugby World Cup's would only feature Tier One sides. Rugby World Cup 2007 and 2011 clearly demonstrated that the global tournament benefits greatly from second and third Tier participants but that they need to be given fair schedules. Australia has little to gain from an Oceania Cup. Meanwhile given that there is money to be made from playing in

Hong Kong or Tokyo the rewards that can be generated from Oceania are likely to be considered as being insignificant.

Asia

Aside from Argentina facing its South American counterparts in the CONSUR A tournament the only comparable example is Asia. Like South America the continent is dominated by one country. Argentina's results in the Americas are similar to that of Japan's in Asia. Japan has won 17 of its 21 matches against Hong Kong, 21 of its 28 matches against South Korea and all of its matches against other Asian opposition.[391] In the professional era Japan has won fifteen and drew one of its eighteen matches against South Korea. Its last loss was in 2002 and since their draw in 2004 Japan has won every match by 19 or more points.[392] Japan's four loses occurred in the professional era but before the first professional Rugby World Cup. The most recent loss was by 17-16 in 1998. With time professional rugby in Japan has improved with a greater quality of foreign players lifting the quality of rugby in Japan and of the Japanese national team. Japan has not only been winning all its matches but has been winning by large scorelines. Its eight games since Rugby World Cup 1999 have all been victories with the lowest margin being 23 points and the highest 89.[393]

By the middle of the 2000-2010 decade it was clear that Japan faced no real danger of losing test matches against Asian opposition. Nevertheless the governing body of Asian rugby, ARFU together with the IRB created the Asian Five Nations championship in 2008. The competition, like in Europe is structured accrding to ability. In Asia the top five teams play in the Top 5, the next best four in Division One, Division Two, Division Three and Division Four and three teams play in Division Five.[394] No matter the division the winner is automatically promoted to the next division and the bottom placed side is automatically relegated. There are no play-off's between divisions. This saw one of Asia's traditional powerhouses, South Korea relegated from the Top 5 in 2010. Unlike the Six Nations championship it gives all teams an equal chance with there being no reward for finishing last. It is reflected in ARFU's 2011-2019 Strategic Plan which has five key points. They are as follows:

1. Grow Rugby in Asia
2. Improve competition standards in Asia
3. Maximise the value of the 2019 RWC
4. Improve governance and leadership
5. Maximize the profile and commercial value of Rugby in the region

Japan has done noticeably better than other sides in the Top 5 in the five year history of the Asian Five Nations. It is undefeated and has rarely been challenged. In 2012 it won 87-0 against Kazakhstan, 106-3 against the United Arab Emirates, 52-8 against South Korea and 67-0 against Hong Kong. The results are similar to that of Argentina in the South American Championship. While Argentina is the only Tier One nation in CONSUR, Japan is the only Tier Two nation in ARFU. All others are Tier Three nations and the pattern of results since the Asian Five Nations started suggests Japan´s dominion faces no threat. Nevertheless, ARFU is serious about developing rugby with the organization stating that its vision is "To create a sustainable, vibrant and competitive rugby culture for all stakeholders, which supports and develops the game in the Region".[395] When Japan hosts Rugby World Cup 2019 it will be representing Asia and is likely to still hold two key records – being the only Asian nation to have played in a Rugby World Cup and having competed at every Rugby World Cup tournament. Japan and Argentina are important for their regions with the leadership of both unions constituting a key part of developing the global game and it further underlines what Argentina has to offer as a World Cup host.

15

Evolution

The evolving state of rugby union means that for the first time tournaments can be staged in all of the IRB´s regions. The sport´s showcase tournament need not be staged exclusively, or mainly, in the traditional areas of the old Five Nations and Tri Nations any longer. The host nation or nations of Rugby World Cup 2023 could theoretically be from anywhere except from Asia due to Japan hosting the 2019 tournament. Already there have been countries showing interest in being the host nation. Countries from Africa, Europe, North America and South America have either confirmed their interest in hosting or have been suggested as firm possibilities. This is a marked evolution from a decade ago when the number of bidding nations was not only far smaller but was also from a far narrower list of countries. France, for instance, won the hosting rights for Rugby World Cup 2007 over England. Conversely England won 2015 and Japan won 2019 while Italy and South Africa both missed out.

The exact reason for choosing England and Japan over Italy and South Africa has never been elaborated on. Rather England was said to be chosen due to the economic benefits it can generate in comparison to the three alternatives and Japan was chosen to see the tournament moved to a new place. Both decisions were made in no small part due to New Zealand hosting 2011. Firstly Englands bid was larger than the others, reportedly offering the IRB an estimated profit of £300 million.[396] Secondly, Japan won over Italy and South Africa due to the controversial decision which saw New Zealand chosen over Japan for the hosting rights of Rugby World Cup 2011. The decision for the 2015 and 2019 tournaments was about stability and growth. England offered one and Japan the other. With Japan confirmed as a host nation rugby had come out of its shackles and broken new ground.[397]

New Continent
There is no reason why Japan 2019 needs to be an exception to the rule. Rather, it can be a new start for global rugby. Bringing the Rugby World Cup to a new continent is an acknowledgement that rugby is becoming increasingly global and that markets beyond those who hold two votes each in the IRB council are key to the future. 2019 is an extraordinary change but a necessary one. It is ending the out of date system which has seen Rugby World Cup's go from Oceania to Europe and back with South Africa thrown in between. Indeed, the pattern almost continued for 2019 and the possibility exists that it will with Japan 2019 potentially being followed by South Africa and Ireland for 2023 and 2027 or possibly to Italy or Russia.

With professionalism has come change. Stadiums are larger, television audiences are larger and rugby is bigger than ever before. The growth has been occurring worldwide with playing numbers and television audiences on the rise making the Rugby World Cup a genuine global event and a genuine showcase event for the sport. Additional countries continue to play Rugby World Cup qualification matches with Armenia, Greece, India, Mexico and Pakistan all involved in qualification matches for New Zealand 2011 for the first time in their history. This has coincided with teams previously considered not capable of winning a Rugby World Cup tournament now being potential contenders. The likelihood of a repeat of Rugby World Cup 2003 which saw the Five Nations and the Tri Nations qualify for the Quarter Finals is increasingly unlikely.

The idea of Ireland hosting a Rugby World Cup came about due to two distinct factors - New Zealand's success in hosting the Rugby World Cup 2011 and the opening of Croke Park in Dublin for rugby from 2007-2010. New Zealand and the Republic of Ireland have similar populations. A July 2012 estimate suggests the Republic of Ireland has roughly 400,000 more people than New Zealand. It also ranks the Republic of Ireland as the worlds 119th most populated country, six places above New Zealand.[398] This figure excludes Northern Ireland which is not a political part of the Republic but is united for rugby. The Irish rugby team represents both the Republic of Ireland and Northern Ireland. Northern Ireland has a population of 1.81 million[399] which combined with the Republic of Ireland gives the island a total population of slightly more than 6.5 million, or a population of over two million more than New Zealand. Irish Rugby Football Union (IRFU) chief executive Philip Browne said "The Rugby World Cup in New Zealand showed what a country of four million people could achieve in terms of attracting visitors and showcasing the potential of a country."[400]

The IRFU, like the three other home unions has a history of concentrating its home matches in its capital city. Dublin has hosted the vast majority of Ireland's test matches in the professional era. It played thirty-two tests in a row at Lansdowne Road between 1996 and 2002 before Ireland played outside of the capital in 2002. Of its eighty-six home internationals between January 1996 and March 2012 all except four were played in Dublin. Romania played in Limerick in 2002, Italy played in Limerick in 2003 and in Belfast in 2007 and Canada played in Limerick in 2008.[401] The success of Croke Park hosting rugby matches is central to a potential Rugby World Cup in Ireland and it has been confirmed that should Ireland host a Rugby World Cup that it would host the final.[402] It would be supported by other Gaelic Athletic Association (GAA) stadiums which will be made available. They are the Páirc Uí Chaoimh in Cork, the Gaelic Grounds in Limerick, Fitzgerald Stadium in Killarney, Pearse Stadium in Galway and Casement Park in Belfast. The six GAA venues would likely be used in conjunction with four rugby venues – the Aviva Stadium and the RDS in Dublin, Thomond Park in Limerick and Ravenhill in Belfast.[403] Similar to England 2015, the majority of the proposed venues have no experience in hosting international rugby.

Croke Park hosted fourteen international rugby matches during the redevelopment of the Republic of Ireland's national rugby and soccer stadium, Lansdowne Road. Demolition and redevelopment meant Ireland needed a different venue in Dublin. The closure of the venue now known as Aviva Stadium saw internationals transferred to the larger Croke Park from 2007-2010. The stadium is Ireland's largest but was historically off limits to rugby and soccer due to the GAA strictly prohibiting non-Irish sports from being played in its stadiums. The GAA benefitted tremendously from the redevelopment of Lansdowne Road, earning €36million from rugby and soccer's four year use of Croke Park.[404] It gives security to an Irish bid with the above mentioned ten venues in six cities being adequate for the IRFU to host a Rugby World Cup, and do so without having a sub-host such as Scotland or Wales.

From a global perspective it would be hard to justify Rugby World Cup 2023 going to the Republic of Ireland and Northern Ireland only eight years after England hosted with Wales as a subhost. Should Europe host the tournament it would need to be moved east to either Italy or Russia. Italy would be the safer option. It is a Tier One rugby nation which has competed at every Rugby World Cup. It also has a proven record in hosting Six Nations matches and Tier One touring teams in November internationals. It remains to be seen whether or not Italy will bid for Rugby World Cup 2023 but there have already been signs that it is not the right time for Italy to bid again. In February 2012 Italian Prime Minister Mario Monti withdrew Italy's bid to bring the 2020 Olympic Games to Rome. He refused to fund the games, in saying "after a difficult evaluation we've arrived at the unanimous conclusion that the government believes it would not be responsible in the current conditions in Italy to take on these guarantees. We don't feel capable of taking on a financial commitment that could burden the Italian finances over the coming years."[405]

Government support is paramount to a country hosting a Rugby World Cup. Italy could well obtain it but there is great uncertainty due to the decision to not bid for the Olympic Games. In the case of Ireland obtaining GAA support is vital and now that the IRFU has the GAA's backing it can go ahead and bid. It would have reason to be confident knowing that the Irish economy would be boosted from World Cup visitors. However, like in Italy so much uncertainty exists in Ireland due to the economic situation in Europe. Ireland has a debt of over €60 billion[406] which places a level of uncertainty over Ireland being selected to host a Rugby World Cup in the immediate future. Many questions remain over Irish debt while, conversely, Argentine debt is today under control which makes a bid for 2023 plausible unlike a bid for 2011.

However, despite significant progress, England was overwhelmingly preferred over Italy for Rugby World Cup 2015. Italy has never hosted a World Cup tournament or a match while England hosted seven matches in 1991 and nine matches in 1999. Sergio Parisse supported Italy hosting the World Cup, wanting rugby to continue growing in the country and wanting rugby to expand beyond the traditional eight. During Italy's presentation to the IRB Organization he said "Italy now is a country where when you talk about Italy, you talk especially about soccer and rugby is going to be little by little a big sport in Italy and I think the World Cup is going to be fantastic for the development of Italian rugby. I think Italy is, like France, a country with a good tradition, it is a younger country of rugby and I think the World Cup is going to be the key for the future to have Italy a big country of rugby."[407]

Parisse wanted the World Cup to act as a launching pad to take rugby to a new level in the country. Italy has had limited success, but nonetheless success in the Six Nations and has performed much better against Tier Two nations over time due directly to its participation in the Six Nations. Italy hosted and lost 22-17 to Canada in 2000, 17-9 to Samoa in 2001 but defeated Canada 51-6 in 2004 and 41-6 in 2006 and defeated Samoa 24-6 in 2009. Italy has been to every Rugby World Cup but does not tick all the boxes that Argentina does. The teams on field progress and the union's success at seeing crowds increase have significantly improved the profile of the sport in Italy. The country however is European and should it host in 2023 it would continue the cycle that has had Europe hosting every second edition of the World Cup. With the Americas yet to host England 2015 will be Europe's fourth World Cup.

South Africa bid against Italy and also lost. It also unsuccessfully bid for Rugby World Cup 2011. The organizer of South Africa's 2011 bid, François Pienaar said in 2005 that "to stage a successful IRB Rugby World Cup, a prospective host must provide two elements - the passion to fill the stands and generate revenue, and infrastructure and stadiums worthy of a global event. Our submission is that South Africa has both."[408] South Africa certainly did fullfil Pienaar's stated requirements and the country was ready made due to its hosting of the 2010 FIFA World Cup. It however was not selected for rugby's showpiece in 2011, 2015 or 2019 which firmly suggests a return to South Africa is not a popular option with the IRB Council. Should South Africa host Rugby World Cup 2023 it would mark a change but like Ireland it would also continue with the hosting history of Rugby World Cup's. Both would mean that the tradition that no new nation has hosted a World Cup match since 1995 would be maintained with the exception of Japan 2019.

Breaking the cycle would be a major step towards embracing the global game, a step that will underline the sport as a growing one and encourage its continual expansion into new markets. When England has its third turn at hosting Rugby World Cup games the Americas will have hosted eight FIFA World Cup's, second only to Europe. South America will have hosted five FIFA World Cups in four countries - Uruguay 1930, Brazil 1950, Chile 1962, Argentina 1978 and Brazil 2014. North America will have hosted three with Mexico hosting in 1970 and 1986 and the USA hosting in 1994. The America's decorated history in hosting soccer's premier event is encouraging from a rugby perspective. The wave of popularity in Argentina can be fully embraced in 2023 and it would not be a move away from an established market due to Argentina's First Tier status and rugby tradition.

FIFA took the unexpected step of awarding the 2018 FIFA World Cup to Russia and the very surprising one of awarding Qatar with hosting rights for the 2022 tournament. It was looking to new markets to encourage growth. It had reason to believe it need not return to a tried and tested soccer nation such as England or Portugal and Spain. Both bids lost out to Russia, a nation with no hosting experience unlike England which hosted the 1966 tournament and Spain which hosted in 1982. The IRB could have taken a similar approach and awarded Italy the hosting rights for 2015 but did not. Similarly, FIFA could have opted for a return to Japan, South Korea or the USA but opted for Qatar for 2022. It means Asia will host its second FIFA World Cup twenty years after its first and will see West Asia or the Middle East, host it's first.

During the bidding process Qatar had actually been widely expected to not win hosting rights after FIFA branded it high risk in 2010.[409] The key to the name World Cup is the use of world in its title. Although the decision was not universally popular it was, no doubt, one taken to underline the importance of the word. Rugby can emulate this with Japan and Argentina hosting in 2019 and 2023 and can do so without the same level of risk. The simple difference between Russia and Qatar in soccer and Japan and Argentina in rugby is that the rugby nations have played at every World Cup while the soccer ones have not. In the case of Qatar the nation has in fact never qualified for a FIFA World Cup.

Make a Statement
FIFA made a bold statement and so can rugby. It involves a key question that the IRB Council must consider - is rugby truely a global sport? This is the central question that the authorities need to answer when determining future Rugby World Cup hosts. If the answer is yes then the question is why will Australia, England, France, New Zealand, Ireland, Scotland and Wales have all hosted or co-hosted two or more World Cup's before the Americas continents have ever hosted one? On the other hand, if the answer is no then there is a clear need to encourage new host nations and new host regions rather than utilize the safety net of returning to previous hosts. Surely new hosts are needed to demonstrate that, whether percieved or not, rugby has the world in mind and is looking well beyond the traditional frontiers. This is where Argentina stands out head and shoulders above all other potential hosts as it has the best record of all Rugby World Cup nations yet to host a World Cup and meets the general criteria ranging from the state of rugby in the country to comercial viability to rugby history and to stadiums.

The Americas have not only hosted a large number of FIFA World Cup tournaments but the region has also been highly successful in the tournaments themselves. Nine of the nineteen FIFA World Cup's to this day have been won by South American countries. Brazil has won five times and both Argentina and Uruguay have won twice each. Two other Americas countries have made it to the Semi Finals - Chile and the USA. The remaining ten FIFA World Cup's have all been won by European countries. Rugby, in contrast has had World Cup

Champions from Africa, Europe and Oceania. It has also had a Semi Finalist from South America and there are arguably considerably more chances of Argentina winning a Rugby World Cup than there are of any African, Asian, North American or Oceanian country winning a FIFA World Cup. No African country has ever made the Semi Finals with its best performers coming from Cameroon in 1990, Senegal in 2002 and Ghana in 2010. All three countries reached the Quarter Finals. South Korea is one of only two non-European and South American countries to have reached the Semi Finals stage. It qualified for the 2002 Semi Finals while the USA qualified in 1994. The best performance from Oceania came in 2006 when Australia made it to the second round. Since then, Australia has played in Asia rather than Oceania.

European and South American domination in soccer is overwhelming. But despite such a lack of genuine global competitiveness, Soccer World Cup hosts are increasingly becoming global. FIFA has actively encouraged bids from non-traditional places. This resulted in the USA hosting the 1994 World Cup, Japan and South Korea co-hosting the 2002 event, South Africa hosting in 2010 and Russia and Qatar in 2018 and 2022. During this twenty-eight year period, from 1994-2022 five of the eight FIFA World Cup's have been rewarded to countries with no previous World Cup hosting experience. The three other hosts are France in 1998, Germany in 2006 and Brazil in 2014. All three hosted their second World Cup. France had hosted in 1938, Brazil in 1950 and West Germany in 1974. These represented gaps of sixty years for France, sixty-four for Brazil and thirty-two years for Germany, albeit a unified Germany. In comparison New Zealand's wait between 1987 and 2011 was twenty-four years and although England hosted key matches in 1999 its wait between finals in 1991 and 2015 will also be twenty-four years.

FIFA's move away from Europe and South America has overlooked ability almost without exception. South Africa hosted the 2010 World Cup despite having failed to qualify for the 2006 tournament. Similarly Russia and formerly the Soviet Union missed out on qualifying in 1974, 1978, 1998, 2006 and 2010 and last made the Quarter Finals in 1970. None of South Africa, Russia or Qatar won hosting rights due to their national soccer team's performances. Neither did the USA, Japan or South Korea. They were all selected to encourage development not because they had naturally embraced self-development and had transferred that into results at World Cup's. Before 2002 Japan's only appearance was in 1998 while South Korea had played in four tournaments without making it past the group stage. Similarly, the USA had not delivered at World Cup's.

Before 1994 the USA had only qualified for four FIFA World Cup's and had never made the knock-out stages. It failed to qualify for every World Cup from 1954-1986 but was the host nation after returning in 1990. Japan prepares for Rugby World Cup 2019 in a different manner altogether. Japan is yet to make the Quarter Finals of a Rugby World Cup but is Asia's finest rugby nation, has the full-support of all of Asian rugby[410] and has shown onfield improvement such as its 2011 victory in the Pacific Nations Cup. Its only weakness is its lack of results at Rugby World Cup's, unlike Argentina. The IRB needs to stand tall and make a statement to the world. Not only can future tournament hosts come from new places but they ought to as well. Rugby World Cup 2023 should go to Argentina. It would be making a huge statement - having a Rugby World Cup in the Soccer continent.

Outdoing Soccer
If Argentina 2023 happens then rugby will be more global than soccer. It would mean a World Cup has been hosted in each of the sports five recognized regions. Qatar 2022 will mark ninety-two years of FIFA World Cup's, during which period most, but not all, regions will have hosted a World Cup. The FIFA World Cup has a history dating back to 1930, fifty-seven more years than the Rugby World Cup. Whilst the first three Rugby World Cup's were hosted in three different continents, the first eight FIFA World Cup's were all hosted in either South America or Europe. Moreover, until the USA hosted in 1994 Mexico was the only other non-South American or European country to have hosted. The pattern is set to continue with South American hosting in 2014 and Europe in 2018. So much is the lack of globality in Soccer host nations that by 2022 eighteen of the twenty-two World Cup's will have been hosted in either Europe or Latin America.

FIFA has improved greatly with the 1994, 2002, 2010 and 2022 tournaments being played outside of Europe and South America but its record would not be as good as rugby's should Argentina host Rugby World Cup 2023. Both sports operate on a regional basis with regional governing bodies. FIFA is divided into six regions. They are the Asia (Asian Football Confederation - the AFC), Africa (the Confederation of African Football – the CAF), North America (Confederation of North, Central American and Caribbean Association Football - CONCACEF), South America (Confederación Sudamericana de Fútbol - CONMEBOL), Oceania (Oceania Football Confederation   OFC) and Europe (Union of European Football Associations - UEFA). Of these regions Oceania has never hosted a World Cup but it is not without trying. Australia, officially now a part of the AFC is, nonetheless an Oceanian country. It bid to host the 2022 FIFA World Cup and was quite confident of winning the hosting rights to the tournament. The union and Australian soccer fans alike were shocked with the decision. Not because they lost but by the extent and because the winner was Qatar. Australia was eliminated in the first round of voting having only received one vote.[411]

Oceania is unquestionably a far more powerful player in global rugby than it is in global soccer. But considering how much rugby has grown in the professional era this would logically be more reason for Australia to host a FIFA World Cup. It would certainly do plenty for the sport in the region, with benefits reaching neighbouring countries including rugby powers Fiji, New Zealand, Samoa and Tonga. Although both FIFA and the IRB divide playing nations into regions the difference between the two is that there are two governing bodies in the Americas for rugby. The regions are combined for Rugby World Cup Qualification and other tournaments including Rugby Sevens events. Argentina 2023 would be not only representing CONSUR but also NACRA and rugby is therefore in the position of being able to have a World Cup hosted in each of its regions before soccer.

Time Zone
The geographical positioning of Argentina in relation to Tier One rugby nations makes the country uniquely positive for scheduling kick-off times for matches. Argentina's location in the Americas with the rugby markets of Oceania to the west and Europe and Southern Africa to the East enables the country the luxury of producing a schedule which would give teams favorable playing times, something Africa and Europe cannot do for Oceania and vice-versa. Argentina's centrality to these markets allows for a genuine spreading out of matches to suit to the demands of the market. With the advent of professionalism rugby has had to adjust to provide for the preferred demands of the market. This has seen more matches played at night to cater to the demands of pay-tv and an evolving audience.

In places like Australia and New Zealand this has meant day matches are rare and night matches are the norm at international level. Previously teams played afternoon matches without exception. For instance, in 1992 New Zealand hosted Ireland with afternoon kick-off's in Dunedin and Wellington. The following year it hosted the British & Irish Lions in the afternoon and in 1994 it was France's turn. However in 2002 Ireland played two tests in New Zealand at night to enable live coverage in Ireland at better hours. The time difference between New Zealand and Ireland of eleven hours in June makes it hard to schedule matches. A mid afternoon kick-off of 2:30pm in New Zealand converts to a 3:30am kick-off in

Ireland. On the other hand a 7:30pm kick-off in New Zealand offers the friendlier and more financially sound option of an 8:30am kick-off in Ireland. England, Scotland and Wales share the same timezone as Ireland while France and Italy are one hour ahead and South Africa is the same as France and Italy in September and October when Rugby World Cup's are played. As such New Zealand offers unfriendly hours for hosting international rugby matches. There are more losers than there are winners but this did not stop Rugby World Cup 2011 from being a highly successful tournament.

It also enables matches to be broadcast live in the European and African markets at better times than by having games played earlier. Broadcasters believe it is better for business to have matches at latter times and this directly affected the match schedule for both France 2007 and New Zealand 2011. For France 2007 a number of matches had 9:00pm kick-off's (local time) which meant for the best possible viewing hours for a global audience. France v Argentina to was 9pm local time which translated into 9pm in Johannesburg, 8pm in London, 4pm in Buenos Aires, 3pm in Toronto, midday in Los Angeles, 7am in Auckland and 5am in Sydney. The scheduling was aimed at delivering a key match at globally accessible hours and an earlier kick-off would certainly have meant lower viewing numbers. The first game of the second day of the tournament took place at 1.45pm the following day between New Zealand and Italy. The reason behind the early kick-off was to meet the needs, as best as possible, of the audience. It meant it was an 11:45pm kick-off in New Zealand on a Saturday night which is far better than a 3am kick-off on a Sunday morning.

For Rugby World Cup 2011, New Zealand emulated this extensively. Unfortunately for the tournament organizers they confronted a major problem which cannot be overcome - New Zealand's global position. The country's location meant key matches needed to start latter than normal. Matches starting at 8pm New Zealand time corresponded to 10am in France and 9am in the United Kingdom and Ireland. There was, however, a problem of matches on the same day. On Sunday September 11 South Africa v Wales kicked-off at 8:30pm and took place after Ireland v USA and Australia v Italy on the same day. The 3:30pm kick-off time for Australia v Italy meant Italians wanting to watch their team live had to tune in at 5:30am. Viewers in Ireland had a 7am kick-off for their teams match while viewers in New York had to watch the match at 2am. The key match of Argentina v England on the second day of the competition kicked-off at 5:30am in Buenos Aires and 9:30am in London. It was chosen as being the best possible time to suit all markets. An earlier kick-off would have been negative for both countries playing in the match. Scotland v Romania was played on the same day with a 1pm kick-off which corresponded to 2am in Glasgow and 4am in Bucharest which made live viewing tough for fans of both sides.

In January 2009 Rugby NZ 2011 chief executive Martin Snedden said "There are some critical issues around broadcasting to do with the value of broadcasting rights in New Zealand and other countries and how they are affected by kickoff times or what days they are played on. If we can, we will endeavour to play major European team matches in the evenings of Saturday and Sunday so the broadcasts go back into Europe on Saturday and Sunday mornings."[412] Tournament organizers will face similar problems in 2015 when trying to find appropriate times for matches involving the likes of Australia, Fiji, Japan, New Zealand, Samoa and Tonga. Similarly, organizers of Rugby World Cup 2019 will need to find a way of accommodating the audiences but to a lesser extent than New Zealand due to the nine hour time difference between Tokyo and London.

Argentina Time Zone Compared to Key Markets

Argentina	Toronto	London	Paris	Bucharest	Tokyo	Sydney	Auckland
2:30pm	1:30pm	6:30pm	7:30pm	8:30pm	2:30am	3:30am	5:30am
3:30pm	2:30pm	7:30pm	8:30pm	9:30pm	3:30am	4:30am	6:30am
4:30pm	3:30pm	8:30pm	9:30pm	10:30pm	4:30am	5:30am	7:30am
5:30pm	4:30pm	9:30pm	10:30pm	11:30pm	5:30am	6:30am	8:30am
6:30pm	5:30pm	10:30pm	11:30pm	12:30am	6:30am	7:30am	9:30am
7:30pm	6:30pm	11:30pm	12:30am	1:30am	7:30am	8:30am	10:30am
8:30pm	7:30pm	12:30am	1:30am	2:30am	8:30am	9:30am	11:30am

As shown in the above chart Argentina's time zone provides opportunities for friendlier match times than all previous World Cup hosts. Despite the size of the country Argentina has only one time zone. The time zone means that tournament organizers would have the luxury of a genuine three day weekend with Friday night matches involving one or more of the likes of Australia, Fiji, Japan, New Zealand, Samoa or Tonga corresponding to superior scheduling options. For the first time in history, the Rugby World Cup could have two matches take place on a Friday which would be in the interests of everybody to better distribute the games and for teams to then have greater rest time between matches. Rather than having four matches on a Saturday and three on a Sunday, it would be possible to have two on a Friday, three on a Saturday and three on a Sunday. 9pm in Buenos Aires would be midday in New Zealand, Fiji and Tonga, 10am in Sydney and

9am in Tokyo. It would also be 2am in Paris and therefore not an option but a 5pm kick-off would mean 10pm in France and 9pm in the United Kingdom and Ireland. Having a match such as New Zealand v France kick-off at 5pm would work well by being 8am in New Zealand and 10pm in France. In other words, Argentina´s time zone is not only favorable for all major rugby markets but it also means finding a balance between two powerful teams from vastly different time zones is possible and friendlier than in all previous Rugby World Cup´s.

Afternoon kick-offs would be favorable for European and African sides while evening kick-off´s are favorable for teams from Asia and Oceania. Competing teams from both North and South America could play in either the afternoon or evening and still have good viewing hours for viewers in their countries. Another bonus is that Tier One sides could more easily be scheduled to play mid-week matches. This has been a tremendous problem for tournament organizers due to the comprabale lack of marketability between a Tier One nation and lower Tiers. It has inevitably resulted in shorter rest times between matches. The players have been unfairly treated due to where they come from rather than all having an equal or relatively equal amount of days to prepare for matches. A World Cup in Argentina could ultimately do what many in from the First Tier fear – enhance the possibility of Tier Two nations defeating them. There would be a decreased need for Tier Two and Three coaches to drastically change their starting lineups as there would be more time to recover and be ready for the subsequent match. Giving Tier Two and Three nations a chance to perform as equals is what sports are supposed to be about. The best way to grow is to actively encourage growth. Argentina 2023 can do just this due to its unique time zone.

The times would enable a match involving a European Tier One side or South Africa to be significantly more marketable to a television audience by kicking-off in the evening, local time, instead of at or around breakfast time in the case of a World Cup in New Zealand. As such, a schedule could be produced with minimal matches played at times that disadvantage viewers from a particular country. Consider the following sample draw for Rugby World Cup 2023. To simplify matters it has been done by using the same twenty nations that competed at Rugby World Cup 2011. They have been distributed fairly according to global rugby trends and with IRB World Rankings being taken into account. Times are local and thus fifteen hours behind New Zealand, five hours behind France and four hours behind the United Kingdom (GMT - Greenwich Mean Time).

Sample Draw for RWC 2023

Pool A	Pool B	Pool C	Pool D
Australia	England	South Africa	New Zealand
France	Argentina	Ireland	Wales
Fiji	Italy	Scotland	Samoa
USA	Canada	Georgia	Japan
Namibia	Russia	Tonga	Romania

Sample Match Schedule for RWC 2023

Date	Match	Kick-Off
Friday September 7	Argentina v England	6:30pm
	Australia v Fiji	8:30pm
Saturday September 8	Ireland v Georgia	2:30pm
	France v USA	4:30pm
	New Zealand v Wales	6:30pm
Sunday September 9	Italy v Russia	2:30pm
	South Africa v Scotland	4:30pm
	Japan v Samoa	7:30pm
Tuesday September 10	England v Canada	5:30pm
	Fiji v Namibia	7:30pm
Wednesday September 11	Wales v Romania	5:30pm
	Ireland v Tonga	7:30pm
Friday September 13	Australia v France	6:30pm
	New Zealand v Japan	8:30pm
Saturday September 14	South Africa v Georgia	4:30pm
	Argentina v Russia	7:30pm
Sunday September 15	Scotland v Tonga	4:30pm
	USA v Namibia	6:30pm
Monday September 16	Samoa v Romania	3:30pm
	Italy v Canada	5:30pm
Thursday September 19	Scotland v Georgia	3:30pm
	Wales v Japan	6:30pm
Friday September 20	South Africa v Ireland	6:30pm
	Australia v USA	8:30pm
Saturday September 21	England v Italy	5:30pm
	New Zealand v Samoa	8:30pm
Sunday September 22	France v Namibia	5:30pm
	Argentina v Canada	8:30pm
Tuesday September 24	Georgia v Tonga	5:30pm
	Japan v Romania	7:30pm
Wednesday September 25	England v Russia	4:30pm
	Fiji v USA	7:30pm
Friday September 27	Argentina v Italy	5:30pm
	Wales v Samoa	7:30pm
Saturday September 28	Scotland v Ireland	6:30pm
	Australia v Namibia	8:30pm
Sunday September 29	Canada v Russia	2:30pm

		South Africa v Tonga	4:30pm
		France v Fiji	6:30pm
		New Zealand v Romania	8:30pm

Solo Host

The confirmation of New Zealand as the host nation for Rugby World Cup 2011 was a wake up call for all Tier One unions. It was the third of seven Rugby World Cup's to be hosted by one country and, importantly, was easily the smallest population of all represented nations to have hosted a World Cup. It was a simple but a revolutionary change for rugby. Size need not matter so long as one can demonstrate that it has the capacity to successfully stage the event. New Zealand 2011 is testament to this and will likely be remembered for this into the future. The NZRU delivered a global event in a small and isolated country but the subsequent Rugby World Cup will be in a country with a population over 51 million[413] and moves are well underway for Wales to subhost matches. It is not through necessity. England has significantly more stadiums than New Zealand both in terms of quantity and size.

Eden Park was upgraded to 60,000 for the tournament with the second largest being Wellington, with a capacity of 40,000 for the tournament. Between them the two stadiums hosted nineteen of the competitions forty-eight matches while North Harbour Stadium, also in Auckland, hosted four matches.[414] Although the tournament's slogan was a stadium of four million, Auckland and Wellington hosted 47.9% of the competitions matches, including all eight of the play-offs games. The allocation of matches to venues was well planned with Tier One v Tier One matches all being played at Auckland, Dunedin or Wellington to capitalize on the larger capacities and quality of the stadiums. Originally Auckland, Christchurch and Wellington had been allocated five pool matches each but with Christchurch not able to host matches the games were moved. Dunedin, Invercargill, North Harbour, Nelson and Wellington all hosted one additional match. Of the five matches three were Tier One v Tier One and they were moved to Auckland, Dunedin and Wellington.[415]

Conversely in France 2007 larger stadiums enabled the organizers more flexibility and this saw a wider distribution of matches with the Stade de France hosting three pool matches, the same number as Lens, Lyon, Nantes, Saint Ettiene and Cardiff. The other French venues, Bordeaux, Marseilles, Montpellier, Toulouse and the Parc des Princes (Paris) hosted four pool matches each while Edinburgh hosted two. Matches were more spread around than in New Zealand due to size. New Zealand utilized five venues with a capacity of 20,000 or less.[416]

The capacity of seven of France's ten venues were separated by less than eight thousand and all were sizeble in comparison to those used in New Zealand 2011.[417] Of New Zealand's twelve venues only Auckland and Wellington were larger than France's smallest venue.[418]

The size of New Zealand's stadiums restricted the distribution of matches notably but England's interest in utilizing the Millenium Stadium for Rugby World Cup 2015 is a different situation altogether. England's successful bid identified a World Cup featuring fourteen venues across England and Wales. The exact list of venues is yet to be confirmed but it has been widely speculated that there will be three venues in London from Emirates Stadium, the Olympic Stadium, Twickenham and Wembley Stadium. Other venues appearing in line for matches are located in the cities of Coventry, Gloucester, Leeds, Leicester, Liverpool, Manchester, Newcastle and Southampton.[419] The venues are spread throughout England but the rugby strong-hold of the western midlands is without a sizeable stadium. Kingsholm in Gloucester has been singled out as a host venue but will be the smallest to host matches and will almost certainly not host Tier One matches at all.

Crucially Gloucester is located near Wales and the RFU believes the best thing to do for rugby the local population is to have the Millenium Stadium host matches. England Rugby 2015 General Manager for Rugby Services and Venue Operations, Simon Jelowitz said "One of the key strategic goals is to find real top-flight venues right across the country and to get as many people as possible engaged in watching the sport at its very best. The mixture of football and rugby venues will allow us to increase capacity which, in turn, means more people have access to tickets. Utilizing larger venues also allows us to look into a pricing model that is affordable and appealing to a wide range of budgets. To that end, we have also looked to include the Millennium Stadium within the tournament venue selection process. Whilst we acknowledge that this is not located in England, it will give all those supporters in the southwest of the country easy access to a fantastic stadium with a capacity of over 70,000 and allows us to host some of the bigger games outside of London."[420] WRU chairman David Pickering had earlier echoed the plans on using Cardiff. He said "I am so pleased that thousands of Welsh rugby fans will now be able to claim real involvement in this great competition. Our proximity to the west of England and London means the Millennium Stadium makes enormous sense as a venue for these important fixtures."[421]

There are two separate issues of credibility that need to be addressed. The first is that Wales and England are separate rugby unions operating within defined geographical borders. Although the stadium in question is large and arguably the world's finest rugby stadium this does not justify using a foreign venue. It's location would facilitate matters for organizers but Cardiff is nonetheless 77KM from Gloucester. Coventry, in comparison is 80KM from Gloucester. Coventry's Ricoh Arena has previously hosted Heineken Cup matches and has a capacity of 32,600[422] making it larger than Dunedin which hosted Argentina v England in 2011. The use of the Millenium Stadium would therefore be of greater value to the population of Wales rather than the population of England and is quite simply surplus to requirements to hosting a World Cup within England. The lack of English international matches outside of London makes the Millenium Stadium a safety net. It is a rugby hotbed of significantly lower risk than the likes of Leeds, Liverpool, Manchester or Newcastle in Northern England. Marketing a game is easier and the potential risk of a big match not attracting a strong attendance is lower in Cardiff than in Northern England.

The second credibility issue is the tournament itself. By allocating matches outside of England the Rugby World Cup is not going to be a genuine English tournament. The potential of a repeat of France's Quarter Final from 2007 in Cardiff is real. England could be forced, like France, into playing abroad during its own Rugby World Cup. The 2007 France v New Zealand match could have easily been in Lyon or Marseilles while the possibility of a smaller French venue such as Nantes or Toulouse was not entirely off limits. The attendances in France 2007 underlined the ability of France to host the tournament on its own. There is no reason why England cannot host a Rugby World Cup alone. Small venues do not necessarily mean negative publicity. Some of the better matches in Rugby World Cup 2011 were in smaller stadia. For instance Canada v Tonga in Whangarei was a genuine success. It was played at a venue similar to Gloucester. Matches involving Tier Two v Tier Two or Tier Three need not be played in large stadiums. France was able to attract strong crowds across its venues but New Zealand did have a few problems. A number of matches were not strongly attended. For instance, despite good weather Fiji v Namibia attracted 10,100 in Rotorua. A similar sized crowd of 10,267 attended Scotland v Georgia in Invercargill.[423] The low attendance can be accredited to it being a mid-week match played on a wet and cold evening.

Low attendances are not a rugby phenomenom but are a sporting one in general. Not all matches are sell outs in rugby or soccer. For instance England's opening match for the 2010 FIFA World Cup had a visible number of vacant seats. The match was played in Rustenburg against the USA. Officially there was a crowd of 38,646 at the stadium[424] which South Africa Explored lists as seating 44,000.[425] The crowd for England v USA was not full but was large in comparison to other matches in Rustenburg. New Zealand v Slovenia attracted a crowd of 23,871.[426] The stadium was a similar size to venues in Nelspruit and Polokwane both of which also hosted matches far from capacity. Slovenia v Algeria in Polokwane officially had a crowd of 30,325 people[427] and Chile v Honduras in Nelspruit was played in front of a crowd of 32,664.[428]

Over 10,000 unsold tickets is a significant number and, it suggests, that South Africa had more large venues than it needed. It could have hosted the FIFA World Cup successfully with a 25,000 seater venue used instead of one that fits 40,000 supporters. Nelspruit, Polokwane and Rustenburg were the three smallest venues used in the tournament yet all had problems justifying the money that had gone into their construction or redevelopment ahead of the tournament. England 2015 is not going to see new stadiums contructed. All stadiums currently exist and are either ready or require upgrading but nothing substantial. The lesson of Rugby World Cup 2011 and the 2010 FIFA World Cup is that larger does not always mean better. Careful planning is crucial with matches being properly distributed according to stadium size to suit the marketability of individual teams. A stadium of 40,000 was not needed for New Zealand v Slovenia in the FIFA World Cup and nor would such a venue be needed for a comparable Rugby World Cup fixture such as Japan v Russia. This makes the selection of the Millenium Stadium for England 2019 extremely controversial.

Wales´s selection in the first instance is problematic. There are no guarantees that the Millenium Stadium will be packed for matches. In 2007 neither Scotland nor Wales justified having matches that France could have hosted on its own. The BBC reported a crowd of 32,245 at the Millenium Stadium for Wales v Japan[429] compared to 72,000 for Wales v Australia five days earlier.[430] Despite being played in France a larger crowd attended Wales v Fiji in Nantes with the BBC listing the attendance at 34,000.[431] Despite not succeeding in attracting home supporters to a World Cup match against Japan, Wales is desired by Jelowitz who is attempting to organize a match schedule to, in his words, give more people access to more tickets. The drive for a large stadium is arguably going to work if it is for big matches, specifically, Tier One v Tier One. This would mean having key matches in Wales rather than England which is certain to effect the prestige of the tournament.

Should Argentina host Rugby World Cup 2023 it would genuinely be able to host the tournament on its own. No subhosts from neighbouring countries or from far away would be required. The growth of the brand name of Los Pumas has been well managed by the UAR which has actively sought the use of more venues throughout the country. This does not mean that Argentina would not listen to its neighbors about potentially having matches sub-hosted in Uruguay or Chile. Montevideo's proximity to Buenos Aires could see it host matches. However it is not an Argentine city and therefore should only be used if no alternative can be found within Argentina itself. Argentina has a list of complete stadiums which could host Rugby World Cup matches and, overall, they are significantly larger than those for Rugby World Cup 2011 in New Zealand. Existing stadiums of differing sizes will enable an Argentine hosted Rugby World Cup to find a balance between having large stadia for Tier One v Tier One matches and having appropriately sized venues for Tier Two v Tier Three matches. Part IV will investigate a potential list of twelve–fourteen stadiums to see if Argentina meets the final component of hosting a Rugby World Cup – having sufficient venues.

Part IV
Venues

16

Level 1 Stadiums

Rugby World Cup venues can be broken down into three categories. They are ranked in terms of size from Level 1 to Level 3. Each category is vitally important to successfully host a Rugby World Cup. Level 1 Stadiums are the core venues which are used to host the biggest matches of the tournament. Matches include the opening match, play-off's and Tier One v Tier One pool matches. The number of Level 1 stadiums has varied from tournament to tournament but the minimum number to host a tournament is three. Level 2 stadiums are crucial for hosting big matches including Tier One v Tier Two teams and the occasional Tier One v Tier One match. They also often host the same number of matches as Level 1 stadiums, and in some tournaments they have hosted more. It is important that host nations have at least three Level 2 stadiums. Level 3 stadiums are supplementary venues. They are used to host two or three matches each, including the majority of Tier Two vs Tier Three matches and, occassionaly Tier One teams play at such a venue. Some Rugby World Cup's have seen stadiums of over 40,000 in capacity used as Level 3 stadiums but such venues need not be large. A small venue seating 20,000 is suitable.

Level 1 Stadiums have a capacity of 40,000 or more. A stadium of this size is appropriate to receive key matches and meets market demands according to previous Rugby World Cup's. Some Tier One v Tier One matches can be in smaller venues and others require larger ones but, overall, 40,000 is a good size for a stadium to warrant hosting a key match such as a World Cup Quarter Final. The IRB's only stipulated requirement of Level 1 stadiums is that a country can host the final in a venue with a minimal capacity of 60,000.[432] This was made clear during the bidding stages for Rugby World Cup 2011 when New Zealand was bidding despite its largest Stadium at the time seating fewer than 50,000 people. The NZRU's bid included a promise to have a 60,000 seater stadium for the tournament. It was also vital that New Zealand had a quality stadium that would attract supporters and to ensure a lasting legacy after the completion of the tournament. The late Jock Hobbs said in 2006 that "To maximize the benefits of hosting the tournament, Rugby World Cup 2011 needs to be flawlessly delivered and we need to have a centre-stage, world-class, 60,000-seat stadium that all of New Zealand can be proud of."[433]

It was the Fourth Rugby World Cup in the professional era while Rugby World Cup 2003 was the first tournament hosted by two or less nations since 1995. It featured eleven venues, like the 1987 tournament. In comparison there were nineteen for 1991, nine for 1995 and eighteen for 1999.[434] The 2003 tournament saw the ARU utilizing venues nationwide with five venues falling into the category of Level 1 stadiums. They were located in four cities with Sydney having two while Brisbane, Melbourne and Perth had one each. Between them these five venues hosted thirty-three of the tournaments forty-eight matches.[435] But many of the matches were far from being at capacity. Brisbane's capacity of 52,500 was approached but never reached. 48,788 attended Australia v Romania compared to 30,990 for Fiji vs USA. Melbourne's largest crowd also featured the home side and Australia v Ireland was full. The stadium was at less than half capacity for Wales v Canada however as 24,874 attended the match at a stadium seating more than 50,000. Perth's highest attendance was 38,834 for England v South Africa but none of its other four matches saw more than 26,000 in attendance.[436] Perth suffered from being isolated from the rest of the venues but also because its stadium's capacity of 43,000 was too big. It also saw the city's Super Rugby team, the Western Force move to the smaller nib Stadium, which seats 20,000, in 2010.

Sydney hosted a total of twelve matches and overall it had the best crowds. There were not noticeably low turnouts in any of its matches. The smallest crowd was 28,576 for Georgia v Uruguay at the Sydney Football Stadium. Now known as Allianz Stadium the stadium has a capacity of 42,000 people. The Olympic Stadium is much larger, seating 83,500[437] and had a solid tournament recording five crowds of over 80,000 out of its seven matches. The 2003 Final received a record attendance of 82,957 for a Rugby World Cup match. The lowest crowd at the stadium was 62,712 for the Bronze Final between France and New Zealand[438] but it was nevertheless too large for any other stadium used for the tournament.

On the other side of the coin the two Quarter Finals in Melbourne did not receive the same numbers of supporters as the key pool matches played at the venue.

France v Ireland had close to 20,000 unsold seats and attracted a crowd of 33,134. New Zealand v South Africa did better the previous day as 40,734 attended the match.[439] The selection of Melbourne for the two Quarter Finals was sensible in terms of promoting rugby in the state of Victoria. The city is also amongst the largest three in the country. It is not a rugby thriving city though and in 2003 the sport had a lower profile in Melbourne than in 2012. The attendances for the Quarter Finals suggest that alternate venues could have better served the tournament with Sydney potentially hosting at least one and maybe a different city with a smaller capacity hosting the other.

One of the major factors behind the attendances in Australia 2003 was the lack of regular rugby played at a high level in much of the country. Neither Melbourne nor Perth were hosting test matches annually at this stage and before the tournament Melbourne had, in fact, not hosted an international match since 1998. Perth, in contrast has hosted four tests in the professional era with Ireland visiting in 1999 and 2003 and South Africa in 1998 and 2001. Having both cities used as Level 1 venues was problematic and was something that would not be repeated in Rugby World Cup 2007. Many of the ten French venues hosted French international matches in the years leading up to France 2007. France played in Marseille every year from 2000-2008. It played in Lyon in 2006, in Lens in 2003, in Nantes in 2005, in Saint Etienne in 2001 and in Toulouse in 2005. The option to play outside of Paris actively prepared the population for the tournament. The domestic situation was also favorable due to the use of larger stadia by Top 14 clubs.

The tournament was hosted very differently to Australia 2003. Aside from the obvious difference of having two sub-hosts, France 2007 was also a far more distributed tournament than Australia 2003. All French venues hosted three or four pool matches and only three hosted five or more matches in total – Marseille, the Parc des Princes and the Stade de France. The three venues were joined by Cardiff and Edinburgh to give Rugby World Cup 2007 five Level 1 stadiums. Marseilles, the Parc des Princess, Cardiff and Edinburgh hosted one Tier One v Tier One pool match each while the Stade de France hosted three.[440] The tournament's other genuine Tier One v Tier One match was played in Saint Etienne while Bordeaux, Lens, Montpellier and Nantes hosted a key match between a Tier One team and a Pacific Island nation.

France's consistent venue size meant it had no Level 3 Stadiums at all. The FFR was happy to have Level 2 Stadiums host as many matches as Level 1 stadiums and overall it did very well in promoting matches. 97% of all the tickets for the tournament's forty-two matches in France were sold.[441] The venue with the worst attendances was Montpellier which was, nevertheless, close to capacity for two of its four matches.[442] Its highest attended match was Australia v Fiji which had a crowd of 32,232[443] while the stadium fits 32,900.[444] Aside from Georgia v Namibia no other Pool match had a noticeable number of unsold seats. The match was played in wet conditions and was a midweek match but its status as a game without a Tier One side did not see a poor turnout however as 32,549 attended the match.[445] It was similar to other matches such as Italy v Romania which had over 44,000 at Marseilles. It could have been played elsewhere but like the 2007 Bronze Final despite having a noticeable amount of unsold tickets there were still more people in attendance than the capacities of other stadiums.

From a Level 1 perspective New Zealand had similar ideas to France before Christchurch's matches had to be relocated. The NZRU had Eden Park, Christchurch and Dunedin as the country's Level 1 venues. All would host key pool matches and games in the knock-out stage. Auckland, Christchurch and Wellington were allocated five pool matches each, including all Tier One v Tier One matches. This changed after the earthquake to give New Zealand two Level 1 stadiums for the tournament. Eden Park and Wellington were supported by two Level 2 stadiums – Dunedin and North Harbour while two matches were relocated to Level 3 stadiums. Of all the relocated matches only one went to a Level 1 Stadium – Argentina v Scotland.[446] It meant that New Zealand's largest cities had congested weekends with multiple venues hosting two matches over three days. For instance North Harbour hosted France v Japan on September 10 and Australia v Italy on September 11. Wellington hosted Australia v USA on September 23 and Argentina v Scotland on September 25. It then hosted France v Tonga on October 01 and New Zealand v Canada on October 02. This did not occur at all in France 2007 due to its high supply of Level 2 stadiums.

Argentina has more Level 1 Stadiums than New Zealand and its overall a range of stadiums is well suited to the demands of hosting a Rugby World Cup. Of the eight venues that hosted the 2011 Copa América five were Level 1 stadiums. The same five venues are suitable for rugby and Los Pumas have played international rugby at each venue in the professional era. They are not, however the only Level 1 stadiums in the country and the UAR's policy of playing outside of Buenos Aires has been successful in increasing the profile of rugby in Argentina. As such Argentina will be in a better position to successfully host key Tier One v Tier One matches across the country than Australia was in 2003 and that England is likely to be in 2015.

In 2012 alone the UAR has not used the same venue twice, even including the two friendly matches against Stade Français. All eight cities that Argentina played in in 2012 are suitable for a Rugby World Cup and, crucially, the majority of venues are Level 1 stadiums but not all of them. A Rugby World Cup in Argentina could work best by having five or six Level 1 stadiums host three or four pool matches each and have support from four Level 2 stadiums and the numbers being made up from Level 3 stadia. Considering the country's Level 1 stadiums and international rugby matches played in the country there appears to be five cities that should host Rugby World Cup matches – Buenos Aires, La Plata, Rosario, Córdoba and Mendoza.

Buenos Aires
Argentina's capital city has traditionally hosted two Pumas tests per year, and sometimes more. In the professional era Buenos Aires has hosted well over half of all Argentina's home matches. Outside of the South American Championship it hosted virtually all matches until Rugby World Cup 2003. Between Rugby World Cup 1995 and 2003 only two Pumas matches against Tier One or Two teams were not in Buenos Aires. But from 2004 onwards other cities started hosting international rugby and doing so with increased regularity.[447] Buenos Aires city missed out on hosting a test in the 2012 Rugby Championship but did play host to Stade Français and in future seasons is certain to play host to Pumas matches. Over time Buenos Aires is likely to be comparable to how the NZRU uses Auckland. It will be a regular host potentially hosting two matches but never more. Like Auckland, it is easily the country's largest city and like New Zealand it is far from being the only city with sufficient stadia for test rugby.

Buenos Aires City has necessary infrastructure to be a hub for a Rugby World Cup. It is not only Argentina's capital and largest city but is also the continents second largest after São Paulo. Its population of 13.8 million[448] makes it easily the country's largest city. It is the economic centre of the country and the transport hub for Argentina both domestically and internationally and is an important tourist city which has been refered to as the Paris of South America.[449] It is also an important rugby city packed with historical rugby clubs which Los Pumas continue to hold training sessions at when in the country. Buenos Aires would without doubt open up and welcome visitors and proudly host a Rugby World Cup. Its high supply of hotels, restaurants and other forms of entertainment will make for a great experience for visiting World Cup supporters.

Since 2003 all host nations have utilized at least two stadiums in the hub city of the tournament. This will continue in London for 2015 and Tokyo for 2019 with both cities looking to use three stadiums each, compared to two used in Sydney, Paris and Auckland from 2003-2011. Buenos Aires can replicate the 2003-2011 tournaments and certainly has the population and stadiums to do so. It is noticeably larger than both Sydney and Auckland which have populations of 4.63million[450] and 1.5 million[451] respectively. Greater Buenos Aires is also larger than Greater Paris. Officially Paris has a population of 2.25 million[452] but with the Greater are of Paris included its total population is slightly above 12 million.[453] The use of multiple stadiums in a tournament's main city is not limited to rugby. The 2010 FIFA World Cup was similar in that the city that hosted the final, Johannesburg has a population of 3.2 million[454] that is increased when combined with surrounding areas. The city had two venues for the tournament with matches being played at both Soccer City and Ellis Park.

Buenos Aires has a number of stadiums that could be candidates to host World Cup matches. A potential venue is the Estadio José Amalfitani, often referred to as Vélez Sarsfield Stadium. It hosted Pumas matches annually from 2002-2010 and also hosted three matches at the 1978 FIFA World Cup and seven matches at the 2001 FIFA World Youth Championship including the final. The stadium first hosted international rugby in 1986 in a match that Los Pumas won 15-13 against France. In total, Argentina has played twenty-nine test matches at the stadium that was the unofficial home of Los Pumas for the majority of the decade ending in 2010. It has hosted at least one test match per year during this period and has always been the venue for the match considered to be the biggest home match of the year. It is a Level 1 stadium with a capacity of 49,540[455] and has been filled for numerous Pumas test matches. The possibility certainly exists for it to be used for Rugby World Cup 2023.

Should Vélez Sarsfeld be used it would be the junior partner for another Buenos Aires stadium due to it having a capacity lower than 60,000. The country's largest stadium is River Plate Stadium, also known as the Estadio Monumental Antonio Vespucio Liberti, and El Monumental de Nuñez. It is an appropriate venue to be used to open a Rugby World Cup and host the final. It is Argentina's equivalent of Croke Park, Eden Park, the Millenium Stadium or the Stade de France as it is the country's national stadium. It is also the usual home of the Argentine soccer team and is an important historical stadium that was first opened in 1938. It has been downsized since hosting the FIFA World Cup Final to now have a capacity of 64,000[456] which meets the demands of the IRB to host a Rugby World Cup Final. Japan is likely to stage the 2019 Rugby World Cup Final at Nissan Stadium in Yokohama which seats 72,327[457] and like River Plate Stadium has an athletics track.

River Plate Stadium has previously hosted international rugby matches with Los Pumas playing one test per year from 2000-2002. It could potentially be used very similarly to the Stade de France in Rugby World Cup 2007. The FFR had three pool matches at the stadium as well as one Quarter Final, both Semi Finals and the Final. The Parc de Princes also hosted Tier One v Tier One matches and the Bronze Final. River Plate Stadium could be potentially be joined by Vélez Sarsfeld or another in Avallaneda, to give Greater Buenos Aires two stadiums to host up to four pool matches each and playoffs matches. Potentially the better option would be Avallenada due to it having a much more modern Level 1 stadium than Vélez Sarsfeld. As it stands, River Plate Stadium would appear to be an appropriate venue to host the 2023 Rugby World Cup Final but it could, of course, be upgraded to have a larger seating capacity and improved facilities.

A strong option to support River Plate Stadium in Buenos Aires is the Estadio Libertadores de América Stadium in Avellaneda, also in Greater Buenos Aires. The stadium is new, having been constructed from 2007-2009 as a redevelopment to the original stadium which was first constructed in 1928. It has a capacity for up to 57,098 people which can be reduced to 48,000 to provide an all-seater environment.[458] With a reduced capacity it would still be a Level 1 Stadium and would be larger than the venues used by Australia, France and New Zealand to support their respective tournament's principal venue in the hub city. It would enable the possibility of having two Tier One v Tier One matches in Greater Buenos Aires on the same weekend. This would make it easier than in some previous tournaments when one venue has hosted pool matches on consecutive days.

The Estadio Libertadores de América and the city of Avallaneda hosted international rugby for the first time ever in June 2011 as Los Pumas took on the French Barbarians. The stadium was selected instead of Vélez Sarsfeld and provided better aesthetics due to the venues young age. Like Vélez Sarsfeld it provides the specators with superb viewing due to the proximity of the stands to the field. Both venues are rectangular rather than oval or round like River Plate Stadium. While it is a part of Greater Buenos Aires, Avellaneda is separate from the autonomous city of Buenos Aires, also known as the Buenos Aires Federal District. As such it is considered to be a separate city even though they are joined to form a conurbation. Avellaneda is on the Southern edge of the Autonomous City of Buenos Aires which is home to River Plate Stadium. Should River Plate Stadium and the Estadio Libertadores de América both act as host venues the population of Greater Buenos Aires would have sufficient opportunities to attend matches. Visiting teams would also have a greater chance of playing in the largest Argentine city.

La Plata
One of South America´s newest and most impressive stadiums is the Estadio Unico Ciudad de La Plata in the capital of Buenos Aires Province, La Plata. The stadium has quickly emerged as a powerful player in Argentine sport having been selected to open the 2011 Copa América and host Argentina´s home test against New Zealand in the 2012 Rugby Championship. It was selected for both events for two reasons. The first being the quality of the stadium and the second being the city´s proximity to Greater Buenos Aires. The stadium had a capacity of 53,000 for the Copa América[459] making it a Level 1 Stadium. It´s size and modernity makes it an ideal venue to host Rugby World Cup matches. It has the potential to host key pool matches as well as play-off´s matches such as Quarter Finals and potentially the Bronze Final. It is a comparable stadium to Loftus Versfeld Stadium in Pretoria, which hosted five matches at Rugby World Cup 1995, including one Quarter Final and the Bronze Final and hosted six matches at the 2010 FIFA World Cup. Like Pretoria, La Plata is located close to the country´s largest city. Both are located less than one hour away and can take similar approaches towards hosting a World Cup tournament. Pretoria joined the two Johannesburg venues in hosting the 2010 FIFA World Cup and La Plata could certainly do the same for Rugby World Cup 2023.

The Estadio Unico has facilities that are unmatched elsewhere in the country and are rarely seen anywhere. It is a stadium for all events and not just sport. The spectators´ experience is enhanced by multiple giant LED television screens that show live action to supporters in all areas of the stadium. The state of the art technology is not found in any other stadium in The Rugby Championship or in any venues from the Six Nations Championship. The infrastructure is found only in La Plata, Germany and Japan. The screens enable the live projection of play taking place on the field and also show advertising, graphics and animations with the highest video quality possible. The screens are 7 metres in length and 5 metres in height[460] providing spectators with a unique experience that no other venue in the history of rugby has provided too date.

La Plata could potentially host up to four pool matches and would likely be attractive to visiting supporters. It would be appropriate for Tier One v Tier One matches but also Tier One v Tier Two matches. In Rugby World Cup 2007, for instance, South Africa started its campaign at the Parc des Princess against Samoa on a Sunday and then faced England at the Stade de France five days later on the Friday. La Plata could host an identical fixture with a Tier One side such as England, Ireland, New Zealand or South Africa playing back-to-back in La Plata and Buenos Aires before travelling outside of the province to play in other parts of the country. It could also do the opposite by hosting a Tier One v Tier One match on the final weekend similar to Argentina v Ireland from 2007. Ireland played two matches in Bordeaux before playing at the Stade de France and the Parc des Princes. Argentina offers similar possibilities and both Avallenada and La Plata could be used in a similar way to the Parc des Princes. It would also simplify attending matches for visiting fans who could easily plan their way to follow their team.

Should La Plata join two stadiums from Greater Buenos Aires it would mean there would be three Level 1 Stadiums in a small part of the country. However it is more than justified due to the quality of the stadium in La Plata and the cities population. La Plata is the sixth largest city in the country with a population of 731,000.[461] Nevertheless Argentina has sufficient Level 1 stadia in other parts of the country to ensure the big name teams are able to be well spread throughout the country. Argentina's second, third and fourth largest cities all hosted Los Pumas in 2012 and all did so by utilizing stadiums with a capacity of 40,000 or above. The same venues would be a key part of an Argentine bid to host Rugby World Cup 2023 and would significantly cut down on congestion for visitors and make for a higher availability of tickets. The spin off for the local population would not only be a greater chance of seeing star players from Tier One teams but also that the cost of attending matches would not need to be so high.

Rosario
Argentina's third largest city, Rosario has increasingly become linked to Los Pumas. The city has been contributing a growing number of players to Los Pumas and in recent years the city has been central to the UAR's plans to see rugby expand in Argentina. Rosario is increasingly going to host big matches and it is a strong option for a Rugby World Cup in Argentina in 2023. The Estadio Dr. Lisandro de la Torre, also known as the Estadio Gigante de Arroyito stadium is a Level 1 venue, seating 41,654[462] and is the largest stadium in Rosario. It is an important Argentine stadium historically and adds greatly to the strength of an Argentine bid to host a Rugby World Cup.

The stadium hosted matches at the 1978 FIFA World Cup and at the 1987 Copa América. Rosario did not feature in the 2011 Copa América but the stadium hosted a key FIFA World Cup qualifying match in 2009 against Brazil. In 2008 the Estadio Gigante de Arroyito hosted an important rugby test match for the first time as Argentina took on Scotland in what was Argentina's first match since France 2007. A strong crowd saw the home team win 21-15 but a lack of home internationals in Argentina meant the city would have to wait four years to host a Pumas test again. In 2012 Los Pumas returned to Rosario to face Australia in The Rugby Championship. The UAR's decision to play against the Wallabies in Rosario speaks volumes of rugby in the city and also of the stadium itself. It was widely considered as being the most winnable test in the Rugby Championship for the South Americans.

Rosario is a large city. With a population of 1.25 million[463] it is Argentina's third largest city. It is located in the Santa Fé province, around 300KM northwest of Buenos Aires and 400KM east of Córdoba. Morover, the main highway from Buenos Aires to Tucumán and to Santa Fé City passes through Rosario. The location of Rosario and the size of the Estadio Gigante de Arroyito would greatly simplify the task of planning a match schedule for a Rugby World Cup. It need not have a team based in the city for multiple matches as it would be accessible to teams going from playing in the capital to playing in Northern or Western Argentina or vice-versa. A key part on delivering a succesful World Cup is simplying travel times for both teams and fans. Rosario can significantly do this by combining with Level 1 venues in Buenos Aires province and Córdoba as well as Level 2 and 3 venues to the north.

Given the size of the Estadio Gigante de Arroyito, it could be used to stage four pool matches in the same way as the earlier mentioned venues from Rugby World Cup 2003 and 2011. However the ideal situation may well be for Rosario to be used in a more comparable way to the venues in France 2007. It could potentially host one of the most important pool matches to determine a Quarter Finalist such as an equivalent match to Wales v Fiji or Scotland v Italy from Rugby World Cup 2007 or Argentina v England from Rugby World Cup 2011. Part of making a Rugby World Cup great is having such matches spread around and not concentrated in only one or two cities. It also adds to the experience of visiting fans who can not only follow their team but also see more of the country. Rosario can play a key role in making this possible.

Córdoba
While Rosario is the largest city in the litoral region[464] of Argentina, Córdoba is the largest in the broadly defined region of the north and the second largest in the country. With a population of 1.39 million[465] the city is guaranteed to feature at a Rugby World Cup in Argentina. Its largest stadium is the Estadio Mario Alberto Kempes, formerly known as Estadio Córdoba, the Estadio Olímpico Chateau

Carreras, or the Estadio Olímpico. It was constructed in 1976 for the 1978 FIFA World Cup and hosted eight out of the tournament's thirty-eight World Cup matches. Since 1978 it has continued to host high profile soccer matches including the 1987 Copa América, the 2001 World FIFA Junior Championship and the 2011 Copa América. It was upgraded significantly in preparation for the 2011 Copa América giving the city a significantly larger and better stadium. Its capacity of 57,000[466] makes it the largest stadium outside of Buenos Aires.

In addition to having an extensive history in soccer, the stadium has also been used by the UAR. Argentina has played three international rugby matches at the stadium – v Fiji in 2003, Italy in 2008 and France in 2012. Despite missing all European based players who featured in The Rugby Championship, the stadium had a strong crowd for the June 2012 international against France. It is certain to have Pumas matches with more regularity with a test in The Rugby Championship quite possibly to be played in 2013 or 2014. It could also be a strategically important venue for a Rugby World Cup. Its location in Northern Argentina could see it used as the major venue outside of Buenos Aires and La Plata and it is large enough to be considered for Quarter Finals. It could be Argentina's equivalent of Wellington, Marseille or Brisbane. This would see Córdoba potentially hosting four pool matches involving at least one Tier One v Tier One match-up. The capacity of the stadium and the size of the city make Córdoba a prime candidate to host Quarter Finals. Should the city do so then it would likely host fewer pool matches similar to Buenos Aires and La Plata.

Córdoba's location is of great interest to Argentina successfully bidding for a Rugby World Cup. It is in the northern half of the country but is central to other major cities aside from the capital. It is 465KM east of Mendoza and 410KM from San Juan. It is 400KM west from Rosario and 560KM south of Tucumán. It is therefore not very close to any other potential host city but has the advantage of being central to all of them and it could act as a bridge between them. Visiting fans would be able to follow their teams and take in three or four different cities with a team able to go north, west or east from Córdoba to play its next match. In comparison Dunedin only had Invercargill close to it. All other venues were more than 600KM away.

Mendoza
The country's fourth largest city and the largest in the west is Mendoza. With a population of 894,000[467] it is larger than all cities from Rugby World Cup 2011 except for Auckland. Mendoza is an important Argentine city and is famous

worldwide for the production of the malbec variety of red wine. No country produces more Malbec than Argentina and the region of Mendoza produces over two-thirds of all wine from the country. There is more to the city than wine with sport in general being important. No Argentine city is larger in the Andes and the city is located near a number of ski resorts. It is also home to one of the country´s key sports stadiums, the Estadio Malvinas Argentinas.

The stadium came under the global rugby spotlight in August 2012 as Argentina made its debut appearance in The Rugby Championship. The stadium is an important landmark in Argentina due to its name and also its sporting role. The stadium takes on the Argentine name for the Falkland Islands and it was a host venue at the 1978 FIFA World Cup. It hosted six matches at the tournament and also hosted games at the 2001 FIFA World Youth Championship and the 2011 Copa América. It was constructed in preparation for the FIFA World Cup and opened in 1976. Like most large venues across Argentina, the Estadio Malvinas Argentinas has not only a history in hosting important soccer fixtures, but it has also hosted international rugby. Before hosting ther Springboks in 2012 it had also hosted Italy in 2007.

The venue qualifies as a Level 1 stadium Estadio Malvinas Argentinas has a capacity at present of 40,268.[468] Its size makes it large enough to be considered to host a Quarter Final in addition to four pool matches. Mendoza is very similar to both Córdoba and Rosario in that it is a large city with an appropriate stadium ready to be used for a Rugby World Cup and is located in a different patr of the country with different potential Level 2 and 3 venues being located near each city. The Malvinas Argentinas would merit a key Tier One v Tier One match similar to Perth hosting England v South Africa in 2003. Like Perth Mendoza is located far from other main cities. Mendoza is 1,100KM west of Buenos Aires and 380KM east of Chile´s capital, Santiago. Córdoba would be the closest Level 1 venue, located 500KM north-east of Mendoza. But the city is not isolated like Perth. A probable Level 2 venue, San Juan is around 150KM to the north of Mendoza. Together San Juan and Mendoza are good options for Western Argentina which can significantly decrease what could be a tough travel demand.

Australia got around the problem of distances by only having teams from one pool play in Perth. Argentina could do the same thing with Mendoza or it could utilize the stadium in conjunction with San Juan and Córdoba and other cities in Northern Argentina. A team such as Ireland could play two matches in Mendoza then its third pool match in Córdoba and its final pool match in Tucumán, Rosario or Buenos Aires. A qualifying team such as Europe 1 could face Ireland in Mendoza then play another qualifying team in San Juan before moving on to play in Tucumán or Salta. Similarly a Tier One team such as France could begin in Buenos Aires then play two matches in cities such as Santa Fé and Córdoba before finishing in Mendoza. There will be plenty of time for competition organizers to devise a match schedule that takes this into account and greatly reduces the chances of having low attendances at matches.

Argentina's limitations in terms of geography are manageable and are far from being a negative. While Mendoza to Buenos Aires is further than Auckland to Chrstchurch there are no geographical barriers such as the Cook Strait which separates New Zealand's North and South Islands. The 900KM distance makes it hard but it did not receive criticism from visitors at Rugby World Cup 2011 despite the voyage including a three hour ferry ride. Many Irish supporters made the trip from Rotorua after Ireland's match against Russia to Dunedin to see Ireland's final pool match, against Italy. Ireland then played in Wellington in a Quarter Final. Such distances are actually similar in size to those separating the Level 1 venues listed in Argentina. In addition the two Quarter-Final venues used for Rugby World Cup 2003, Melbourne and Brisbane are over 1500KM apart with a flight time of 3.5 hours. In comparison, by plane the trip from Buenos Aires to Mendoza is less than 2 hours. In other words Mendoza is located far but not comparatively and it can be used effectively with organizers drawing up match schedules knowing which teams will likely have the larger number of travelling supporters. They will be able to travel by land or air to follow their team.

Level 1 Stadiums

City	Stadium	Capacity	Number of potential RWC pool Matches
Avallenada	Libertadores	48,000	Three
Buenos Aires	River Plate	64,000	Three
Córdoba	Mario Kempes	57,000	Three
La Plata	Único	53,000	Three
Mendoza	Malvinas Argentinas	40,268	Four
Rosario	Gigante de Arroyito	41,654	Four

17

Level 2 Stadiums

Chapter 16 outlined a list of potential venues to act as core venues. No country can host a Rugby World Cup without them and Argentina certainly appears to be a strong candidate based on the venues listed. But hosting a Rugby World Cup goes beyond having large stadiums in different parts of a country. There is also a need to have several venues which can host key matches and ensure a smooth tournament by being able to cope with the heavy load of weekend matches during the pool stage. Such venues need to be big but not as big as Level 1 Stadiums. A working stadium size is a capacity of between 25,000 and 40,000. Stadiums of this size enable a broad range of matches to be played and they have played host to Tier One teams at every Rugby World Cup in the professional era. The fundamental importance of venues of this size is to ensure that attendances are positive and that attracting visitors is a possible task. Previous Rugby World Cup´s in the professional era have demonstrated this unlike World Cup´s operated by FIFA.

Australia 2003 utilized three Level 2 stadiums – Adelaide, Canberra and Townsville. They were used in differing ways. Adelaide only hosted two matches and did so on the same weekend. In an effort to promote rugby in the city and in the state of South Australia, the ARU allocated it with Australia v Namibia playing on a Saturday and also gave it a Tier One v Tier One match as Australia´s pool rivals Argentina and Ireland played on the Sunday. Canberra hosted four matches, three of which involved Italy. The city´s fourth match was also from the same pool as Wales faced Tonga. Townsville hosted three matches, all of which featured Japan. The share size of Australia certainly played a key part in determining which teams played in which venues and against whom. It resulted in a high concentration of matches in Level 1 Stadiums and too many matches lacked strong attendances.

France 2007 took a different approach. The size of France certainly simplified the organizers task but so did the number of Level 2 stadiums. France had seven stadiums seating between 32,000 and 42,000 with five of them lower than the 40,000 mark. The key to France making it's Rugby World Cup the most successful ever was its distribution of matches. None of the seven venues hosted play-off's matches at all yet between them they hosted half of the tournaments matches. The allocation of matches saw all seven venues host either three or four pool matches each. It enabled each venue to host matches involving Tier One teams and every venue had at least one genuinely even fought pool match. The organizers focused more on full stadiums than large ones and this saw Wales v Canada in Nantes and Australia v Canada in Bordeaux compared to Wales v Canada and New Zealand v Canada in Melbourne in 2003.

France only gave Lens, Lyon, Nantes and Saint Etienne three matches. While Bordeaux, Montpellier and Toulouse all hosted four each. The reason for this is the comparable strength of rugby in these cities. Lyon is larger than Toulouse as a city and its stadium, the Stade de Gerland also has a larger capacity than the Stadium Municipal in Toulouse. By organizing a tournament according to the market France succeeded where Australia had failed. It did so evidently without using Level 3 stadiums at all. New Zealand, in contrast did not have the population to emulate France 2007 but it did have a large number of Level 2 stadiums. New Zealand used a total of five Level 2 stadiums and like in France they all hosted three or four pool matches each. The NZRU distributed teams according to their marketability to have different Tier One teams play in different parts of New Zealand. Hamilton, New Plymouth and Rotorua hosted three pool matches each while Dunedin and North Harbour hosted four. The largest of these venues – Dunedin, Hamilton and North Harbour all hosted one or two key pool matches featuring either a Tier One v Tier one or a Tier One v Tier Two match. New Plymouth and Rotorua acted to fill the gap required on weekends.

Argentina offers a list of Level 2 venues that is similar to France but not equal. Unlike New Zealand it has a number of venues seating over 30,000 that can simplify the task of hosting key pool matches on weekends. New Zealand hosted seventeen pool matches at a total of five Level 2 stadiums[469] while it hosted eleven pool matches at its two Level 1 stadiums. Despite there being no set number of required Level 2 stadiums it would appear likely that a country needs to host at least thirteen matches at Level 2 venues. The number can be higher depending on the individual cases but hosting fewer will require a higher number of Level 1 stadiums which would subsequently mean the potential of having low attendances would increase. If Argentina was to utilize the venues covered in the previous chapter and host fourteen matches in Level 2 stadia it would likely need four venues of the Level 2 variety.

Argentina could utilize four Level 2 stadiums that could host three or four pool matches each to maximize the likelihood of a successful tournament. The geography of Argentina means that there could be one Level 2 stadium in each of the four general regions - Buenos Aires province, the Litoral, the North and the West. Distribution is highly important to minimize the travel for teams backing up from their previous match to cut down on travel time. It is also crucial to ensure a broad spread of matches in not only different cities but also different regions. In Argentina the four mentioned regions all have Level 1 stadiums that can be well supported by nearby Level 2 stadiums. Furthermore Argentina's Level 2 stadiums are far from being white elephants. They would also all be stadiums familiar to international rugby – Mar del Plata, Santa Fé, San Juan and Tucumán.

Mar del Plata
The host city of the 2011 Rugby Sevens World Cup is a venue certain to be seriously considered for a Rugby World Cup in Argentina. The city's largest stadium is the Estadio José María Minella, also known as the Estadio Mundialista. It was built in time for the 1976 FIFA World Cup and hosted six matches amongst them were high profile games such as France v Italy and Brazil vs Spain. It also hosted seven matches in the 2001 FIFA Junior World Cup. Like all of the Level 1 Stadiums having World Cup Rugby played in Mar del Plata would be a significant achieved for the sport. The stadium is not large enough to be called a Level 1 venue but it is nevertheless large enough to still be chosen for home soccer international matches. It hosted Argentina v Ecuador in 2011.

The stadium has a capacity of 35,354[470] making it comparable to the majority of the venues used by France in 2007. Like the French venues it is likely to be a good choice to host three or four pool matches in the event that Argentina hosts Rugby World Cup 2023. It has played host to international rugby matches previously. The most recent match was in 2010 against Scotland. It was not selected for the 2012 internationals but remains a possible venue to host Pumas tests in the coming years. The city is also a popular beach destination, which can contribute to the World Cup experience. Mar del Plata is located 400KM south of Buenos Aires and 340KM from La Plata. It is a large city with a population of 609,000, making it the seventh largest in Argentina.[471]

Its best potential use as a World Cup venue could well be supporting the larger stadiums in Buenos Aires and La Plata. If so it could mean that Mar del Plata would host three matches. It could be a venue for a midweek match featuring a Tier One side coming off a Tier One v Tier One match or a standard weekend match. Its proximity to the capital and the nature of the city would work in favor of a schedule that is drawn up to the advantage of the Tier Two and Tier Three competing nations. For instance if New Zealand were to play Wales in La Plata on a Friday or Saturday it could then play against a regional qualifier on a Tuesday or Wednesday. This being the case, the stadium could work well with two such matches and a third being a higher profile game similar to how France used Saint Etienne in 2007.

Santa Fé

The Estadio Brigadier General Estanislao López, also known as the Cementerio des Elefantes in Santa Fé City is a quality stadium, more than capable of hosting Rugby World Cup matches. The stadium underwent a dramatic upgrade for the 2011 Copa América. Its capacity increased from 32,000 to 40,000[472] and it importantly had new facilities installed to significantly modernize the stadium. Its capacity technically makes it a Level 1 stadium but only just. It could host Quarter Finals but it would be unlikely to do so due to its location in the same province as Rosario. Santa Fé is 147KM north of Rosario and the size of both venues mean it will be highly useful for distributing matches around Argentina. The two cities can provide Argentina's key venues in the Litoral region and be supported by a Level 3 stadium such as Resistencia as will be looked at in the final chapter.

The Estadio Brigadier General Estanislao López has played host to important rugby matches previously. In 2007 Los Pumas played at the stadium for the first time, facing Ireland in front of a large crowd. It was also one of three venues used to host the 2010 IRB Junior World Championship. It hosted ten matches with the others being played at the Club Atlético Estudiantes in Paraná and the Estadio Newell's Old Boys in Rosario. The stadium missed out on hosting a Pumas test in 2012 but did host Argentina v Stade Français and like the Level 1 stadiums it is a strong contender to host more Pumas matches now that Argentina is playing twice as many home tests than previously. The two main reasons for the stadium not hosting a test in 2012 is quite possibly the cities population and location close to Rosario. Santa Fé is Argentina's nineth largest city but it has a larger stadium than those found in larger cities including Mar del Plata, Salta and Tucumán. Its population of 521,000 makes it the second largest city in the Litoral.[473]

The stadiums capacity and infrastructure in general are more than adapt to host a key World Cup match. The venue would be suited to hosting four pool matches and strategically it would simplify the creation of a match schedule. While Mendoza can be supported by San Juan, Rosario can be supported by Santa Fé and given its location in comparison to Buenos Aires Santa Fé could be used very effectively. It could host a similar set of matches as the Stade Chaban-Delmas in Bordeaux or the Stadium Municipal in Toulouse. Both venues hosted Tier One v Tier Two matches and Tier Two v Tier Two matches. Santa Fé could be similar to this with a Tier One team easily backing up after playing in Rosario or even Buenos Aires. Tier Two teams, in contrast, could come from matches in Resistencia or move on to play matches there. Resistencia is slightly less than 500KM to the north of Santa Fé, close to the border with Paraguay.

Santa Fé boosts Argentina's credibility as being able to spread around the tournaments biggest matches during the pool stage. It could host a match on the opening weekend when traditionally eight matches are played. France 2007 hosted eight matches in eight stadiums while neither Australia nor New Zealand did in 2003 or 2007. Argentina can not only do so but it can by utilizing different parts of the country. An opening weekend could be a genuine showcase of what Argentina has to offer with matches spread throughout the four regions with each region hosting matches on two of the three days to open the tournament. France opened its Rugby World Cup by having all the Tier One teams playing in different parts of the country. The two Tier One v Tier One fixtures were in Paris and Marseille. The remaining matches saw the Tier One sides all evenly distributed throughout France. Australia played in Lyon, England in Lens, Ireland in Bordeaux, Scotland in Saint Etienne, South Africa at the Parc des Princes and Wales in Nantes. All of these cities stadiums are comparable to Santa Fé.

San Juan
Despite being the tenth largest city in Argentina San Juan was selected as one of eight venues for the 2011 Copa América. It had a new stadium constructed for the tournament – the Estadio del Bicentenario which with a capacity of 25,000[474] is a Level 2 stadium. The size of the stadium is the same as New Plymouth which hosted three matches in Rugby World Cup 2011. But San Juan is a noticeably larger city than New Plymouth. It has a population of 461,000[475] making it larger than all cities from Rugby World Cup 2011 except Auckland. It is a part of the Cuyo region which competes in the Campeonato Argentino. The region also consists of Mendoza, San Luis and La Rioja. San Juan and Mendoza are the

largest cities and they also have the largest stadiums. The UAR´s use of both makes it a logical decision to have the two represent the region at Rugby World Cup 2023.

Considering the location of the city and the size of its stadium San Juan could be used in a similar way to New Plymouth and it could potentially host a fourth pool match. New Plymouth, with a population of well below 100,000[476] hosted three differing matches – Tier One v Tier Two, Tier Two v Tier Three and Tier One v Tier Three.[477] An identical format would be highly plausible and an additional match would not be out of the question at all. San Juan is more than big enough to merit four pool matches and the stadium is only 5,000 smaller than both Dunedin and Hamilton which hosted key matches in 2011. It is however different to the New Zealand stadiums due to Argentina having many more to choose from. The UAR has used San Juan twice over the past two years and should continue using it into the future. The stadiums size suits the city fine due to Argentina having nine larger cities and San Juan´s best soccer club, San Martín only arrived in Argentina´s top flight in the 2011-2012 Season.

Seven days after facing Italy in San Juan in 2012 Los Pumas faced France in Córdoba. The distance between the cities is 420KM. Argentina and France then played in Tucumán a further seven days latter and some 520KM north of Córdoba. The example of how the UAR scheduled Argentina´s June internationals is encouraging from a global perspective. Competing teams at a Rugby World Cup in Argentina could have similar schedules. This cuts down on the simple fact that San Juan is 1,150KM west of Buenos Aires and is not particularly close to other Level 2 stadiums. With the advantage of planning by using the benefit of hindsight from previous tournaments Argentina´s task of taking on the responsibility of hosting a Rugby World Cup can be made easier by seeing how previous tournaments were run and what things went well and what things did not. With well planned, logical match scheduling San Juan can play its part in Argentina hosting Rugby World Cup 2023.

Tucumán
The province of Tucumán is a rugby stronghold and is often said to be the heartland of Argentine rugby. The province´s capital city, San Miguel de Tucumán does not have a team in Argentina´s national soccer championship, the Campeonato de Primeira División. Conversely, in rugby Tucumán has a solid record. It is a multiple time Argentine national champion with Los Naranjas having won the Campeonato Argentino nine times between 1985 and 2010.[478] The city has also produced many notable Pumas players including Omar

Hasan, Julio Farías Cabello and José Maria Nuñez Piossek. It is nothing less than Argentina´s version of Toulouse. Like the southwestern French city, San Miguel de Tucumán would be a rugby city hosting a Rugby World Cup rather than a soccer city like Marseille for instance.

Although the name of the city is San Miguel de Tucumán it is commonly refered to simply as Tucumán. The city is the largest in Northern Argentina and the fifth largest in the country. It is a large city with a population of 800,000[479] which means it should host the maximum of four pool matches. Its largest stadium is the Estadio Monumental Presidente José Fierro which has a capacity of 32,700,[480] making it comparable to Montpellier. It is a Level 2 Stadium in terms of capacity but it is one in need of renovation and, indeed, the stadium is scheduled to be upgraded to have modern facilities and a larger capacity.[481] Improved facilities will add to the strength of an Argentine bid to host Rugby World Cup 2023. The stadium is not likely to be considered to host Quarter Finals matches but it could be in line to host an important pool match and also a Pumas pool match.

It has played host to three Pumas test matches in the professional era – v Wales in 2004, Scotland in 2010 and France in 2012. All matches were well attended despite there being some outside complications. The 2010 match was played on the same day as Argentina v Nigeria in the FIFA World Cup, while the 2012 match featured a depleted Pumas squad due to the resting of players ahead of The Rugby Championship. The indication is that the people will strongly get behind Rugby World Cup matches played in the city. The stadium´s size and the city´s location imply that it would be the most used venue in Northern Argentina. The city is located 1,300KM from Buenos Aires and 500KM from Córdoba. It is therefore close enough to Córdoba for it to be used in conjunction when compiling a match schedule. More importantly, it is 227KM south of Salta which is another city that would be highly likely to host matches.

Tucumán´s location between Córdoba and Salta is ideal for organizers due to the three of them each being a different stadium level. This is vital to ensuring the right stadiums are allocated for the right matches. Visiting teams could perhaps play two pool matches in the region. A possible scenario would see Tier One sides playing against Tier Two or Tier Three sides in Tucumán or Salta and playing against a Tier One side in Córdoba or even Mendoza. For instance Tucumán could host a team such as Scotland for its first two pool matches before that team would play once in Salta before flying to Buenos Aires to play its final match. Similarly, a team playing in Córdoba or even Santá Fe which is 700KM from Tucumán, could travel to the north for their final pool match. Distances in Argentina do seem large but they need to be taken with comparisons. One such example is that of 2007 when Argentina played Namibia in Marselle and then Ireland in Paris the following weekend. The distance between the two is 770KM.

Level Two Stadiums

City	Stadium	Capacity	No. of potential RWC Matches
Mar del Plata	Estadio José María Minella	35,354	Three
San Juan	Estadio del Bicentenario	25,000	Three
Santa Fé	Estadio Brigadier General Estanislao López	40,000	Four
Tucumán	Estadio Monumental Presidente José Fierro	32,700	Four

18

Level 3 Stadiums

All things big and small are crucial in planning an event and Level 3 stadiums are true to this rule for Rugby World Cup's. In the history of the tournament there have been matches which struggled to attract crowds. Overall the majority of these matches have been of the Tier Two v Tier Three variety. Some have involved Tier One sides but overall the pattern is that matches not featuring Tier One teams are the hardest to promote. In 2007 it was Tonga's two matches in Montpellier while in 2011 it was Namibia's matches in Rotorua. Looking back to 2003 it was clear that there were too many Level 1 Stadiums and too few Level 3 Stadiums. While Australia 2003 featured nine matches at Level 2 Stadiums it featured six at Level 3 Stadiums.[482] This was the case despite Australia utilizing three Level 3 Stadiums.

The master of the Level 3 venues was New Zealand which hosted twelve of the tournament's forty pool matches at such stadiums. Of the twelve stadiums used for the tournament five were Level 3 stadiums[483] and overall the venues delivered a highly positive result of strong crowds. Canada's win over Tonga was one of the highlights of the pool matches and it was played in Whangarei. Scotland v Romania and Canada v Japan were two other memorable matches from the pool stage and they were also played at Level 3 Stadiums. It is not likely that these matches could have filled Level 1 or arguably 2 Stadiums but they were all either at capacity or close to meeting the capacity of the respective Level 3 Stadiums. Even New Zealand's rugby culture was not enough to see all matches played in front of capacity crowds. But by distributing matches relatively evenly throughout the country, the various communities responded by generally attending matches well.

The size of a Level 3 Stadium has a maximum capacity of below 25,000. The minimum capacity of such a stadium is arguably 15,000. Invercargill, Napier and Palmerston North had capacities of around this mark and future editions of Rugby World Cup's are not likely to be played in smaller stadiums. Future editions of Rugby World Cup's are also not likely to have as many Level 3 Stadiums but they are, nonetheless, likely to have some. Both England and Japan have indicated their plans to have at least one Level 3 Stadium for Rugby World Cup 2015 and 2019. England has firm plans on playing matches in Gloucester and Japan wants to host matches in Fukuoka and Sendai.

In the case of Argentina the previous chapters indicated that the country could host a Rugby World Cup by utilizing six Level 1 Stadiums and four Level 2 Stadiums. The IRB's minimum requirement of stadiums is ten and so technically Argentina would not need Level 3 stadiums. However given that the purpose of planning a tournament is to ensure that matters are both well attended and well distributed history has shown that it is wise to stage the less marketable matches at Level 3 Stadiums. Doing so increases the likelihood that matches will be well attended and not be played in empty stadiums. This is true in all countries and in all sports.

France 2007 proved that the minimum number of Level 3 Stadiums is zero but there has been no clear example to resolutely establish an appropriate maximum number of Level 3 Stadiums for a Rugby World Cup. France 2007 also showed the advantage of having no venues over or under used. The fixed number of three or four pool matches should be a lesson to all future Rugby World Cup hosts. Argentina could complete a list of twelve venues to host a Rugby World Cup by using two Level 3 Stadiums. There are a number of options to choose from around the country. The options extend beyond cities in Buenos Aires province, the Litoral, North and West to include the possibility of playing in Patagonia.

Bahía Blanca
A Level 3 option in Buenos Aires province is the city of Bahía Blanca. Despite not being one of Argentina's ten largest cities, Bahía Blanca is nevertheless an option worth considering as a host venue because of its attractions, size and location. The greater city area of Gran Bahía Blanca[484] has a population of 300,000[485] making it a large city in comparison to the majority of those which hosted matches in Rugby World Cup 2011. The city is located 575KM south of the capital and 580KM north of Puerto Madryn, the city which hosted Argentina v Wales in 2006. Its geographical position opens the possibility of genuinely utilizing two Level 3 venues to the South of Buenos Aires. Its location would

also assist in allocating Level 2 venues because Bahía Blanca is also located 420KM west of Mar del Plata. Used together the three cities of Bahia Blanca, Mar del Plata and Puerto Madryn provide Argentina with the opportunity of staging matches in the southern half of the country.

The largest stadium in Bahía Blanca, the Estadio Roberto Natalio Carminatti, also known as the Estadio Aurinegro was constructed in 1942 and has a seating capacity at present of 20,000[486] making it a good size for Tier Two v Tier Three matches. If used Bahía Blanca would likely host midweek matches with lower Tier teams playing in the city after facing Tier One sides in Buenos Aires, La Plata, Mar del Plata or potentially even Puerto Madryn. If utilized Bahía Blanca would host three matches with no chance of a fourth. It is simply not large enough to merit more matches nor does it have the same history as other centres around Argentina. It is, however a solid example of the potential within Argentina of not only hosting Rugby World Cup 2023 but doing so correctly by having matches spread well and played at appropriate sized venues.

A lot of changes could happen over the coming decade but as it stands Bahía Blanca is yet to host an international rugby match. If the progress of Los Pumas as a team and rugby as a sport in Argentina continue then the chances of the UAR scheduling a match against a Tier One side in Bahía Blanca are extremely low. The possibility does exist for the city to host a lower ranked team and it could well be used at some point in time for the South American Championship. The lack of international rugby in the Bahía Blana aside it is nonetheless an important city for rugby as it is the home of the Unión de Rugby del Sur (URS), or the Southern Rugby Union in English. The city has also contributed to rugby at the highest level. It has produced international rugby players such as Bernardo Stortoni.

Puerto Madryn
A venue with an equally low chance of hosting international rugby in the coming years is Puerto Madryn. However it is not a stranger to test rugby. The UAR opted to play the first of two tests against Wales at the Estadio Raúl Conti in June 2006. It was the first ever test match in Patagonia and was noteworthy due to not only the location of the city but also its population making the city the smallest to ever host a home Pumas test match.[487] The UAR made the decision to play at the venue as part of its push to move matches around Argentina. Puerto Madryn was picked specifically for Wales because it has a large Welsh speaking population. The locals welcomed the Welsh team with open arms putting on a festival week

in the city. They were treated like the home side until match day when a crowd of 15,000 packed the stadium in support of Los Pumas.

The experience could be considered worth replicating should Argentina hsot Rugby World Cup 2023. The venue could not justify hosting many games and at most it could host two. Logically it would be well suited to hosting Wales against a Tier Three team and possibly have that team face a Tier Two side or have Wales play twice in the city to give it two World Cup matches. New Zealand planned similarly for Rugby World Cup 2011 with Nelson, for instance, originally scheduled to host two matches – Italy v Russia and Italy v USA. The city is smaller than Puerto Madryn and the capacity of Trafalgar Park for Rugby World Cup 2011 was similar to the Estadio Raúl Conti. Trafalgar Park's regular capacity was increased with temporary seating for the tournament but the venue was still too large for Italy v Russia which had a crowd of 12,418.[488] The drawing power of Italy was not sufficient to attract a capacity crowd for its matches in Nelson. Historical examples can be found elsewhere. Argentina v Samoa from Rugby World Cup 1999 was played at Stradey Park in Llanelli which seated less than Nelson. The venue would stand no chance of hosting a comparable fixture ever again. However in 1999 neither Argentina nor Samoa was thought to have drawing power in Wales and the venue selection was suitable for the time.

Looking at it from this perspective an argument can be made for Puerto Madryn to be a justifiable Rugby World Cup venue. With temporary seating, as in the 2006 Pumas v Wales match the venue could be comparable to Nelson. Arguably it would be a better option than Italy playing in Nelson because of the city's history. Nelson, unlike Puerto Madryn has no such association with Italy. There is no Italian speaking population in the city to rival that of the Welsh descendents in Puerto Madryn. Whether or not Puerto Madryn would be needed to provide support to the larger venues is another question altogether. However the Welsh experience in 2006 would appear to suggest the city's value as a place that the Welsh rugby team is unlikely to ever experience again. It could strongly be argued that Wales should indeed play its second and third pool matches in the city just like Italy did in Nelson in 2011.

Puerto Madryn's southern location would make it the final frontier. No city further south would be considered to host Rugby World Cup matches. It would likely be selected due to its Welsh speaking community with this alone deciding whether or not it would host matches. Its location would likely be highly influencial in whether or not Bahía Blanca would also be used. In 2011 after playing its two matches in Nelson, Italy travelled to Dunedin to face Ireland five days latter. The distance between the cities is close to 800KM, compared to 1,100KM from Puerto Madryn to Buenos Aires. Similar things could not happen in Puerto Madryn but it is far from being a strong option given the alternatives. If it were indeed to go ahead then a likely scenario would be Wales having its four pool matches organized so that it would play its second and third matches in Puerto Madryn against the qualifying teams from Tier Two and Three nations in its pool. This would mean two of Buenos Aires, La Plata and Mar del Plata would likely be used for Wales's first and fourth pool matches. If so the Tier Two and Tier Three teams would likely play their match in Bahía Blanca.

Resistencia

Argentina's litoral has a number of options worth considering for hosting Rugby World Cup matches. The two strongest are arguably Paraná and Resistencia. Paraná currently does not have an adequate stadium but this could potentially change in the coming years. However, due to its close proximity to Santa Fé it is not the best option for the region. Instead Resistencia would appear to be a strong and real option to act as a Level 3 venue. The city is located in Chaco province on the border with Corrientes province. The cities of Resistencia and Corrientes are 15KM apart with one being on either side of the Paraná River. Greater Corrientes has a population of 316,000[489] while Greater Resistencia had 359,000 in 2001.[490] Greater Resistencia is Argentina's eleventh largest city and combined with Greater Corrientes the total population makes it larger than the likes of Mar del Plata and Santa Fé and similar in size to La Plata. Combined the two cities could certainly make a strong case to have one act as a host venue to represent North-Eastern Argentina should the country host a Rugby World Cup. They cover the area bordering Southern Paraguay and located 160KM to the north of Resistencia is another noticeable Argentine city, Formosa.

The Estadio Centenario was opened in Resistencia in 2011. It is a strong candidate to host Rugby World Cup 2023 matches. Having matches played at the stadium would mean that Paraguay would join Bolivia, Chile and Uruguay in having a World Cup venue located close to its borders. The stadium has a capacity of 23,000 and meets all the required standards of the AFA to merit hosting matches at the highest level of Argentine soccer.[491] Its facilities are good for rugby with the fans being seated close to the action. The venue is in the sights of the UAR and is a candidate to host June internationals in the coming years. It hosted one of two matches against the French Barbarians in 2011 and the stadium was full. It was not the first time international rugby had been staged in the region but it was the highest profile match as the previous encounters had been against Tier Three South American opposition.

The size of the Estadio Centenario is ideal to act as a Level 3 stadium to join Rosario and Santa Fé to give Argentina's litoral region three venues – one of each variety. Between them they would ensure a steady geographical distribution to have teams spread throughout Argentina. Resistencia is 1000KM north of Buenos Aires, 500KM north of Santa Fé, 700KM east of Salta and Tucumán and 800KM North East of Córdoba making it workable into a match schedule. Resistencia could justifiably host three pool matches with it receiving teams from the other litoral venues or the Northern Argentine venues. In between moving from one region to the other they could play in Resistencia. Rather than have potentially difficult matches from a marketing standpoint played in large stadiums, Resistencia would, like San Juan, be a solid option to give the Rugby World Cup stability. Aside from the obvious choice of using the city to stage Tier Two v Tier Three matches Resistencia would also be suited to having a Tier One v Tier Two match if need be.

Salta
The previous two chapters put forward four potential venues to cover the large area covering Northern and Western Argentina. They were Córdoba, Mendoza, San Juan and Tucumán. The region has a number of cities and stadiums worth considering to be used as Level 3 Stadiums. Four are considered as Northern cities and one is a part of the west. They are Catamarca, Salta, Santiago del Estero, San Luis and San Salvador de Jujuy. Of these cities two have hosted Los Pumas tests and one of them should certainly be a venue to host Rugby World Cup matches. Of the four, two hosted matches in the 2011 Copa América - Salta and San Salvador de Jujuy. One of these two would be certain to host matches in a Rugby World Cup in Argentina and there is also the real possibility of both hosting.

Arguably the strongest candidate is Salta. It is the largest of the four with a population of 527,000 which also makes it the eighth largest city in the country.[492] On population alone Salta would have to be a host city for a Rugby World Cup in Argentina. But the city is also a strong candidate due to its standing in Argentine rugby. It has produced noteable players such as Juan Figallo and despite not having the largest stadium out of the five mentioned cities it is the one which has hosted the highest profile rugby match - Argentina v England in 2009. It was a genuine case of taking a game to the people and the result was an exhibition of just how successful a Rugby World Cup in Argentina could be. The local newspapers were devoting little space to soccer while rugby was covering far more than just the sports sections.[493] The occasion caught the imagination of the local population and is sure to see future June tests staged in the city.

Like Tucumán, Salta is a city in which rugby enjoys a noticeable profile. Its location 220KM to the North of Tucumán means it is ideally placed to act as a supporting venue for Northern Argentina. The city's largest stadium, the Estadio Padre Ernesto Martearena was also used as a host venue for the 2011 Copa América. It hosted two matches and ten years earlier hosted seven matches in the FIFA World Youth Championship. The stadium has a capacity of 20,408[494] which would make it a similar option to Resistencia for hosting matches. Like Resistencia Salta could host three pool matches and between them they could stage the four Tier Two v Tier Three matches and also host one other match each, either a Tier One v Tier Three match or a Tier One v Tier Two match.

Similar to Argentina having the possibility of utilizing Bahía Blanca, Mar del Plata and Puerto Madryn to give Southern Argentina three host venues, Northern Argentina could do the same thing. 68KM north of Salta is San Salvador de Jujuy, often simply refered to by the provincial name of Jujuy. It has previously hosted international rugby, hosting Italy A in 2005. Like Salta it has a stadium that featured in the 2011 Copa América and it also hosted two matches. The Estadio 23 de Agosto has the credentials to host up to three pool matches. It has a capacity of 23,000 and was upgraded with improved facilities for the Copa América. It would be suitable for the same matches as Resistencia and Salta. The city and stadium are good options which suggest that the only question to address is whether or not Jujuy would be needed or if Salta on its own is enough. With six Level 1 stadiums and four Level 2 stadiums already having been identified as strong options it is probable that Argentina only need two Level 3 stadiums to stage a Rugby World Cup using twelve venues. This being the case Salta and Resistencia would be the most feasible options.

The opportunity nevertheless would be realistic for the UAR and the IRB to prefer to make use of an addition Level 3 stadium. If so then Jujuy could well be used as the third option or, similarly, it could be argued that Puerto Madryn and Bahía Blanca ought to host matches too. Such a scenario would mean that the Level 3 venues would host two matches rather than three and fewer matches would be allocated to Level 2 stadiums. Argentina has the cities and stadiums in place to enable such decisions to be debated. There are multiple options which could be investigated extensively by the sports authorities to see Argentina 2023 deliver the best possible event for Argentina and the global rugby community.

International

The venues covered so far in Part IV show that when compared to the host nations from 1987-2019, Argentina has sufficient venues to host a Rugby World Cup tournament on its own. The possibility, nevertheless, exists for a Rugby World Cup in Argentina to have subhosts similar to what France did in 2007 and what both England and Japan are planning on doing for both 2015 and 2019. Despite being surplus to the requirements of having between ten and twelve stadia Uruguay could potentially be used in a bid to make Argentina 2023 a true South American event. The country has large stadiums but should games be subhosted the idea would not be to ensure larger crowds, but to take the games to the people. It would be strictly used for the purpose of being a Level 3 venue.

The home venue of Los Teros, the Estadio Charrúa in Montevideo has a capacity of 14,000 and regularly sees crowds of around the 10,000 mark attend Uruguay´s home matches. The venue was used for Uruguay´s home World Cup Qualifying matches for Rugby World Cup 2011 with good crowds attending matches against the United States of America, Kazakhstan and Romania. This is not to imply that a Level 2 or Level 1 stadium is out of the question. Uruguay´s national stadium could well make a claim to stage matches. However, there is no need given Argentina´s abundance of potential venues. As such should Uruguay host matches it would be in a supporting capacity with the Estadio Charrúa being a potential venue for two pool matches in a similar way to Gloucester potential use by England for Rugby World Cup 2015. Montevideo is located 230KM from Buenos Aires and is easily accessed via a ferry ride from the Argentine capital.

The possibility also exists of Argentina having its western neighbours host some matches. Santiago could similarly be used to host two pool matches. The city has a lot of different stadiums with potentialy the Estadio San Carlos de Apoquindo being suitable to be considered to host World Cup matches. It has a capacity of 18,000 which is smaller than the probable Level 3 stadiums that Argentina would use to stage matches. However, if the historical rules of Rugby World Cup´s continue unchanged then South America will get an automatic participant in a Rugby World Cup hosted by Argentina. With South Africa´s return in 1995 Africa was allotted a qualifying place which saw two African nations play at the 1995 tournament. This would mean that CONSUR would have a place as Argentina would automatically qualify. This being the case rugby authorities might be seriously temped into having one of Chile, Uruguay, both or possibly even Brazil act to host two matches.

Such a scenario is far from being a long shot. It is, however, a questionable road to take. The overuse of subhosts has spoiled previous Rugby World Cup's and could well do the same thing in 2015 and 2019. Rugby World Cup's in the professional era have established that they are better products when they are centralized and organized by one union. Subhosts should not be encouraged and should only be sought if there are no other real alternatives. In the case of Argentina 2023 like in England 2015 this is not the case. Both can host a Rugby World Cup without utilizing venues from outside their borders. The Millenium Stadium may well deliver impressive crowds in 2015 but the experience from 2007 suggests otherwise and as such the UAR should not need to collaborate with Chile or Uruguay at all.

Argentina will, however need to find at least two Level 3 venues to host a Rugby World Cup. This should not be a problem at all. Arguably the best options are Salta and Resistencia due to their locations, stadiums and populations. A suggested list of twelve stadiums for the UAR to work with to launch a bid for Rugby World Cup 2023 would include these two venues as they should provide a solid foundation for protecting against potential weaknesses such as using stadiums with temporary seating or relying on venues that have no experience in hosting important rugby matches. In contrary to the norm, Resistencia and Salta would complete a list of venues that have previous experience hosting Los Pumas for either test rugby or matches against visiting Barbarians teams.

Level 3 Stadiums

City	Stadium	Capacity	No. of potential RWC Matches
Resistencia	Estadio Centenario	23,000	Three
Salta	Padre Ernesto Martearena	20,408	Three

As shown in the following table, the twelve suggested venues for Argentina 2023 are more than good enough to host rugby's showcase tournament. In comparison to the three previous editions of the Rugby World Cup the stadium list covered in Part IV gives Argentina 2023 a larger stadium capacity than Australia 2003 and New Zealand 2007. It averages over 40,000 per stadium compared to 38,576 for Australia and 26,916 for New Zealand. It has a larger capacity than Australia 2003 despite Australia using eleven rather than twelve stadiums. The numbers suggest that Argentina has sufficient stadiums to successfully host a Rugby World Cup. The increasing name of Los Pumas in global rugby and what has already been achieved makes Argentina not only a strong option but one that would be very hard to say no to.

Australia 2003	France 2007	New Zealand 2011	Argentina 2023
Sydney 83,500	Paris 80,000	Auckland 60,000	Buenos Aires 64,000
Melbourne 53,351	Marseilles 60,000	Wellington 40,000	Córdoba 57,000
Brisbane 52,500	Paris 47,870	North Harbour 30,000	La Plata 53,000
Perth 43,000	Lens 41,400	Dunedin 30,000	Avellaneda 48,000
Sydney 42,000	Lyon 41,100	Hamilton 30,000	Rosario 41,654
Adelaide 33,597	Nantes 38,100	Rotorua 26,000	Mendoza 40,268
Townsville 31,500	Toulouse 35,700	N. Plymouth 25,000	Santa Fé 40,000
Canberra 25,000	St. Etienne 35,615	Nelson 18,000	Mar del Plata 35,354
Gosford 20,000	Bordeaux 34,440	Whangarei 17,000	Tucumán 32,700
Wollongong 20,000	Montpellier 33,650	Invercargill 17,000	San Juan 25,000
Launceston 19,891	Cardiff 72,000	Napier 15,000	Resistencia 23,000
	Edinburgh 67,800	Palm. North 15,000	Salta 20,408
Total = 424,339	Total = 587,635	Total = 323,000	Total = 480,384
Average = 38,576	**Average = 48,969**	**Average = 26,916**	**Average = 40,032**

The question of which matches would be played where was a theme throughout Part IV and there are a number of possibilities. Instead of covering all possibilities this book will come to its conclusion by covering one. The potential match schedule put forward in Chapter 15 has been maintained to see that it is easier to interpret. The twelve match venues and their suggested number of matches laid out in Part IV have been utilized to distribute the stadiums to complete a potential match schedule. The play-off's have not been included. The same twelve venues put forward in Chapter 15 have been used.

Venues added to Sample Match Schedule for RWC 2023

Date	Match	Venue	Kick-Off
Friday September 8	Argentina v England	Buenos Aires	6:30pm
	Australia v Fiji	Córdoba	8:30pm
Saturday September 9	Ireland v Georgia	Mendoza	2:30pm
	France v USA	Rosario	4:30pm
	New Zealand v Wales	La Plata	6:30pm
Sunday September 10	Italy v Russia	Santa Fé	2:30pm
	South Africa v Scotland	Avellaneda	4:30pm
	Japan v Samoa	Tucumán	7:30pm
Tuesday September 12	England v Canada	Rosario	5:30pm
	Fiji v Namibia	Salta	7:30pm
Wednesday September 13	Wales v Romania	Mar del Plata	5:30pm

	Ireland v Tonga	San Juan	7:30pm
Friday September 15	Australia v France	Buenos Aires	6:30pm
	New Zealand v Japan	Santa Fé	8:30pm
Saturday September 16	South Africa v Georgia	Rosario	4:30pm
	Argentina v Russia	Mendoza	7:30pm
Sunday September 17	Scotland v Tonga	Tucumán	4:30pm
	USA v Namibia	Resistencia	6:30pm
Monday September 18	Samoa v Romania	Salta	3:30pm
	Italy v Canada	San Juan	5:30pm
Thursday September 21	Scotland v Georgia	Tucumán	3:30pm
	Wales v Japan	Mar del Plata	6:30pm
Friday September 22	South Africa v Ireland	Buenos Aires	6:30pm
	Australia v USA	Salta	8:30pm
Saturday September 23	England v Italy	Avallenada	5:30pm
	New Zealand v Samoa	Mendoza	8:30pm
Sunday September 24	France v Namibia	La Plata	5:30pm
	Argentina v Canada	Córdoba	8:30pm
Tuesday September 26	Georgia v Tonga	Resistencia	5:30pm
	Japan v Romania	Tucumán	7:30pm
Wednesday September 27	England v Russia	Rosario	4:30pm
	Fiji v USA	San Juan	7:30pm
Friday September 29	Argentina v Italy	La Plata	5:30pm
	Wales v Samoa	Rosario	7:30pm
Saturday September 30	Scotland v Ireland	Córdoba	6:30pm
	Australia v Namibia	Santa Fé	8:30pm
Sunday October 1	Canada v Russia	Resistencia	2:30pm
	South Africa v Tonga	Mar del Plata	4:30pm
	France v Fiji	Avallenada	6:30pm
	New Zealand v Romania	Mendoza	8:30pm
Saturday October 7	Quarter Final 1	Córdoba	6:30pm
	Quarter Final 2	Mendoza	8:30pm
Sunday October 8	Quarter Final 3	Córdoba	6:30pm
	Quarter Final 4	Rosario	8:30pm
Saturday October 14	Semi Final 1	Buenos Aires	6:30pm
Sunday October 15	Semi Final 2	Buenos Aires	8:30pm
Friday October 20	Bronze Final	La Plata	8:30pm
Saturday October 21	RWC Final	Buenos Aires	8:30pm

Acknowledgements

I would like to thank the following people who have in some way contributed to my life in a way that has led to me writing this book.

John 'Taffy' Davies and Ernie Tait fostered my interest in the sport and introduced me to debating in sporting terms which ultimately led to me writing this book.

I am forever grateful to Andrew Orme and Alan Jones.

Ian Cook, Nestór Cadario, Stuart Pearson, Peter Tanner and Linzi Wallace are five influential people on me from a rugby perspective. Conversations with them significantly stimulated my desire for rugby to become more global.

Robert Deuchars challenged me intellectually in a way that significantly changed me.

Bryn Harrow helped me a lot with the blog.

Thanks to Francisco Bosch, Fernando Portugal, Dallen Stanford and Seta Tuiveluka for their contributions to the blog.

Thanks to Tárcio Miranda Corá, Douglas Demame and João Paulo Minchio for helping me on Brazilian websites.

A special thanks to my friends from Franca Rugby and others I have come to know from playing in Brazil.

Endnotes

All web addresses cited were current on September 15 2012, unless otherwise specified.

[1] IRB Organisation See. http://bit.ly/Pzs0oC

[2] "The Long Road to the Rugby World Cup – 1987 Rugby World Cup", *New Zealand History Online*. See http://bit.ly/UuLOxQ

[3] Record Broadcast Levels for RWC 2011 http://bit.ly/POrkLT

[4] For a complete list of the IRB Council see: http://bit.ly/qGoIr4

[5] "New Zealand Handed 2011 Rugby World Cup", *BBC*, Thursday, 17 November 2005, http://bbc.in/QNIVTV

[6] "Japan Fumes as Kiwis win 2011 World Cup vote", *The Independent*, Friday 18 November 2005, http://ind.pn/NLbfbI

[7] The IRB World Rankings has 97 nations, one less than the number of member unions due to the recent addition of American Samoa. The union is yet to be added to the World Rankings and is expected to be added in 2013 when it will begin international competition against lower ranked Oceania unions. It became an IRB member Union in 2012.

[8] For a complete list of IRB unions see: http://bit.ly/RTsZ1j

[9] "Historia Del Rugby em Argentina", *Argentinaxplora*, http://bit.ly/Vu2OSN

[10] "El rugby em Argentina – 1ra parte", *San Isidro Club*. http://bit.ly/RNugfT

[11] While in Rhodesia, contemporary Zimbabwe, in 1965 a local journalist created the term Pumas by calling the animal on the players uniforms a Puma rather than a Jaguar. The name remains used to this day as the nickname of the Argentine rugby team.

[12] Argentina played against South African teams in non-internationals as early as 1959. Argenina hosted the Junior Springboks in 1959 and played against them in South Africa in 1965. Argentina played against the SA Gazelles in two away matches in 1971 and hosted them in 1972. Argentina won two matches against the SA Gazelles - 12-0 in Pretoria in 1971 and 18-16 in Buenos Aires in 1972.

[13] See Hastings, Max and Jenkins, Simon "The Battle for the Falklands", 1984, W. W. Norton & Company

[14] "UK regret over Falklands dead ", *BBC*, Sunday 01 April 2007, http://bbc.in/QNJ0qr

[15] "Jaguars and Johnno" John Griffiths, *ESPN Scrum*, July 18 2012, http://es.pn/Pdl1AI

[16] "Pumas enter the Rugby Championship with strong pedigree", *SANZAR*, 22 November 2011, http://bit.ly/VtZdnV

[17] For a complete list of all Argentine international matches see "statsguru", *espnscrum*, http://bit.ly/VtZQO5

[18] New Zealand's Semi Final loss against Australia saw the coaches replaced. Kieran Crowley, Steve McDowell, Alan Whetton and Captain Gary Whetton were not wanted for international duty in 1992.

[19] Paraguay scored four points rather than Five because the scoring system used to reward four points for a try. It was changed in 1992 to be worth five points.

[20] "1987: France 30-24 Australia" , *BBC*, Wednesday 24 September 2003, http://bbc.in/obOBWB

[21] The team competed under the name Western Samoa in Rugby World Cup 1991 and 1995. In subsequent World Cup's the country has been referred to as Manu Samoa or simply Samoa.

[22] Diego Dominguez scored 1010 international points in 76 test match appearances. Four players have scored more in the history of test rugby – Dan Carter (New Zealand), Jonny Wilkinson (England), Neil Jenkins (Wales) and Ronan O'Gara (Ireland).

[23] See Howitt, Bob "*SANZAR Saga: Ten Years of Super 12 and Tri-Nations Rugby*", 2005, Harper Collins Publishers

[24] For a full list of URBA affiliated and invited members See http://bit.ly/SgI2Gi

[25] "Noriega to start for Warratahs", *Sports Illustrated*, February 22 2002, http://bit.ly/qmeg3

[26] The result is the largest defeat that Argentina has ever suffered.

[27] "Pumas dread management change", *The Standard*, Friday December 02, 2005, http://bit.ly/PYm5Ia

[28] Stradey Park was the setting for Wales's 1972 win over New Zealand.

[29] "Pumas mauled", *Sports Illustrated*, Sunday October 24, 1999 http://bit.ly/QNHXXL

[30] They were as follows - Alejandro Allub (Perpignan, France), Lisandro Arbizu (Brive, France), Rolando Martín (Richmond, England), Agustín Pichot (Richmond, England), Mauricio Reggiardo

(Castres, France) Omar Hasan was, at the time, playing in his native Tucumán but had previously played Super 12 rugby for the Wellington Hurricanes in New Zealand in 1997 and the ACT Brumbies in Australia in 1998.

[31] Diego Albanese, Felipe Contepomi, Ignácio Corleto, Mario Ledesma, Carlos Ignácio Fernández Lobbe, Gonzalo Longo, Gonzalo Quesada, Eduardo Simone, and Martín Scelzo all played against Ireland as amateurs and all became Professional players.

[32] A list compiled by ESPN Scrum details Argentina's largest attendances for international matches. The top three are all matches played at River Plate Stadium from 2000-2002 as Argentina hosted one member of SANZAR in each of these years and attracted strong crowds. http://bit.ly/RTqgVw

[33] "New Zealand vs Argentina at Estádio Monumental Antonio V Liberti", *New Zealand Rugby Museum*, Saturday, 1 December 2001 http://bit.ly/PzqWBa

[34] "Italy's schedule not unfair, ARU says", *The Age*, April 13 2003 http://bit.ly/SneUOV

[35] "Kirwan rails at injustice", *BBC*, Wednesday October 22 2003, http://bbc.in/Qaye03

[36] "IRB admits to unfair draw", BBC, Monday November 03 2003, http://bbc.in/OTBcBQ

[37] "Bad Blood", *Independent*, Saturday November 22 2008, http://bit.ly/Pdlh2F

[38] Docklands Stadium is the original name of the Sporting venue that hostsed this particular rugby match in 2003. At the time the stadium was known as the Telstra Dome for commercial reasons and is today known as Etihad Stadium.

[39] "International Rules: In a hybrid game, powerful Australia stops speedy Ireland", *New York Times*, November 01 2003, http://nyti.ms/RTtg4f

[40] Mario Ledesma talked about the painful feeling of losing against Ireland and how a number of players got together in late 2003 and started planning for Rugby World Cup 2007. Ledesma's comments can be seen on a documentary dvd. "Pumas de Bronze, Corazón de Ouro", *ESPN Deportes*, 2003 (dvd)

[41] Six of the starting team against Chile and two from the bench played against Wales. They were Matias Albina, Lucas Borges, Pablo Bouza, German Bustos, Manuel Contepomi, Martín Durand, Lucio Lopéz Fleming, Eusébio Guiñazú, José Maria Nuñez Piossek and Hernán Senillosa.

[42] "Argentina Halt France Winning Run ", *CNN*, Saturday November 20 2004, http://bit.ly/UqlMHF

[43] "Last-ditch drop goal by O'Gara puts euphoric Ireland past Argentina ". *The Observer*, Sunday November 28 2004, http://bit.ly/RTr6S8

[44] "Lions 25-25 Argentina", *BBC*, Monday May 23 2005, http://bbc.in/OTBB75

[45] Bernardo Stortoni and Mariano Sambucetti played the 2004-2005 Season for Bristol and Martín Schusterman played for Plymouth Albion. The quartet of Pablo Bouza, Nicolás Fernández Miranda, Federico Genoud and Francisco Leonelli were all based in Argentina though Bouza joined the Harlequins and Leonelli joined Edinburgh for the 2005-2006 season.

[46] "Argentina Tests in the Balance", *The Telegraph*, May 28 2006, http://bit.ly/PYmREU

[47] "Worries for Argentina", *TVNZ*, Sunday May 28, 2006, http://bit.ly/PdkL4L

[48] "The Welsh in Patagonia", *BBC*, August 15, 2008, http://bbc.in/Qxtqig

[49] "Wales & Argentina", *Wales Cymru*, http://bit.ly/UuOPyf

[50] Agustín Pichot, Felipe Contepomi, Gonzalo Longo, Mario Ledesma, Ignacio Fernández Lobbe and Martin Durand signed the letter. "Pumas are losing their patience", *Wales Online*, August 04 2006, http://bit.ly/QayNXF

[51] "Pumas crisis may take heat out of autumn fixture dispute", *The Guardian*, Thursday May 25 2006, http://bit.ly/Vu2mnF

[52] "Todeschini tortures poor England", *CNN*, November 11 2006, http://bit.ly/POr7s1

[53] IBID.

[54] "Cusworth states´ Pumas case for a place at top table", *The Guardian*, Thursday November 09 2006, http://bit.ly/Qaz2lr

[55] "Pichot calls for 'Seven Nations' ", ESPN Scrum, November 26 2006, http://es.pn/QsZRkX

[56] "Argentina centre Gaitan suffers heart attack", *BBC*, August 20 2007 http://bit.ly/2ep2z7

[57] "Argentina beat Belgium", *Planet Rugby*, August 26 2007 http://bit.ly/SeMyRf

[58] "Argentina shock France in World Cup opener", *The Telegraph*, September 07 2007, http://bit.ly/POqfUc

[59] "France 12-17 Argentina", *BBC*, Friday September 07 2007, http://bbc.in/SgIcNP

[60] IBID.

[61] "Conmovieron", *La Nacion*, Saturday September 08 2007 http://bit.ly/QxuqDd

[62] "Argentina Moves Soccer's 'Superclasico' so Fans Can Watch Rugby", *Bloomberg*, October 02 2007, http://bloom.bg/SN4aUM

[63] "French rugby aims to emulate soccer", *Sports Illustrated*, Thursday November 04 1999, http://bit.ly/UqlvnW

[64] "Rugby: Randall wants to keep his job", *New Zealand Herald*, Saturday November 06 1999, http://bit.ly/POqsqw

[65] IBID.

[66] "Rugby World Cup 2011: Australia vs Wales as it happened", *The Guardian*, Friday November 21 2001, http://bit.ly/nWK82f

[67] "Victory for Wales in the Bronze Final can lead to great things", *Wales Online*, October 21 2011, http://bit.ly/Vu1HT8

[68] "IRB chief calls for 'neglected' Argentina to join Tri Nations", *ABC News*, October 09 2007, http://bit.ly/QsZvKT

[69] "Los Pumas fueron recibidos como héroes", *Clarin*, Sunday October 21 2007 http://bit.ly/OTCsVn

[70] "Cristina y Néstor Kirchner recebieron a Los Pumas en la Casa Rosada", *Los Andes*, Tuesday October 23 2007 http://bit.ly/ONKnZU

[71] See ESPN Scrum Team Records: http://bit.ly/OTCblm

[72] "Report shows Rugby´s growth in new markets", *IRB*, Tuesday April 05 2011, http://bit.ly/RTsc0c

[73] "Les Cusworth steps up to coach Argentina", *The Telegraph*, December 03 2007, http://bit.ly/2udKmD

[74] "IRB announces 3N boost for Argentina", Monday March 29 2010, http://bit.ly/9jvdGH

[75] "Phelan named new Argentina coach", *BBC*, Thursday March 13 2008, http://bbc.in/SnekRg

[76] "Rugby-Argentina invited to play South Africa in Mandela match", *Reuters*, Tuesday February 26 2008, http://reut.rs/u5YI2Q

[77] The IRB changed the qualifying for Rugby World Cup 2011. Instead of the eight Quarter Finalists qualifying automatically it was extended to the top three from each pool. This meant that Argentina, Australia, England, Fiji, France, Ireland, Italy, New Zealand, Scotland, South Africa, Tonga, and Wales were all qualified for New Zealand 2011.

[78] "Fightback in vain as England succumb to Pumas", *The Guardian*, Saturday June 13 2009, http://bit.ly/39VBb

[79] "IRB Welcomes Argentina Four Nations Invite", *IRB*, Monday September 14 2009, http://bit.ly/3Vy11j

[80] "Argentina, Namibia to feature in Vodacom Cup", *Mail & Guardian*, December 11 2009, http://bit.ly/SN4u68

[81] The six players were Agustín Creevy, Santiago Fernández, Genaro Fessia, Agustín Figuerola, Mariano Galarza and Martín Rodríguez Gurruchaga

[82] Many of Scotland's key wins in recent years have occurred in dreadful conditions. Scotland's wins over Australia at Murrayfield and Newcastle were both influenced by the conditions. Scotland's win over Italy at Rugby World Cup 2007 was also a match dominated by rain. The Scot's win in Mar del Plata was also played in far from ideal conditions.

[83] The name Aviva Stadium was given to the renovated Lansdowne Road in 2009. The old stadium was demolished in 2007 and the new one opened in 2010. Aviva signed a ten year deal for the naming rights of the stadium in 2009. See "Lansdowne to be renamed Aviva Stadium", *Irish Times*, February 12 2009, http://bit.ly/coTjx

[84] "Rugby World Cup 2011: Argentina star Juan Martin Hernandez out of tournament with knee injury
", *The Telegraph*, August 10 2011, http://bit.ly/poLhlG

[85] "Jonny Wilkinson says balls used at Rugby World Cup in New Zealand were 'horribly unprofessional'", *The Telegraph*, November 07 2011, http://bit.ly/sITp9r

[86] "Christchurch pays tribute to 185 quake victims one year on... in a city that still lies in ruins", *Mail Online*, February 22 2012, http://bit.ly/xDCnez

[87] "Christchurch loses Rugby World Cup games", *Stuff*, March 16 2011 http://bit.ly/hQJf2A

[88] Planet rugby predicted England to win by 40 points. "*Preview: England v Georgia*" Planet Rugby, September 17 2011, http://bit.ly/o8skRY

[89] "Scoreboard flatters England as Georgia take fight to Six Nations", *The Sydney Morning Herald*, September 18 2011, champions http://bit.ly/RNxP5C

[90] "RWC Preview: All Blacks vs Argentina", *TVNZ*, Sunday October 09 2011, http://bit.ly/ONL8SV

[91] "2011 RWC QF 4, New Zealand v Argentina preview & latest betting specials", Bet365, October 7 2011, http://bit.ly/SN4Dqc

[92] "Preview: New Zealand vs Argentina", *Planet Rugby*, October 07 2011, http://bit.ly/RamTMY

[93] "RWC Preview: All Blacks v Pumas", *Sky Sport*, Saturday 08 October 2011, http://bit.ly/n8YH3Z

[94] "Record crowds confirm Top 14´s popularity and plans for foreign expansion", *French Rugby Club*, July 18 2009, http://bit.ly/SN4GCc

[95] "Crowds on the increase in Aviva Premiership rugby", *Aviva Premiership Rugby*, May 29 2012, http://bit.ly/N6wzFc

[96] The complete Pumas squad for The Rugby Championship was as follows

France - Patricio Albacete (Toulouse), Lucas González Amorosino (Montpellier), Marcelo Bosch (Biarritz), Maximilano Bustos (Montpellier), Martín Bustos Moyano (Montpellier), Rafael Carballo (Bordeaux-Begles), Manuel Carizza (Biarritz)*, Agustín Creevy (Montpellier), Santiago Fernández (Montpellier), Juan Martín Fernández Lobbe (Toulon), Juan Figallo (Montpellier), Agustín Figuerola (Brive), Alvaro Galindo (Racing Métro), Eusebio Guiñazú (Biarritz) *, Juan Martín Hernández (Racing Métro), Juan Imhoff (Racing Métro), Juan Manuel Leguizamón (Lyon OU), Juan Pablo Orlandi (Racing Métro), Martín Rodriguez Gurruchaga (Stade Français), Rodrigo Roncero (Stade Français)*, Nicolas Sánchez (Bordeaux-Begles), Nicolas Vergallo (Toulouse)

England - Horacio Agulla (Bath), Marcos Ayerza (Leicester Tigers), Gonzalo Camacho (Exeter Chiefs)

Wales - Tomás Vallejos Cinalli (Scarlets)

Argentina - Julio Farías Cabello (Tucumán), Tomás Cubelli (Belgrano Athletic), Tomás De La Vega (CUBA), Martín Landajo (CASI), Tomás Leonardí (SIC), Manuel Montero (Pucurá), Bruno Postigliano (La Plata), Leonardo Senatore (GER)

* Players released ahead of The Rugby Championship or to retire after the competition. Carizza and Guiñazú were given the choice of extending their contracts with Biarritz or playing for Argentina. They both decided to play for their country. Roncero had retired after the completion of the 2011-2012 French club Season but came out of retirement for The Rugby Championship.

[97] An elite professional competition is one in which the majority of players are Tier One players. This is the case in the Aviva Premiership, Pro 12, Super Rugby and the Top 14. An elite competition need not necessarily be organized by a Tier One union, however. Italy is a Tier One union with a league that is above amateur status. It is not, however as good of as league as that found in Japan and Japan is a Tier Two rugby nation.

[98] South Africa scored 189 points in Pool A of Rugby World Cup 2007. The pool included England, Samoa, Tonga and the United States of America. In 2011 South Africa scored 166 points in D. The pool featured Fiji, Namibia, Samoa and Wales.

[99] The Georgian players based in France were as follows:

First Division (Top 14) - Giorgi Chkhaidze (Montpellier), Akvsenti Giorgadze (Castres), Mamuka Gorgodze (Montpellier), Vasil Kakovin (Brive), Davit Khinchagishvili (Brive), Viktor Kolelishvili (Clermont Espoirs*), Davit Kubriashvili (Toulon), Goderdzi Shvelidze (Montpellier), Davit Zirakashvili (Clermont).

*Espoirs is the development team

Second Division (Pro d2) - Levan Datunashvili (Aurillac), Lasha Malaghuradze (Béziers)

Lower Divisions (Fédérale1, Fédérale 2 and Fédérale 3) Irakli Abuseridze (Auxerre), Dimitri Basilaia (Aubenas), Revaz Gigauri (Figeac), Davit Kacharava (Nice), Merab Kvirikashvili (Figeac), Irakli Machkhaneli (Mâcon), Vakhtang Maisuradze (Saint Nazaire), Giorgi Nemsadze (Montauban), Shalva Sutiashvili (Massy), Malkhaz Urjukashvili (Gourdon), Ilia Zedginidze (Carqueiranne), Tedore Zibzibadze (Périgueux)

[100] "Romania join the professional era", *The Telegraph*, October 07 2003, http://bit.ly/3WMNES

[101] Phelan named all of Horacio Agulla, Patrício Albacete, Marcos Ayerza, Marcelo Bosch, Martín Bustos Moyano, Maximilano Bustos, Gonzalo Camacho, Rafael Carballo, Manuel Carizza, Agustín Creevy, Juan Fernández Lobbe, Santiago Fernández, Juan Figallo Agustín Figuerola, Álvaro Galindo, Lucas González Amorosino, Juan Martín Hernández, Juan Orlandi, Martín Rodríguez Gurruchaga, Nicolas Sánchez, Tomás Vallejos and Nicolas Vergallo for The Rugby Championship. None of them, however, would play against Italy or France in June.

[102] The complete squad for the June international series was as follows - Belisario Agulla (Agen, France), Gabriel Ascárate (Los Pampas XV), Rodrigo Báez (Los Pampas XV), Facundo Barrea (Los Pampas XV), Andrés Bordoy (Pau, France), Rodrigo Bruno (Los Pampas XV), Felipe Contepomi (Stade Français, France), Tomás Cubelli (Los Pampas XV), Tomás De la Vega (Los Pampas XV), Julio Farías Cabello (Los Pampas XV), Genaro Fessia (Los Pampas XV), Francisco Gómez Kodela (Biarritz, France), Agustín Gozio (London Scottish, England), Eusebio Guiñazú (Biarritz, France), Santiago Guzmán (Los Pampas XV), Pablo Henn (Brive, France), Martín Landajo (Los Pampas XV), Tomás Leonardi (Los Pampas XV), Esteban Lozada (Agen, France), Benjamin Macome (Los Pampas XV), Ignacio Mieres (Exeter Chiefs, England), Román Miralles (Los Pampas XV), Manuel Montero (Los Pampas XV), Matías Orlando (Los Pampas XV), Bruno Postiglioni (Los Pampas XV), Rodrigo Roncero (Stade Français, France), Leonardo Senatore (Los Pampas XV), Francisco Nahuel Tetaz Chaparro (Stade Français, France), Joaquín Tuculet (Sale Sharks, England), Benjamin Urdapilleta (Harlequins, England)

[103] "Graham Henry to Pumas – Score more tries", *Stuff*, May 31 2012, http://bit.ly/LHrcJc

[104] The players from Los Pampas XV to train in Pensacola were Tomas Cubelli, Tomas De La Veja, Julio Farías Cabello, Eusebio Guiñazú, Martín Landajo, Tomás Leonardi, Bruno Postiglioni and Leonardo Senatore.

[105] "Albacete: "Va a ser como un Mundial con el peor fixture de tu vida"", *ESPN Scrum*, June 27 2012, http://es.pn/LR3ayg

[106] "Pumas show commitment is in their DNA", *Rugby Heaven*, September 17 2012, http://bit.ly/QzAv2a

[107] "Saint-Andre: Los Pumas Superaron a Francia", *ESPN Scrum*, September 13 2012, http://es.pn/OkGNAM

[108] "Argentina to host JWC 2010", *IRB*, Monday June 01 2009, http://bit.ly/PdmlTW

[109] IBID.

[110] IBID.

[111] "JWC opening day attracting record attendance", *IRB*, Monday June 07 2010, http://bit.ly/PYpIhf

[112] "IRB North American 4 schedule announced", *IRB*, Tuesday March 18 2008, http://bit.ly/QNJLQo

[113] "Americas Rugby Championship set for kick-off", *IRB*, Tuesday October 05 2010, http://bit.ly/dhjcSI

[114] Argentina's seven players from the squad to play in Rugby World Cup 2011 were Maximilano Bustos, Julio Farías Cabello, Genaro Fessia, Agustín Gosio, Juan Imhoff, Nicolás Sánchez and Leonardo Senatore. Five of them also went on to play professional rugby in England or France after the World Cup.

Maximilano Bustos and Agustín Creevy joined Montpellier, Agustín Gosio joined London Scottish, Juan Imhoff joined Racing Métro, Nicolás Sánchez joined Bordeaux-Begles and Leonardo Senatore joined Toulon.

[115] "¿Americas Cup en Mar del Plata?", *Try Scrum*. http://bit.ly/P8YOX6

[116] "Sevens Explosion – World Cup History Part 1: Dallaglio and co sweep to inaugural win", *Ultimate Rugby Sevens*, Tuesday February 24 2009, http://ur7s.com/news/107

[117] Starmer-Smith, Nigel (ed) "*Rugby - A Way of Life, An Illustrated History of Rugby*", (Lennard Books, 1986, PP144.

[118] IBID P142

[119] McLaren, Bill "Talking of Rugby", (Stanley Paul), 1991, P 166

[120] "World Cup Sevens: Lomu enlivens an out-of-step event" *The Telegraph*, January 29 2011, http://bit.ly/UHu5BV

[121] "HSBC Sevens World Series expands to 10 rounds", *IRB*, Tuesday June 26 2012, http://bit.ly/KKdRoP

[122] IBID.

[123] FIBA World Cup Champions History, *FIBA*, 2007, P3 http://bit.ly/dtGl6C

[124] See "Fiba Archive" for a list of complete results: http://bit.ly/Rancr3

[125] FIBA World Cup Champions History, *FIBA*, 2007, P3 http://bit.ly/dtGl6C

[126] IBID. PP8-9

[127] "ESP - Spain selected to host 2014 FIBA World Championship", *FIBA*, May 23 2009, http://bit.ly/QNK1iq

[128] Ranking Men after all 2011 FIBA Zones Championships, FIBA, http://bit.ly/1fVkn2

[129] "História do Pan", UOL, http://bit.ly/ONLzMX

[130] "History of the Pan Am Games",*Guadalajara 2011 Pan Am Games*, http://bit.ly/RTv8tR

[131] "Troubling Times in Mar Del Plata ", Los Angeles Times, March 12 1995, http://lat.ms/RTv9hx

[132] "História do Pan", UOL, http://bit.ly/SgIWm1

[133] "FIFA World Cup", *FIFA*, http://bit.ly/ONLCII

[134] "1978 World Cup: A First title for Argentina", *CBS Sports*, Wednesday November 25, 2009, http://bit.ly/SeNwgn

[135] "Argentina´s dirty war: the museum of horrors", The Telegraph, May 17 2008. http://bit.ly/27iIAk

[136] "1978 World Cup: A First title for Argentina", *CBS Sports*, Wednesday November 25, 2009, http://bit.ly/SeNwgn

[137] "Jorge Rafael Videla convicted of baby thefts", The Guardian, Friday July 06 2012 http://bit.ly/NEMlEE

[138] "There Is No Scoffing at Argentina's Triumph: World Cup Victory Takes Some of the Taint Off Controversial 1978 Decision", Los Angeles Times, July 01 1986, http://lat.ms/SeNDsh

[139] "We fixed it! Peru senator claims 1978 World Cup game against Argentina was rigged", Mail Online, February 09 2012, http://bit.ly/zyrSaU

[140] "FIFA World Cup host Decision", FIFA, http://bit.ly/Pztm2I

[141] The Argentine military overthrew democracy in Argentina six times in the twentieth century. The origin of the first coup in 1930 was electoral fraud. Having lost the provincial election to the Radical Party the Conservative Party resorted to fraud to stay in power. Other coup d´etat´s followed in 1943, 1955, 1962, 1966 and 1976 as Argentina was not able to complete a transition to be a developed country despite having high living standards in the early twentieth century.

"Explorations in Economic History", *Elsevier*, 2010, PP 179-197.
http://cdi.mecon.gov.ar/doc/sd/4.pdf

[142] "Guerrillas and Generals: The "Dirty War" in Argentina", (Paul H Lewis), Praeger October 30, 2001

[143] "Military Rebellion in Argentina: Between Coups and Consolidation", (Norden, Deborah), University of Nebraska Press January 1, 1996

[144] "Timeline: Argentina´s Road to Ruin", *The Washington Post*, August 03 2003, http://wapo.st/SngUGP

[145] "Profile: Carlos Menem", *BBC*, April 28 2003, http://bbc.in/PztpLY

[146] "Timeline: Argentina´s Road to Ruin",*The Washington Post*, August 03 2003, http://wapo.st/SngUGP

[147] IBID.

[148] "Timeline: Argentina´ economic crisis", *The Guardian*, Thursday December 20 2001, http://bit.ly/yZwEG6

[149] "How Argentina survived economic meltdown", *BBC*, July 11 2011, http://bbc.in/pu4cWv

[150] "Argentina", *The New York Times*, April 19 2012, http://nyti.ms/PMp1WT

[151] IBID.

[152] "Argentina: unemployment", New Statesman, February 29 2012, http://bit.ly/POtT0t

[153] "Unemployment Rate", *CIA World Fact Book*, http://1.usa.gov/BAiyE

[154] IBID.

[155] "Area", *CIA World Fact Book*, http://1.usa.gov/Qxw7QW

[156] "Population", *CIA World Fact Book*, http://1.usa.gov/UuUq7z

[157] Taken from XE Universal Currency Converter on Saturday September 22 2012, http://bit.ly/Rao5Qo

[158] "Top 10 best value destinations for 2011", *Lonely Planet*, May 05 2011, http://bit.ly/NLcyra

[159] "Rugby World Cup visitors spend $390 million", *Scoop*, Tuesday February 14 2012, http://bit.ly/OktTbR

[160] "Glory at what price?", *The Economist*, September 18 2011, http://econ.st/q5N59p

[161] "Eden Park Redevelopment", *Fletcher Construction*, http://bit.ly/TmOU7E

[162] "RWCL welcomes RNZ 2011 financial results", *Rugby World Cup*, May 30 2012 http://bit.ly/L1Wxv9

[163] "Olympics worth the price tag? The Montreal Legacy", *CNN*, Thursday July 19 2012, http://bit.ly/OAlGNj

[164] "Population", *CIA World Factbook*, http://1.usa.gov/UuTXCt

[165] "Not Our Fault, Coke Tells Greeks", *Chicago Tribune*, September 24 1990, http://bit.ly/Qt0quY

[166] "Euro Crisis Explained", *BBC*, June 18 2012, http://bbc.in/jQFXqu

[167] "Greece Blames Olympics for Stoking Debt Crisis", *Voice of America*, June 01 2012, http://bit.ly/JSIhG6

[168] "Argentina Getting There and Around", Lonely Planet, http://bit.ly/SN56IK

[169] "Car Hire in Argentina", *rentalcars.com*, http://bit.ly/ONM7CA

[170] See the complete list here: http://bit.ly/SnhDHY

[171] "Argentine High Speed Railway, Argentina", *Future Rail*, http://bit.ly/PYrajx

[172] IBID.

[173] "Argentina´s High Speed Trains: Delayed and Derailed", *World Policy Journal*, April 20 2012, http://bit.ly/HY2qcP

[174] The players not from Buenos Aires were - Omar Hasan (Tucumán), Juan Manuel Leguizamón (Santiago del Estero), Martín Schusterman (San Juan), Federico Todechini (Rosario)

Eusebio Guiñazú of Mendoza was a replacement for the Bronze Final match only.

[175] The twelve players not from Buenos Aires Aires were - Maximilano Bustos (Santa Fé), Manuel Carizza (Rosario), Julio Farías Cabello (Tucumán), Genaro Fessia (Córdoba), Juan Figallo (Salta), Juan Imhoff (Rosario), Juan Manuel Leguizamón (Santiago del Estero), Martín Rodríguez Gurruchaga (Rosario), Nicolas Sánchez (Tucumán), Leonardo Senatore (Rosario), Tomás Vallejos Cinalli (Rosario), Nicolas Vergallo (Rosario)

[176] "URBA-PLADAR 2010", *Periodismo Rugby*, December 15 2009, http://bit.ly/Uqn5X2

[177] "JUGADORES QUE RENUNCIEN A LA BECA PODRAN JUGAR EN SUS CLUBES", *Terra*, April 15 2011, http://bit.ly/TmPPFb

[178] "Argentina get Springbok opener in Four Nations", *The Independent*, Sunday 09 October 2011 http://ind.pn/r9h5df

[179] "¿Los Pampas cambian de torneo?", *ESPN Scrum*, August 29 2012, http://es.pn/RYtIUL

[180] "Saint-Andre: Los Pumas Superaron a Francia", *ESPN Scrum*, September 13 2012, http://es.pn/OkGNAM

[181] "Necesitamos El apoyo Del estado", *ámbito financiero*, Wednesday July 27 2011, http://bit.ly/SeOCZj

[182] In the 2010 competition five teams out of fourteen posted a profit. In 2011 nine teams posted a profit. "Hamish Riach backs retaining provincial rugby", *The Press*, Agusut 01 2012, http://bit.ly/NHCUdP

[183] "Pampas XV win Vodacom Cup!",*Super Sport*, May 13 2011, http://bit.ly/l2TpgF

[184] The nine Pampas players who made the World Cup squad were tighthead prop Maximilano Bustos, hooker Agustín Creevy, second rower Mariano Galarza, backrowers Julio Farías Cabello, Genaro Fessia and Leonardo Senatore, flyhalf Nicolás Sánchez, wing Juan Imhoff and centre Agustín Gosio.

[185] The seventeen Pampas players selected for the June 2012 internationals were Gabriel Ascárate, Rodrigo Báez, Facundo Barrea, Rodrigo Bruno, Tomás Cubelli, Tomás De la Veja, Julio Farías Cabello, Genaro Fessia, Santiago Guzmán, Martín Landajo, Tomás Leonardi, Benjamin Macome, Román Miralles, Manuel Montero, Matías Orlando, Bruno Postiglioni and Leonardo Senatore

[186] "Super Rugby the next target for rising Argentina", *Rugby Heaven*, November 23 2011, http://bit.ly/v1fkYv

[187] IBID.

[188] "LA UAR Tendrá 10 Jugadores contratadas", *UAR*, February 17 2012, http://bit.ly/zE8ebt

[189] IBID.

[190] IBID.

[191] "French defeat gives hope to all", *BBC*, September 09 2007, http://bbc.in/SN5h6U

[192] "Coach asks Argentina to stay calm", *BBC*, Saturday September 08 2007, http://bbc.in/SgJNmQ

[193] IBID.

[194] "Rugby: Pay is a bonus to players", *NZ Herald*, Sunday May 19 2012, http://bit.ly/QaFg4V

[195] "EXCLUSIVE: Sportsmail reveals the payments that led to the rift in England camp", *Daily Mail*, November 23 2011, http://bit.ly/sMmRVr

[196] IBID.

[197] "Wales players given £100k World Cup bonus incentive", *BBC*, August 05 2011 http://bbc.in/PzuhQA

[198] "Wallabies offered bigger bonus to win RWC", *Rugby Heaven*, July 15 2011, http://bit.ly/quaYIA

[199] "All Blacks: Injured stars to get medals - but French get the cash", *NZ Herald*, Tuesday October 18 2011, http://bit.ly/SN5k2C

[200] "Rugby: Pay is a bonus to players", *NZ Herald*, Sunday May 19 2012, http://bit.ly/QaFg4V

[201] "Agustin Pichot: How the Pumas learnt to roar", *The Independent*, Saturday November 14 2009, http://ind.pn/1GurME

[202] The official announcement: http://bit.ly/rjrkke

[203] "Support for grassroots rugby in Madagascar", *IRB*, Monday July 09 2012, http://bit.ly/POvao8

[204] Lisandro Arbizu, Octavio Bartolucci, Roberto Grau, Omar Hasan, Gonzalo Quesada, Mauricio Reggiardo, Martín Scelzo and Eduardo Simone played as professional players in 1999.

[205] "World Cup Words", *CNN Sports Illustrated*, Monday November 08 1999, http://bit.ly/QNLFka

[206] "WRU axe falls on Warriors", *BBC*, Tuesday June 1 2004, http://bbc.in/OkulqK

[207] Argentina had ten professional forwards in 2003 and eight professional backs.

Forwards: - Rimas Alvarez Kairelis (Perpignan, France), Ignácio Fernández Lobbe (Castres, France), Roberto Grau (Dax, France), Omar Hasan (Agen, France), Mario Ledesma (Narbonne, France), Gonzalo Longo (Narbonne, France), Federico Méndez (Natal Sharks, South África), Mauricio Reggiardo (Castres, France), Rodrigo Roncero (Gloucester, England), Martín Scelzo (Narbonne, France)

Backs: - Diego Albanese (Leeds Tykes, England), Felipe Contepomi (Bristol, England), Ignácio Corleto (Stade Français, France), Martín Gaitan (Biarritz, France), José Maria Nuñez Piossek (Bristol, England), José Orengo (Grenoble, France), Agustín Pichot (Bristol, England), Gonzalo Quesada (Béziers, France)

[208] Leinster is the reigning European Champion after having won the final in May 2012. It was the province's second straight title and third overall. Ulster was European Champions in 1999 and Munster won in 2006 and 2008.

[209] The Ospreys are the current Rabo Direct Pro 12 champions having won the title in May 2012. It made the Welsh region the most successful team overall in the competitions history with four titles. Fellow Welsh region the Scarlets was champion in 2004 while Irish sides have won the six other editions of the tournament. Munster is a three time champion having won in 2003, 2009 and 2011. Leinster is a two time champion following victories in 2002 and 2008. While Ulster won the 2006 championship.

[210] "Magners League Dream team Announced", *Rabo Direct Pro 12*, May 11 2007, http://bit.ly/Vu7EPY

[211] "Magners League Dream team' Announced", *Rabo Direct Pro 12*, May 25 2008, http://bit.ly/PYslj6

[212] "Leinster Player Archive", *Rabo Direct Pro 12*, http://bit.ly/Qt0XwP

[213] For a complete list of the all time top points scorers for Leinster see here: http://bit.ly/RNB9Oq

[214] "Contepomi: 'This is my last year of contract here, so we'll have to see...'", Independent, Wednesday October 01 2008, http://bit.ly/Vu7Q1M

[215] "Leinster unveil new signing Galarza", *RTE Sport*, Friday August 20 2010, http://bit.ly/POvqUd

[216] For a complete list of his matches for Leinster see here: http://bit.ly/QaGld3

[217] "Pucciariello calls time on four fantastic seasons", *Limerick Leader*, Friday August 10 2012, http://bit.ly/Qt0Zor

[218] "IRFU to restrict player imports to Ulster, Leinster and Munster", *BBC*, December 21 2011, http://bbc.in/xppVpg

[219] "SRU should be thoroughly ashamed for casting Caledonia into international exile", *Herald Scotland*, Saturday May 15 2004, http://bit.ly/QxxgYE

[220] "Gordon McKie exits as Scottish Rugby chief executive", *BBC*, June 14 2011, http://bbc.in/HaKMjP

[221] "Professional Rugby Continues To Flourish In Spite Of The Recession, But According To George Hook, There Is A Large Cloud On The Horizon... ", *The Cork News*, April 26 2012, http://bit.ly/Qxxpva

[222] The eight players who did not played the 2011-2012 season in Scotland were as follows - Joe Ansbro (London Irish, England), Max Evans (Castres, France), Alex Groove (Worcester Warriors, England), Scott Lawson (Gloucester, England), Alasdair Strokosch (Gloucester, England), Sean Lamont (Scarlets, Wales), Euan Murray (Newcastle Falcons, England), Richie Vernon (Sale Sharks, England)

[223] "Replicating the Irish rugby model may not be easy", *Caledonian Mercury*, May 23 2012, http://bit.ly/KWSoEZ

[224] For a complete list of his Rabo Direct Pro 12 appearances see here: http://bit.ly/ONMT2q

[225] "Aramburu eyes last hurrah in Warriors PRO12 crunch", *Rabo Direct Pro 12*, April 30 2012, http://bit.ly/UqnE35

[226] "Glasgow Warriors 24-3 Connacht", *Glasgow Warriors*, May 04 2012, http://bit.ly/Vu8coR

[227] "Glasgow swoop for Jose Maria Nunez Piossek", *The Telegraph*, September 30 2008, http://bit.ly/SePrBB

[228] "Glasgow Warriors Francisco Leonelli Morey", *Rabo Direct Pro 12*, http://bit.ly/PzuWl8

[229] "Edinburgh Francisco Leonelli Morey", *Rabo Direct Pro 12*, http://bit.ly/RNBTTH

[230] "Edinburgh Lucio Lopez-Fleming ", *Rabo Direct Pro 12*, http://bit.ly/ONN9yi

[231] "Edinburgh Esteban Lozada ", *Rabo Direct Pro 12*, http://bit.ly/QNMhpW

[232] "Edinburgh Augusto Allori ", *Rabo Direct Pro 12*, http://bit.ly/RapgQ6

[233] "Professional Rugby Continues To Flourish In Spite Of The Recession, But According To George Hook, There Is A Large Cloud On The Horizon... ", *The Cork News*, April 26 2012, http://bit.ly/Qxxpva

[234] "Rugby : L'inflation des budgets en Top 14", *Sud Ouest*, Thursday August 11 2011, http://bit.ly/RapkPF

[235] "Italians may join Magners League", *BBC*, Friday December 05 2008, http://bbc.in/Vu8P1J

[236] "Two Italian teams to join Magners League", *BBC*, Monday March 08 2010, http://bbc.in/8YXDK3

[237] IBID.

[238] "Italian side Aironi to pull out of Pro12 after their licence is revoked", *BBC*, April 06 2012, http://bbc.in/I7pfcu

[239] "French coach for new Italian Pro12 team", *Planet Rugby*, June 01 2012 http://bit.ly/SN5HKz

[240] "Agustin Pichot: How the Pumas learnt to roar", *The Independent*, Saturday November 14 2009, http://ind.pn/1GurME

[241] IBID.

[242] "Agustín Pichot", *PREMIERSHIP RUGBY: SQUADS*, HTTP://BIT.LY/ONNXNS

[243] "Felipe Contepomi", *PREMIERSHIP RUGBY: SQUADS*, http://bit.ly/QaI7uI

[244] "Gonzalo Tiesi", *PREMIERSHIP RUGBY: SQUADS*, http://bit.ly/Okv5Mx

[245] "Three London Irish Players Named in Sky Sports Dream Team", *London Irish*, Wednesday May 06 2009 http://bit.ly/SePFIL

[246] "Marcos Ayerza", *Leicester Tigers*, http://bit.ly/Snkpgl

[247] "Three London Irish Players Named in Sky Sports Dream Team", *London Irish*, Wednesday May 06 2009, http://bit.ly/SePFIL

[248] "Rodrigo Roncero", PREMIERSHIP RUGBY: SQUADS, http://bit.ly/UuXEYF

[249] "Martín Scelzo", *PREMIERSHIP RUGBY: SQUADS*, http://bit.ly/QNMBVA

[250] "Sale Sharks crowned GUINNESS PREMIERSHIP champions", *Aviva Premership*, May 27 2006, http://bit.ly/PYtC9G

[251] "Ignacio Fernandez Lobbe", *PREMIERSHIP RUGBY: SQUADS*, HTTP://BIT.LY/UQO5UA

[252] "Juan Martin Fernandez Lobbe", *PREMIERSHIP RUGBY: SQUADS*, HTTP://BIT.LY/PYTLDR

[253] "Three London Irish Players Named in Sky Sports Dream Team", *London Irish*, Wednesday May 06 2009, http://bit.ly/SePFIL

[254] "Juan Manuel Leguizamon", *PREMIERSHIP RUGBY: SQUADS*, http://bit.ly/QaIc1n

[255] "Horacio Agulla", *Leicester Tigers*, http://bit.ly/RNCPY3

[256] "Agulla wins Supporters' Awards Double", *Leicester Tigers*, May 02 2012, http://bit.ly/ItoWZh

[257] "Agulla lands second Goldsmiths award", *Leicester Tigers*, April 12 2012, http://bit.ly/IEMs6f

[258] "Aviva Premiership Rugby Award Winners", *Aviva Premiership*, May 08 2012, http://bit.ly/KDiG3P

[259] "Gonzalo Camacho", *PREMIERSHIP RUGBY: SQUADS*, HTTP://BIT.LY/OTHFN9

[260] "Aviva Premiership Rugby Award Winners", *Aviva Premiership*, May 08 2012, http://bit.ly/KDiG3P

[261] "Ignacio Mieres", PREMIERSHIP RUGBY: SQUADS, HTTP://BIT.LY/QXYKFK

[262] "Rugby : L'inflation des budgets en Top 14", *Sud Ouest*, Thursday August 11 2011, http://bit.ly/RapkPF

[263] "Salary Cap", *Aviva Premiership*, http://bit.ly/ITLDlF

[264] "Canal Plus retains Top 14 with multi-million dollar deal", *Sports Pro*, May 11 2011, http://bit.ly/UHE6yY

[265] "Saracens 19 Harlequins 24: match report", *The Telegraph*, March 31 2012, http://bit.ly/HFxuZM

[266] "Perpignan 29 Toulon 25: Match Report", *The telegraph*, April 09 2011, http://bit.ly/Pdu8Be

[267] "Rugby : L'inflation des budgets en Top 14", *Sud Ouest*, Thursday August 11 2011, http://bit.ly/RapkPF

[268] IBID.

[269] The European Parliament Constituency divides mainland France into six regions. They are the North-West, West, East, Wouth-West, South-East, Loire-Massif Central and Ile-De-France. The area called South-Western France encompasses the regions of Aquitaine, Languedoc-Roussillon and the Midi-Pyrénées. See here: http://bit.ly/TmXVxs

[270] "Gloom over French Soccer Contrasts with Rugby´s Rise", *Time*, Sunday May 16 2010, http://ti.me/cIzOgF

[271] "Munster to play in Toulouse", *Munster Rugby*, September 22 2011, http://bit.ly/ofySsL

[272] "Population Castres", *Cartes France*, http://bit.ly/PYy9Jm

[273] The complete list of clubs in the 2011-2012 season with players from Argentina reads as follows:

Agen - Belisario Agulla, Miguel Avramovic, Martín Scelzo
Bordeaux-Begles Rafael Carballo, Nicolás Sánchez
Brive - Pablo Cardinali, Agustín Figuerola, Pablo Henn
Biarritz Marcelo Bosch, Manuel Carizza, Francisco Goméz Kodela, Eusebio Guiñazú
Clermont - Gonzalo Canale*
Lyon - Juan Manuel Leguizamón
Montpellier - Lucas González Amorosino, Maximilano Bustos, Martín Bustos Moyano, Agustín Creevy, Santiago Fernández, Juan Figallo
Perpignan - Rimas Alvarez Kairelis
Racing Métro - Santiago Dellapé*, Alvaro Galindo, Juan Martín Hernández, Juan Imhoff, Juan Pablo Orlandi
Stade Français - Francisco Nahuel Tetaz Chaparro, Felipe Contepomi, Martín Rodríguez Gurruchaga, Sergio Parisse*, Rodrigo Roncero, Gonzalo Tiesi
Toulon - Juan Martín Fernández Lobbe, Leonadro Senatore
Toulouse - Patricio Albacete, Alberto Vernet Basualdo, Eusebio Guiñazú, Nicolás Vergallo

* Born in Argentina but plays for Italy.

[274] The nineteen Pumas in the 2011-2012 Top 14 who played at the 2011 World Cup are Patrício Albacete, Lucas González Amorosino, Marcelo Bosch, Maximilano Bustos, Manuel Carizza, Felipe Contepomi, Agustín Creevy, Santiago Fernández, Juan Martín Fernández Lobbe, Juan Figallo, Martín Rodríguez Gurruchaga, Juan Imhoff, Juan Manuel Leguizamón, Rodrigo Roncero, Nicolas Sánchez, Martín Scelzo, Leonardo Senatore, Gonzalo Tiesi and Nicolas Vergallo.

Four others played at Rugby World Cup 2007 but not Rugby World Cup 2011. They are Alberto Vernet Basualdo, Eusébio Guiñazú, Juan Martín Hernández and Rimas Alvarez Kairelis.

[275] "Rugby: ce qui change cette saison en Top 14", *L'Express*, August 13 2010, http://bit.ly/c38uHX

[276] "Gloom over French Soccer Contrasts with Rugby´s Rise", *Time*, Sunday May 16 2010, http://ti.me/cIzOgF

[277] "France Confronts Its Rugby Fears With Argentina", *The New York Times*, November 19 2010, http://nyti.ms/OkxtCV

[278] "MARIO LEDESMA FICHE JOUEUR", *rugbyrama*, http://bit.ly/PzytQp

[279] "Une 53e soirée de revê", rugbyrama, November 19 2007, http://bit.ly/Uqqghj

[280] "Top 14 : Hernandez joueur de l'année", *Le Post*, December 03 2007, http://huff.to/OTLMsk

[281] "La nuit du rugby 2008, les résultats", *Sports.fr*, May 19 2008, http://bit.ly/OTLTEv

[282] "Nuit du rugby 2009 : les lauréats", *LNR*, October 05 2009, http://bit.ly/SnpLIB

[283] "RWC 2011 legacy programme to benefit islands", Rugby World Cup, Thursday May 03 2012, http://bit.ly/TmZV99

[284] Taken from *ESPN Scrum*, http://bit.ly/OkxMh8

[285] "Chile and Hong Kong to host next two JWRT", *IRB*, Friday July 13 2012, http://bit.ly/Lei5Ap

[286] "History of Rugby Canada", *Rugby Canada*, http://bit.ly/PduN5U

[287] "World Ranking Analysis", *IRB*, http://bit.ly/qUdh2D

[288] "History of Rugby Canada", *Rugby Canada*, http://bit.ly/PduN5U

[289] "Northern Rocks: Canadian Rugby", *BBC*, http://bbc.in/NLfQuy

[290] "Wales 42-17 Canada", *BBC*, September 09 2007, http://bbc.in/RNI0XY

[291] "Minnows facing cull for 2011 Cup", *BBC*, Thursday September 27 2007, http://bbc.in/RTHDpo

[292] "World Cup to remain at 20 teams", *BBC*, Friday November 30 2007, http://bbc.in/VugrRQ

[293] "Rugby World Cup 2011 Pool A: Tonga 20-25 Canada", *BBC*, September 14 2011, http://bbc.in/P6MwNJ

[294] "Canada shock Tonga in RWC upset", *TVNZ*, Wednesday September 14 2011, http://bit.ly/mUbYG1

[295] "Japan coach Kirwan targets 'at least two' World Cup wins", ITV, http://itv.co/Qt36Zp

[296] "Italy rallies to defeat Canada in rugby test match at BMO Field", *The Globe and Mail*, Friday June 15 2012, http://bit.ly/ONQGwL

[297] "Canada's rugby team gets comeback win over U.S.", *National Post*, August 06 2011, http://natpo.st/nAJgXL

[298] The complete squad was as follows.

Canadian based: Hubert Buydens, Nanyak Dala, Brian Erichsen, Matt Evans, Ed Fairhurst, Scott Franklin, Ryan Hamilton, Ciaran Hearn, Nathan Hirayama, Adam Kleeberger, Jeremy Kyne, Jason Marshall, Ander Monro, Taylor Paris, Pat Riordan, Mike Scholz , Ryan Smith, Andrew Tiedemann, Conor Trainor, Frank Walsh and Sean White

Professionals - Aaron Carpenter (Plymouth Albion, England), Jamie Cudmore (Clermont, France), Tyler Hotson (Plymouth Albion, England), Jamie Mackenzie (Esther, England), Phil Mackenzie (Esther, England), Chauncey O'Toole (Ospreys, Wales), James Pritchard (Bedford, England), Jebb Sinclair (London Irish, England), DTH van der Merwe (Glasgow Warriors, Scotland)

[299] "Glasgow Warriors DTH van der Merwe ", *Rabo Direct Pro 12*, http://bit.ly/UqqDZc

[300] "Could rugby union take off in the US?", *BBC*, September 07 2011, http://bbc.in/op2iYC

[301] "Report shows Rugby's growth in new markets", *IRB*, Tuesday April 05 2011, http://bit.ly/RTsc0c

[302] "NBC Announces RWC Schedule", *Rugby Mag*, Tuesday August 09 2011, http://bit.ly/Tn0f7F

[303] "Emotional 9/11 memorial for US rugby team", *Sydney Morning Herald*, September 11 2011, http://bit.ly/mPy2GQ

[304] The team that defeated Russia featured ten players who had played some or all of the season before the World Cup professionally. They were as follows - Todd Clever (Suntory Sungoliath, Japan), Paul Emerick (Ulster, Northern Ireland), Mike MacDonald (Leeds, England), Matekitonga Moeakiola (Bobigny, France), James Paterson (Highlanders, New Zealand)
Hayden Smith (Saracens, England), Louis Stanfill (Mogliani, Italy), John van der Giessen (Bath, England), Taku Ngwenya (Biarritz, France), Chris Wyles (Saracens, England)

[305] "USA Sevens declared giant success", *IRB*, Sunday February 12 2012, http://bit.ly/ONR7He

[306] IBID.

[307] "JWRT raises the profile of Rugby in USA", *IRB*, Sunday July 01 2012, http://bit.ly/LqXQRx

[308] "USA Rugby to Offer Fulltime Contracts to 23 Athletes in 2012", *USA Rugby*, November 30 2011, http://bit.ly/OTMu95

[309] "United States ready to launch BID to host 2023 Rugby World Cup", *The Guardian*, Thursday December 01 2011, http://bit.ly/sQTbI1

[310] "USA falls to Italy", *USA Rugby*, June 23 2012, http://bit.ly/RatW8v

[311] Home Page, *Montevideo Cricket Club*, http://bit.ly/SN7xeq

[312] "Campeones", *Unión de Rugby de Uruguay*, http://bit.ly/OkxXJf

[313] "I Am Alive: The Crash of Uruguayan Air Force Flight 571", *History.com*, http://bit.ly/c9lkq2

[314] Parrado Nando "Milagre Nos Andes: *72 Dias na Montanha e Minha Longa Volta para Casa* ", 2006, LIS Gráfica E Editora LTDA, Chapter 8-9.

[315] IBID, PP284-285.

[316] IBID, P 286.

[317] "I Am Alive: The Crash of Uruguayan Air Force Flight 571", *History.com*, http://bit.ly/c9lkq2

[318] Parrado Nando "Milagre Nos Andes: *72 Dias na Montanha e Minha Longa Volta para Casa* ", 2006, LIS Gráfica E Editora LTDA, P314.

[319] IBID, PP23-28.

[320] For a full list of attendances for World Cup matches played in Scotland in 1991, 1999 and 2007 see here: http://bit.ly/SeUdiy

[321] "International Individual Records", *Super Sport*, August 20 2012, http://bit.ly/POEeJY

[322] "Fiche Joueur Rodrigo Capó Ortega", *itsrugby*, October 31 2011, http://www.itsrugby.fr/joueur-446.html

[323] "Portugal make history to qualify", *IRB*, Monday March 26 2007, http://bit.ly/QaQxlN

[324] "Russia and Uruguay return to IRB Nations Cup", *IRB*, Friday May 25 2012, http://bit.ly/MVKxfp

[325] "Statsguru", *ESPN Scrum*, http://bit.ly/ONRdPb

[326] "Campeonato Argentino de Mayores", *UAR*, http://bit.ly/wekaij

[327] "World Rankings Analysis", *IRB*, http://bit.ly/qUdh2D

[328] "Chile jugó un partidazo frente a Tonga", *Feruchi*, September 20 2010, http://bit.ly/POENmW

[329] "Rugby en Chile", Feruchi, http://bit.ly/ONRqlr

[330] "Country Comparison: Population", *CIA World Fact Book*, http://1.usa.gov/ONRoKf

[331] "Institucional", *Unión de Rugby Del Uruguay*, http://bit.ly/Okymv2

[332] "2008: Uruguay Spoil Chile's Party", *IRB*, http://bit.ly/Uqr5Xu

[333] "Chile to host IRB Junior World Trophy", *IRB*, Friday August 31 2007, http://bit.ly/SgPHo4

[334] "Chile and Hong Kong to host next two JWRT", *IRB*, Friday July 13 2012, http://bit.ly/Lei5Ap

[335] "Enrique Larenas"No teníamos em La cabeza poder ganarle a Argentina"", *Feruchi*, May 07 2012, http://bit.ly/RauCus

[336] "Ontário Blues in Argentina", *scrum*, May 08 2012, http://bit.ly/ISlfNZ

[337] "Country Comparison: Population", *CIA World Fact Book*, http://1.usa.gov/POEqsB

[338] "O Future para o Rugby no Brasil", *Globoesporte*, Friday September 16 2011, http://glo.bo/Qt3rvn

[339] "Numero de clubes de rugby aumenta qause oito vezes em sete anos no Brasil", *Mais Revista Homen*, August 24 2012, http://bit.ly/RTJn1I

[340] "Resultados – Masculino 2010", *Raça Ribeirão Rugby*, http://bit.ly/Tn17cs

[341] "Interview with Fernando Portugal", *Rugby World Cup: Argentina 2023*, Friday November 05 2010, http://bit.ly/Qt3s2k

[342] "Time da França contrata revelação da seleçãobrasileira de rúgbi", *Globo Esporte*, August 24 2012 http://glo.bo/P2TMqu

[343] "World Rankings Analysis", *IRB*, http://bit.ly/qUdh2D

[344] "CBRu quer a Copa do Mundo de Rugby de 2023 no Brasil!", *Blog do Rugby*, October 21 2011, http://bit.ly/Qt3uHu

[345] "Interview with Fernando Portugal", *Rugby World Cup: Argentina 2023*, Friday November 05 2010, http://bit.ly/Qt3s2k

[346] "IRB World Rankings", *IRB*, August 20 2012, http://bit.ly/zYwVw

[347] "IRB announces increased funding for the game ", *IRB*, Friday January 25 2008, http://bit.ly/QaRlag

[348] "Russia qualify for their first Rugby World Cup", *BBC*, Sunday February 28 2010, http://bbc.in/cXs8Zh

[349] "Namibia secure place at RWC 2011", *IRB*, Saturday November 28 2009, http://bit.ly/POF5u6

[350] "IRB World Rankings", *IRB*, November 09 2009, http://bit.ly/QNRzla

[351] "IRB World Rankings used for RWC 2011 draw", *IRB*, Friday February 22 2008, http://bit.ly/pvDBCn

[352] "Rugby World Cup venues revealed", *Television New Zealand*, Thursday March 12 2009 http://bit.ly/dC8ueF

[353] "RWC 2015 draw adds spice to season", *IRB*, Monday May 21 2012, http://bit.ly/UHIFJy

[354] "RWC 2015 draw adds extra spice to season", *IRB*, Monday May 21 2012, http://bit.ly/UHIFJy

[355] "IRB World Rankings – Archive", *IRB*, December 06 2004 http://bit.ly/Uv8b6h

[356] "RWC Qualifying Reperchage", *IRB*, http://bit.ly/Tn25Wi

[357] "RWC Qualifying Oceania", *IRB*, http://bit.ly/RNKA0d

[358] "Oceania sets RWC 2015 qualification process", *IRB*, Wednesday May 02 2012, http://bit.ly/Izj9TW

[359] The Cook Islands was the higest ranked of the six at the time in 55th position. The Solomon Islands were 70th, Niue was 71st, Tahiti was 86th and Vanuatu was 94th. American Samoa was not included as it was yet to play an official international rugby match since it became a full member of the IRB in 2012.

"IRB World Rankings", *IRB*, August 20 2012, http://bit.ly/zYwVw

[360] "Samoa and Fiji through to RWC 2007", *IRB*, Friday October 21 2005 http://bit.ly/PYCcFs

[361] In total Argentina has played 102 matches in the South American Championship, winning every time. The complete list is as follows:

1951 Brazil, Chile, Uruguay
1958 Chile, Peru, Uruguay
1961 Brazil, Chile Uruguay
1964 Brazil, Chile, Uruguay
1967 Chile, Uruguay
1969 Chile Uruguay
1971 Brazil, Chile, Paraguay, Uruguay
1973 Brazil, Chile, Paraguay, Uruguay
1975 Brazil, Chile, Paraguay, Uruguay
1977 Brazil, Chile, Paraguay, Uruguay
1979 Brazil, Chile, Paraguay, Uruguay
1983 Chile, Paraguay, Uruguay
1985 Chile, Paraguay, Uruguay
1987 Chile, Paraguay, Uruguay
1989 Brazil, Chile, Paraguay, Uruguay
1991 Brazil, Chile, Paraguay, Uruguay

1993 Brazil, Chile, Paraguay, Uruguay
1995 Chile, Paraguay, Uruguay
1996 Chile, Paraguay, Uruguay
1997 Chile, Paraguay, Uruguay
1998 Chile, Paraguay, Uruguay
1999 Chile, Peru, Uruguay
2000 Chile, Uruguay
2001 Chile, Paraguay, Uruguay
2002 Chile, Paraguay, Uruguay
2003 Chile, Paraguay, Uruguay
2004 Chile, Uruguay, Venezuela
2005 Chile, Uruguay
2006 Chile, Uruguay
2007 Chile
2008 Chile, Uruguay
2009 Chile, Uruguay
2010 Chile, Uruguay
2011 Chile, Uruguay
2011 Brazil, Chile, Uruguay

[362] The union members of the CAR can be divided into IRB members, IRB associate members and members which are not affiliated with the IRB. They are as follows:

Full IRB Members – Botsuana, Cameroon, Cote d´Ivoire, Kenya, Madagascar, Mauritius, Morocco, Namíbia, Nigéria, Senegal, South Africa, Swaziland, Tunísia, Uganda, Zâmbia, Zimbabwe.

IRB Associate members – Burundi, Ghana, Mali, Mauritânia, Rwanda, Tanzânia, Togo.

Non-affiliates IRB members – Algeria, Benin, Burkina Faso, Central African Republic, Chad, Democratic Republic of the Congo, Egypt, Gabon, Libya, Niger, Republic of the Congo, Seychelles

In addition there are two members affiliated with the IRB which are French territories. They are Mayotte and Réunion.

[363] "Competitions", *CAR*, http://bit.ly/Uv8YEi

[364] "RWC Qualifying Africa", *IRB*, http://bit.ly/UqrzwE

[365] "Madagascar climb rankings after shock win", *IRB*, Monday July 09 2012, http://bit.ly/RMwwRd

[366] At the time of writing Nambia was 22nd in the world and Botsuana was 77th. "IRB World Rankings", *IRB*, Monday August 20 2012, http://bit.ly/zYwVw

[367] "Exit-bound Namibia ask for help in form of tougher tests", *Sydney Morning Herald*, September 25 2011 http://bit.ly/Qt3Q0C

[368] FORU's members can be divided into two categories – full IRB members and associate members.

Full IRB members: American Samoa, Australia, the Cook Islands, Fiji, New Zealand, Niue, Papua New Guinea, Samoa, the Solomon Islands, Tahiti, Tonga and Vanuatu.

Associate members: New Caledonia, Tuvalu, Wallis and Futuna.

[369] Taken from the sites home page, *Federation of Oceania Rugby Unions*, http://bit.ly/vD67Uy

[370] The six competitions within the FORU region are the Pacific Rugby Cup, the Pacific Nations Cup, the Oceania Cup, the Oceania Under 19's Championship, the Oceania Sevens Championship and the Oceania Womens Sevens Championship.

[371] "Tournaments Home", *Federation of Oceania Rugby Unions*, http://bit.ly/Tn2NTl

[372] At time of writing the higest ranked nation was Papua New Guinea in 51st position. "IRB World Rankings", *IRB*, August 27 2012, http://bit.ly/zYwVw

[373] "Samoa qualify for Rugby World Cup 2011", IRB, Saturday July 18 2009, http://bit.ly/QxDI26

[374] Three players from the match played in Rugby World Cup 2011. They were John Afoa, Stephen Donald and Corey Flynn.

[375] "Australia A out of Pacific Nations Cup", *ESPN Scrum*, December 17 2008, http://es.pn/PzApZ2

[376] Taken from Statsguru: http://bit.ly/SeVs19

[377] Taken from Statsguru: http://bit.ly/Ravjnu

[378] "360th All Black Test", *Rugby Museum*, August 28 2012, http://bit.ly/POG5hV

[379] Tonga could have hosted Scotland in 2012 but it was deemed to not have the same level of facilities found in Fiji and Samoa so instead the match between the teams was made a home match for Scotland in Aberdeen.

The complete list of home tests for Tonga from June 2015 to August 2012 can be seen on scrumguru: http://bit.ly/RNL9qW

[380] Tonga's complete list of matches between the 2007 and 2011 Rugby World Cup's is:

2008 Fiji, Japan, Samoa
2009 Fiji, Japan, Portugal, Samoa

2010 Chile, Japan, Fiji, Samoa
2011 Fiji (3 matches), Japan, Samoa, USA

[381] The four matches between Australia and Tonga were played in 1973, 1993 and 1998. Curiously Tonga won the first test between the nations, 16-11 in Brisbane in 1973.

[382] Argentina has hosted Uruguay thirteen times and an additional thirteen tests have been played in a neutral country in South or North America. See here: http://bit.ly/Qt3Xt4

[383] Taken from Rugby Museum: http://bit.ly/OTOqOY

[384] "473rd All Black Test", *Rugby Museum*, August 28 2012, http://bit.ly/Tn308Y

[385] "Junior All Blacks wear out Fiji", *Fiji Rugby*, Saturday June 03 2006, http://bit.ly/UHK5DP

[386] "RFU defend extra England – All Blacks Test ", *The Telegraph*, January 23 2008, http://bit.ly/RavwqO

[387] "Hong Kong to host Bledisloe Cup match", *The New York Times*, Monday March 03 2008, http://nyti.ms/QxE3BP

[388] FIRA´s member nations are as follows – Andorra, Armenia, Austria, Azerbaijan, Belgium, Bosnia & Herzegovina, Bulgaria, Croatia, Cyprus, Czech Republic, Denmark, England, Estonia, Finland, France, Georgia, Germany, Greece, Hungary, Iceland, Ireland (The Republic of Ireland and Northern Ireland combined), Israel, Italy, Latvia, Liechtenstein, Lithuania, Luxembourg, Malta, Moldova, Monaco, Netherlands, Norway, Poland, Portugal, Romania, Russia, San Marino, Scotland, Serbia, Slovakia, Slovenia, Spain, Sweden, Switzerland, Turkey, Ukraine, Wales

[389] The countries competing in the 2012-2014 European Nations Cup are Belgium, Georgia, Portugal, Romania, Russia and Spain. Of them all except Beglium have played in a Rugby World Cup previously.

[390] In the amateur era Italy played Russia (or the Soviet Union) a total of fifteen times. Since them there have been three matches – qualification matches for Rugby World Cup 1999 and 2007 and their Pool match at Rugby World Cup 2011.

[391] In total Japan has faced nine Asian teams in officially recognized international rugby matches. They are the Arabian Gulf, Chinese Taipei, Hong Kong, Kazakhstan, Singapore, South Korea, Sri Lanka, Thailand and the United Arab Emirates.

[392] Taken from statsguru: http://bit.ly/NLhpbH
In many cases the matches that Japan have lost have featured a Japanese team that is far from being at full strength.

[393] Japan´s complete list of matches against Hong Kong from 1999-2012 are as follows:

Japan 91-3 Hong Kong, May 08 2005

Hong Kong 3-52 Japan November 18 2006
Japan 73-3 Hong Kong May 18 2007
Japan 75-29 Hong Kong, May 18 2008
Hong Kong 6-59 Japan, May 02 2009
Japan 94-5 Hong Kong, May 22 2009
Hong Kong 22-45, April 30 2011
Japan 67-0 Hong Kong, May 19 2012

[394] In 2012 the divisions were as follows:

Top 5: Japan, Kazakhstan, Hong Kong, South Korea and the United Arab Emirates.

Division One: Chinese Taipei, Philippines, Singapore and Sri Lanka.

Division Two: China, Iran, Malaysia and Thailand

Division Three: Guan, India, Indonesia and Pakistan

Division Four: Jordan, Lebanon, Qatar and Uzbekistan

Division Five: Brunei, Cambodia and Laos

[395] "About ARFU", *ARFU*, http://www.arfu.com/page.php?id=3&ABOUT%20ARFU

[396] "England to host 2015 Rugby World Cup with Japan chosen for 2019", *The Telegraph*, July 28 2009, http://bit.ly/GGUhy

[397] IBID.

[398] The data was taken from the CIA World Fact Book country comparison. http://1.usa.gov/SN8jbh

[399] "Northern Ireland population now stands at 1.81m", *BBC*, July 16 2012, http://bbc.in/Lsd9gj

[400] "We´ll hand you the World Cup!", *The Irish Sun*, Sunday September 02 2012, http://bit.ly/PzASKM

[401] For a complete list of Irish home internationals during this period see here: http://bit.ly/QNSIsU

[402] "We´ll hand you the World Cup!", *The Irish Sun*, Sunday September 02 2012, http://bit.ly/PzASKM

[403] IBID.

[404] "GAA back rugby world cup bid ", *Independent*, Sunday September 02 2012, http://bit.ly/SyJalc

[405] "Italy government won´t back 2020 Olympic bid", *RTE*, Tuesday February 14 2012, http://bit.ly/RavU8S

[406] "Irish debt-relief decision in October", *Irish Times*, July 10 2012, http://bit.ly/OsEECL

[407] "RWC 2015 2019 Tender Presentation Reaction", *IRB*, Wednesday May 13 2009, http://bit.ly/SgR8Tp

[408] "Support 2011 rugby bid: Pienaar", *South Africa London*, September 05 2005, http://bit.ly/QNSDFQ

[409] "Blow to Qatar´s 2022 bid as FIFA brands it "high risk"", *Arabian Business*, Thursday November 18 2010, http://bit.ly/a4gqRB

[410] "Full cross-party support for RWC 2019", *ARFU*, http://bit.ly/RTMnva

[411] The decision to award the hosting rights to Qatar also raised concerns over transparency and democratic credibility.

"We Shouldn´t be embaraased by Cup defeat but other´s should" , *National Times*, December 03 2010, http://bit.ly/QNSL8e

[412] "TV powers push for late kick-off´s", *Rugby Heaven*, January 25 2009, http://bit.ly/Okzn6m

[413] The combined population of England and Wales passed 56 million in 2011 according to a census. England accounted for 53 million and Wales 3.1 million.

"England and Wales population up", *BBC*, July 16 2012, http://bbc.in/P9ub2S

[414] Eden Park hosted the following eleven matches - New Zealand v Tonga, Australia v Ireland, New Zealand v France, Fiji v Samoa, England v Scotland, Quarter Final 2 (England v France), Quarter Final 4 (New Zealand v Argentina), Semi Final 1 (New Zealand v Australia), Semi Final 2 (France v Wales), Bronze Final (Australia v Wales), Rugby World Cup Final (New Zealand v France).

North Harbour Stadium hosted the following matches - France v Japan, Australia v Italy, South Africa v Namibia, South Africa v Samoa

Wellington hosted the following eight matches - South Africa v Wales, South Africa v Fiji, Australia v USA, Argentina v Scotland, France v Tonga, New Zealand v Canada, Quarter Final 1 (Ireland v Wales), Quarter Final 3 (South Africa v Australia)

"Rugby World Cup 2011 venue: Stadium Wellington, Wellington", *3 news*, Friday August 05 2011, http://bit.ly/QxEPPa

[415] Argentina v England was moved to Dunedin, Argentina v Scotland was moved to Wellington and Australia v Italy was moved to Auckland (North Harbour). The other relocated matches were

England v Georgia which was moved to Dunedin and Australia v Russia which was moved to Nelson.

[416] The official site of the Rugby World Cup, www.rugbyworldcup.com, lists the capacities of the twelve New Zealand stadiums as follows - Auckland Eden Park(60,000), Auckland North Harbour (30,000), Dunedin (30,000), Hamilton (30,000), Invercargill (17,000), Napier (15,000), Nelson (18,000), New Plymouth (25,000), Palmerston North (15,000), Rotorua (26,000), Wellington (40,000), Whangarei (20,000)

They were not entirely accurate, however. For instance, other sources suggest that Napier had a capacity of 22,000 for the tournament. Nevertheless Napier's two matches did not attract crowds of larger than 15,000. According to local newspaper Hawkes Bay Today the official attendance for France v Canada was 14,230 and for Canada v Japan it was 14,335.

"Mayor laments crowd restrictions", *Hawke's Bay Today*, Monday September 03 2012, http://bit.ly/Qt4qeV

[417] Bordeaux, Lens, Lyon, Montpellier, Nantes, Saint Etienne and Toulouse all had capacities of between 30,000 and 42,000.

"Rugby World Cup 2007 Venues", *World Stadiums*, http://bit.ly/Qt4r2q

[418] "World Cup venues: a guide to the cities and stadiums in New Zealand", *Mai Online*, September 05 2011, http://bit.ly/oYA0Ok

[419] ESPN Scrum listed twelve venues that will host Rugby World Cup 2015 matches in July 2009. http://es.pn/VuIKB0

[420] "Selecting the perfect venues for RWC 2015", *IRB*, Wednesday July 25 2012, http://bit.ly/Q3qvwx

[421] "Millenium Stadium chosen as RWC 2015 venue", *BBC*, May 24 2011, http://bbc.in/xM80fz

[422] "Capacity and facility information", *Ricoh Arena*, http://bit.ly/RNMXjH

[423] The ten lowest attended matches at Rugby World Cup 2011 were as follows

- 10,100 Fiji v Namibia, Rotorua
- 10,267 Scotland v Georgia, Invercargill
- 12,418 Italy v Russia, Nelson
- 12,592 Scotland v Romania, Invercargill
- 12,752 Samoa v Namibia, Rotorua
- 13,288 Georgia v Romania, Palmerston North
- 13,710 Wales v Namibia, New Plymouth
- 13,754 Argentina v Georgia, Palmerston North
- 14,230 France v Canada, Napier
- 14,335 Canada v Japan, Napier

"Mayor laments crowd restrictions", *Hawke's Bay Today*, Monday September 03 2012, http://bit.ly/Qt4qeV

[424] "Match Report England-USA", *2010 FIFA World Cup South Africa*, June 12 2010, http://bit.ly/ONT6LC

[425] "Royal Bafokeng Stadium", *SA Venues*, http://bit.ly/Qt4s6z

[426] "Match Report Slovenia – New Zealand", *2010 FIFA World Cup South Africa*, June 15 2012, http://bit.ly/fC6MZO

[427] "Match Report Slovenia – Algeria", *2010 FIFA World Cup South Africa*, June 13 2012, http://bit.ly/QxFdgC

[428] "Match Report Chile – Honduras", *2010 FIFA World Cup South Africa*, June 16 2012, http://bit.ly/Vumjut

[429] "Wales 72-18 Japan", *BBC*, Thursday September 20 2007, http://bbc.in/SgRGIW

[430] "Wales 20-32 Australia", *BBC*, Saturday September 15 2007, http://bbc.in/Vumnue

[431] "Wales 34-38 Fiji", *BBC*, September 29 2007, http://bbc.in/QxFi3U

[432] "IRB happy to temporarily bed down in garden of Eden", *New Zealand Herald*, Monday March 05 2007, http://bit.ly/SN8GTo

[433] "World-class Eden Park viotal to Cup: rugby chief", *New Zealand Herald*, Wednesday Deember 13 2006, http://bit.ly/PYEPau

[434] The complete list of venues for the first four Rugby World Cup's is as follows

Rugby World Cup 1987
Australia – Brisbane, Sydney
New Zealand – Auckland, Wellington, Christchurch, Dunedin, Rotorua, Napier, Hamilton, Invercargill, Palmerston North

Rugby World Cup 1991
England – London, Leicester, Gloucester, Otley
France – Paris, Toulouse, Lille, Agen, Bayonne, Béziers, Brive, Grenoble
Ireland – Dublin, Belfast
Scotland - Edinburgh
Wales – Cardiff, Llanelli, Pontypool, Pontypridd

Rugby World Cup 1995
South Africa – Johannesburg, Cape Town, Durban, Pretoria, Bloemfontein, East London, Rustenburg, Stellenbosch

Rugby World Cup 1999
Wales – Cardiff, Llanelli, Wrexham
England – London, Bristol, Huddersfield, Leicester
France - Paris, Béziers, Bordeaux, Lens, Toulouse
Ireland – Dublin, Belfast, Limerick
Scotland – Edinburgh, Galashiels, Glasgow

[435] Brisbane hosted nine matches. They were as follows - France v Fiji, Fiji v USA, Australia v Romania, Scotland v USA, New Zealand v Tonga, South Africa v Samoa, England v Uruguay, Quarter Final 2 (Australia v Scotland), Quarter Final 4 (England v Wales)

Melbourne hosted seven matches. They were as follows - New Zealand v Italy, Wales v Canada, New Zealand v Canada, England v Samoa, Australia v Ireland, Quarter Final 1 New Zealand v South Africa, Quarter Final 3 France v Ireland

Perth hosted five matches. They were as follows - South Africa v Uruguay, England v Georgia, Samoa v Uruguay, South Africa v England, Georgia v Samoa

Sydney hosted twelve matches with five at Allianz Stadium and seven at ANZ Stadium. They were as follows

ANZ Stadium - Australia v Argentina, France v Scotland, New Zealand v Wales, Semi Final 1 Australia v New Zealand, Semi Final 2 England v France, Bronze Final France v New Zealand, World Cup Final Australia v England

Allianz Stadium - Ireland v Namibia, Argentina v Romania, South Africa v Georgia, Georgia v Uruguay, Scotland v Fiji

[436] Match attendances taken from ESPN Scrum: http://bit.ly/SgSflZ

[437] "ANZ Stadium: creating history every day", *ANZ Stadium*, http://bit.ly/Qt4Py0

[438] Match attendances taken from ESPN Scrum: http://bit.ly/SgSflZ

[439] IBID.

[440] The distribuition of Tier One v Tier One pool matches in France 2007 was as follows
- France v Argentina, Stade de France
- England v South Africa, Stade de France
- France v Ireland, Stade de France
- Ireland v Argentina, Parc des Princes
  New Zealand v Italy, Marseille
- Scotland v New Zealand, Edinburgh
- Wales v Australia, Cardiff
- Scotland v Italy, Saint Etienne

[441] "RWC 2007 confirmed as record breaker", *IRB*, Monday February 18 2008, http://bit.ly/NLiDDW

[442] Montpellier hosted four matches. They were attended as follows
Tonga v USA, (25,214), Tonga v Samoa (24,128), Australia v Fiji (32,232), South Africa v USA (30,485)

Match attendances taken from ESPN Scrum: http://bit.ly/OkxMh8

[443] Montpellier hosted four matches. They were attended as follows
Tonga v USA, (25,214), Tonga v Samoa (24,128), Australia v Fiji (32,232), South Africa v USA (30,485)

Match attendances taken from ESPN Scrum: http://bit.ly/OkxMh8

[444] "Le Stade", *MHSCFoot*, http://bit.ly/QaXgMx

[445] Match attendances taken from ESPN Scrum: http://bit.ly/OkxMh8

[446] Christchurch's Five matches were relocated as follows
Argentina v England, Dunedin, Australia v Italy, North Harbour, England v Georgia, Dunedin, Argentina v Scotland, Wellington, Australia v Russia, Nelson

Invercargill also hosted an extra match. It has been scheduled to host two matches but also hosted Scotland v Georgia which had been scheduled to be played in Dunedin.

[447] International matches played outside of Buenos Aires in the Professional era from 1996-2012 are as follows
- August 08 2008 Argentina v Romania, Rosario
- August 18 2003 Argentina v Fiji, Córdoba
- June 12 2004 Argentina v Wales, Tucumán
- June 11 2005 Argentina v Italy, Salta
- June 17 2005 Argentina v Italy, Córdoba
- June 11 2006 Argentina v Wales, Puerto Madryn
- May 26 2007 Argentina v Ireland, Santa Fé
- June 09 2007 Argentina v Italy, Mendoza
- June 07 2008 Argentina v Scotland, Rosario
- June 28 2008 Argentina v Italy, Córdoba
- June 13 2009 Argentina v England, Salta
- June 12 2010 Argentina v Scotland, Tucumán
- June 19 2010 Argentina v Scotland, Mar del Plata
- June 09 2012 Argentina v Italy, San Juan
- June 16 2012 Argentina v France Córdoba
- June 23 2012 Argentina v France, Tucumán
- August 25 2012 Argentina v South Africa, Mendoza

- September 29 Argentina v New Zealand, La Plata
- October 06 Argentina v Australia, Rosario

* This list does not include matches in the South American Championship.

[448] The official Argentine Census for 2010 lists Buenos Aires as having a population of 13.8 million. Censo 2010, http://bit.ly/POJKw8

[449] "Buenos Aires Travel Guide", *Travel + Leisure*, http://bit.ly/erGdvY

[450] The Australian Bureau of Statistics published findings showing that Sydney´s population had grown to 4.63 million in June 2011.

"3218.0 – Regional Population Growth, Australia 2010-2011", *The Australian Bureau of Statistics*, March 30 2012, http://bit.ly/Qt53oF

[451] "Auckland´s population reaches 1.5 million", *Television New Zealand*, Wednesday February 01 2012, http://bit.ly/w4h3LM

[452] "La population par arrondissement de 1990 á 2011", *INSEE*, http://bit.ly/olxVhh

[453] "Resúltats du recensement de la population - 2009 ", *INSEE*, http://bit.ly/QNULNF

[454] "A brief History", *City of Johanesburg*, September 06 2012, http://bit.ly/PYGGvW

[455] "Home Page", *Club Atlético Vélez Sarsfeld*, http://bit.ly/dfg3U3

[456] "El Club", *Club Atlético River Plate*, http://bit.ly/jORFEb

[457] "Overview of the Facility", *Nissan Stadium*, http://bit.ly/RTQdo1

[458] "Stadium", *Independiente*, http://bit.ly/Uveh6J

[459] "Ciudad de La Plata – La Plata", *Copa America Argentina 2011*, http://bit.ly/gioAd1

[460] "Características", *Estadio Único Ciudad de La Plata*, http://bit.ly/e4hHZU

[461] [461] "Argentina: Las 10 Ciudades más Grandes", *Taringa*, http://bit.ly/yDJpBc

[462] "El Club - Gigante de Arroyito", *Buenos Aires Canalla*, http://bit.ly/SeYiD7

[463] "Argentina: Las 10 Ciudades más Grandes", *Taringa*, http://bit.ly/yDJpBc

[464] The Litoral region covers the five provinces of Chacho, Correintes, Entre Rios, Formosa, Missiones and Santa Fé in Northeastern Argentina.

[465] "Argentina: Las 10 Ciudades más Grandes", *Taringa*, http://bit.ly/yDJpBc

[466] "Alberto Mario Kempes - Córdoba", *Copa America Argentina 2011*, http://bit.ly/iphy0p

[467] "Argentina: Las 10 Ciudades más Grandes", *Taringa*, http://bit.ly/yDJpBc

[468] "Malvinas Argentinas - Mendoza", *Copa America Argentina 2011*, http://bit.ly/Uqtt0l

[469] The complete list of Level 2 Stadiums used in Rugby World Cup 2011 and their matches are as follows

Dunedin - Argentina v England, England v Georgia, England v Romania, Ireland v Italy
Hamilton - New Zealand v Japan, Wales v Samoa, Wales v Fiji
New Plymouth - Ireland v USA, USA v Russia, Wales v Romania
North Harbour - France v Japan ,Australia v Italy, South Africa v Namibia, South Africa v Samoa
Rotorua Fiji v Namibia, Samoa v Namibia, Ireland v Russia

[470] "Los 10 mejores estádios de Argentina", *Taringa*, http://bit.ly/POKyB9

[471] "Argentina: Las 10 Ciudades más Grandes", *Taringa*, http://bit.ly/yDJpBc

[472] "Los 10 mejores estádios de Argentina", *Taringa*, http://bit.ly/POKyB9

[473] "Argentina: Las 10 Ciudades más Grandes", *Taringa*, http://bit.ly/yDJpBc

[474] "Estádio del Bicentenario – San Juan", *Copa America Argentina 2011*, http://bit.ly/m1TnfE

[475] "Argentina: Las 10 Ciudades más Grandes", *Taringa*, http://bit.ly/yDJpBc

[476] In 2006 the population was officially listed at 68,901. "Quick Stats About New Plymouth District", *Statistics New Zealand*, http://bit.ly/QaYN57

[477] New Plymouth´s matches were as follows
- Tier One v Tier Two (Ireland v USA)
- Tier Two v Tier Three (USA v Russia)
- Tier One v Tier Three (Wales v Namibia)

[478] Tucumán won the Argentine Provincial Championship, known as the Campeonato Argentino in 1985, 1987, 1988, 1989, 1990, 1992, 1993, 2005 and 2010.

[479] "Argentina: Las 10 Ciudades más Grandes", *Taringa*, http://bit.ly/yDJpBc

[480] "Estádio Monumental José Fierro", *Club Atlético Tucumán*, http://bit.ly/fzrUuj

[481] IBID.

[482] The complete list of Rugby World Cup 2003 matches played at Level 3 Stadiums was as follows

Gosford - Ireland v Romania, Argentina v Namibia, USA v Japan
Wollongong - Canada v Tonga, France v USA
Launceston - Romania v Namibia

[483] New Zealand's Level 3 Stadiums used at Rugby World Cup 2011 were as follows

Invercargill - Scotland v Romania, Scotland v Georgia, Argentina v Romania
Napier - France v Canada, Canada v Japan
Nelson - Italy v Russia, Italy v USA, Australia v Russia
Palmerston North - Georgia v Romania, Argentina v Georgia
Whangarei - Tonga v Canada, Tonga v Japan

[484] Gran Bahia Blanca consists of Bahía Blanca, Ingeniero White, Grunbein, Villa Espora and Villa Bordeu.

[485] "Bahía Blanca – History and Legends", *Welcome Argentina*, http://bit.ly/1IcOLL

[486] El Estadio Aurinegro, *PasionAurinegra*, http://bit.ly/RTS0cK

[487] In the 2001 Census Puerto Madryn had a population of 57,688. http://bit.ly/SgTjWV

The next smallest city to have hosted test rugby is Puerto Iguazú which has a population of 82,000.

[488] "Rugby World Cup 2011 Pool C: Italy 53-17 Russia", *BBC*, September 20 2011, http://bbc.in/P8guRB

[489] "Corrientes – El Grande Del Litoral", *Taringa*, http://bit.ly/UqtOjD

[490] "Megapost Resistencia mi ciudad [Chaco-Arg]", *Taringa*, http://bit.ly/VupNgy

[491] "Estádio Centenario", *Club Atlético Sarmiento*, http://bit.ly/SeYPoG

[492] "Argentina: Las 10 Ciudades más Grandes", *Taringa*, http://bit.ly/yDJpBc

[493] "Argentine rugby fans deserve annual test", *The Telegraph*, June 15 2009, http://bit.ly/R4CxY

[494] "Padre Ernesto Martearena – Salta", *Copa America Argentina 2011*, http://bit.ly/pWG9MK

Also from MX Publishing

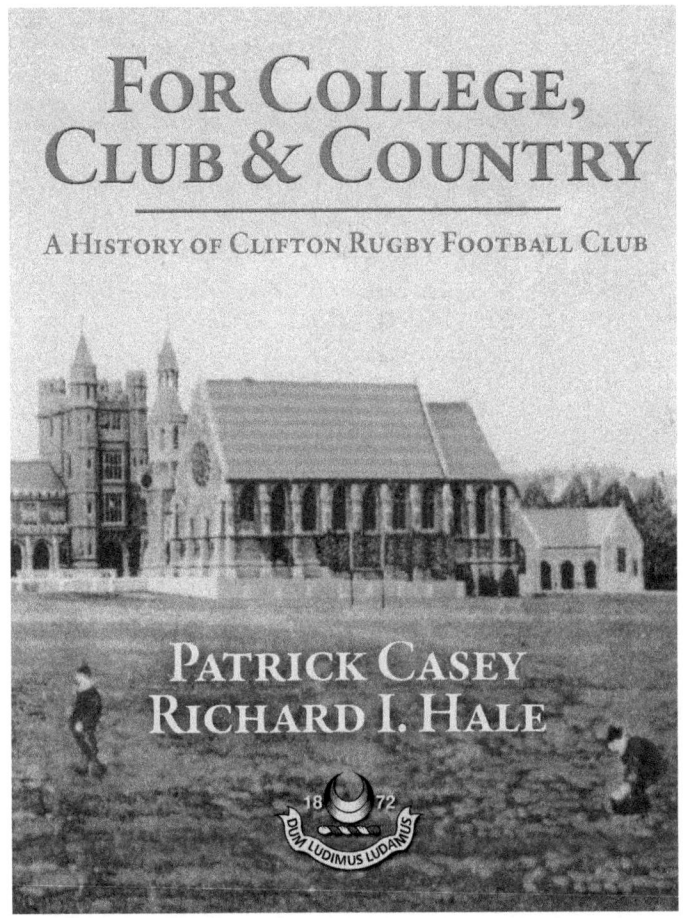

"Richly illustrated with team photographs over more than 100 years, this is a fascinating piece of social history based around one of the oldest rugby clubs in the country. Providing moving accounts of club members who lost their lives in the two World Wars, this is an important and fascinating history of a club that has retained a strong community focus". - The Bookbag

Also from MX Publishing

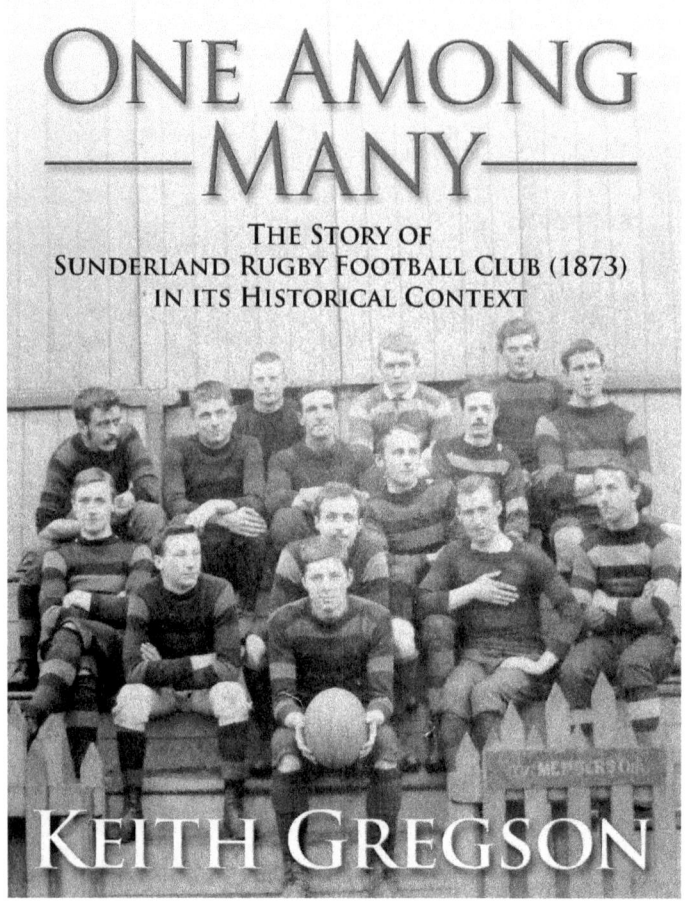

The story of a typical English rugby club set in its historical context linked to the tale of the rare survival of a multi-sport Victorian complex. This will be of interest and use to local people, sports enthusiasts and serious sports historians.

Also from MX Publishing

A fascinating insight into the early years of Rugby Football - carefully reproduced and enhanced with notes and commentaries. During the 1890s, The Times newspaper described Fletcher Robinson as a household name within rugby circles. Hence he was well qualified to write an anecdotal account of the origin of Rugby Union.

www.ingramcontent.com/pod-product-compliance
Ingram Content Group UK Ltd.
Pitfield, Milton Keynes, MK11 3LW, UK
UKHW040847260326
46938JUK00009B/95